CAMBRIDGE LIBRARY COLLECTION

Books of enduring scholarly value

History

The books reissued in this series include accounts of historical events and
movements by eye-witnesses and contemporaries, as well as landmark studies
that assembled significant source materials or developed new historiographical
methods. The series includes work in social, political and military history on
a wide range of periods and regions, giving modern scholars ready access to
influential publications of the past.

The English Village Community

The Yorkshire-born barrister, banker and economic historian Frederic Seebohm
(1833–1912) first came to attention with his work on the Reformation intellectuals
Colet, Erasmus and More. In this work, first published and then reissued in 1883,
Seebohm's focus is on the agrarian history of medieval England, with special
reference to problems of early land tenure and the social system that developed
from it. Seebohm stresses the continuity between Roman settlement and English
villages, and he regards the manor, whose lands were cultivated by serfs, as the
original form of landed property among the Anglo-Saxons and other Germanic
peoples. He was the first British historian to provide a detailed description of the
structure and economic life of the large manor, based on the unpaid labour of
the serfs, and of the relations between the manor and the community. The book
remains an influential treatment of the feudal system.

Cambridge University Press has long been a pioneer in the reissuing of out-of-print titles from its own backlist, producing digital reprints of books that are still sought after by scholars and students but could not be reprinted economically using traditional technology. The Cambridge Library Collection extends this activity to a wider range of books which are still of importance to researchers and professionals, either for the source material they contain, or as landmarks in the history of their academic discipline.

Drawing from the world-renowned collections in the Cambridge University Library and other partner libraries, and guided by the advice of experts in each subject area, Cambridge University Press is using state-of-the-art scanning machines in its own Printing House to capture the content of each book selected for inclusion. The files are processed to give a consistently clear, crisp image, and the books finished to the high quality standard for which the Press is recognised around the world. The latest print-on-demand technology ensures that the books will remain available indefinitely, and that orders for single or multiple copies can quickly be supplied.

The Cambridge Library Collection brings back to life books of enduring scholarly value (including out-of-copyright works originally issued by other publishers) across a wide range of disciplines in the humanities and social sciences and in science and technology.

The English Village Community

Examined in its Relation to the Manorial and Tribal Systems and to the Common or Open Field System of Husbandry

FREDERIC SEEBOHM

CAMBRIDGE
UNIVERSITY PRESS

CAMBRIDGE UNIVERSITY PRESS

Cambridge, New York, Melbourne, Madrid, Cape Town,
Singapore, São Paolo, Delhi, Mexico City

Published in the United States of America by Cambridge University Press, New York

www.cambridge.org
Information on this title: www.cambridge.org/9781108036344

© in this compilation Cambridge University Press 2012

This edition first published 1883
This digitally printed version 2012

ISBN 978-1-108-03634-4 Paperback

THE

ENGLISH VILLAGE COMMUNITY.

LONDON : PRINTED BY
SPOTTISWOODE AND CO., NEW-STREET SQUARE
AND PARLIAMENT STREET

Reduced Tracing
of the
TITHE MAP
of
HITCHIN TOWNSHIP
about 1816.

Hyde Mill

1 Croft Field	21 Reel Shot
2 Welshmans Croft	22 Wymondley Highway Shot
3 Little Welshmans Croft	23 Beggarly Shot
4 Bury Field	24 Beech Tree Field
5 Bury Field Lammas	25 Herne Shot
6 Bearton (Buryton?) Old homestead	26 Purwell Grove
7 Bearton Green	27 Riddy Shot
8 Dᵒ Dᵒ Field	28 Standhill Field
9 Cock Mead Lammas	29 Spittal Field Common
10 Cow Common Lammas	30 Standhill Common
11 Walsworth Holmes	31 Burford Common
12 Great Wimbush Field	32 Red Hill Shot
13 Lammas	33 Sparrow Bush Shot
14 Short Shadwell Shot	34 Hag Dell Shot
15 Long Dᵒ	35 West Mill Field
16 Great Benslow Hills	36 Chalk Dell Shot
17 Little Dᵒ	37 Chalk Dell
18 Nettle Dell	38 Chalk Dell Lane Shot
19 Little Wimbush Field	39 The Linces
20 Benslow Hill Shot	40 Below Linces
	41 Duck Land
	42 Gaping Hill
	43 Fox Holes
	44 Crow Furlong
	45 Manley Highway Shot
	46 Moor Mead Bottom
	47 Moor Mead
	48 Great Moor Mead
	49 Sweeting Valley
	50 Furzen Hedges
	51 Temple Hedges
	52 Butts Close

WALSWORTH HAMLET

BURY FIELD

R. Hiz

Purwell R.

Purwell Mill

PURWELL FIELD

Wymondley Highway

SPITAL FIELD

MUCH WYMONDLEY

Ippollitts Brook

Scale of a Mile (each division being an Acre)

FURLONG

London Longmans & Cᵒ

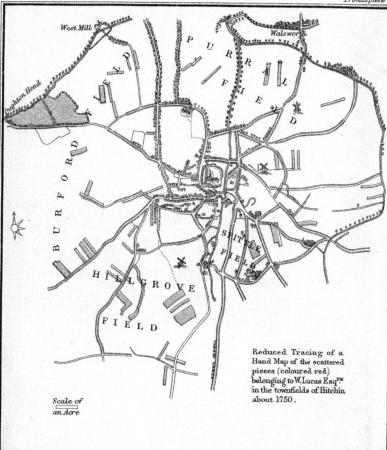

West Mill

Walsworth

P U R R
F I E
L D

Prighton Head

B U R F O R D   F I E L D

H I L G R O V E

F I E L D

SHITTLE
FIELD

Reduced Tracing of a
Hand Map of the scattered
pieces (coloured red)
belonging to W. Lucas Esqre
in the townfields of Hitchin
about 1750.

Scale of
an Acre

Enlarged Plan of the normal acre strip in the open fields
afterwards adopted as the statute acre.
(Scale 4 inches to a Furlong)

Rods or Poles   10   20   30   40

A Rood of 40 square rods

Rods or Poles   10   20   30   40

An Acre = being 4 Roods side by side

| 1 | 2 | 3 | 4 | 5 | 6 | 7 | 8 | 9 | 10 |

An Acre = being 10 square chains

A Furlong (Furrow-long) or Quarentena of 40 rods length.

THE

ENGLISH VILLAGE COMMUNITY

EXAMINED IN ITS RELATIONS TO THE MANORIAL AND
TRIBAL SYSTEMS AND TO THE COMMON OR OPEN
FIELD SYSTEM OF HUSBANDRY.

AN ESSAY IN ECONOMIC HISTORY

BY

FREDERIC SEEBOHM.

SECOND EDITION.

LONDON:
LONGMANS, GREEN, AND CO.
1883.

DEDICATED BY PERMISSION

TO THE

SOCIETY OF ANTIQUARIES OF LONDON.

PREFACE.

————◦◦◦————

WHEN I had the honour to lay the two papers which have expanded into this volume before the Society of Antiquaries, it was with a confession and an apology which, in publishing and dedicating to them this Essay, I now repeat.

I confessed to having approached the subject not as an antiquary but as a student of Economic History, and even with a directly political interest. To learn the meaning of the old order of things, with its 'community' and 'equality' as a key to a right understanding of the new order of things, with its contrasting individual independence and inequality, this was the object which in the first instance tempted me to poach upon antiquarian manors, and it must be my apology for treating from an economic point of view a subject which has also an antiquarian interest.

To statesmen, whether of England or of the new Englands across the oceans, the importance can hardly be over-estimated of a sound appreciation of the nature of that remarkable economic evolution in the course of which the great English speaking nations have, so to speak, become charged in our time with the trial of the experiment—let us hope also with the solution of the problem—of *freedom* and *democracy*, using the words in the highest political sense as the antipodes of *Paternal Government* and *Communism*.

Perhaps, without presumption, it may be said that the future happiness of the human race—the success or failure of the planet—is in no small degree dependent upon the ultimate course of what seems, to us at least, to be the main stream of human progress, upon whether it shall be guided by the foresight of statesmen into safe channels or misguided, diverted, or obstructed, till some great social or political convulsion proves that its force and its direction have been misunderstood.

It may indeed be but too true that, in spite of the economic lessons of the past—

> The weary Titan ! with deaf
> Ears, and labour dimmed eyes,
> Regarding neither to right
> Nor left, goes passively by,
> Staggering on to her goal ;
> Bearing on shoulders immense,
> Atlantëan, the load,
> Wellnigh not to be borne,
> Of the too vast orb of her fate.

And she may continue to do so, however clearly and truthfully the economic lessons of the past may be dinned into her ear. But still the deep sense I have endeavoured to describe in these few sentences of the importance of a sound understanding of English Economic History as the true basis of much of the practical politics of the future will be accepted, I trust, as a sufficient reason why, ill-furnished as I have constantly found myself for the task, I should have ventured to devote some years of scant leisure to the production of this imperfect Essay.

It is simply an attempt to set English Economic History upon right lines at its historical commencement by trying to solve the still open question whether it began with the *freedom* or with the *serfdom* of the masses of the people—whether the village communities living in the 'hams' and 'tons' of England were, at the outset of English history, *free* village communities or communities in *serfdom* under a manorial lordship; and further, what were their relations to the tribal communities of the Western and less easily conquered portions of the island.

On the answer to this question depends fundamentally the view to be taken by historians (let us say by politicians also) of the nature of the economic evolution which has taken place in England since the English Conquest. If answered in one way, English Economic History begins with free village communities which gradually degenerated into the serfdom of the Middle Ages. If answered in the other way, it begins with the serfdom of the masses of the rural population under Saxon rule—a serfdom from which it has taken 1,000 years of English economic evolution to set them free.

Much learning and labour have already been expended upon this question, and fresh light has been recently streaming in upon it from many sides.

A real flash of light was struck when German students perceived the connexion between the widely prevalent common or open field system of husbandry, and the village community which for centuries had used it as a shell. Whatever may be the ultimate verdict upon G. L. von Maurer's theory of the German 'mark,' there can be no doubt of its service as a working hypothesis by means of which the study of the economic problem has been materially advanced.

A great step was taken as regards the English problem when Mr. Kemble, followed by Mr. Freeman and others, attempted to trace in English constitutional history the development of ancient German free institutions, and to solve the English problem upon the lines of the German 'mark.' The merit of this attempt will not be destroyed even though doubt should be thrown upon the correctness of this suggested solution of the problem, and though other and non-German elements should prove to have been larger factors in English economic history. The caution observed by Professor Stubbs in the early chapters of his great work on English Constitutional History may be said to have at least reopened the question whether the German 'mark system' ever really took root in England.

Another step was gained on somewhat new lines when Professor Nasse, of Bonn, pointed out to English

students (who hitherto had not realised the fact) that
the English and German land systems were the same,
and that in England also the open-field system of
husbandry was the shell of the mediæval village community. The importance of this view is obvious,
and it is to be regretted that no English student has
as yet followed it up by an adequate examination of
the remarkably rich materials which lie at the dis-
posal of English Economic History.

A new flash of light at once lit up the subject
and greatly widened its interest when Sir Henry S.
Maine, carrying with him to India his profound insight
into ' Ancient Law,' recognised the fundamental
analogies between the ' village communities ' of the
East and the West, and sought to use actually surviving Indian institutions as typical representatives
of ancient stages of similar Western institutions. Undoubtedly much more light may be looked for from
the same direction.

Further, Sir Henry S. Maine has opened fresh
ground, and perhaps (if he will permit me to say so)
even to some extent narrowed the area within which
the theory of archaic free village communities can
be applied, by widening the range of investigation in
yet another direction. In his lectures on the ' Early
History of Institutions ' he has turned his telescope
upon the *tribal* communities, and especially the ' tribal
system ' of the Brehon laws, and tried to dissolve
parts of its mysterious nebulæ into stars—a work in
which he has been followed by Mr. W. F. Skene
with results which give a peculiar interest to the third

volume of that learned writer's valuable work on
' Celtic Scotland.'

Lastly, under the close examination of Dr. Landau
and Professors Hanssen and Meitzen, the open-field
system itself has been found in Germany to take
several distinct forms, corresponding, in part at least,
with differences in economic conditions, if not directly
with various stages in economic development, from
the early tribal to the later manorial system.

It is very much to be desired that the open-field
system of the various districts of France should be
carefully studied in the same way. An examination
of its widely extended modern remains could hardly
fail to throw important light upon the contents of the
cartularies which have been published in the ' Collection de Documents Inédits sur l'histoire de France,'
amongst which the ' *Polyptique d'Irminon*,' with
M. Guérard's invaluable preface, is pre-eminently
useful.

In the meantime, whilst students had perhaps been
too exclusively absorbed in working in the rich mine
of early German institutions, Mr. Coote has done
service in recalling attention in his ' Neglected Fact
in English History ' and his ' Romans of Britain ' to
the evidences which remain of the survival of Roman
influences in English institutions, even though it may
be true that some of his conclusions may require re-
consideration. The details of the later Roman provincial government, and of the economic conditions
of the German and British provinces, remain so
obscure even after the labours of Mommsen, Mar-

quardt, and Madvig, that he who attempts to build a bridge across the gulf of the Teutonic conquests between Roman and English institutions still builds it somewhat at a venture.

It is interesting to find that problems connected with early English and German Economic History are engaging the careful and independent research also of American students. The contributions of Mr. Denman Ross, of Cambridge, Massachusetts, and Professor Allen, of the University of Wisconsin, will be welcomed by fellow-students of these questions in the old country.

It has seemed to me that the time may have come when an inquiry directed strictly upon economic lines, and carefully following the English evidence, might strike a light of its own, in the strength of which the various side lights might perhaps be gathered together and some clear result obtained, at least as regards the main course of economic evolution in England.

The English, like the Continental village community, as we have said, inhabited a shell—an open-field system—into the nooks and corners of which it was curiously bound and fitted, and from which it was apparently inseparable.

The remains of this cast-off shell still survive in parishes where no Enclosure Act happens to have swept them away. The common or open field system can even now be studied on the ground within the township in which I am writing as well as in many others.

Men are still living who have held and worked farms under its inconvenient rules, and who know the meaning of its terms and eccentric details. Making use of this circumstance the method pursued in this Essay will be, first, to become familiar with the little distinctive marks and traits of the English open-field system, so that they may be readily recognised wherever they present themselves; and then, proceeding from the known to the unknown, carefully to trace back the shell by searching and watching for its marks and traits as far into the past as evidence can be found. Using the knowledge so acquired about the shell as the key, the inquiry will turn upon its *occupant.* Examining how the mediæval English village community in serfdom fitted itself into the shell, and then again working back from the known to the unknown, it may be perhaps possible to discern whether, within historical times, it once had been free, or whether its serfdom was as old as the shell.

The relation of the ' tribal system ' in Wales, in Ireland, and in Germany to the open-field system, and so also to the village community, will be a necessary branch of the inquiry. It will embrace also both the German and the Roman sources of serfdom and of the manorial system of land management.

It may at least be possible that Economic History may sometimes find secure stepping stones over what may be impassable gulfs in constitutional history;

and it obviously does not follow that a continuity lost, perhaps, to the one may not have been preserved by the other. The result of a strictly economic inquiry may, as already suggested, prove that more things went to the 'making of England' than were imported in the keels of the English invaders of Britain. But whatever the result—whatever modifications of former theories the facts here brought into view, after full consideration by others, may suggest—I trust that this Essay will not be regarded as controversial in its aim or its spirit. I had rather that it were accepted simply as fellow-work, as a stone added at the eleventh hour to a structure in the building of which others, some of whose names I have mentioned, have laboured during the length and heat of the day.

In conclusion, I have to tender my best thanks to Sir Henry S. Maine for the kind interest he has taken, and the sound advice he has given, during the preparation of this Essay for the press; also to Mr. Elton, for similar unsolicited help generously given. To my friend George von Bunsen, and to Professor Meitzen, of Berlin, I am deeply indebted as regards the German branches of my subject, and to Mr. T. Hodgkin and Mr. H. Pelham as regards the Roman side of it. For the ever ready assistance of my friend Mr. H. Bradshaw, of Cambridge, Mr. Selby, of the Record Office, and Mr. Thompson, of the British Museum, in reference to the manuscripts under their charge, I cannot be too grateful. Nor must I omit to acknowledge the care with which Messrs. Stuart Moore and Kirk have undertaken for me the task of revising the text and translations of the many extracts from mediæval documents contained in this volume.

F. Seebohm.

The Hermitage, Hitchin:
May, 1883.

CONTENTS.

CHAPTER I.

THE ENGLISH OPEN-FIELD SYSTEM EXAMINED IN ITS
MODERN REMAINS.

CHAPTER II.

THE ENGLISH OPEN-FIELD SYSTEM TRACED BACK TO THE DOMES-
DAY SURVEY—IT IS THE SHELL OF SERFDOM—THE MANOR
WITH A VILLAGE COMMUNITY IN VILLENAGE UPON IT.

CHAPTER III.

THE DOMESDAY SURVEY (A.D. 1086).

CHAPTER IV.

THE OPEN-FIELD SYSTEM TRACED IN SAXON TIMES—THE SCATTERING OF THE STRIPS ORIGINATED IN THE METHODS OF CO-ARATION.

CHAPTER VIII.

CONNEXION BETWEEN THE ROMAN LAND SYSTEM AND THE LATER MANORIAL SYSTEM.

CHAPTER IX.

THE GERMAN SIDE OF THE CONTINENTAL EVIDENCE.

CHAPTER X.

THE CONNEXION BETWEEN THE OPEN-FIELD SYSTEM AND SERFDOM OF ENGLAND AND OF THE ROMAN PROVINCES OF GERMANY AND GAUL.

CHAPTER XI.

RESULT OF THE EVIDENCE.

LIST OF MAPS AND PLATES.

THE

ENGLISH VILLAGE COMMUNITY.

CHAPTER I.

THE ENGLISH OPEN FIELD SYSTEM EXAMINED IN ITS MODERN REMAINS.

I. THE DISTINCTIVE MARKS OF THE OPEN FIELD SYSTEM.

THE distinctive marks of the open or common field system once prevalent in England will be most easily learned by the study of an example.

The township of Hitchin, in Hertfordshire, will answer the purpose. From the time of Edward the Confessor—and probably from much earlier times—with intervals of private ownership, it has been a royal manor.[1] And the Queen being still the lady of the manor, the remains of its open fields have never been swept away by the ruthless broom of an Enclosure Act.

Annexed is a reduced tracing of a map of the

---

[1] The lesser manors included in it are clearly only *sub*-manors, and | for the present purpose do not destroy its original unity.

township without the hamlets, made about the year 1816, and showing all the divisions into which its fields were then cut up.

It will be seen at once that it presents almost the features of a spider's web. A great part of the township at that date, probably nearly the whole of it in earlier times, was divided up into little narrow strips.

Divided into strips or seliones, *i.e.* acres, by balks.

These strips, common to open fields all over England, were separated from each other not by hedges, but by green balks of unploughed turf, and are of great historical interest. They vary more or less in size even in the same fields, as in the examples given on the map of a portion of the Hitchin Purwell field. There are ' long ' strips and ' short' strips. But taking them generally, and comparing them with the statute acre of the scale at the corner of the map, it will be seen at once that the normal strip is roughly identical with it. The length of the statute acre of the scale is a furlong of 40 rods or poles. It is 4 rods in width. Now 40 rods in length and 1 rod in width make 40 square rods, or a *rood*; and thus, as there are 4 rods in breadth, the acre of the scale with which the normal strips coincide is an *acre* made up of 4 roods lying side by side.

Eorm of the acre.

Thus the strips are in fact roughly cut ' acres,' of the proper shape for ploughing. For the furlong is the ' furrow long,' *i.e.* the length of the drive of the plough before it is turned ; and that this by long custom was fixed at 40 rods, is shown by the use of the Latin word ' *quarentena* ' for furlong. The word ' rood' naturally corresponds with as many furrows in the ploughing as are contained in the breadth of one rod. And four of these roods lying side by side made

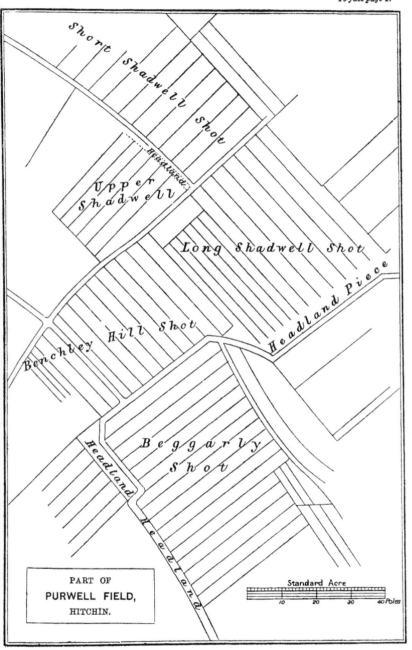

Short Shadwell Shot

Headland

Upper Shadwell

Long Shadwell Shot

Benchley Hill Shot

Headland Piece

Headland

Beggarly Shot

Headland

PART OF
PURWELL FIELD,
HITCHIN.

Standard Acre

10   20   30   40 Poles

the acre strip in the open fields, and still make up
the statute acre.

This form of the acre is very ancient. Six hundred
years ago, in the earliest English law fixing the size
of the statute acre (33 Ed. I.), it is declared that
' 40 perches in length and 4 in breadth make an acre.' [1]
And further, we shall find that more than a thousand
years ago in Bavaria the shape of the strip in the open
fields for ploughing was also 40 rods in length and 4
rods in width, but the rod was in that case the Greek
and Roman rod of 10 ft. instead of the English rod of
$16\frac{1}{2}$ ft.

But to return to the English strips. In many
places the open fields were formerly divided into half-
acre strips, which were called ' half-acres.' That is to
say, a turf balk separated every two rods or roods in
the ploughing, the length of the furrow remaining
the same.

The strips in the open fields are generally known
by country folk as ' balks,' and the Latin word used
in terriers and cartularies for the strip is generally
' *selio*,' corresponding with the French word ' *sillon*,'
(meaning furrow). In Scotland and Ireland the same
strips generally are known as ' rigs,' and the open
field system is known accordingly as the ' run-rig '
system.

The whole arable area of an uninclosed township
was usually divided up by turf balks into as many
thousands of these strips as its limits would contain,
and the tithing maps of many parishes besides Hitchin,
dating sixty or eighty years ago, show remains of

---

[1] *Statutes, Record Com.* Ed. i. p. 206.

them still existing, although the process of ploughing up the balks and throwing many strips together had gradually been going on for centuries.

Shots or furlongs, or quarentenæ.   Next, it will be seen that the strips on the map lie side by side in groups, forming larger divisions of the field. These larger divisions are called 'shots,' or 'furlongs,' and in Latin documents '*quarentenæ*,' being always a furrow-long in width. Throughout their whole length the furrows in the ploughing run parallel from end to end; the balks which divide them into strips being, as the word implies, simply two or three furrows left unploughed between them.[1]

The shots or furlongs are divided from one another by broader balks, generally overgrown with bushes.

This grouping of the strips in furlongs or shots is a further invariable feature of the English open field *Headlands.* system. And it involves another little feature which is also universally met with, viz. the *headland*.

It will be seen on the map that mostly a common field-way gives access to the strips; *i.e.* it runs along the side of the furlong and the ends of the strips. But this is not always the case; and when it is not, then there is a strip running along the length of the furlong inside its boundaries and across the ends of the strips composing it.[2] This is the *headland*. Sometimes when the strips of the one furlong run at right angles to the strips of its neighbour, the first strip in the one furlong does

---

[1] *Balc* is a Welsh word; and when the plough is accidentally turned aside, and leaves a sod of grass unturned between the furrows, the plough is said by the Welsh ploughman speaking Welsh, to '*balc*' (balco).

[2] See the map of a portion of the Purwell field.

'LINCHES' IN THE OPEN FIELDS OF CLOTHALL, HERTS.

duty as the headland giving access to the strips in the other. In either case all the owners of the strips in a furlong have the right to turn their plough upon the headland, and thus the owner of the headland must wait until all the other strips are ploughed before he can plough his own. The Latin term for the headland is '*forera*;' the Welsh, '*pen tir*;' the Scotch, '*head-rig*;' and the German (from the turning of the plough upon it), '*anwende.*'

A less universal but equally peculiar feature of the open field system in hilly districts is the 'lynch,' and it may often be observed remaining when every other trace of an open field has been removed by enclosure. Its right of survival lies in its indestructibility. When a hill-side formed part of the open field the strips almost always were made to run, not up and down the hill, but horizontally along it ; and in ploughing, the custom for ages was always to turn the sod of the furrow downhill, the plough consequently always returning one way idle. If the whole hill-side were ploughed in one field, this would result in a gradual travelling of the soil from the top to the bottom of the field, and it might not be noticed. But as in the open field system the hill-side was ploughed in strips with unploughed balks between them, no sod could pass in the ploughing from one strip to the next ; but the process of moving the sod downwards would go on age after age just the same within each individual strip. In other words, every year's ploughing took a sod from the higher edge of the strip and put it on the lower edge ; and the result was that the strips became in time long level terraces one above the other, and the balks between them grew into steep rough banks of long grass covered often with natural self-sown brambles and bushes. These banks between the plough-made terraces are generally called *lynches*, or *linces*; and the word is often applied to the terraced strips themselves, which go by the name of ' the linces.'[1]

Butts.

Where the strips abruptly meet others, or *abut* upon a boundary at right angles, they are sometimes called *butts*.

Two other small details marking the open field system require only to be simply mentioned.

Gored acres.

Corners of the fields which, from their shape, could not be cut up into the usual acre or half-acre strips, were sometimes divided into tapering strips pointed at one end, and called 'gores,' or 'gored acres.' In other cases little odds and ends of unused land remained, which from time immemorial were called ' no

No man's land.

man's land,' or ' any one's land,' or 'Jack's land,' as the case might be.

Thus there are plenty of outward marks and traits by which the open common field may be recognised wherever it occurs,—the acre or half-acre

---

[1] Striking examples of these lynches may be seen from the railroad at Luton in Bedfordshire, and between Cambridge and Hitchin, as well as in various other parts of England. They may be seen often on the steep sides of the Sussex Downs and the Chiltern Hills. Great numbers of them are to be noticed from the French line between Calais and Paris. In some cases on the steep chalk downs, terraces for ploughing have evidently been artificially cut; but even in these cases there must always have been a gradual natural growth of the lynches by annual accretion from the ploughing. In old times, in order to secure the turning of the sod downhill, the plough, after cutting a furrow, returned as stated one way idle; but in more recent times a plough called a ' turn-wrist ' plough ' came into use, which by reversing its share could be used both ways, to the great saving of time.

HITCHIN.
PURWELL FIELD.

PROPRIETORS' NAMES,
WITH THEIR
NUMBERS.

	NO.
Byde, Esq.	1
Carter, Esq.	2
Mrs. Simpson	3
Rev. Mr. Whitehurst...	4
Mr. Rd. Tristram ...	5
Late Mr. Gravely Hurst	6
Mr. Charles Baron ...	7
Jno. Radcliffe, Esq. ...	8
Wm. Lucas Brewer ...	9
Late Thomas Smith ...	10
Mrs. Ann Newman ...	11
Thomas Goldsmith ...	12
Thomas Lyle	13
Francis Thatcher ...	14
Mr. Jno. Foster	15
Mrs. Field	16
Mr. Vincent	17
Mr. Wm. Malein ...	18
Late Wm. Lucas ...	19
Benjn. Dobbs	20
Mr. Ransom	21
Mr. Warbe	22
Late Widow Paternoster	23
James Joyner	24
Mr. James	25
Mr. Jno. Collinson ...	26
Late Andrew Oakley ...	27
Wm. Dimsey	28
Mr. Collins	29
Mrs. Barrington ...	30
Charity Land	31
Mr. Bradley	32
Mr. Capreol	33
Mr. Cooper	34
Mr. Lane	35
Mr. Peirson	36
Late Mr. Turner ...	37
Mr. Jno. Turner ...	38
Mr. Gray	39
Widow Jevis	40
Mr. Jno. Overitt ...	41
Mr. Palmer	42
Mr. Worner Green ...	43
Mrs. Flack	44
Late Hurst	45
Widow Dobbs	46
Mr. Hatton	47
Mr. Wm. Thomas ...	48

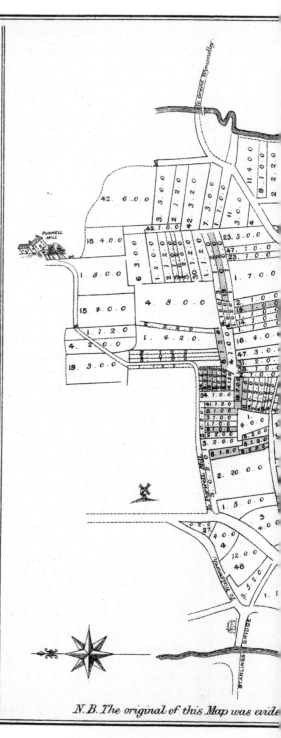

N.B. The original of this Map was evide

...tly not drawn to a scale, It was made early in this Century.

Spottiswoode & Co. Lith. London.

strips or *seliones*, the gored shape of some of them,
the balks and sometimes lynches between them, the
shots or furlongs (*quarentenæ*) in which they lie in
groups, the headlands which give access to the
strips when they lie off the field-ways, the butts, and
lastly the odds and ends of ' no man's land.'

II. SCATTERED AND INTERMIXED OWNERSHIP IN THE OPEN FIELDS.

Passing from these little outward marks to the
matter of ownership, a most inconvenient peculiarity
presents itself, which is by far the most remarkable
and important feature of the open field system wherever it is found. It is the fact that neither the strips
nor the furlongs represented a complete holding or
property, but that the several holdings were made up
of a multitude of strips scattered about on all sides of
the township, one in this furlong and another in that,
intermixed, and it might almost be said entangled
together, as though some one blindfold had thrown
them about on all sides of him.

The extent to which this was the case in the
Hitchin common fields, even so late as the beginning
of the present century, will be realised by reference
to the map annexed. It is a reduced tracing of a
map showing the ownership of the strips in one division of the open fields of Hitchin called the *Purwell*
field. The strips are numbered, and correspond with
the owners' names given in the tally at the side.
The strips belonging to two of the owners are also
coloured, so as at once to catch the eye, and the area
of each separate piece is marked upon it. The num-

ber of scattered pieces held by each owner is also given in the note below; and as the map embraces only about one-third of the Hitchin fields, it should be noticed that each owner probably held in the parish three times as many separate pieces as are there described![1] Further, at the side of the map of the Hitchin township, is a reduced tracing of a plan of the estate of a single landowner in the townfields of Hitchin, which shows very clearly the curious scattering of the strips in a single ownership all over the fields, notwithstanding that the tendency towards consolidation of the holdings by exchanges and purchases had evidently made some progress.

III. THE OPEN FIELDS WERE THE COMMON FIELDS OF A VILLAGE COMMUNITY OR TOWNSHIP UNDER A MANOR.

The next fact to be noted is that under the English system the open fields were the common fields—the arable land—of a village community or township under a manorial lordship. This could hardly be more clearly illustrated than by the Hitchin example.

---

[1] The number of parcels held by each owner was as follows:—

Owner	Parcels	Owner	Parcels	Owner	Parcels	Owner	Parcels
No. 1 .	. 38	No. 14 .	. 5	No. 27 .	. 1	No. 39 .	. 1
2 .	. 35	15 .	. 8	28 .	. 0	40 .	. 1
3 .	. 28	16 .	. 7	29 .	. 1	41 .	. 6
4 .	. 25	17 .	. 2	30 .	. 3	42 .	. 3
5 .	. 3	18 .	. 1	31 .	. 2	43 .	. 2
6 .	. 8	19 .	. 12	32 .	. 1	44 .	. 1
7 .	. 4	20 .	. 1	33 .	. 3	45 .	. 1
8 .	. 28	21 .	. 3	34 .	.. 6	46 .	. 2
9 .	. 6	22 .	. 1	35 .	. 4	47 .	. 7
10 .	. 1	23 .	. 4	36 .	. 1	48 .	. 1
11 .	. 10	24 .	. 0	37 .	. 2		——
12 .	. 2	25 .	. 0	38 .	. 2	Total	289
13 .	. 5	26 .	. 1				

The Hitchin manor was, as already stated, a royal Chap. I.
manor. The *Court Leet* and *View of Frankpledge*
were held concurrently with the *Court Baron* of the
manor. Periodically at this joint court a record was Periodical
made on the presentment of the jurors and homage present-
of various particulars relating to both the manor the jurors
and township.

The record for the year 1819 will be found at
length in Appendix A, and it may be taken as a common form.

The jurors and homage first present that the manor
comprises the township of Hitchin and hamlet of
Walsworth, and includes within it three lesser manors;
also that it extends into other hamlets and parishes.

They then record the *boundaries* of the township The
(including the hamlet of Walsworth) as follows, viz.:— boundaries.

> ' From Orton Head to Burford Ray,
>   and from thence to a Water Mill called Hide Mill,
>   ,,   ,,   ,, Willberry Hills,
>   ,,   ,,   ,, a place called Bossendell,
>   ,,   ,,   ,, a Water Mill called Purwell Mill,
>   ,,   ,,   ,, a Brook or River called Ippollitt's Brook,
>   ,,   ,,   ,, Maydencroft Lane,
>   ,,   ,,   ,, a place called Wellhead,
>   ,,   ,,   ,, a place called Stubborn Bush,
>   ,,   ,,   ,, a place called Offley Cross,
>   ,,   ,,   ,, Five Borough Hills [Five Barrows],
>   ,,   ,,   back to Orton Head, where the boundaries
>   commenced.'

The form in which these boundaries are given is
of great antiquity. It is a form used by the Romans
two thousand years ago, and almost continuously
followed from that time to this.[1] Its importance for

---

[1] *Hyginus de Condicionibus Agro-* 114. ' Nam invenimus sæpe in pub-
rum. Die Schriften der Römischen licis instrumentis significanter in-
Feldmesser (Lachmann, &c.), i. p. scripta territoria, ita ut *ex colliculo*

the purpose in hand will be manifest as the inquiry proceeds.

The courts. The jurisdiction of the Court Leet and View of Frankpledge is recorded to extend within the foregoing boundaries, *i.e.* over the township, that of the Court Baron beyond them over the whole manor, which was more extensive than the township. The Court Leet is therefore the Court of the township, the Court Baron that of the manor.

It is then stated that in the Court Leet at Michaelmas the jurors of the king elect and present to the lord—

The officers. Two constables,

Six headboroughs (two for each of the three wards),

Two ale-conners,

Two leather-searchers and sealers, and

A bellman, who is also the watchman and crier of the town.

All the foregoing presentments have reference to the township, and are those of 'the jurors of our lord the King (*i.e.* of the Court Leet), and the homage of the Court' [Baron] of the manor.

Reliefs, fines, &c. Then come presentments of the homage of the Court of the Manor alone, describing the reliefs of freeholders and the fines, &c., of copyholders under the manor, and various particulars as to powers of leasing,

---

qui appellatur ille ad flumen illud, et super flumen illud ad rivum illum aut viam illam, et per viam illam ad infima montis illius, qui locus appellatur ille, et inde per jugum montis illius in summum, et super summum montis per divergia aquæ ad locum, *qui appellatur ille, et inde deorsum versus ad locum illum, et inde ad compitum illius, et inde per monumentum illius, ad locum unde primum cœpit scriptura esse.'* See as an early example, ' Sententia Minuciorum,' *Corpus Inscript. Lat.* i. 199.

forfeiture, cutting timber, heriots, &c. ; the freedom
of grain from toll in the market, the provision by the
lord of the *common pound* and the *stocks* for the use
of the tenants of the manor, and the right of the
lord with the consent of the homage to grant out
portions of the waste by copy of court roll at a rent
and the customary services.

Next the *commons* are described.

(1) The portions coloured dark green on the map
are described as *Green Commons*, and those coloured
light green as *Lammas Meadows* ;[1] and every occupier
of an ancient messuage or cottage in the township
has certain defined rights of common thereon, the
obligation to find the common bull falling upon the
rectory, and a common herdsman being elected by
the homage at a Court Baron.

(2) The *common fields* are stated to be—

{Purwell field,
{Welshman's croft,
{Burford field,
{Spital field,
{Moremead field,
{Bury field ;

and it is recorded that these common fields have
immemorially been, and ought to be, kept and cultivated in three successive seasons of *tilth grain*, *etch*
grain, and *fallow* : Purwell field and Welshman's
croft being fallow one year ; Burford field and Spital
field the next year ; Moremead field and Bury field
the year after, and so on in regular rotation.

---

[1] The lammas meadows are | land for the purpose of the hay
divided into strips like the arable | crop.

It is stated that every occupier of unenclosed land in any of the common fields of the township may pasture his sheep over the rest of the field after the corn is cut and carried, and when it is fallow. If he choose to enclose his own portion of the common field he may do so, but he then gives up for ever his right of pasture over the rest. It is under this custom that the strips and balks are gradually disappearing.

The ancient messuages and cottages in the hamlet of Walsworth had their separate green common and herdsman, but (at this date) no common fields, because they had already been some time ago enclosed.

It will be seen from the map how very small a proportion of the land of the township was in meadow or pasture. The open arable fields occupied nearly the whole of it. The community to which it belonged, and to whose wants it was fitted, was evidently a community occupied mainly in agriculture.

Another feature requiring notice was the fact that in the open fields freehold and copyhold land were intermixed ; some of the strips being freehold, whilst the next strip was copyhold, instead of all the freehold and all the copyhold lying together. And in the same way the lands belonging to the three lesser or sub-manors lay intermixed, and not all apart by themselves. The open field system overrode the whole.

Thus, if the Hitchin example may be taken as a typical one of the English open field system, it may be regarded generally as having belonged to a village or township under a manor. We may assume that the holdings were composed of numbers of strips scattered over the three open fields; and that the husbandry was controlled by those rules as to rotation of crops and fallow in three seasons which marked the three-field system, and secured uniformity of tillage throughout each field. Lastly, whilst fallow after the crop was gathered, the open fields were probably everywhere subject to the common rights of pasture. The sheep of the whole township wandered and pastured all over the strips and balks of its fields, while the cows of the township were daily driven by a common herdsman to the green commons, or, after Lammas Day, when the hay crop of the owners was secured, to the lammas meadows.

IV. THE WIDE PREVALENCE OF THE SYSTEM THROUGH GREAT BRITAIN.

But before the attempt is made to trace back the system, it may be well to ask what evidence there is as to its wide prevalence in England, and with what reason the particular example of the Hitchin township may be taken as generally typical.

In the first place, an examination into the details of an Enclosure Act will make clear the point that the system as above described is the system which it was the object of the Enclosure Acts to remove. They were generally drawn in the same form, commencing with the recital that the open and common fields lie dispersed in small pieces intermixed with each other and inconveniently situated, that divers persons own parts of them, and are entitled to rights of common on them, so that in their present state they are incapable of improvement, and that it is desired that they may be divided and enclosed, a specific share being set out and allowed to each owner. For this purpose Enclosure Commissioners are appointed, and under their award the balks are ploughed up, the fields divided into blocks for the several owners, hedges planted, and the whole face of the country changed.

The common fields of twenty-two parishes within ten miles of Hitchin were enclosed in this way between 1766 and 1832. All the Acts were of the same character.[1] And as, taking the whole of England, with, roughly speaking, its 10,000 parishes, nearly 4,000 Enclosure Acts were passed between 1760

Number of Acts.

---

[1] These Enclosure Acts were as follows:—

Date of Enclosure Acts	Names of Parishes whose open fields were thereby enclosed
1766	Hexton [Herts].
1795	Henlow [Beds].
1796	Norton [Herts].
1797	Campton-cum-Shefford [Beds].
1797	King's Walden [Herts].
1797	Weston [Herts].
1802	Hinxworth [Herts].
1802	{ Shitlington [Beds]. Holwell [Beds].
1804	Arlsey [Beds].
1807	Offley [Herts].
1808	Luton [Beds].
1809	Barton-in-the-Clay [Beds].
1810	Codicote [Herts]. Welwyn [Herts]. Knebworth [Herts].
1811	Pirton [Herts].
1811	{ Great Wymondley [Herts]. Little Wymondley [Herts]. Ippollitts [Herts].
1827	Langford [Beds].
1832	Clifton [Beds].

and 1844,[1] it will at once be understood how gene- CHAP. I.
rally prevalent was this form of the open field system
so late as the days of the grandfathers of this generation.

The old 'Statistical Account of Scotland,' obtained eighty years ago by inquiry in every parish,
shows that at its date, under the name of 'run-rig,'
a simpler form of the open field system still lingered
on here and there more or less all over Scotland. Wide ex-
Traces of it still exist in the Highlands, and there tent of
open field
are well-known remains of its strips and balks also system.
in Wales. The run-rig system is still prevalent in
some parts of Ireland. But at present we confine
our attention to the form which the system assumed
in England, and for this purpose the Hitchin example
may fairly be taken as typical.

Now, judged from a modern point of view, it will
readily be understood that the open field system, and
especially its peculiarity of straggling or scattered
ownership, regarded from a modern agricultural point Unecono-
of view, was absurdly uneconomical. The waste of mical;
time in getting about from one part of a farm to
another; the uselessness of one owner attempting
to clean his own land when it could be sown with
thistles from the seed blown from the neighbouring
strips of a less careful and thrifty owner; the
quarrelling about headlands and rights of way, or

---

[1] Porter's *Progress of the Nation*, p. 146 :—

1760–69 .	.	. 385		1820–29 .	.	. 205
1770–79 .	.	. 660		1830–39 .	.	. 136
1780–89 .	.	. 246		1840–44 .	.	. 66
1790–99 .	.	. 469				——
1800–9 .	.	. 847				3,867
1810–19	.	. 853				

paths made without right; the constant encroach-
ments of unscrupulous or overbearing holders upon the
balks—all this made the system so inconvenient, that
Arthur Young, coming across it in France, could
hardly keep his temper as he described with what
perverse ingenuity it seemed to be contrived as
though purposely to make agriculture as awkward
and uneconomical as possible.

but must
have had
meaning
once.

But these now inconvenient traits of the open
field system must once have had a meaning, a
use, and even a convenience which were the cause of
their original arrangement. Like the apparently
meaningless sentinel described by Prince Bismarck
uselessly pacing up and down the middle of a lawn in
the garden of the Russian palace, there must have been
an originally sufficient reason to account for the
beginning of what is now useless and absurd. And
just as in that case, search in the military archives disclosed that once upon a time, in the days of Catherine
the Great, a solitary snowdrop had appeared on the
lawn, to guard which a sentinel was posted by an
order which had never been revoked ; so a similar
search will doubtless disclose an ancient original
reason for even the (at first sight) most unreasonable
features of the open field system.

CHAPTER II.

*THE ENGLISH OPEN FIELD SYSTEM TRACED BACK
TO THE DOMESDAY SURVEY—IT IS THE SHELL
OF SERFDOM—THE MANOR WITH A VILLAGE COM-
MUNITY IN VILLENAGE UPON IT.*

I. THE IDENTITY OF THE SYSTEM WITH THAT
OF THE MIDDLE AGES.

THAT this open field system, the remains of which have now been examined, was identical with that which existed in the Middle Ages might easily be proved by a continuous chain of examples. But it will be enough for the present purpose to pick out a few typical instances, using them as stepping-stones.

It would be easy to quote Tusser's description of '*Champion Farming*' in the sixteenth century. In his 'Five Hundred Points of Good Husbandry' he describes the respective merits of 'several,' and 'champion' or open field farming. But as he describes the latter as a system already out of date in his time, and as rapidly giving way to the more economical system of 'several' or enclosed fields, we may pass on at once to evidence another couple of centuries earlier in date.

Of the fact that the open field system 500 years ago (in the fourteenth century), with its divisions into furlongs and subdivision into acre or half-acre strips, existed in England, the 'Vision of Piers the Plowman' may be appealed to as a witness.

Piers the Plowman.

What was 'the faire felde ful of folke,' in which the poet saw 'alle maner of men' 'worchyng and wandryng,' some 'putten hem to the plow,' whilst others 'in settyng and in sowyng swonken ful harde'?[1] A modern English field shut in by hedges would not suit the vision in the least. It was clearly enough the open field into which all the villagers turned out on the bright spring morning, and over which they would be scattered, some working and some looking on. In no other 'faire felde' would he see such folk of all sorts, the '[hus]bondemen,' bakers and brewers, butchers, woolwebsters and weavers of linen, tailors, tinkers, and tollers in market, masons, dikers, and delvers; while the cooks cried 'Hote pies hote!' and tavern-keepers set in competition their wines and roast meat at the alehouse.[2]

Then as to the division of the fields into furlongs; remembering that the wide balks between them and along the headlands were often covered with 'brakes and brambles,' the point is at once settled by the *naïve* confession of the priest who scarce knew perfectly his Paternoster, and could 'ne solfe ne synge' 'ne seyntes lyues rede,' yet knew well enough the 'rymes of Robyn hood,' and how to 'fynde an hare in a *fourlonge*.'[3]

---

[1] *Prologus,* lines 17 to 21.   [2] *Prologus,* 216 to end.
[3] *Passus,* v. 400 to 428.

Further, a chance indication that the furlongs were divided into half-acre strips occurs most naturally in that part of the story where the folk in the fair field, sick of priests and parsons and other false guides, come at last to Piers the plowman, and beg him to show them the way to truth ; and he replies that he must first plow and sow his ' half-acre :'

> I have an *half acre* to erye · bi the heighe way:
> Hadde I eried this half acre · and sowen it after,
> I wolde wende with you · and the way teche.[1]

And if there should remain a shadow of doubt whether Piers' half-acre must necessarily have been one of the strips between the balks into which the furlongs were divided, even this is cleared up by the perfect little picture which follows of the folk in the field helping him to plow it. For in its unconscious truthfulness of graphic detail, after saying,—

> Now is perkyn and his pilgrymes · to the plowe faren:
> To erie his halue acre · holpyn hym manye,

the very first lines in the list of services rendered explain that—

> Dikeres and delueres · digged up the balkes.[2]

This incidental evidence of ' Piers the Plowman' is fully borne out by a manuscript *terrier* of one of the open fields near Cambridge, belonging to the later years of the fourteenth or beginning of the fifteenth century.[3] It gives the names of the owners and occupiers of all the seliones or strips. They are

---

[1] *Passus*, vi. 4 to 6.
[2] *Passus*, vi. 107–9.
[3] I am indebted to Mr. Brad-shaw for having called my attention to this MS., which is now in the Cambridge University Library.

Chap. II. divided by balks of turf. They lie in furlongs or *quarentenæ*. They have frequently headlands or *foreræ*. Some of the strips are gored, and called *gored acres*. Many of them are described as *butts*. Indeed, were it not that the country round Cambridge being flat there are no *lynches*, almost every one of the features of the system is distinctly visible in this terrier.

The system already decaying.
But this terrier also contains evidence that the system was even then in a state of decay and disintegration. The balks were disappearing, and the strips, though still remembered as strips, were becoming merged in larger portions, so that they lie thrown together *sine balca*. The mention is frequent of iii. seliones which used to be v., ii. which used to be iv., iii. which used to be viii., and so on. Evidently the meaning and use of the half-acre strips are already gone.

It will be well, therefore, to take another leap, and at once to pass behind the Black Death—that great watershed in economic history—so as to examine the details of the system *before* rather than after it had sustained the tremendous shock which the death in one year of half the population may well have given to it.

Winslow Manor rolls of Ed. III.
A remarkably excellent opportunity for inquiry is presented by a complete set of manor rolls during the reign of Edward III. for the Manor of Winslow in Buckinghamshire, preserved in the Cambridge University Library.[1]

---

[1] MS. Dd. 7. 22. I am much indebted to Mr. Bradshaw for the loan of this MS. from the Library.

No evidence could possibly be more to the purpose. Belonging to the Abbey of St. Albans, the rolls were kept with scrupulous accuracy and care. Every change of ownership during the long reign of Edward III. is recorded in regular form ; and the year 1348-9—the year of the Black Death—occurring in the course of this reign, and occasioning more changes of ownership than usual, the MS. presents, if one may appropriate a geological expression, something like an economic section of the manor, revealing with unusual clearness the various economic strata in which its holdings were arranged.

Before examining these holdings it is needful only to state that here, as in the later examples, the fields of the manor are open fields, divided into furlongs, which in their turn are made up with apparently almost absolute regularity of half-acre strips. Whenever (with very rare exceptions) a change of ownership takes place, and the contents of the holding are described, they turn out to be made up of half-acre pieces, or seliones, scattered all over the fields.

The open field.

The typical entry on these rolls in such cases is that A. B. surrenders to the lord, or has died holding, a messuage and so many acres of land, of which a half-acre lies in such and such a field, and often in such and such a furlong, between land of C. D. and E. F., another half-acre somewhere else between two other persons' land, another half-acre somewhere else, and so on. If the holding be of 1½ acres it is found to be in 3 half-acre pieces, if of 4 acres, in 8 half-acre pieces, and so on, scattered over the fields. Sometimes amongst the half-acres are mentioned still smaller portions, roods and even half-roods or doles

Half-acre strips

(chiefly of pasture or meadow land), belonging to the holdings, but the division into half-acre strips was clearly the rule.

There can be no doubt, therefore, of the identity of the system seen at work in these manor rolls with that of which some of the *débris* may still be examined in unenclosed parishes to-day.

II. THE WINSLOW MANOR ROLLS OF THE REIGN OF EDWARD III.—EXAMPLE OF A VIRGATE OR YARD-LAND.

Starting with the fact that the fields of the manor of Winslow and its hamlets [1] were open fields divided into furlongs and half-acre strips, the chief object of inquiry will be the nature of the holdings of its various classes of tenants.

Demesne and villen-age. In the first place the land of the manor was divided, like that of almost all other manors, into two distinct parts—land in the *lord's demesne*, and land in *villenage*.

The land in demesne may be described as the home farm of the lord of the manor, including such portions of it as he may have chosen to let off to tenants for longer or shorter terms, and at money rents in free tenure.

The land in villenage is also in the occupation of tenants, but it is held in villenage, at the will of the lord, and at customary services. It lies in open fields. These are divided into three seasons, according to the

---

[1] The MS. is headed 'Extracta Rotulorum de Halimotis tentis apud Manerium de Wynselowe tempore Edwardi tercii a Conquestu,' and it embraced *Wynselowe, Horelwode, Greneburgh, Shipton, Nova Villa de Wynselowe, Onyng,* and *Muston.*

three-field system. There is a *west field, east field,*
and *south field.* The demesne land lies also in these
three fields,[1] probably more or less intermixed, as in
many cases, with the strips in villenage, but sometimes in separate furlongs or shots from the latter.

Throughout the pages of the manor rolls, in recording transfers of holdings in villenage, the common
form is always adhered to of a surrender by the old
tenant to the lord, and a re-grant of the holding to
the new tenant, to be held by him at the will of the
lord in villenage at the usual services. Where the
change of holding occurs on the death of a tenant, the
common form recites that the holding has reverted to
the lord, who re-grants it to the new tenant as before
in villenage.

Further examination at once discloses a marked
difference in kind between some classes of holdings
in villenage and others.

In some cases the holding handed over is simply
described by the one comprehensive word '*virgata*'
(the Latin equivalent for 'yard-land'), without any
further description. The 'virgate' of A. B. is transferred to C. D. in one lump ; *i.e.* the holding is an
indivisible whole, evidently so well known as to need
no description of its contents.

In other cases the holding is in the same way
described as a '*half-virgate,*' without any details being
needful as to its contents.

But in the case of all other holdings the contents
are described in detail half-acre by half-acre, each
half-acre being identified by the names of the holders

---

[1] See entry under 44 Ed. III.

of the strips on either side of it. They vary in size from one half-acre to 8 or 10 or 12 half-acres, and in a few cases more. The greater number of them are, however, evidently the holdings of small cottier tenants. A few cases occur, but only a few, where a messuage is held without land.

What is a virgate or yard-land? But the question of interest is what may be the nature of the holdings called virgates and half-vir-gates—these well-known *bundles* of land, which, as already said, need no description of their contents. Fortunately in one single case a virgate or yard-land —that of John Moldeson—loses its indivisible unity and is let out again by the lord to several persons in portions. These being new holdings, and no longer making up a virgate, it became needful to describe their contents on the rolls.[1] Thus the details of which a virgate was made up are accidentally exposed to view.

Putting the broken pieces of it together, this vir-gate of John Moldeson is found to have consisted of a messuage in the village of Shipton, in the manor of Winslow, and the following half-acre strips of land scattered all over the open fields of the manor.

The vir-gate or yard-land of John Moldeson.

Where situated.	Between the Land of
½ acre in *Clayforlong.*	*John Boveton* and *William Jonynges.*
½ acre in *Brereforlong.*	*Richard Lif* and *John Mayn.*
½ acre at *Anamanlond* by the king's highway (juxta regiam viam).	
½ acre at *Lofthorn.*	*John Watekyns* and *John Mayn.*
½ acre at *le Wawes.*	*John Hikkes* and *Henry Warde.*
½ acre at *Michelpeysforlong.*	*Henry Warde* and *John Watekyns.*
½ acre above *le Snoute.*	*John Watekyns* and *John Mayn.*
½ acre in *le Snouthale.*	*John Watekyns* and *Henry Warde.*
½ acre above *Livershulle.*	*John Watekyns* and *Henry Warde.*
½ acre above *Narowe-aldemed.*	*John Watekyns* and *Henry Warde.*

[1] Sub anno 35 Ed. III.

The virgate or yard-land of John Moldeson, continued.

Where situated.	*Between the Land of*
½ acre in *Shiptondene.*	*John Hikkes* and *John Howeprest.*
½ acre in *Waterforough.*	*John Watekyns* and *John Mayn.*
2 roods below *Chircheheigh.*	*John Watekyns* and *Henry Warde.*
½ acre at *Fyveacres.*	*John Watekyns* and *John Mayn.*
½ acre at *Sherdeforlong.*	*John Watekyns* and *Henry Warde.*
½ acre at *Thorlong.*	*John Watekyns* and *Henry Warde.*
½ acre (of pasture) in *Farnhamesden.*	*John Watekyns* and *Henry Warde.*
½ acre (of pasture) in three parcels.	
1 acre (of pasture) below *Estattemore.*	
½ acre (of pasture) at *Brodemore.*	*John Watekyns* and *Henry Warde.*
½ acre (of meadow) at *Risshemede.*	*John Watekyns* and *Henry Warde.*
2 doles (of meadow) in *Shrovedoles.*	*John Watekyns* and *Henry Warde.*
½ acre below *le Knolle.*	*John Watekyns* and *Henry Warde.*
½ acre above *Brodealdemade.*	*John Watekyns* and *John Mayn.*
½ acre above *Brodelangelonde.*	*John Watekyns* and *John Mayn.*
½ acre at *Merslade.*	*John Watekyns* and *Henry Warde.*
½ acre above *Langebenehullesdene.*	*John Watekyns* and *Henry Warde.*
½ acre above *Hoggestonforde.*	*John Watekyns* and *Henry Warde.*
½ acre at *Clayforde.*	*John Watekyns* and *John Mayn.*
½ acre at *Narwelanglonde.*	*John Watekyns* and *Henry Warde.*
½ acre at *Wodewey.*	*John Watekyns* and *John Mayn.*
½ acre *Benethenhystrete.*	*William Jonynges* and *Henry Boviton.*
½ acre *Benethenhystrete.*	*John Watekyns* and *John Mayn.*
½ acre at *Langeslo.*	*John Watekyns* and *John Mayn.*
½ acre at *Lowe.*	*John Watekyns* and *Henry Warde.*
½ acre at *le Knolle.*	*John Watekyns* and *Henry Warde.*
½ acre above *Brodealdemede.*	*John Watekyns* and *John Mayn.*
½ acre at *Shortslo.*	*John Watekyns* and *Henry Warde.*
½ acre at *Eldeleyen.*	*John Watekyns* and *John Janekyns.*
½ acre above *Langeblakgrove.*	*John Watekyns* and *Henry Warde.*
½ acre at *Blakeputtis.*	*John Watekyns* and *John Mayn.*
½ acre above *Medeforlong.*	*John Watekyns* and *Henry Warde.*
½ acre at *le Thorn.*	*John Watekyns* and *Henry Warde.*
½ acre above *Overlitellonde.*	*John Watekyns* and *John Mayn.*
½ acre above *le Brodelitellonde.*	*John Watekyns* and *Henry Warde.*
½ acre above *Overlitellonde.*	*John Watekyns* and *John Mayn.*
½ acre above *Medeforlong.*	*John Watekyns* and *Henry Warde.*
½ acre at *le Thorn.*	*John Watekyns* and *Henry Warde.*
½ acre at *Hoggestonforde.*	*John Watekyns* and *Henry Warde.*
½ acre above *Eldeleyes.*	*John Watekyns* and *Henry Warde.*
½ acre above *Cokwell.*	*John Watekyns* and *John Mayn.*

Where situated.	*Between the Land of*
½ acre at *Brodefarnham.*	John Watekyns and Henry Warde.
½ acre at *Langefarnham.*	John Watekyns and Henry Warde.
½ acre above *Farnhamshide.*	Henry Boveton and Richard Atte Halle.
½ acre at *Howeshamme.*	John Watekyns and Henry Warde.
½ acre at *Stonysticch.*	John Watekyns and Henry Warde.
½ acre at *Coppedemore.*	John Watekyns and Henry Warde.
½ acre at *Brerebuttes.*	John Watekyns and Henry Warde.
½ acre at *Wodeforlonge.*	John Watekyns and John Mayn.
½ acre at *Porteweye.*	John Watekyns and John Mayn.
½ acre at *Litebenhulle.*	Henry Boveton and Matthew atte Lane.
½ acre at *Michilblakegrove.*	John Watekyns and Henry Warde.
½ acre at *Litelblakegrove.*	John Watekyns and Henry Warde.
½ acre at *Brodereten.*	John Watekyns and John Mayn.
½ acre at *Brodeliteldon.*	John Watekyns and John Mayn.
½ acre at *Stoteford.*	John Watekyns and John Mayn.
½ acre at *Brodelangelonde.*	John Watekyns and John Mayn.
½ acre above *Litelbelesden.*	John Watekyns and John Mayn.
½ acre in *Anamaneslonde.*	John Watekyns and Henry Warde.
½ acre at *Litelpeisaere.*	John Watekyns and Henry Warde.
1 rood in *le Trendel.*	John Watekyns and Henry Warde.
½ acre at *Merslade.*	John Watekyns and Henry Warde.
½ acre at *Merslade.*	John Watekyns and Henry Warde.
½ acre at *Brodelitellonde.*	John Watekyns and Henry Warde.
½ acre below *le Knolle.*	John Watekyns and Henry Warde.
½ acre above *le Brodealdemede.*	John Watekyns and John Mayn.

Summary of the contents of a virgate or yard-land.

Thus the virgate or yard-land of John Moldeson was composed of a messuage and

> 68 half-acre strips of arable land,
> 3 rood strips of arable land,
> 2 doles,
> 1 acre of pasture,
> 3 half-acres of pasture, and
> 1 half-acre of meadow,

scattered all over the open fields in their various furlongs.

But it may be asked, how can it be proved that the other virgates were like the one virgate of John

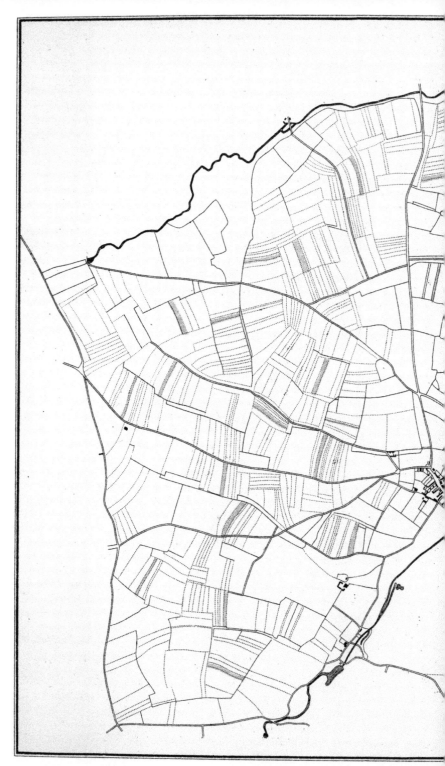

A NORMAL
VIRGATE OR YARDLAND

The normal holding of the villanus,
consisting of a messuage and 30
scattered acres coloured red, by way
of example on the Map of the open
fields of Hitchin.

Scale of a Mile (each division being an Acre)

FURLONG

Edwᵈ Weller

Longmans & Cᵒ

Moldeson thus by chance described and exposed to
view on the manor rolls? Is it right to assume that
this virgate may be taken as a pattern of the rest? The
answer is, that in the description of its 72 half-acre
strips the 144 neighbouring strips are incidentally involved. And as 66 of its strips had on one side of
them 66 other strips of another tenant, viz. John
Watekyns, and on the other side 43 of the next strips
belonged to Henry Warde, and 23 to John Mayn, Rotation
and 8 of the strips only had other neighbours, it is in the
order of
evident that the virgate of John Moldeson was one of a the strips.
system of similar virgates formed of scattered half-acre
strips, arranged in a certain regular order of rotation,
in which John Moldeson came 66 times next to John
Watekyns, and two other neighbours followed him,
one 43 and the other 23 times, in similar succession.

Thus the Winslow virgates were intermixed, and A virgate
each was *a holding of a messuage in the village, and* or yard-
land is a
between 30 *and* 40 *modern acres of land, not con-* bundle of
30 or 40
tiguous, but scattered in half-acre pieces all over the acres in
scattered
common fields. The half-virgate consisted in the same acre or
half-acre
way of a messuage in the village with half as many strips.
strips scattered over the same fields. The intermixed
ownership complained of in the Inclosure Acts, and
surviving in the Hitchin maps, need no longer surprise us.

We know now what a virgate or yard-land was. The
We shall find that its normal area was 30 scattered normal
virgate
acres—10 acres in each of the three fields. Using was of
30 acres.
again the map of the Hitchin fields, we may mark
upon it the contents of a normal virgate by way of
impressing upon the eye the nature of this peculiar
holding. It must always be remembered that when

the fields were divided into half-acres instead of acres the number of its scattered strips would be doubled.

It is not possible to ascertain from a mere record of the changes in the holdings precisely how many of these virgates and half-virgates there were in the manor of Winslow. But in the year of the Black Death it may be assumed that the mortality fell with something like equality upon all classes of tenants, 153 changes of holding from the death of previous holders being recorded in 1348–9. Out of these, 28 were holders of virgates and 14 of half-virgates. The virgates and half-virgates of these holders who died of the Black Death must have included more than 2,400 half-acre strips in the open fields; and adding up the contents of the other holdings of tenants who died that year, it would seem that about two-thirds of the whole area which changed hands in that memorable year were included in the virgates and half-virgates. It may be inferred, therefore, that about the same proportion of the whole area of the open fields must have been included in the virgates and half-virgates whose holders died or survived. Clearly, then, the mass of the land in the open fields was held in these two grades of holdings.[1]

Two-thirds of the land held in virgates and half-virgates.

Thus much, then, may be learned from the Winslow manor rolls with respect to the virgates and half-virgates. Not only were they holdings each composed of a messuage and the scattered strips belonging to it in the open fields, not only did they form the

They are held in villenage.

---

[1] The number of tenants with smaller holdings was considerably larger than the number of holders of virgates and half-virgates, but their holdings were so small that in the aggregate they held a much smaller acreage than the other class.

two chief grades of holdings with equality in each grade, but also they were all alike held in *villenage.* They were not holdings of the lord's demesne land, but of the land in villenage. The holders, besides their virgates and half-virgates, often, it is true, held other land, part of the lord's demesne, as free tenants at an annual rent. But such free holdings were no part of their *virgates.* The virgates and half-virgates were held in villenage. Of these they were not *free* tenants, but *villein* tenants. So also the lesser cottage holdings were held in villenage. But the holders of virgates and half-virgates were the highest grades in the hierarchy of tenants in villenage. They not only held the greater part of the open fields in their bundles of scattered strips; the rolls also show that they almost exclusively served as jurors in the ' Halimot,' or Court of the Manor; though occasionally one or two other villein tenants with smaller holdings were associated with them.[1]

It is possible that just as villein tenants could hold in free tenure land in the lord's demesne, so free men might hold virgates in villenage and retain their personal freedom; but those at all events of the holders of virgates who were *nativi, i.e.* villeins by descent were *adscripti glebæ.* They held their holdings at the will of the lord, and were bound to perform the customary services. If they allowed their houses to

The villein holders, ' villani,' are ' adscripti glebæ.'

---

[1] Out of 43 jurymen who had served in 1346, 1347, and 1348, 27 died of the Black Death in 1348–9. Out of these 27 who died, and whose holdings therefore can be traced, 16 held virgates, 8 held half-virgates, and of the other 3 one held 1 messuage and 2 cottages, another a messuage and 15 acres in villenage (equivalent to a half-virgate), and the third 8 acres arable and 2½ of meadow.

get out of repair they were guilty of *waste*, and the jury were fined if they did not report the neglect.[1]

Yet the entries in the rolls prove that their holdings were hereditary, passing by the lord's re-grant from father to son by the rule of primogeniture, on payment of the customary heriot or relief.[2]

Widows had dower, and widowers were *tenants by the curtesy*, as in the case of freeholds. The holders in villenage, even 'nativi,' could make wills which were proved before the *cellerarius* of the abbey, and had done so time out of mind, while the wills of free tenants were proved at St. Albans.[3]

These things all look like a certain recognition of freedom within the restraints of the villenage. But if the 'nativi' married without the lord's consent they were fined. If they sold an ox without licence, again they were fined. If they left the manor without licence they were searched for, and if found arrested as fugitives and brought back.[4] If their daughters lost their chastity [5] the lord again had his fine. And

---

[1] Cases of this are numerous after the Black Death. See in 27 Ed. III. one case, in 28 Edward III. 11 cases, in 30 Ed. III. five cases.

[2] All the 153 holdings which changed hands on the death of the tenants of the Black Death were re-granted to the single heir of the deceased holder or to a reversioner, or in default of such were retained by the lord. In no case was there a subdivision by inheritance. The *heriot* of a virgate was generally an ox, or money payment of its value. But the amount was often reduced 'propter paupertatem;' and some- times when a succeeding tenant could not pay, a half-acre was deducted from the virgate and held by the lord instead of the heriot.

[3] See under 23 Ed. III. a record of the unanimous finding of the jury to this effect.

[4] The instances of fugitive villeins are very numerous for years after the Black Death; and inquiry into cases of this class formed a prominent part of the business transacted at the halimotes.

[5] There were 22 cases of 'Lerewyt' recorded on the manor rolls in the first 10 years of Edward III.

in all these cases the whole jury were fined if they neglected to report the delinquent.

Their services were no doubt limited and defined by custom, and so late as the reign of Edward III. mostly discharged by a money payment in lieu of the actual service, but they rested nominally on the will of the lord ; and sometimes to test their obedience the relaxed rein was tightened, and trivial orders were issued, such as that they should go off to the woods and pick nuts for the lord.[1] In case of dispute a court was held under the great ash tree at St. Albans, and the decision of this superior manorial court at head-quarters settled the question.[2] This villenage of the Winslow tenants was, no doubt, in the fourteenth century mild in its character ; the silent working of economic laws was breaking it up ; but it was villenage still. It was serfdom, but it was serfdom in the last stages of its relaxation and decay.

Already, any harking back by the landlord upon older and stricter rules—any return, for instance, to the actual services instead of the money payments in lieu of them—produced resentment and insubordination amongst the villein tenants. Murmurs were already heard in the courts, and symptoms appear on the rolls in the year following the Black Death which clearly indicate the presence of smouldering embers very likely soon to burst into flame.[3] The rebellion under Wat Tyler was, in fact, not far ahead. But in this inquiry we are looking backwards into earlier times, in order to learn what English serfdom was when fully in force, rather than in the days when

---

[1] See a case in 25 Ed. III.   [2] See a case of this in 6 Ed. III.
[3] See under 6 Ed. III.

it was breaking up. In the meantime the practical knowledge gained from the Winslow manor rolls, how a community in serfdom fitted as it were into the open field system as into an outer shell, and still more the knowledge of what the virgate and half-virgate in villenage really were, drawn from actual examples, may prove a useful key in unlocking still further the riddle of earlier serfdom.

III. THE HUNDRED ROLLS OF EDWARD I., EMBRACING FIVE MIDLAND COUNTIES.

The facts thus learned from the Winslow Manor Rolls throw just that flash of light upon the otherwise dry details of the Hundred Rolls of Edward I. which is needful to make the picture they give in detail of the manors in parts of five midland counties vivid and clear.

English economic history is rich in its materials; and of all the records of the economic condition of England, next to the Domesday Survey, the Hundred *Surveys of* Rolls are the most important and remarkable. The *manors in* *five* second volume, in its 1,000 folio pages, contains *inter* *counties,* *alia* a true and clear description of every manor in a *A.D. 1279.* large district, embracing portions of Oxfordshire, Berkshire, Bedfordshire, Huntingdonshire, and Cambridgeshire, in about the year 1279; and as in most cases the name of every tenant is recorded, with the character of his holding and a description of his payments and services, the picture of each manor has almost the detail and accuracy of a photograph. Turning over its pages, the mass of detail may at first appear confused and bewildering, and in one sense it is so, because

it relates to a system which, however simple when
fully at work, becomes broken up and entangled
whilst in process of disintegration.   But the key to it
once mastered, the original features of the system may
still be recognised.   Even the broken pieces fall into
their proper places, and the general economic outlines
of the several manors stand out sharply and clearly
marked.

Speaking generally, in its chief economic features
every manor is alike, as in the record itself one
common form of survey serves for them all.   Hence
the Winslow example gives the requisite key to the
whole.   Bringing to the record the knowledge of how
the open fields were everywhere divided into furlongs,
and acre or half-acre strips, and that virgates and
half-virgates were equal bundles of strips scattered
all over the fields, the description of the manors in
the Hundred Rolls becomes perfectly intelligible.

In the first place the manor consists, as in the
Winslow example, of two parts—the land in demesne
and the land in villenage.

The land in demesne consists of the home farm,
and portions, irregular in area, let out from it to what
are called free tenants (*libere tenentes*), some of them
being nevertheless villeins holding their portions of
the demesne lands in free tenure at certain rents in
addition to their regular holdings.

The land in villenage, as in the Winslow manor, is
held mostly in virgates and half-virgates, and below
these cottiers hold smaller holdings, also in villenage.

In describing the tenants in villenage there is first
a statement that A. B. holds a *virgate* in villenage at
such and such payments and services, which are often

very minutely described. The money value of each service and the total value of them all is in many cases also carefully given. This description of the holding and services of A. B. is then followed by a list of persons who also *each* hold a virgate at the same services as A. B.

Secondly, there is a similar statement in detail that C. D. holds a *half-virgate* in villenage, and that such and such are his payments and services, followed by a similar list of persons who also *each* hold a half-virgate at the same services as C. D.

Cottier tenants.

Then follows a list of the little cottier tenants, and their holdings and services. Amongst some of these cottage holdings there is equality, some are irregular, and some consist of a cottage and nothing else.

These holdings are all in villenage, but, as before mentioned, the names of the villein tenants often occur again in the list of free tenants (*libere tenentes*) of portions of the lord's demesne or of recently reclaimed land (*terra assarta*).

This may be taken as a fair description of the common type of manor throughout the Hundred Rolls, with local variations.

With exceptional variations the manors are all of one type.

The chief of these is that in many places in Cambridgeshire and Huntingdonshire the holdings of the *villani*, instead of being described as virgates and half-virgates, are described by their acreage. There are so many holders of 30, 20, 15, 10, or other number of acres each. They are not the less in grades, with equality in each grade, but the holdings bear no distinctive name.

There is also in these counties a class of tenants, partly above the *villani*, called *sochemanni*, which we shall find again when we reach the Domesday Survey. But upon exceptional local circumstances it is not needful to dwell here.

The fact is, then, that in the Hundred Rolls of Edward I. there is disclosed over the much wider area of five midland counties almost precisely the same state of things as that which existed in the manor of Winslow late in the reign of Edward III. That manor was under the ecclesiastical lordship of an abbey, but here in the Hundred Rolls the same state of things exists under all kinds of ownership. Manors of the king or the nobility, of abbeys, and of private and lesser landowners, are all substantially alike. In all there is the division of the manor into demesne land and land in villenage. In all the mass of the land in villenage is held in the grades of holdings mostly called virgates and half-virgates, with equality in each grade both as to the holding and the services. In all alike are found the smaller cottage holdings, also in villenage ; and lastly, in all alike there are the free tenants of larger or smaller portions of the demesne land.

If the picture of a manor and its open fields and virgates or yard-lands in villenage—*i.e.* both of the shell and of the community in serfdom inhabiting the shell — drawn in detail from the single Winslow example, has thrown light upon the Hundred Rolls, these latter, embracing hundreds of manors in the midland counties of England, give the picture a typical value, proving that it is true, not for one manor only, but, speaking generally, for all the manors of central England.

The open field system is the shell of serfdom.

They also give additional information on the relation of the holdings to the *hide,* and reveal more clearly than the Winslow manor rolls the nature of the serfdom under which the villein tenants held their virgates. Before passing from the Hundred Rolls it will be worth while to examine the new facts they give us, and to devote a section to an examination of the *services.*

IV. THE HUNDRED ROLLS (*continued*)—RELATION OF THE VIRGATE TO THE HIDE AND CARUCATE.

Before passing to the villein services described in the Hundred Rolls, evidence may be cited from them showing the relation of the virgate or yard-land— which is now known to be the normal holding of the normal tenant in villenage—to the *hide* and *carucate.* If to the knowledge of what a virgate was, can be added an equally clear understanding of what a *hide* was, another valuable step will be gained.

In the rolls for Huntingdonshire a series of entries occurs, describing, contrary to the usual practice of the compilers, the number of acres in a virgate, and the number of virgates in a hide, in several manors.

These entries are given below,[1] and they show clearly—

(1) That the bundle of scattered strips called a virgate did not always contain the same number of acres.

(2) That the *hide* did not always contain the same number of virgates.

But at the same time it is evident that the hide in

---

[1] For Table of entries see next page.

Huntingdonshire most often contained 120 acres or thereabouts. It did so in twelve cases out of nineteen. In one case it contained the double of 120, *i.e.* 240 acres. In six cases only the contents varied irregularly from the normal amount.

Chap. II.

The normal *hide* four virgates or 120 acres; the double hide of 240 acres : but there are local variations.

Taking the normal hides of 120 acres, five of them were made up of four virgates of thirty acres each, which we may take to have been *normal* virgates. In one case there were eight virgates of fifteen acres each in the hide. In other places these probably would have been called half-virgates, as at Winslow.

There were occasionally five virgates and sometimes six virgates in the hide, and the fact of these variations will be found to have a meaning hereafter ; but in the meantime we may gather from the instances given in the Hundred Rolls for Huntingdonshire, that the *normal* hide consisted as a rule of four virgates of about thirty acres each. The really important

Rot. Hund.	No. of virgates in each hide	Acres in a virgate	Acres in a hide
II. p. 629	VI.	40	240
	VI.	28	168
	IV.	48	192
631	VI.	30	180
635	VI.	25	150
636	IV.	30	120
	V.	25	125
637	VIII.	15	120
640	IV.	30	120
640	V.	25	125
645	IV.	30	120
646	V.	26	130
648	IV.	30	120
653	IV.	30	120
654	IV.	30	120
656	VI.	24	144
658	V.	25	125
660	V.	25	125
661	VI.	20	120

consequence resulting from this is the recognition of the fact that as the *virgate* was a bundle of so many scattered strips in the open fields, the *hide*, so far as it consisted of actual virgates in villenage, was also a bundle—a compound and fourfold bundle—of scattered strips in the open fields.

Whilst, however, marking this relation of the virgate to the hide, regarded as actual holdings in villenage, it is necessary to observe also that throughout the Hundred Rolls the assessed value of the manors is generally stated in hides and virgates; and that, in the estimate thus given of the *hidage* of a manor as a whole, the demesne land as well as the land in villenage is taken into account. In this case the hide and virgate are used as measures of assessment, and it does not follow that all land that was measured or estimated by the hide and virgate was actually divided up by balks into acres, although the demesne land itself was in fact, as we have seen, often in the open fields, and intermixed with the strips in villenage. Distinction must therefore be made between the hide and virgate as actual holdings and the hide and virgate as customary land measures, used for recording the assessed values or the extent of manors, just as in the case of the acre.

The virgate and the hide were probably, like the acre, actual holdings before they were adopted as abstract land measures. It may be even possible to learn or to guess what fact made a particular number of acres the most convenient holding.

The scutage. In the Hundred Rolls for Oxfordshire there is frequent reference to the payment of the tax called *scutage*. The normal amount of this is assumed

The ancient hidage or assessment of taxation.

to be 40*s.* for each *knight's fee*, or *scutum*. And it
appears that the knight's fee was assumed to contain
four normal hides. There is an entry, ' One hide
gives scutage for a fourth part of one scutum.' And
as four virgates went usually to each hide, so each
virgate should contribute $\frac{1}{16}$ of a scutum. There are
several entries which state that when the scutage is
40*s.* each virgate pays 2*s.* 6*d.*, which is $\frac{1}{16}$ of 40*s.*[1]

And these figures seem to lead one step further, Connexion between acreage of holdings and the coinage.
and to connect the normal acreage of the hide of
120A., and of the virgate of 30A., with the scutage of
40*s.* per knight's fee ; for when these normal acreages
were adhered to in practice the assessment would be
one penny per acre, and the double hide of 240 acres
would pay one pound. In other words, in choosing
the acreage of the standard hide and virgate, a number of acres was probably assumed, corresponding
with the monetary system, so that the number of
pence in the ' scutum' should correspond with the
number of acres assessed to its payment. We shall
find this correspondence of acreage with the coinage
by no means confined to this single instance.

But there remains the question, why the acreage
in the virgate and hide as actual holdings, and the

---

[1] *Hundred Rolls, Oxon.*

II. 708. Every virgate gives scutage 2*s.* 6*d.* when the scutage is 40*s.*

2 virgates give	„	5*s.*	„	„	40*s.*
1 virgate gives	„	2*s.* 6*d.*	„	„	40*s.*
4 virgates give	„	10*s.*	„	„	40*s.*
2 „ „	„	5*s.*	„	„	40*s.*,&c.
II. 709. 4 „ „	„	8*s.*	„	„	40*s.*
5 „ „	„	11*s.* 5*d.*	„	„	40*s.*

II. 830. 1 hide gives scutage for a fourth part of a scutum.

From these instances it is evident that normally 4 virgates = 1 hide, and
4 hides make a knight's fee.

CHAP. II.

Carucate, or land of a plough team, used instead of the hide for later taxation,

and varied according to the soil.

Services often commuted into money payments.

number of virgates in the hide, were not constant. Their actual contents and relations were evidently ruled by some other reason than the number of pence in a pound.

A trace at least of the original reason of the varying contents and relations of the hide and virgate is to be found in the Hundred Rolls, as, indeed, almost everywhere else, in the use of another word in the place of *hide*, when, instead of the anciently assessed hidage of a manor, its more modern actual taxable value is examined into and expressed. This new word is ' carucate '—*the land of a plough or plough team,*— ' caruca ' being the mediæval Latin term for both plough and plough team.

The Hundred Rolls for Bedfordshire afford several examples in point. In some cases the carucate seems to be identical with the normal hide of 120 acres, but other instances show that the carucate varied in area.[1] It is the land cultivated by a plough team ; varying in acreage, therefore, according to the lightness or heaviness of the soil, and according to the strength of the team.

V. THE HUNDRED ROLLS (*continued*)—THE SERVICES OF THE VILLEIN TENANTS.

In the Hundred Rolls for Bedfordshire and Buckinghamshire the services of the villein tenants

---

[1] *Hundred Rolls, Beds.*

II. 321. Carucate of 120 acres.	II. 328. Carucate of 200 acres.
324 ,, 80 ,,	329 ,, 80 ,,
325 ,, 100 ,,	332 ,, 100 ,,
326 ,, 120 ,,	

are almost always commuted into money payments.
From each virgate a payment of from 16*s.* to 20*s.* is
described as due, or services to that value (*vel opera
ad valorem*), showing that the actual services have
become the exception, and the money payments the
rule. But in many cases distinguishing marks of
serfdom still remained in the fine upon the marriage
of a daughter, the heriot on the death of the holder,
and the restraint on the sale of animals.[1]

In Huntingdonshire and Oxfordshire, on the other
hand, the services, whilst often having their money
value assigned, are mostly given in great detail, as
though still frequently enforced.

Speaking generally, the chief services, notwith _Of three_
standing variations in detail, may be classed under _kinds._
three different heads.

(1) There is the *weekly work* at ploughing, reap- _Week_
ing, carrying, usually for two or three days a week, _work._
and most at harvest-time. In other cases there are
so many days' work required between certain dates.

(2) There are *precariæ*, or ' boon-days,' some- _Precariæ._
times called *bene works*—special or extra services
which the lord has a right to require, sometimes the
lord providing food for the day, and sometimes the
tenant providing for himself.

(3) There are *payments in kind or in money* at _Fixed dues_
specified times, such as Christmas, Easter, Martinmas, _in money_
and Michaelmas dues ; *churchshot*, an ancient ecclesias- _or in kind._

---

[1] *Hundred Rolls, Bedfordshire.*
—' Et sunt illi villani ita servi quod
non possunt maritare filias nisi ad
voluntatem domini ' (II. 329).
   ' Nec pullos sibi pullatos mas-

(II. 328).
   Buckinghamshire. — ' Sunt ad
voluntatem domini, et ad alia faci-
enda quæ ad servilem conditionem
pertinent ' (II. 335-6). And so on.

tical due ; besides contributions towards the lord's taxes in the shape of *tallage* or *scutage*.

Sometimes the services are to be performed with one or two labourers, showing that the cottier tenants were labourers under the holders of virgates, or indicating possibly in some cases the remains of a slave class.

The chief weekly services were those of ploughing, the tenants sometimes supplying oxen to the lord's plough team, sometimes using their own ploughs, two or more joining their oxen for the purpose. This co-operation is a marked feature of the services, and is found also in connexion with reaping and carrying.

The cottier tenants in respect of their smaller holdings often worked for their lord one day a week, and having no plough, or oxen, their services did not include ploughing.

Annexed are typical instances of the services of both classes of tenants. They are taken from three counties, and placed side by side for comparison.

EXAMPLES OF VILLEIN SERVICES.

OXFORDSHIRE	HUNTINGDONSHIRE	CAMBRIDGESHIRE
Of a Villanus holding a Virgate.[1]	*Of a Villanus holding a Virgate.*[2]	*Of a Villanus holding ½ Virgate of 15 acres.*[3]
A. B. holds a virgate, and owes— 82 days' work [about *s. d.* 2 days a week] between Michaelmas and June 24, valued at ½*d.* = . . 3 5 11½ days' work [rather more than 2 days a week] be-	A. B. holds 1 virgate in villenage— By paying 12*d.* at Michaelmas. By doing works from Michaelmas to Easter, with the exception of the fortnight after Christmas, viz. 2 days each week,	A. B. holds a ½ virgate of customable land containing 15 acres, and does 3 days' work each week throughout the year, and 3 precariæ, with

[1] II. 744 *b*. [2] II. 642 *a*. [3] II. 554 *b*.

OXFORDSHIRE	HUNTINGDONSHIRE	CAMBRIDGESHIRE
Of a Villanus holding a Virgate.	*Of a Villanus holding a Virgate.*	*Of a Villanus holding ½ Virgate of 15 acres.*

		s.	*d.*
tween June 24 and August 1, valued at 1*d.* = . .			11½
19 days' work [2½ days a week] between August 1 and Michaelmas, valued at 1½*d.* = .		2	4½
6 precariæ, with one man, valued at .			12
1 precaria, with 2 men, for reaping, with food from the lord, valued at .			2
Half a carriage for carrying the wheat			1
Half a carriage for the hay . .			1
The ploughing and harrowing of an acre . . .			6
1 ploughing called ' *graserthe* ' . .			1½
1 day's harrowing of oat[land] . .			1
1 horse [load] of wood . . .			½
Making 1 quarter of malt, and drying it			1
1 day's work at washing and shearing sheep, valued at .			½
1 day's hoeing . .			½
3 days' mowing .			6
1 day's nutting .			½
1 day's work in carrying to the stack .			½

Tallage once a year at the lord's will.

HUNTINGDONSHIRE

with one man each day.

Item, he shall plough with his own plough one selion and a half on every Friday in the aforesaid time.

Item, he shall harrow the same day as much as he has ploughed.

He shall do works from Easter to Pentecost, 2 days each week, with one man each day.

And he shall plough one selion each Friday in the same time.

He shall do works from Pentecost till August 1, for 3 days each week, with one man each day, either hoeing the corn, or mowing and lifting (*levand*).

He shall do works from August 1 till September 8, for 3 days each week, with two men each day.

He shall make 1 ' *lovebonum* ' with all his family except his wife, finding his own food. And from September 8 to Michaelmas he works 3 days each week, with one man each day. He shall carry [with a horse or horses] as far as Bolnhurst, and from Bolnhurst to Torneye.

CAMBRIDGESHIRE

meals found by the lord, and gives at Martinmas 1*d.*, and a hen at Christmas, and 8 eggs at Easter; and the same works and customs if ' *ad firmam* ' are valued at 9*s.* per annum.

(20 others each hold 15 acres with like services.)

OXFORDSHIRE	HUNTINGDONSHIRE	CAMBRIDGESHIRE
	Of a Villanus holding a Virgate. Also he gives ½ bushel of corn as '*bensed*' in winter-time. Also 10 bushels of oats at Martinmas as '*fodderkorn*.' Also 7 *d.* as '*loksilver*,' that is for 2*d.* a loaf, and 5 hens. Also 1 *d.* on Ash-Wednesday, as '*fispeni*' (fishpenny). Also 20 eggs at Easter. Also 10 eggs on St. Botolph's Day (June 17). Also in Easter week 2*d.* towards digging the vineyard. Also in Pentecost week 1*d.* towards upholding the mill-dam (*stagnum*) of Newetone. If he sell a bull calf he shall give the lord abbot 4*d.*, and this according to custom. He gives '*merchetum*' and '*herietum*,' and is tallaged at Michaelmas according to the will of the said abbot. He gives 2*d.* as '*sumewode silver*' at Christmas.	
Of a Cotarius.[1] A. B. holds one croft, and owes from Michaelmas to August 1, each workable week, one day's work of whatever kind the lord requires.	*Of a Cotarius.*[2] A. B. holds 1 acre at 12*d.*, and works 4 days in autumn with one man. He is tallaged '*quando*	*Of a Cotarius.*[3] A. B. is a cotarius, and holds 1 cottage and 1 acre, for which he gives—

[1] II. 758 *a.*   [2] II. 613 *b.*   [3] II. 535 *b.*

OXFORDSHIRE	HUNTINGDONSHIRE	CAMBRIDGESHIRE
Of a Cotarius.	*Of a Cotarius.*	*Of a Cotarius.*
At Martinmas gives 1 cock and 3 hens for churchshot, and ought to drive to certain places, and to carry writs,[1] his food being found by the lord; also to wash and shear sheep, receiving a loaf and a half, and being partaker of the cheese with the *servi*; and to hoe. In the autumn, to work and receive like as each *servus* works and receives for the whole week.[2] (10 cottiers do like services).	*Rex talliat burgos suos.'* He gives '*garshaves*' each year for pigs killed and sold, viz. for a pig a year old, ½*d.* And when there is pannage in the lord's wood he gives for a pig of a year old, 1*d.* And if he keeps his pigs alive beyond a year, he gives nothing.	1 day's work on Monday in every week unless a festival prevents him. 1 hen at Christmas. 5 eggs at Easter.

VI. DESCRIPTION IN FLETA OF A MANOR IN THE TIME OF EDWARD I.

Contemporary in date with the Hundred Rolls is the anonymous work bearing the title of ' *Fleta*,' which may be described as the *vade mecum* of the landlords of the time of Edward I. It was designed to put them in possession of necessary legal knowledge; and mixed up with this are practical directions regarding the management of their estates. The writer advises landlords on taking possession of their manors to have a survey made of their property, so that they may know the extent of their rights and income.

Landlords view of a manor.

If in the Hundred Rolls we have photographic details of hundreds of individual manors surveyed

---

[1] In another manor in Huntingdonshire certain cottiers ought to make summonses. II. 616.

[2] The Latin text is badly printed here, but the original has been inspected.

for purposes of royal taxation, so here is a picture of an ordinary or typical manor—a generalisation of the ordinary features of a manor—drawn by a contemporary hand, and regarding all things from a landlord's point of view.

The manor as described in Fleta is a territorial unit, with its own courts and local customs known only on the spot. Therefore the extent is to be taken upon the testimony of 'faithful and sworn tenants of the lord.' And inquiry is to be made [1]—

Survey of a manor.

(1) Of castles and buildings in the demesne (*intrinsecis*) within and without the moat, with gardens, curtilages, dovecotes, fish-ponds, &c.

(2) What fields (*campi*) and *culturæ* there are in demesne, and how many acres of arable in each *cultura* of meadow and of pasture.

(3) What common pasture there is outside the demesne (*forinseca*), and what beasts the lord can place thereon [he, like his tenants, being as to this limited in his rights by custom].

(4) Of parks and demesne woods, which the lord at his will can cultivate and reclaim (*assartare*).

(5) Of woods outside the demesne (*forinsecis*), in which others have common rights, how much the lord may approve.

(6) Of pannage, herbage, and honey, and all other issues of the forests, woods, moors, heaths, and wastes.

(7) Of mills [belonging to the lord, and having a monopoly of grinding for the tenants at fixed charges], fishponds, rivers (*ripariis*), and fisheries several and common.

(8) Of pleas and perquisites belonging to the county, manor, and forest courts.

(9) Of churches belonging to the lord's advowson.

(10) Of heriots, fairs, markets, tolls, day-works (*operationes*), services, foreign (*forinseci*) customs, and gifts (*exhenniis*).

(11) Of warrens, liberties, parks, coneyburrows, wardships, reliefs, and yearly fees.

Then regarding the tenants,—

Free tenants.

(1) *De libere tenentibus*, or free tenants, how many are *intrinseci* and how many *forinseci*; what lands they hold of the lord, and

---

[1] *Fleta*, lib. 2, c. 71. Compare also '*Extenta Manerii:*' *Statutes of the Realm*, i. p. 242.

what of others, and by what service; whether by *socage*, or by *military* service, or by fee farm, or 'in eleemosynam'; who hold by charter, and who not; what rents they pay; which of them do suit at the lord's court, &c.; and what accrues to the lord at their death.

(2) *De custumariis*, or villein tenants; how many there are, and what is their suit; how much each has, and what it is worth, both *de antiquo dominico* and *de novo perquisito*; to what amount they can be tallaged without reducing them to poverty and ruin; what is the value of their '*operationes*' and '*consuetudines*' —their day-works and customary duties—and what rent they pay; and which of them can be tallaged '*ratione sanguinis nativi*,' and who not.

Villein tenants.

Then there follows a statement of the duties of the usual officials of the manor.

Officers.

First there is the *seneschal*,[1] or steward, whose duty it is to hold the Manor Courts and the View of Frankpledge, and there to inquire if there be any withdrawals of customs, services, and rents, or of suits to the lord's courts, markets, and mills, and as to alienations of lands. He is also to check the amount of seed required by the *præpositus* for each manor, for under the seneschal there may be several manors.

The seneschal, or steward;

On his appointment he must make himself acquainted with the condition of the manorial ploughs and plough teams. He must see that the land is properly arranged, whether on the three field or the two-field system. If it be divided into *three parts*, 180 acres should go to each carucate, viz. 60 acres to be ploughed in winter, 60 in Lent, and 60 in summer for fallow. If in *two parts*, there should be 160 acres to the carucate, half for fallow, half for winter and Lent sowing, *i.e.* 80 acres in each of the two 'fields.'

who arranges the ploughing and the plough teams.

---

[1] *Fleta*, lib. 2, c. 72.

Besides the manorial ploughs and plough teams he must know also how many tenant or villein ploughs (*carucæ adjutrices*) there are, and how often they are bound to aid the lord in each manor.

He is also to inquire as to the stock in each manor, whereof an inventory indented is to be drawn up between him and the serjeant; and as to any deficiency of beasts, which he is at once to make good with the lord's consent.

The seneschal thus had jurisdiction over all the manors of the lord. But each single manor should have its own *præpositus*.

The best husbandman is to be elected by the *villata*, or body of tenants, as *præpositus*, and he is to be responsible for the cultivation of the arable land. He must see that the ploughs are yoked early in the morning—both the demesne and the villein ploughs—and that the land is properly ploughed (*pure et conjunctim*) and sown. He is a villein tenant, and acts on behalf of the villeins, but he is overlooked by the lord's bailiff.

The *bailiff's*[1] duties are stated to be—To rise early and have the ploughs yoked, then walk in the fields to see that all is right. He is to inspect the ploughs, whether those of the demesne or the villein or auxiliary ploughs, seeing that they be not unyoked before their day's work ends, failing which he will be called to account. At sowing-time the bailiff, *præpositus*, and reaper must go with the ploughs through the whole day's work until they have completed their proper quantity of ploughing for the day,

---

[1] *Fleta*, lib. 2. c. 73.

which is to be measured, and if the ploughmen have made any errors or defaults, and can make no excuses, the reaper is to see that such faults do not go uncorrected and unpunished.

Such is the picture, given by Fleta, of the manorial machine at work grinding through its daily labour on the days set apart for service on the lord's demesne.

The other side of the picture, the work of the *villani* for themselves on other days, the yoking of their oxen in the common plough team, and the ploughing and sowing of their own scattered strips ; whether this was arranged with equal regard to rigid custom, or whether in Fleta's time the co-operation had become to some extent broken up, so that each villein tenant made his own arrangements by contract with his fellows, or otherwise—this inferior side of the picture is left undrawn.

In the meantime, returning to the question of the holdings in villenage, an additional reason for the variations in their acreage is found in the statement already alluded to, viz. that the extent of the actual carucate, or land of one plough team, was dependent, among other things, upon whether the system of husbandry was the two-field or the three-field system, each plough team being able to cultivate a larger acreage on the former than on the latter system.

VII. S.E. OF ENGLAND—THE HIDE AND VIRGATE UNDER OTHER NAMES (THE RECORDS OF BATTLE ABBEY AND ST. PAUL'S).

Passing now to the south-eastern counties, there are in the Record Office valuable MSS. relating to the

E

estates of Battle Abbey.[1]   There are two distinct surveys of these estates, made respectively in the reigns of Edward I. and Henry VI.

The date of the earliest MS. is from 12 to 15 Edward I. (1284–7).   It is, therefore, almost contemporaneous with the Hundred Rolls.   The estates lay in various counties ; but wherever situated, the same general phenomena as those already described are found.

Confining attention to the regular grades of holdings in villenage, the following are examples from the Battle Abbey estates.

The abbot had an estate at Brichwolton (or Brightwalton), in Berkshire.   In the survey of it 10 holders of a virgate each are recorded as *virgarii*, and in the MS. of Henry VI., 5 holders of half-virgates are in the same way called *dimidii virgarii.*

There was another estate at 'Apeldreham,' in Sussex.   Here, under the heading 'Isti subscripti dicuntur *Yherdlinges,*' there is a list of 5 holders of virgates, 4 holders of $1\frac{1}{2}$ virgates each, and one of $\frac{1}{2}$ a virgate.

At 'Alsiston,' in Sussex, a manor nestling under the chalk downs, the holdings were as follows :—

1 wista and 1 great wista.	1 wista.
½ hide.	½ hide.
1 hide.	½ hide.
½ hide and 1 wista.	½ hide.
3 wistas and 1 great wista.	1 wista.
½ hide.	½ hide.
½ hide.	The præpositus 1 wista
½ hide.	(without services).
½ hide.	

---

[1] Augmentation Office, *Miscellaneous Books,* Nos. 56 and 57.

In the description of the services, those for each half-hide are first given, and then there follows a note that each half-hide contains two wistas ; wherefore the services of each wista are half those above mentioned.

There is another manor (Blechinton, near the coast), where there were—

> 2 holdings of half-hides,
> 9 of wistas,
> 6 of half-wistas,

and two other manors where the holders were in one case 5, all of half-hides ; and in the other case one of a hide and 4 of half-hides.

These are valuable examples of hides and half-hides, as still actual holdings in villenage, whilst apparently instead of virgates in some of these Sussex manors a new holding—the wista—occurs. And among the documents of Battle Abbey given by Dugdale there is the following statement, viz., that 8 virgates = 1 hide, and 4 virgates = 1 wista (*great* wista?). Supposing the virgate here, as mostly elsewhere, to have been, normally, a bundle of 30 acres, it is clear that in this hide of 8 virgates we get another instance of the *double hide of* 240 *acres* ; whilst the ' *great* The double wista ' of 4 virgates would correspond with the single $\begin{smallmatrix}\text{hide of}\\240\text{ acres.}\end{smallmatrix}$ hide of 120 acres, and the wista would equal the ordinary half-hide of two virgates.

We pass to another cartulary, and of earlier date. Domesday In 1222 a visitation was made of the manors belong- $\begin{smallmatrix}\text{of St.}\\\text{Paul's, A.D.}\end{smallmatrix}$ ing to the Dean and Chapter of St. Paul's, London. 1222. The register of this visitation is known as the ' Domesday of St. Paul's.' [1] The manors were scattered in

---

[1] *The Domesday of St. Paul's*, edited by Archdeacon Hale, Camden Society, 1858.

Herts, Essex, Middlesex, and Surrey—all south-eastern counties.

In the survey of Thorp,[1] one of the manors in Essex, after a list of tenants on the demesne land, and others on reclaimed land (*de essarto*), there follows a list of tenants in villenage who are called *hydarii*. As in the Battle Abbey records the *virgarii* were holders of virgates, so these *hydarii* were probably, as their name implies, groups of *villani* holding a hide. But the holdings had in fact become subdivided and irregular. Nevertheless, those belonging to each original hide are bracketed together; and adding together their acreage, it appears that the hide is assumed to contain 120 acres. The following examples will make it clear that the holdings were once hides of four virgates of 30 acres each.

Hides and virgates.

Holdings.

$$
\left.
\begin{array}{l}
\left.\begin{array}{l}\text{xx. } a. \\ \text{x. } a.\end{array}\right\} = 30\ a. \\
\text{xxx. } a. \quad = 30\ a. \\
\tfrac{1}{2}\ \text{hide} \quad = 60\ a.
\end{array}
\right\} = \text{hide of 120 acres.}
$$

$$
\left.
\begin{array}{l}
\text{xxx. } a. \quad = 30\ a. \\
\text{xxx. } a. \quad = 30\ a. \\
\left.\begin{array}{l}\text{xv. } a. \\ \text{xv. } a\end{array}\right\} = 30\ a. \\
\left.\begin{array}{l}\text{v. } a \\ \text{v. } a. \\ \text{vii.}\tfrac{1}{3}\ a. \\ \text{v. } a. \\ \text{vii.}\tfrac{1}{2}\ a.\end{array}\right\} = 30\ a.
\end{array}
\right\} = \text{hide of 120 acres.}
$$

And so on.

Services reckoned by the hide.

The services also were reckoned by the hide, and an abstract of them is here given, from which it will be seen that for some purposes the tenants of the now divided hide still clubbed as it were together to

---

[1] Pp. 38 *et seq.*

perform the services required for the hide ; whilst for others ' each homestead (*domus*) of the hide ' had its separate duties to perform.

The following were the services on the manor of Thorp : [1]—

Each of the *hidarii* ought to plough 8 acres, 4 in winter and 4 in Lent.
  Also to harrow and sow with the lord's seed.
  After Pentecost each house (*domus*) of the hide has to hoe thrice.
  And to reap 4 acres, 2 of rye (*siligine*), and 2 of barley and oats.
  And find a waggon (*carrum*) with 2 men to carry the hard grain, and another to carry the soft grain ; and each waggon (*plaustrum*) shall have 1 sheaf.
Each house of the hide has to mow 3 half-acres.
Each house of the hide has to provide a man to reap until the third [day], if aught remains.
Each house of the hide and of the demesne allotted to tenants has to provide the strongest man whom it has for the lord's '*precariæ*' in autumn, the lord providing him meals twice a day.
All men, both of the hide and of the demesne, have to provide their own ploughs for the lord's '*precariæ,*' the lord providing their meals.
And each hide ought to thresh out seed for the sowing of 4 acres after Michaelmas Day.
Each hide must thresh out so much seed as will suffice for the land ploughed by one team in winter and in Lent.
Each house of the whole village owes a hen at Christmas and eggs at Easter.
These 10 hides ought to repair and keep in repair these houses in the demesne, viz. the Grange, cowhouse, and threshing house.
Each of these *hidarii* owes 2 *doddæ* of oats in the middle of March.
  And 14 loaves for '*mescinga*' (?).
  And a '*companagium*' (flesh, fish, or cheese).
Each hide owes 5*s.* by the year, and ought to make of the lord's wood 4 hurdles of rods for the fold.

The instance of another manor of St. Paul's (Tillingham), in Essex,[2] may be cited as further evidence that sometimes, even where the holdings (as at Winslow) were virgates and half-virgates, their original relation to the hide was not yet forgotten. For after giving the list of tenants in demesne, and of 19

---

tenants holding 30 acres each, who ' faciunt magnas operationes,' *i.e.* do full service, there is a statement that in this manor 30 acres make a virgate, and 120 acres a hide ;[1] so that here also there are 4 virgates to the hide. But there was further in this manor a *double*

Solanda, or double hide. hide, called a ' *solanda*,'[2] presumably of 240 acres. This double hide called a *solanda* is also mentioned in a manor in Middlesex,[3] and in another in Surrey ;[4] and the term *solanda* is probably the same as the well-known ' *sullung*' or ' *solin*' of Kent, meaning a ' plough land.'

It will be remembered that in the Huntingdon-shire Hundred Rolls a double hide of 240 acres was noticed.

The Kentish sullungs and yokes. It may also be mentioned that in Kent[5] the division of the *sullung*, or hide, was called a *yoke*, instead of a yard-land or virgate; suggesting that the divisions of the plough land in some way corresponded with the yokes of oxen in the team.

On the whole little substantial difference appears between the grades of holdings in the south-east of England and those of the midland counties. We may add also that here, as elsewhere, the humbler class of cottier tenants are found beneath the regular holders of hides and virgates, and that on the demesne lands there appears the constantly increasing class of *libere tenentes*. Also passing from the holdings in villen-age to the serfdom under which they were held,

---

[1] ' In manerio isto sexcies xx. acre faciunt hidam, et xxx. acre faciunt virgatam ' (p. 64).

[2] ' Cum vi. hidis trium solan-darum ' (p. 58).

[3] *Sutton*, where mention is made

of a ' solanda quæ per se habet duas hidas ' (p. 93).

[4] *Draitone*, 'cum una hida de solande ' (p. 99).

[5] For the *sullung* of Kent, see Mr. Elton's *Tenures of Kent*.

and speaking generally, the description obtained from
the Hundred Rolls of the services might with little
variation be applied to the different area embraced
in this section.

VIII. THE RELATION OF THE VIRGATE TO THE HIDE
TRACED IN THE CARTULARIES OF GLOUCESTER AND
WORCESTER ABBEYS, AND THE CUSTUMAL OF BLEADON,
IN SOMERSETSHIRE.

Further facts relating to the hide and the virgate
are elicited by extending the inquiry into the west of
England. Turning to the cartulary of the monastery
of St. Peter at Gloucester,[1] there are several ' extents ' *Gloucester surveys of 1266.*
of manors in the west of England of about the year
1266, which give valuable evidence, not only of the
existence of the open fields divided into *three fields* or
seasons, furlongs, and half-acre strips, but also as regards the holdings.

The virgates in this district varied in acreage,
some containing 48 acres, others 40, 38, 36, and
28 acres respectively.[2] In one case it is incidentally mentioned that 4 virgates make a hide.[3] We
have thus in these extents evidence both of the prevalence and of the varying acreage of the virgate in
the extreme west of England, to add to the evidence
already obtained in respect of the midland counties.

So also the register of the Priory of St. Mary, *Worcester surveys of 1240.*
Worcester,[4] dated 1240, affords still earlier evidence
for the west of England of a similar kind.

---

[1] Published in the Rolls Series.
[2] iii. p. cix.
[3] iii. p. 55. ' Quatuor virgatæ terræ continentes unam hidam.'

[4] Edited by Archdeacon Hale, in the Camden Society's Series, 1865.

In the first manor mentioned therein the customary services of the villeins are described as pertaining to each pair of half-virgates, *i.e.* to each original virgate.[1] In the next manor there were 35 holdings in half-virgates, and so in other manors.[2] It is sometimes mentioned how many acres in each field belong to the several half-virgates, thus showing not only the division of the fields into *seasons*, but the scattered contents of the holdings.

Finally, with local variations serfdom in these two western counties was almost identical with that in other parts of England.

Two examples of the services of holders of virgates and half-virgates respectively are appended as before for comparison with others, and also examples of the services of cottier tenants. The list given in the note below of the 'common customs' of the villein tenants of one of the manors of Worcester Priory, describes some of the more general incidents of villenage, and shows how thorough a serfdom it originally was.[3]

---

[1] P. 10 *b*.

[2] P. 14 *b*.

[3] Worcester Cartulary, p. 15 *a*. Of the common customs of the villeins on the manor of Newenham—to give ' *Thac* ' on Martinmas Day; for pigs above a year old (sows excepted), 1*d.*, and for pigs not above a year, ½*d.*; to sell neither ox nor horse without licence; to give 1*d.* toll on selling an ox or horse; also ' aid ' and ' *leyrwite* ' (fine for a daughter's incontinence); to redeem his sons, if they leave the land; to pay ' *gersuma* ' for his daughters; no one to leave the land, nor to make his son a clerk, without licence; natives coming of age, unless they directly serve their father or mother, to perform 3 ' *ben-ripæ* '; and ' *forinseci* ' (*i.e.* villeins not born in the manor) shall do likewise; to carry at the summons of the ' *serviens* ' (bailiff or serjeant) besides the work: and if he carry ' *ex necessitate*,' to be quit of [a day's] work; to give at death his best chattel (*catallum*); the successor to make a fine, as he can; the widow to stay on the land as

To this evidence from the counties of Worcester and Gloucester we may add the evidence of the Custumal of Bleadon, in Somersetshire, also dating from the thirteenth century.

The manor belonged to the Prior of St. Swithin, at Winchester. There were very few *libere tenentes*. The tenants in villenage were *virgarii*, or holders of virgates, and *dimidii-virgarii*, or holders of half-virgates. There were also holders of fardels or quarter-virgates, and half-fardels, or one-eighth-virgates, and other small cottier tenants. Four virgates went to the hide. And the services were very similar to those of the Gloucester and Worcester tenants. They are described at too great length to be inserted here. We may, however, notice the importance amongst other items of the *carrying service* or *averagium*—a service often mentioned among villein services, but here defined with more than usual exactness.[1]

In short, without going further into details, it is obvious that the open field system and the serfdom which lived within it were practically the same in their general features in the west and in the east of England.

The following are the examples of the services in Gloucestershire and Worcestershire :—

---

long as she continues the service ; all to attend their own mill ; ' Cotmanni' to guard and take prisoners [to jail].

[1] ' Et idem faciet *averagium* apud Bristoll' et apud Wellias per totum annum, et apud Pridie, et post hokeday apud Bruggewauter, cum affro suo ducente bladum domini, caseum, et lanam, et cetera omnia quæ sibi serviens præcipere voluerit, et habebit unam quadrantem et dayuam suam quietam. Et debet facere *averagium* apud Axebrugge et ad navem quotiens dominus voluerit, et nichil habebit propter idem averagium.'—*Proceedings of Archæological Institute*, Salisbury, p. 203. App. to *Notice of the Custumal of Bleadon*, pp. 182–210.

VILLEIN SERVICES.

GLOUCESTERSHIRE	WORCESTERSHIRE

Services of a Virgate.[1]

A. B. holds 1 virgate of 48 acres (in the manor of Hartpury), with messuage, and 6 acres of meadow land.

From Michaelmas till August 1 he has to plough one day a week, each day's work being valued at ... $3\frac{1}{2}$ *s. d.*

And to do manual labour 3 days a week, each day's work being valued at ... $\frac{1}{2}$

On the 4th day to carry horse-loads (*summagiare*), if necessary, to Preston and other manors, and Gloucester, each day's work being valued at ... 1

Once a year to carry to Wick, valued at ... 3

To plough one acre called '*Eadacre*,'[2] and to thresh the seed for the said acre, the ploughing and threshing being valued at 4

To do the ploughing called '*beneherthe*' with one meal from the lord, valued *ultra cibum* at . 1

To mow the lord's meadow for 5 days, and more if necessary, each day's work being valued *ultra opus manuale* at . . 1

To lift the lord's hay for 5 days . . . . $2\frac{1}{2}$

To hoe the lord's corn for one day (besides the customary labour), with one man, valued at . $\frac{1}{2}$

To do 1 '*bederipa*' before autumn with 1 man, valued at . . . $1\frac{1}{2}$

Services of a Half-virgate.[3]

Of the villenage of Neweham, with appurtenances (or members), and of the villeins' works and customs.

In this manor are 35 half-virgates with appurtenances, exclusive of the half-virgate belonging to the '*præpositus.*'

Each half-virgate *ad censum* pays on St. Andrew's Day 12*d.* (November 30); on Annunciation Day, 12*d.* (March 25); on St. John's Day, 12*d.* (June 24).

From June 24 till August 1, each villein to work 2 days a week, and, if the serjeant (*serviens*) shall so will, to continue the same work till after August 1.

From August 1 to Michaelmas—

To work 4 days a week.

To do 2 '*benripæ*' (reapings at request), with 1 man.

To plough about Michaelmas a half-acre, to sow it with his own corn, and to harrow it.

Also to plough for winter corn, spring corn, and fallowing, for 1 day, exclusive of the work, and it is called '*benherthe.*'

To give on February 2 one quarter of oats, and $2\frac{1}{2}d.$ as *fisfe*' (fish-fee).

To hoe as [one day's] work after June 24.

All to mow as [one day's] work, and each to receive on mowing day as much grass as he can lift with his scythe, and if his scythe break he shall lose his grass and be amerced.

All to receive 6*d.* for drink.

---

[1] *Gloucester Cartulary*, vol. iii. p. 78.

[2] '*Radacre*' in other places, pp.

[ ] 80, 116.

[3] *Worcester Cartulary*, p. 14 *b.*

VILLEIN SERVICES—*continued.*

GLOUCESTERSHIRE	WORCESTERSHIRE
Services of a Virgate.	*Services of a Half-virgate.*

<table>
<tr><td colspan="2">s. d.</td></tr>
</table>

GLOUCESTERSHIRE

Services of a Virgate.

To work in the lord's har- *s. d.*
vest 5 days a week with
2 men, from August 1 to
Michaelmas, valued per
week at . . .1 3
To do 1 '*bederipa*,' called
'*bondenebedripa*,' with 4
men, valued at . .   6
To do 1 harrowing a year,
called   '*londegginge*,'
valued at . . .   1
To give at Michaelmas an
aid of .   .   .3 3
To [pay] '*pannage*,' viz. for
a pig of a year old .   1
For a younger pig that can
be separated. . .   ½
If he brew for sale, to give
14 gallons of ale as toll.
To sell neither horse nor
ox without licence.
Seller and buyer to give 4*d.* as
toll for a horse sold within
the manor.
To redeem son and daughter at
the will of the lord.
If he die, the lord to have his
best beast of burden as heriot,
and of his widow likewise, if
she outlive her husband.

Services of a Lundinarius.[1]

A. B. holds one '*lundi-
narium*' (in the manor
of Highnam), to wit, a
messuage with curtilage,
4 acres of land, and a
half-acre of meadow,
and has to work one day
a week (probably Mon-
day, Lunæ-dies, Lundi,
whence the title of the
holding), from Michael-
mas to August 1, and
each day's work is
valued at .   .   .

WORCESTERSHIRE

Services of a Half-virgate.

In this manor 8 gallons of beer
are given as toll, besides the
toll of the mills.
Each half-virgate, if *ad operationem*, from Michaelmas till
August 1, to work 2 days a
week.
To plough and sow with
its own corn half an acre,
and to harrow the same.
To plough and harrow one
day in winter, and the
prior to provide the seed;
and, if necessary, each
virgate to harrow as [a
day's work] till ploughing
time.
To plough one day in spring.
And to plough for fallowing
for 1 day (warrectare) as
above.

Services of a Cottarius.[2]

In the manor of Neweham are
10 cottiers (omitting William
the miller and Adam de Neweham), each holding 1 mes-
suage with appurtenances, and
6 acres.
[If *ad operationem*] each to work
2 days a week (excepting
Easter, Pentecost, and Christmas weeks).
To drive, take messages, and
bear loads.
To give '*thac*,' '*thol*,' aid,
and such like.

[1] *Gloucester Cartulary*, vol. iii.
p. 118.

[2] *Worcester Cartulary*, p. 15 *a.*

VILLEIN SERVICES—*continued.*

GLOUCESTERSHIRE	WORCESTERSHIRE
Services of a Lundinarius.	*Services of a Cottarius.*
	s.	*d.*	
To mow the lord's mea-dow for 4 days if necessary, and a day's mowing is valued at . .		2	But they give neither oats nor '*fisfe*.' If '*ad firmam*,' to render at each quarter-day (*terminum*) 6*d*.
To aid in cocking and lifting the hay for 6 days at least, and the day's work is valued at . .		½	
To hoe the lord's corn for 1 day, valued at . .		½	
To do 2 'bederipæ' before August 1, valued at .		2	
From August 1 to Michaelmas to do manual labour 2 days a week, and each day's work is valued at . . .		1½	
To gather rushes on August 1, valued at .		½	
And in all other 'conditions' he shall do as the customers.			
The total value of the service of a 'lundinarius' is	6	8	
To give 4*d*. as aid at Michaelmas.			
(15 other 'lundinarii' hold on a like tenure.)			

IX. CARTULARIES OF NEWMINSTER AND KELSO (XIII. CENTURY)—THE CONNEXION OF THE HOLDINGS WITH THE COMMON PLOUGH TEAM OF EIGHT OXEN.

Passing to the north of England, substantially the same system is found, along with customs and details which still further connect the gradations of the holdings in villenage with the plough team and the yokes of oxen of which it was composed.

North of the Tees, in the district of the old Northumbria, virgates and half-virgates were still the usual holdings, but they were called 'husband-lands.'

The full husband-land, or virgate, was composed of two *bovates*, or *oxgangs*, the bovate or oxgang being thus the eighth of the hide or carucate.

In the cartulary of Newminster,[1] under date 1250, amongst charters giving evidence of the division of the fields into 'seliones,' or strips,[2] the holdings of which were scattered over the fields,[3] as everywhere else, is a grant of land to the abbey containing 8 bovates in all, made up of 4 equal holdings of *two bovates* each.

In the '*Rotulus Redituum*' of the Abbey of Kelso, dated 1290,[4] the holdings were 'husband-lands.' In one place [5]—Selkirk—there were 15 *husband-lands, each containing a bovate.* In another [6]—Bolden—the record of which, with the services of the husband-lands, is referred to several times in the document as typical of the rest, there were 28 husband-lands, owing equal payments and services. The contents are not given, but as the services evidently are doubles of those of Selkirk, it may be inferred that the husband-lands each contained 2 bovates (*i.e.* a virgate), and that so did the usual husband-lands of the Kelso estates. This inference is confirmed by the record for the manor of Reveden, which states that the monks had there 8 husband-lands,[7] from each of which were due the services set out at length at the end of this section; and then goes on to say that formerly each 'husband' took with his 'land' his *stuht,* viz. 2 *oxen,* 1 horse, 3 cháfders of oats, 6 bolls

---

[1] *Surtees Society,* p. 57.
[2] P. 57. [3] P. 59.
[4] Published by the Bannatyne

Club, 1846.
[5] Vol. ii. p. 462.
[6] P. 461.   [7] P. 455.

of barley, and 3 of wheat. ' But when Abbot Richard commuted that service into money, then they returned their *stuht*, and paid each for his husband-land 18*s*. per annum.' The allotment of 2 oxen as *stuht*, or outfit, to the husband-land evidently corresponds with its contents as two bovates.

If the holding of 2 bovates was equivalent to the virgate, and the bovate to the half-virgate or one-eighth of the hide, then the hide should contain 8 bovates or oxgangs ; and as the single oxgang had relation to the single ox, and the virgate or ' two bovates' to the pair of oxen allotted to it by way of ' stuht,' or outfit, so the hide ought to have a similar relation to a team of 8 oxen. Thus, if the full team of 8 oxen can be shown to be the *normal* plough team, a very natural relation would be suggested between the gradations of holdings in villenage, and the number of oxen contributed by the holders of them to the full plough team of the manorial plough. And, in fact, there is ample evidence that it was so.

Full *caruca* or plough team of eight oxen. In the Kelso records there is mention of a ' carucate,' or ' plough-land '[1] (' plough ' being in these records rendered by ' caruca ') ; and this plough-land turns out, upon examination, to contain 4 husband-lands, *i.e.* presumably 8 bovates.

Further, among the 'Ancient Acts of the Scotch Parliament' there is an early statute[2] headed ' *Of Landmen telande with Pluche*,' which ordains that ' *ilk man teland with a pluche of viii. oxin* ' shall sow at the least so much wheat, &c. : showing that the team of 8 oxen was the normal plough team in Scotland.

P. 361.   [2] P. 18.

Again, among the fragments printed under the heading of 'Ancient Scotch Laws and Customs,' without
date, occurs the following record :[1]—

'In the first time that the law was made and or-
'dained they began at the freedom of " halikirk,"
'and since, at the measuring of lands, the " *plew-land* "
'they ordained to contain *viii. oxingang*, &c.'

Even so late as the beginning of the present century, we learn from the old 'Statistical Account of
Scotland' that in many districts the old-fashioned
ploughs were of such great weight that they required 8, 10, and sometimes 12 oxen to draw them.[2]

Information from the same source also explains
the use of the word '*caruca*' for plough. For the
construction of the word involves not 4 yoke of
oxen, but 4 oxen yoked abreast, as are the horses in   Four oxen
the *caruca* so often seen upon Roman coins. And the   yoked
  abreast.
'Statistical Account' informs us that in some districts of Scotland in former times ' the ploughs were
' drawn by 4 oxen or horses *yoked abreast*: one trod
' constantly upon the tilled surface, another went in
' the furrow, and two upon the stubble or white land.
' The driver walked backwards holding his cattle by
' halters, and taking care that each beast had its equal
' share in the draught. This, though it looked awk-
' ward, was contended to be the only mode of yoking
' by which 4 animals could best be compelled to exert
' all their strength.'[3]

The ancient Welsh laws, as we shall see by-and-   So also in
by, also speak of the normal plough team as consist-   Wales.
ing from time immemorial, throughout Wales, of 8

---

[1] *Acts of Parliament of Scotland*, App. V. p. 387.

[2] *Analysis*, p. 232.
[3] Id. p. 232.

oxen yoked 4 to a yoke. The team of 8 oxen seems further to have been the normal manorial plough team throughout England, though in some districts still larger teams were needful when the land was heavy clay.

In the ' Inquisition of the Manors of St. Paul's '[1] it is stated of the demesne land of a manor in Hertfordshire, that the ploughing could be done with two plough teams (*carucæ*), of 8 head each. And in another case in the same county 'with 2 plough ' teams of 8 heads, " cum consuetudinibus villatæ " ' —with the customary services of the villein tenants.'[2] In another, ' with 5 ploughs, of which 3 have 4 oxen ' and 4 horses, and 2 each 6 horses.' In another, ' with 3 ploughs of 8 heads.'

In manors in Essex, on the other hand, where the land is heavier, there are the following instances:[3]—

4 plough	teams,	10 in each.
2 ,,	,,	8 ,,
1 ,,	team,	10.
3 ,,	teams,	8 oxen and 2 horses.
2 ,,	,,	10 oxen and 10 horses for the two.
2 ,,	,,	12 oxen and 8 horses the two.
2 ,, ·	,,	4 horses and 4 oxen in each.
2 ,,	,,	10 each.
1 ,,	team,	6 horses and 4 oxen.

In two manors in Middlesex the teams were as under:[4]—

1 of 8 heads.
2 of 8 oxen and 2 horses.

---

[1] *Domesday of St. Paul's*, p. 1.
[2] *Id.* p. 7.
[3] *Id.* pp. 28, 33, 48, 53, 86.
[4] *Id.* pp. 99, 104.

In the Gloucester cartulary[1] there are the following instances :—

> To each plough team 8 oxen and 4 over.
>   „   „   12   „   1 „
>   „   „   12   „   1 „

All these instances are from documents of the Normal
English
plough
team of
eight oxen.
thirteenth century, and they conspire in confirming
the point that the normal plough team was, by general
consent, of 8 oxen ; though some heavier lands required 10 or 12, and sometimes horses in aid of the
oxen.

Nor do these exceptions at all clash with the
hypothesis of the connexion of the grades of holdings
with the number of oxen contributed by the holders
to the manorial plough team of their village ; for as
the number of oxen in the team sometimes varied
from the normal standard, so also did the number of
virgates in the hide or carucate.

So that, summing up the evidence of this chapter,
daylight seems to have dawned upon the meaning of
the interesting gradation of holdings in villenage in
the open fields. The hide or carucate seems to be Connexion
between
the oxen
and the
holdings.
the holding corresponding with the possession of a
full plough team of 8 oxen. The half-hide corresponds with the possession of one of the 2 yokes
of 4 abreast ; the virgate with the possession of a
pair of oxen, and the half-virgate or bovate with the
possession of a single ox ; all having their fixed relations to the full manorial plough team of 8 oxen.
And this conclusion receives graphic illustration when
the Scotch chronicler Winton thus quaintly describes

---

[1] *Gloucester Cart.* pp. 55, 61, 64.

F

the efforts of King Alexander III. to increase the growth of corn in his kingdom :—

> Yhwmen, pewere karl, or knawe
> That wes of mycht an ox til have
> He gert that man hawe part in pluche:
> Swa wes corn in his land enwche:
> Swa than begouth, and efter lang
> Of land wes mesure, ane oxgang.
> Mychty men that had mâ
> Oxyn, he gert in pluchys ga.
> Be that vertu all his land
> Of corn he gert be abowndand.[1]

Not that Alexander III. was really the originator of the terms 'plow-land' and 'oxgate,' but that he attained his object of increasing the growth of corn by extending into new districts of Scotland, before given up chiefly to grazing, the same methods of husbandry as elsewhere had been at work from time immemorial, just as the monks of Kelso probably had done, by giving each of their villein tenants a 'stuht' of 2 oxen with which to plough their husband-lands.

One point more, however, still remains to be explained before the principle of the open field system can be said to be fully grasped, viz. why the strips of which the hides, virgates, and bovates were composed were scattered in so strange a confusion all over the open fields.

Services on *Kelso* manors.

In the meantime the following examples of the services of the villein tenants of *Kelso* husband-lands and bovates are appended for the purpose of comparison with those of other districts :—

---

[1] *Winton*, vol. i. p. 400 (A.D. 1249–92).

BOLDEN [1]	REVEDEN [2]
At Bolden—	At Reveden—
The monks have 28 'husbands'-lands in the villa of Bolden, each of which used to render 6*s.* 8*d.* at Pentecost and Martinmas, and to do certain services, viz. :	The monks have 8 'husbands'-lands and 1 bovate, each of which performed certain services at one time, viz. :
To reap in autumn for 4 days with all his family, himself and wife.	Each week in summer the carriage with 1 horse to Berwick.
To perform likewise a fifth day's work in autumn with 2 men.	The horse to carry 3 '*bollæ*' of corn, or 2 '*bollæ*' of salt, or 1½ '*bollæ*' of coals.
To carry peat with one waggon for one day from Gordon to the 'pullis.'	In winter the same carriage, but the horse only carried 2 '*bollæ*' of corn, or 1½ '*bollæ*' of salt, or 1 '*bolla*' and '*ferloth*' of coal.
To carry one waggon-load of peat from the 'pullis' to the abbey in summer, and no more.	Each week, when they came from Berwick, each land did one day's work according to order.
To carry once a year with one horse from Berwick.	When they did not go to Berwick, they tilled 2 days a week.
And to have their meals from the abbey when doing this service.	In autumn, when they did not go to Berwick they did 3 days' work.
To till 1½ acre at the grange of Neuton every year.	At that time each ' husband ' took with his land '*stuht*,' viz. :
To harrow with one horse one day.	2 oxen, 1 horse,
To find one man at the sheepwashing and another man at the shearing, without meals.	3 ' celdræ ' of oats, 6 ' bollæ ' of barley, 3 ' bollæ ' of corn.
To answer likewise for foreign service and for other suits.	And afterwards, when Abbot Richard commuted that service into money, they returned their '*stuht*,' and each one gave for his land 18*s.* a year.
To carry corn in autumn with one waggon for one day.	
To carry the abbot's wool from the barony to the abbey.	
To find him carriage over the moor to Lessemahagu.	

[1] *Rot. Red. Kelso*, p. 461.   [2] *Ib.* p. 456.

X. THE BOLDON BOOK, A.D. 1183.

We are now in a position to creep up one step nearer to the time of the Domesday Survey, and in the Boldon Book to examine earlier examples of North Country manors.

The Boldon Book is a survey of the manors belonging to the Bishop of Durham in the year 1183, nearly a century earlier than the date of the Hundred Rolls.

Survey of *Boldon.*

The typical entry which may be taken as the common form used throughout the record relates to the village of Boldon, from which the name of the survey is taken.

It is as follows : [1]—

The services of villani.

In Boldon there are 22 villani, each holding 2 bovates, or 30 acres, and paying 2s. 6d. for 'scat-penynges' [being in fact 1d. per acre], a half '*shaceldra*' of oats, 16d. for 'averpenynges' [in lieu of carrying service], 5 four-wheel waggons of 'woodlade' [lading of wood], 2 cocks, and 10 eggs.

They work 3 days a week throughout the year, excepting Easter week and Pentecost, and 13 days at Christmas.

In autumn they do 4 dayworks at reaping, with all their family except the housewife. Also they reap 3 roods of '*averype*,' and plough and harrow 3 roods of '*averere.*'

Also each villein plough-team ploughs and harrows 2 acres, with allowance of food ('*corrodium*') once from the bishop, and then they are quit of that week's work.

When they do '*magnas precationes*,' they have a food allowance (*corrodium*) from the bishop, and as part of their works do harrowing when necessary, and '*faciunt ladas*' (make loads?). And when they do these each receives 1 loaf.

Also they reap for 1 day at Octon till the evening, and then they receive an allowance of food.

And for the fairs of St. Cuthbert, every 2 villeins erect a booth; and when they make '*logiæ*' and 'wodelade' (load wood), they are quit of other labour.

---

[1] P. 566.

There are 12 '*cotmanni*,' each of whom holds 12 acres, and they work throughout the year 2 days a week except in the aforesaid feasts, and render 12 hens and 60 eggs.

Robertus holds 2 bovates or 36 acres, and renders half a mark.

The *Punder* holds 12 acres, and receives from each plough 1 '*trave*' of corn, and renders 40 hens and 500 eggs.

The *Miller* [renders] 5½ marks.

The '*Villani*' are, if need be, to make a house each year 40 feet long and 15 feet wide, and when they do this each is quit of 4*d.* of his '*averpenynges.*'

The whole '*villa*' renders 17*s.* as '*cornagium*' (*i.e.* tax on horned beasts), and 1 cow '*de metride.*'

The demesne is at farm, together with the stock for 4 ploughs and 4 harrows, and renders for 2 ploughs 16 '*celdræ*' of corn, 16 '*celdræ*' of oats, 8 '*celdræ*' of barley, and for the other 2 ploughs, 10 marks.

Here then at Boldon were 22 villani, each hold- ing two bovates or 30 acres, equivalent to a virgate or yard-land. In another place (Quycham) there are said to be thirty-five '*bovat-villani*,' each of whom held a bovate of 15 acres, and performed such and such services.[1] These correspond with holders of half-virgates.

They hold yard-lands of two bovates, or single bovates.

Below these villani, holding one or two bovates, as in all other similar records, were cottage holdings, some of 12 acres, some of 6 acres each. There seems to have been a certain equality in some places, even in the lowest rank of holdings.

Here then, within about 100 years of the Domes- day Survey, are found the usual grades of holdings in villenage. The services, too, present little variation from those of later records and other parts of England.

From the Boldon Book may be gathered a few points of further information, which may serve to complete the picture of the life of the village com- munity in villenage.

---

[1] P. 579.

Manor sometimes farmed by villani.

The unity of the 'villata' as a self-acting community is illustrated by the fact that in many instances the services of the villani are *farmed* by them from the monastery *as a body*, at a single rent for the whole village[1]—a step in the same direction as the commutation of services and leasing of land to farm tenants, practices already everywhere becoming so usual.

Village officials: the faber.

The corporate character of the 'villata' is also illustrated by frequent mention of the village officials. The *faber*,[2] or blacksmith, whose duty it was to keep in repair the ironwork of the ploughs of the village, usually held his bovate or other holding in respect of his office free from ordinary services. The carpenter[3] also held his holding free, in return for his obligation to repair the woodwork of the ploughs and harrows.

The punder.

The *punder*[4] (pound-keeper) was another official with a recognised position. And, as a matter of course,

The præpositus.

the villein tenant holding the office of *præpositus* for the time being was freed by virtue of his office from the ordinary services of his virgate or two bovates,[5] but resumed them again when his term of

---

[1] P. 568. 'Villani de Southby-dyk tenent villam suam ad firmam et reddunt v. libras, et invenient viii^xx. homines ad metendum in autumpno et xxxvi. quadrigas (*i.e.* waggons) ad quadriganda blada apud Octonam' (*i.e.* a neighbouring village where was probably the bishop's chief granary) (568 *a*).

[2] 'Faber (de Wermouth tenet) xii. acras pro ferramentis carucæ et carbones invenit' (567 *a*).

'Faber (de Queryndonshire) tenet xii. acras pro ferramento carucæ fabricando' (596 *b*).

'Faber 1 bovat' pro suo servicio' (569 *a*).

Compare *Hundred Rolls*, p. 551 *a*, and *Domesday of St. Paul's*, p. 67.

[3] 'Carpentarius (de Wermouth) qui senex habet in vita sua xii. acras pro carucis et herceis (*i.e.* harrows) faciendis' (567 *a*).

[4] 'Punder (de Neubotill) tenet xii. acras et habet de unaquaque caruca de Neubotill, de Bydyk et de Heryngton (*i.e.* three villatæ) unam travam bladi et reddit xl. (vel lx.) gallinas et ccc. ova' (p. 568 *a*).

[5] (In Seggefeeld). 'Johannes præpositus habet ii. bovatas pro servicio suo et si servicium præposituræ dimiserit, reddit et operatur sicut alii Firmarii' (570 *a*).

office ceased, and another villein was elected in his
stead.

In addition to the ordinary agricultural services
in respect of the arable land, there is mention, in the
services of Boldon and other places, of special dues
or payments, probably for rights of grazing or possession of herds of cattle. This kind of payment is
called ' cornagium,' either because it is paid in horned
cattle, or, if in money, in respect of the number of
horned cattle held.

There are also services connected with the bishop's
hunting expeditions. Thus there are persons holding
in ' drengage,' who have to feed a horse and a dog,
and ' to go in the great hunt' (*magna caza*) with two
harriers and 15 ' cordons,' &c.[1]

So of the villani of ' Aucklandshire '[2] it is recorded
that they are ' to furnish for the great hunts of the
' bishop a " cordon " from each bovate, and to make
' the Bishop's hall (*aula*) in the forest, sixty feet long
' and sixteen feet wide between the posts, with a
' buttery, a steward's room, a chamber and " privat."
' Also they make a chapel 40 feet long by 15 wide,
' receiving two shillings, of charity ; and make their
' portion of the hedge (*haya*) round the lodges (*logiæ*).
' On the departure of the bishop they have a full tun
' of beer, or half a tun if he should stay on. They
' also keep the eyries of the hawks in the bailiwick of
' Radulphus Callidus, and put up 18 booths (*bothas*)
' at the fairs of St. Cuthbert.'

The last item, which also occurs in the services
of Boldon, is interesting in connexion with a passage
in a letter of Pope Gregory the Great to the Abbot

---

[1] P. 572.   [2] P. 575.

Mellitus (A.D. 601), in which he requests the Bishop
Augustine to be told that, after due consideration of
the habits of the English nation, he (the Pope) deter-
mines that, ' because they have been used to slaughter
' many oxen in the sacrifices to devils, some solemnity
' must be exchanged for them on this account, as that
' on the day of the dedication, or the nativities of the
' holy martyrs, whose relics are there deposited, they
' may build themselves huts of the boughs of trees,
' about those churches which have been turned to
' that use from temples, and celebrate the solemnity
' with religious feasting, and no more offer beasts to
' the devil, but kill cattle to the praise of God in their
' eating, it being impossible to efface everything at
' once from their obdurate minds : because he who
' tries to rise to the highest place rises by degrees or
' steps, and not by leaps.' [1]

The villeins of St. Cuthbert's successor are found
500 years after Pope Gregory's advice still, as a
portion of their services, yearly putting up the booths
for the fairs held in honour of their patron saint—a
fact which may help us to realise the tenacity of local
custom, and lessen our surprise if we find also that
for the origin of other services we must look back
for as long a period.

XI. THE ' LIBER NIGER ' OF PETERBOROUGH ABBEY,
A.D. 1125.

Fifty or sixty years earlier than the Boldon Book,
was compiled the ' Liber Niger ' [2] of the monastery
of St. Peter de Burgo, the abbey of Peterborough.

---

[1] *Bede,* bk. i. c.xxx.
[2] Published by the Camden Society, 1849, as an appendix to the *Chronicon Petroburgense.*

This record is remarkably exact and full in its details. Its date is from 1125 to 1128 ; and its evidence brings up our knowledge of the English manor and serfdom—the open field and its holdings—almost to the threshold of the Domesday Survey, *i.e.* within about 40 years of it.

The first entry gives the following information : [1]—

In Kateringes, which is assessed at 10 hides, 40 villani held 40 yard-lands (*virgas terræ*, or virgates), and there were 8 cotsetes, each holding 5 acres. The services were as follows :

The holders of virgates for the lord's work plough in spring 4 acres for each virgate. And besides this they find plough teams (*carucæ*) three times in winter, three times for spring plowing, and once in summer. And they have 22 plough teams, wherewith they work. And all of them work 3 days a week. And besides this they render per annum from each virgate of custom 2s. 1½d. And they all render 50 hens and 640 eggs. One tenant of 13 acres renders 16d., and [has] 2 acres of meadow. The mill with the miller renders 20s. The 8 cotsetes work one day a week, and twice a year make malt. Each of them gives a penny for a goat, and if he has a she-goat, a halfpenny. There is a shepherd and a swineherd who hold 8 acres. And in the demesne of the manor (*curiæ*) are 4 plough teams with 32 oxen (*i.e.* 8 to each team), 12 cows with 10 calves, and 2 unemployed animals, and 3 draught cattle, and 300 sheep, and 50 pigs, and as much meadow over as is worth 16s. The church of the village is at the altar of the abbey church. For the love-feast of St. Peter [2] [they give] 4 rams and 2 cows, or 5s.'

This entry may be taken as a typical one.

Here, then, within forty years of the date of the Domesday Survey is clear evidence that the normal holding of the villanus was a virgate. Elsewhere there were semi-villani with half-virgates. [3]

---

[1] P. 157.

[2] The love-feast (*caritas*) of St. Peter may possibly, like the fairs of St. Cuthbert, be a survival of ancient pagan sacrifices allowed to continue by the permission of Pope Gregory the Great. See Hazlitt under 'Wakes' and 'Fairs.' And Du Cange under 'Caritas.'

[3] In the next place mentioned 20 men hold 20 virgates, and 13 hold 6½ virgates among them, or half a virgate each; and so on. In one place 8 villani hold 1 hide and 1 virgate among them (*i.e.* 2 probably hold virgates, and 6 of them half-virgates), and 2 others hold 1 virgate each. In another,

The manorial plough team of eight oxen.

Further, throughout this record fortunately the number of ploughs and oxen on the lord's demesne happens to be mentioned, from which the number of oxen to the team can be inferred. And the result is that in 15 out of 25 manors there were 8 oxen to a team ; in 6 the team had 6 oxen, and in the remaining 4 cases the numbers were odd.

So far as it goes, this evidence proves that, as a rule, 8 oxen made up the full normal manorial plough team in the twelfth as in the thirteenth century. But it should be observed that this seems to hold good only of the ploughs on the lord's demesne—*in dominio curiæ.* The villani held other and apparently smaller ploughs, with about 4 oxen to the team instead of 8, and with these they performed their services.[1]

Smaller teams of the *villani.*

---

20 *pleni villani* [of 1 virgate each] and 29 *semi-villani* [of half-virgate each] hold in all 34 virgates and a half. In another, 8 villani hold 8 bovates, and 3 bovates are waste.

In the rest of the record it is generally assumed that the 'pleni villani' have a virgate each, and the 'dimidii villani' half a virgate each.

[1] The following are instances of the villein plough teams:—

The holders of 40 virgates hold 22 plough teams.

„	20	„	12	„
„	20	„	9	„
„	8	„	2	„

There seems to have been as nearly as possible one plough team to each two virgates, which at two oxen the virgate would give four oxen to the plough instead of eight. Speaking generally, it may therefore be said that there were on the Peterborough manors the greater ploughs of the lord's demense with their separate teams of eight oxen belonging to the lord, and the lesser ploughs of the villani, to work which two clubbed together, for which four oxen made a sufficient team; and it would seem, further, that not only had the villani to work at the great manorial ploughs, but also to do service for their lord with their own lesser ploughs in addition. This seems to explain the expressions used in the Gloucester cartulary that the demesne land of this or that manor can be ploughed with so many ploughs of eight head of oxen in the team ' *cum consuetudinibus villatæ ;* ' and also the mention in Fleta of the ' *carucæ adjutrices* ' of the villani.

But this fact does not appear to clash with the supposed connexion between the hide of 8 bovates and the manorial plough with its team of 8 oxen. It probably simply shows that the connexion between them on which the regular gradation of holdings in villenage depended had its origin at an earlier period, when a simpler condition of the community in villenage existed than that to be found in those days immediately following the Domesday Survey. There were, in fact, many other symptoms that the community in villenage had long been losing its archaic simplicity and wandering from its original type.

One of these symptoms may be found in the fact *Symptoms* observed in the later evidence, that the number of *of the breaking* irregular holdings increased as time went on ; and this *up of serfdom.* applies as well to the number of the free tenants of various portions of the lord's demesne as of the small tenancies in villenage below the regular holdings of the villani. In the 'Liber Niger' these irregular holdings seldom occur at all—a fact in itself very significant.

Another symptom may be noticed in the circumstance mentioned in the Boldon Book, and also in other cartularies, of the land in demesne being as a whole sometimes let or farmed out to the villani. Another was the fact, so apparent in the Hundred Rolls and cartularies, of the substitution of money payments for the services. There is no mention in the 'Liber Niger' of either of these practices.

All these are symptoms that the system was not a system recently introduced, but an old system gradually breaking up, relaxing its rules, and becoming in some points inconsistent with itself.

XII. SUMMARY OF THE POST-DOMESDAY EVIDENCE.

CHAP. II.

Manors every-where.

Land in demesne and in villenage.

Open field system.

Villani with yard-lands, &c.

To sum up the evidence already examined, and reaching to within forty years of the date of the Domesday Survey, it is clear that England was covered with manors. And these manors were in fact, in their simplest form, estates of manorial lords, each with its village community in villenage upon it. The land of the lord's demesne—the home farm belonging to the manor-house—was cultivated chiefly by the services of the *villata*, *i.e.* of the village community, or tenants in villenage. The land of this village community, *i.e.* the land in villenage, lay round the village in open fields. In the village were the messuages or homesteads of the tenants in villenage, and their holdings were composed of bundles of scattered strips in the open fields, with rights of pasture over the latter for their cattle after the crops were gathered, as well as on the green commons of the manor or township.

The tenants in villenage were divided into two distinct classes.

First, there were the villani proper, whose now familiar holdings, the hides, half-hides, virgates, and bovates, were connected with the number of oxen allotted to them or contributed by them to the manorial plough team of 8 oxen, the normal holding, the virgate or yard-land, including about 30 acres in scattered acre or half-acre strips:

And further, these holdings of the villani were indivisible bundles passing with the homestead which formed a part of them by re-grant from the lord from one generation of serfs to another in unbroken regularity, always to a single successor, whether the eldest or the youngest son, according to the custom of each individual manor. They possessed all the unity and indivisibility of an entailed estate, and were sometimes known apparently for generations by the family name of the holders.[1] But the reason underlying all this regular devolution was not the preservation of the family of the tenant, but of the services due from the yard-land to the lord of the manor.

Below the villani proper were the numerous Bordarii, smaller tenants of what may be termed the cottier or cottiers. class—sometimes called in the ' Liber Niger,' as it is important to notice, *bordarii*[2] (probably from the Saxon ' bord,' a cottage). And these cottagers, possessing generally no oxen, and therefore taking no part in the common ploughing, still in some manors seem to have ranked as a lower grade of villani, having small allotments in the open fields,—in some manors 5 acre strips apiece, in other manors more or less.

Lastly, below the villeins and cottiers were, in some Slaves. districts, remains, hardly to be noticed in the later cartularies, of a class of *servi*, or slaves, fast becoming

---

[1] ' Galfridus Snow tenet quoddam tenementum nativum vocatum *Snowes*. . . . Willelmus Biesten tenet tenementum nativum vocatum *Biestes*,' and so on.

Extent of ' Byrchsingeseie,' near Colchester.

Leger Book of St. John the Baptist, Colchester.

Wrest Park MSS., No. 57.

I am indebted to Earl Cowper for the opportunity of referring to this interesting MS., containing valuable examples of extents of manors from the reign of Edward I., and of the services of the tenants. See particularly the extent of ' *Wycham*,' 17 Ed. I., as a good example of the three field system and serfdom.

[2] Pp. 162–4, &c.

Chap. II.

merged in the cottier class above them, or losing themselves among the household servants or labourers upon the lord's demesne.

Open field the shell of serfdom.

Thus the community in villenage fitted into the open field as into its shell—a shell which was long to survive the breaking up of the system of serfdom which lived within it. The *débris* of this shell, as we have seen, still remains upon the open fields of some English villages and townships to-day; but for the full meaning of some of its features, especially of the scattering of the strips in the yard-lands, we have to look still farther back into the past even than the twelfth century.

Analysis of the services.

Passing from the shell to the serfdom which lived within it, we have found it practically alike in the north and south and east and west of England, and from the time of the Black Death back to the threshold of the Domesday Survey. Complicated as are the numerous little details of the services and payments, they fall with great regularity under three distinct heads :—

Week-work.

Boon-work.

Gafol.

1. *Week-work*—*i.e.* work for the lord for so many days a week, mostly three days.
2. *Precariæ*, or *boon-work*—*i.e.* special work at request ('ad precem' or 'at bene'), sometimes counting as part of the week-work, sometimes extra to it.
3. Payments in money or kind or work, rendered by way of rent or 'Gafol'; and various dues, such as *Kirkshot, Hearth-penny, Easter dues*, &c.

The first two of these may be said to be practically quite distinct from the third class, and intimately connected *inter se*. The boon-work would seem to be a necessary corollary of the *limitation* of the week-work. If the lord had had unlimited right to the whole work

of his villein tenant all days a week, and had an unrestricted choice as to what kind of work it should
be, week-work at the lord's bidding might have
covered it all. But custom not only limited the
number of days' work per week, but also limited the
number of days on which the work should consist of
ploughing, reaping, and other work of more than
usual value, involving oxen or piece-work, beyond the
usual work of ordinary days.

The *week-work*, limited or otherwise, was evidently
the most *servile* incident of villenage.

The payments in money or kind, or in work of
the third class, to which the word *gafol*, or tribute,
was applied, were more like modern rent, rates, and
taxes than incidents of serfdom.

Comparing the services of the villani with those
of the cottiers or bordarii, the difference evidently
turns upon the size of the holdings, and the possession
or non-possession of oxen.

Naturally ploughing was a prominent item in the
services of the villanus holding a virgate, with his
' stuht,' or outfit of two oxen. As naturally the services of the bordarius or cottager did not include
ploughing, but were limited to smaller services.

But apparently the services of each class were
equally servile. Both were in villenage, and *week-
work* was the chief mark of the serfdom of both.

Besides the servile week-work and '*gafol*,' &c.,
there were also other incidents of villenage felt to be
restrictions upon freedom, and so of a servile nature.
Of these the most general were—

The requirement of the lord's licence for the marriage of a daughter,
and fine on incontinence.

The prohibition of sale of oxen, &c., without the lord's licence.
The obligation to use the lord's mill, and do service at his court.
The obligation not to leave the land without the lord's licence.

It was the week-work of the villanus, and these restrictions on his personal liberty, which were felt to be serfdom.[1]

All limited
by custom.

But these servile incidents were limited by custom, and this limitation by custom of the lord's demands, as well as the more and more prevalent commutation of services into money payments in later times, were, as has been said, notes and marks of a relaxation of the serfdom. The absence of these limitations would be the note and mark of a more complete serfdom.

Thus, in pursuing this economic inquiry further back into Saxon times, the main question will be whether the older serfdom of the holder of yard-lands was more or less unlimited, and therefore complete, than in the times following upon the Norman conquest.

The evidence has
led up to
the Domesday Survey,

In the meantime the Domesday Survey is the next evidence which lies before us, and judging from the tenacity of custom, and the extreme slowness of economic changes in the later period, it may be approached with the almost certain expectation that no great alteration can well have taken place in the English open-field and manorial system in the forty

---

[1] The question of the *personal status* of the villein tenant is a different one from that of villein *tenure.* Sir H. S. Maine (*Early Law and Custom,* p. 333) and Mr. F. Pollock (in his *Notes on Early English Land Law,* 'Law Mag. and Review' for May 1882) have pointed out that, according to Bracton, free men might be subject to villein tenure and its incidents (except the *merchetum* on marriage of a daughter) and yet personally be free, as contrasted with the 'nativi' or villeins by blood. Compare Bracton f. 4 b with f. 26 a and 208 b. The question of the origin of the confusion of status in serfdom will be referred to hereafter.

years between its date and that of the *Liber Niger*
of Peterborough Abbey.

If this expectation should be realised, the
Domesday Survey, approached as it has been by
the ladder of the later evidence leading step by step
up to it, ought easily to yield up its secrets.

If such should prove to be the case, though losing *and must*
some of its mystery and novelty, the Domesday *give the key to it.*
Survey will gain immensely in general interest and
importance by becoming intelligible. The picture it
gives of the condition of rural England will become
vivid and clear in its outlines, and trustworthy to a
unique degree in its details. For extending as it does,
roughly speaking, to the whole of England south of
the Tees and east of the Severn, and spanning as it
does by its double record the interval between its
date and the time of Edward the Confessor, it will
prove more than ever an invaluable vantage-ground
from which to work back economic inquiries into
the periods before the Norman conquest of England. It may be trusted to do for the earlier Saxon
records what a previous understanding of later records
will have done for it.

CHAPTER III.

THE DOMESDAY SURVEY (A.D. 1086).

I. THERE WERE MANORS EVERYWHERE.

In the Domesday Survey, as might be expected from the evidence of the foregoing chapter, the unit of inquiry is everywhere the manor, and the manor was a landowner's estate, with a township or village community in villenage upon it, under the jurisdiction of the lord of the manor.

But the same person was often the lord of many manors.

1,422 manors were in the ancient demesne of the Crown at the date of the Survey,[1] and most of them had also been Crown manors in the time of Edward the Confessor. Thus, for centuries after the Conquest, the Domesday book was constantly appealed to as evidence that this manor or that was of 'ancient demesne,' *i.e.* that it was a royal manor in the time of Edward the Confessor ; because the tenants of these manors claimed certain privileges and immunities which other tenants did not enjoy.

---

[1] Ellis's *Introduction*, i. p. 225.

The monasteries also at the time of Edward the
Confessor were holders of many manors, often in
various counties, and the Survey shows that they
were generally permitted to retain them after the
Conquest.

Earls and powerful thanes were also at the time of
Edward the Confessor possessors of many manors, and
so were their Norman successors at the date of the
Survey. The resident lord of a manor was often the
mesne tenant of one of these greater lords. However
this might be, every manor had its lord, resident, or
represented by a steward or reeve (*villicus*).

Sometimes the Survey shows that a village or
township, once probably under a single lord, had
become divided between two or more manors ; and
sometimes again, by what was called subinfeudation,
lesser and dependent manors, as in the Hitchin
example, had been carved out of the original manor,
once embracing directly the whole village or township.

But these variations do not interfere with the
general fact that there were manors everywhere, and
that the typical manor was a manorial lord's estate,
with a village or township upon it, under his jurisdiction, and in villenage.

Further, this was clearly the case both after the
Conquest at the date of the Survey, and also before
the Conquest in the time of Edward the Confessor.

What land was extra-manorial or belonged to no
township was probably royal forest or waste. At
the date of the Survey this unappropriated forest, as
well as the numerous royal manors already alluded
to, was included in the royal demesne. Whatever
belonged to the latter was excluded from the jurisdic-

tion of the courts of the hundreds. It acknowledged no lordship but that of the king, and was described in the Survey as *terra regis.*

II. THE DIVISION OF THE MANOR INTO LORD'S DEMESNE AND LAND IN VILLENAGE.

Not only were there manors everywhere, but throughout the Domesday Survey the division of the land of the manor into lord's demesne and land in villenage was all but universal, both in the time of Edward the Confessor and at the later date. It was so equally in the case of manors both in royal and in private hands.

Hides *ad geldum.*

The record generally begins with the number of hides or carucates at which the whole manor was rated according to ancient assessment. Generally, except in the Danish district of England (where the *carucate* only is used), the word *hide* (though often originally meaning, as already mentioned, the same thing as a carucate, viz. the land of one plough) was used in the Survey exclusively as the ancient unit of assessment, while the actual extent of the manor was described in *carucates,* and thus the number of hides often fell far short of the number of carucates.

Actual *carucæ* or plough teams.

In the *Inquisitio Eliensis* the Huntingdonshire manors of the abbey are described as containing so many *hides* ' *ad geldum,*' and so many *carucates* ' *ad arandum,*' thus exactly explaining the use of the terms.

In Kent the ancient assessment was, consistently with later records, given by the number of solins—

sulung being an old word used both long before and afterwards, as we have seen, in the south-east of England for ' plough land.'

Generally, whatever the terms made use of, the basis of the assessment seems to have been the number of plough teams at the time it was made, and (except in the west of England) this probably had been the case also as regards the ancient one quoted in the Survey. The actual circumstances of the manors had at the date of the Survey wandered far away from those at the date of the ancient assessment, and therefore it was needful to state the present actual number of carucates (*carucatæ*) or plough teams (*carucæ*).[1] The devastations of the Norman Conquest had not been wholly repaired at the date of the Survey, and therefore after the number of actual plough teams in demesne and in villenage it is often stated that so many more might be added.

The total number of plough teams being given, information is almost always added how many of them were *in demesne* and how many belonged to the villeins. And it is to be noticed that the plough teams of the villeins were smaller than the typical manorial plough team of 8 oxen, just as was the case on the Peterborough manors, according to the Liber Niger.

In demesne and in villenage.

There were on an average in most counties about half as many ploughs in villenage as there were villeins ; so that, roughly speaking, two villeins, as in

---

[1] Unfortunately the same contracted form serves in the Survey for both *carucata* and *caruca.*

the Peterborough manors, seem to have joined at each villein plough, which thus can hardly have possessed more than 4 oxen in its team.

III. THE FREE TENANTS ON THE LORD'S DEMESNE.

In the Domesday Survey for the greater part of England there is no mention of free tenants, whether ' *liberi homines* ' or ' *libere tenentes* '

Nor, considering the extreme completeness of the Survey, is it easy to explain their absence on any other hypothesis than that of their non-existence.[1] A glance at the map will show that throughout those

---

[1] An elaborate argument was raised by Archdeacon Hale in the valuable introduction to the Camden Society's edition of the *Domesday of St. Paul's*, to show that the values given at the end of the entry for each manor in the Domesday Survey consisted of the rents of free tenants. He based his view on the fact that in two cases quoted by him the amount of the value so given was exceeded by the amount for which the manor, in these cases, was let 'ad firmam;' and, further, upon a comparison of the Domesday values of the manors of St. Paul's with the recorded 'Summæ denariorum' in 1181, and 'Tenants' rents' in 1222. But the figures given are probably a sufficient refutation of the view taken, inasmuch as though the latter have a certain general correspondence with the Domesday values in almost every case, if the view were correct, there must have been a falling off in the number and value of the tenants' rents between the two periods. The falling off for the whole of the 18 manors must have been in this case from 155*l*. 10*s*. T.R.E., and 157*l*. 13*s*. 4*d*. T.R.W., of Domesday amounts, to 112*l*. 16*s*. 4*d*. in 1181, and 126*l*. 10*s*. 3*d*. in 1222. The true reading of these figures, there can hardly be a doubt, is that the amount of *tenants' rents alone* at the later date had become in the interval nearly as great as the *whole value* of the manors (including the land both in demesne and in villenage) at the time of the Domesday Survey. There is abundant evidence of the rapid growth of population, and especially of the class of free tenants, between the eleventh and the thirteenth century. The value of manors is given in many cases in the Hundred Rolls for Oxfordshire (including demesne

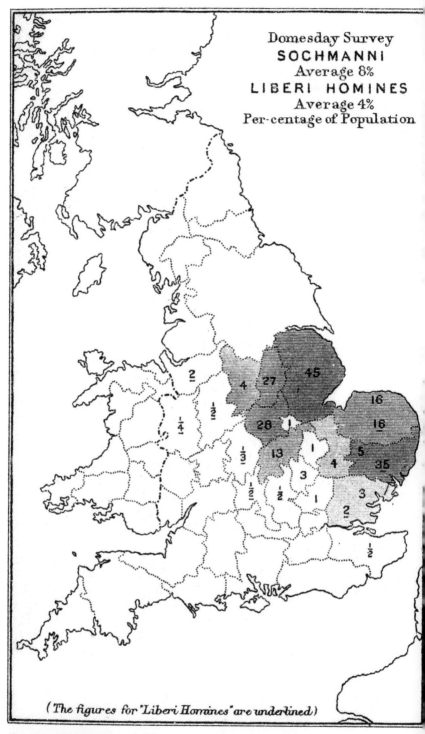

Domesday Survey
SOCHMANNI
Average 8%
LIBERI HOMINES
Average 4%
Per-centage of Population

(The figures for "Liberi Homines" are underlined)

London: Longmans & C.º

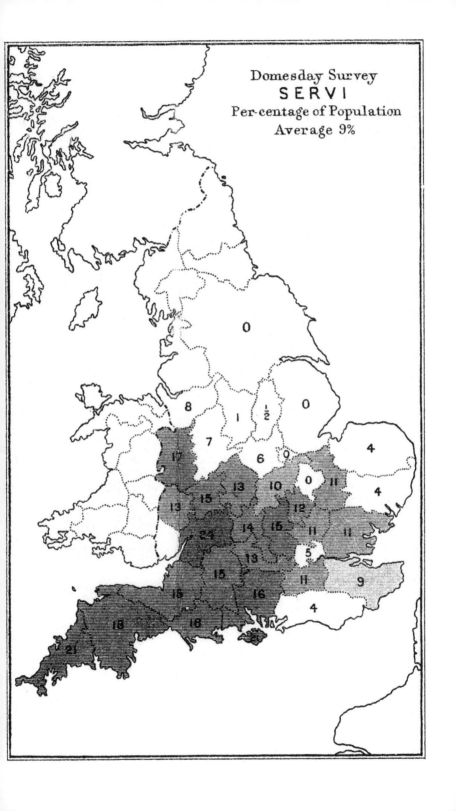

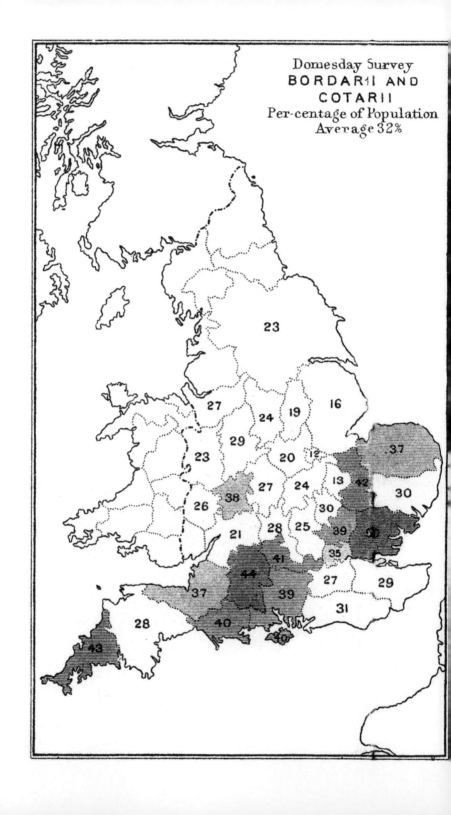

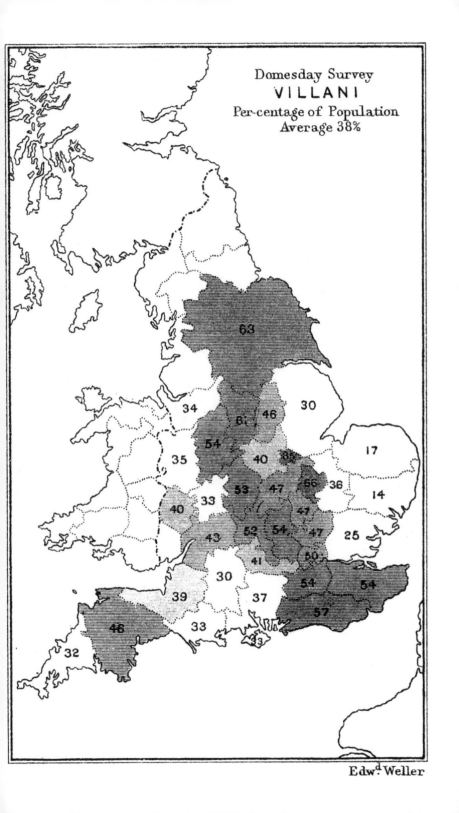

Domesday Survey
VILLANI
Per-centage of Population
Average 38%

Edw.ᵈ Weller

counties of England most completely under Danish influence there were plenty of *liberi homines* and of the allied class of *sochmanni*, but nowhere else. And that these two classes were distinctly and exceptionally Danish there is evidence in a passage in the laws of Edward the Confessor, in which the ' Manbote in ' Danelaga ' is given separately and as different from that of the rest of England, viz. ' de vilano et *soche-* ' *man* xii. oras : de *liberis hominibus* iii. marcas.' [1]

That the existence of these classes in a manor was local and quite exceptional is also confirmed by the place in which they are mentioned in the list of classes of tenants, the numbers of whom were to be recorded. They are placed last of all, even after the ' servi.' Inquiry was to be made, ' quot villani, quot cottarii, ' quot servi, *quot liberi homines, quot sochemanni*.' These were the words used in the statement of the inquiry to be made in the manors of the monks of Ely,

---

land rents and services), and the figures in the following six cases in which the comparison is complete

show a large rise in value, as might be expected :

DOMESDAY SURVEY				HUNDRED ROLLS			
Name		Value		Name		Value	
		£	£			£ s. d.	
P. 156 *b*. Lineham	(T.R.E.)	12 modo	10	P. 743. Lynham	.	27 8 4	
P. 157 *a*. Henestan	,,	20 ,,	18	P. 739. Ennestan	.	38 19 2	
P. 158 *b*. Esthcote	,,	5 ,,	8	P. 730. Estcot .	.	32 3 4	
P. 158 *b*. Fulebroc	,,	16 ,,	16	P. 744. Folebrok	.	28 7 7	
P. 159 *a*. Ideberie	,,	12 ,,	12	P. 734. Iddebir .	.	31 12 10½	
P. 159 *b*. Caningeham	,,	12 ,,	15	P. 733. Keyngham	.	37 4 2	
		£77	,, £79			£195 15 5½	

It is thus almost certain that both surveys were taken on the same plan, and embrace the value of the whole manor in each case.

[1] *Ancient Laws, &c., of England*, Thorpe, 192.

which manors lay in the Danish district; and the two last-mentioned classes were added out of order at the end of a common form, to meet its special needs.[1]

It is remarkable, however, that by common law (which generally represents very ancient custom) the existence of free tenants was essential to the Court Baron of a manor. Without some freemen, according to the old law books, it could not be held.[2] And there is a curious instance, in the Survey, of three sochmanni being lent by one lord to another, so that he might hold his court.[3]

Norman dependants of the lord of the manor and men of the hundred.

This being so, it is curious and important to notice that the survey of the manors of the monks of Ely was to be taken upon the oaths of the sheriff of the county, and of all the barons and of their Norman associates (*eorum Francigenarum*), and of the whole hundred (*tocius centuriatus*), the priests, præpositi, and six villani of each manor (*villa*).[4]

The sochmanni and liberi homines must here be included either among the 'Norman associates' or the 'whole hundred.'

It may be concluded, therefore, that the liberi homines and sochmanni were of Danish or Norman origin, as also probably was the Court Baron itself; whilst in those districts of England not so much under Danish or Norman influence, the demesne lands were not let out until a later period to permanent freeholding tenants. Upon the lord's demesne, and perhaps

---

[1] *Inquisitio Eliensis*, f. 497 a.

[2] *Ellis*, i. 237.

[3] *Ibid.* i. 237, note. *Domesday*, i. 193 b. *Orduuelle*.

[4] Ellis, i. 22. See, as to *Francigenæ, Laws of W. Conq.* iii. Nos.

III. and IV. Thorpe, p. 211. As to the 'centuriatus,' see *Capitulare de Villis Caroli Magni*, s. 62—'Quid de liberis hominibus et centenis.' *Monumenta Germaniæ Historica*, Hanover, 1881, p. 89.

in the manorial hall, may have been the ' *Francigenœ* *eorum* ' belonging to the ' Comitatus,' not necessarily holders of land, but more or less dependants of the lord of the manor. Out of the Danish district nearly all the population on the manor seems clearly to have been tenants in villenage or slaves.

IV. THE CLASSES OF TENANTS IN VILLENAGE.

We turn now to the tenants in villenage, who formed the bulk of the population, and with whom this inquiry has most to do.

The terms of the writ ordering the survey to be made on the Ely manors show clearly what classes of tenants in villenage were expected to be found on the manors. The jury were to inquire—

(1) Quot villani.
(2) Quot cotarii.
(3) Quot servi.

The three classes of tenants in villenage actually mentioned in the Survey are almost universally the—

(1) Villani.
(2) Bordarii [or cottarii].
(3) Servi.

As regards the servi, the map will show that The servi. whilst only embracing nine per cent. of the whole population of England, they were most numerous towards the south-west of England, less and less numerous as the Danish districts were approached, and absent

altogether from Yorkshire, Lincolnshire, and border-
ing districts.

Even when most numerous they were hardly
tenants in villenage.   They seem to have held no
land, and often to have been rather household thralls
of the lord of the manor than *tenants* in any ordinary
sense of the word.[1]

Thus the real tenants in villenage were confined
mainly to the two classes of villani and bordarii, or
cottiers.

The cot-
tiers.

Taking the *bordarii* or cottage tenants first, the
map will show how evenly they were scattered over
the whole country.   They embraced 32 per cent.—
roughly one-third—of the whole population in their
number, and in no county were there less than 12 per
cent. of them.

The villani.

But the *villani* were evidently at the date of the
Survey, and at the earlier date of Edward the Confessor, as they were afterwards, by far the most important and typical tenants in villenage.

They were at the date of the Survey even more
numerous than the cottier class below them.   They
embraced 38 per cent. of the whole population, and,
except where partially displaced by the sochmanni of
the Danish district, were pretty evenly dispersed all
over England.   Except in Norfolk and Suffolk, they
were seldom less than one-third of the popula
tion.   And if at the time of the Survey they were
holders of virgates and half-virgates, as their successors were afterwards, then it follows that they held
by far the largest proportion of the land of England

---

[1] The servi are mentioned
sometimes as on the lord's demesne, and sometimes at the end of the
tenants in villenage.

in their holdings. But before we assume this, some
proof may fairly be required that it was so. In the
meantime it is clear that the classes of tenants in
villenage *bore the same names* at the time of the Survey
as they did afterwards. The presumption evidently
is that they held similar holdings.

V. THE VILLANI WERE HOLDERS OF VIRGATES, ETC.

The compilers of the Survey were not in the habit
of describing in detail the character of the holdings
of the villani. Whilst recording how many villani
there were in a manor, the Domesday Survey does
not, like the Hundred Rolls, usually go on to state
how many of them held a virgate and how many a
half-virgate each.

Still, notwithstanding this general silence of the
Survey on this point, treating the matter manor by
manor, and taking for example the Peterborough
manors, it might be inferred almost with certainty
that as the villani of the *Liber Niger* in 1125 were
holders of virgates and half-virgates, so their fathers
and grandfathers before them must also have held
virgates and half-virgates at the time of the Domesday Survey and of Edward the Confessor. And such
an inference would be strengthened by the occasional
use in the Survey of the terms *integri villani*[1] and
villani dimidii,[2] answering no doubt to the same
terms, and to the *pleni virgarii* and *semi-virgarii* of
the *Liber Niger* and the Battle Abbey records.

---

[1] *Survey*, i. f. 252.   [2] *Ibid*. i. ff. 162, 168, 169 *b*, 252.

That the land was really held at the date of the Survey in hides and virgates may also be gathered from the well-known statement of the Saxon Chronicle that ' *næs an ælpig hide ne an gyrde landes* ' was omitted from the Survey—a statement which does not mean that not a hide nor a yard of land was omitted, but not a hide or a yard-land, *i.e.* a *virgate*.[1] So that it might fairly be inferred from this passage that the virgate was the normal or typical holding of the villanus, and this inference might well cover the whole area of the Survey.

But there is more direct evidence than these general inferences. It so happens that there are a few local exceptions to the general silence of the Survey as regards the holdings of the villani.

Examples in survey of Middlesex.

The most remarkable exception to the general reticence occurs in the survey for Middlesex, the compilers of which go out of their way fortunately to give precisely the desired information. And wherever they do so the holdings are found to be in the now familiar grades of hides, half-hides, virgates, and half-virgates.

The following are a few examples :—

(F. 127 *a.*)—*Hesa.*

The priest holds 1 hide.
3 milites hold 6½ hides.

2 villani	„	2	„	[*i.e.* a hide each].
12 „	„	6	„	[*i.e.* ½ hide each].
20 „	„	5	„	[*i.e.* ¼ hide each, or virgate].
40 „	„	5	„	[*i.e.* ⅛ hide each, or ½ virgate].
16 „	„	2	„	[*i.e.* ⅛ hide each, or ½ virgate].

---

[1] Sub anno MLXXXV. Rolls Edition, by Thorpe, i. p. 353.

(F. 128 *a*.)—*In Villa vbi sedet Æcclesia Sti. Petri (Westminster).*

> 9 villani each of a virgate.
> 1 villanus of 1 hide.
> 9 villani each of ½ virgate.
> 1 cotarius of 5 acres.
> 41 cotarii with gardens.

(F. 128 *b*.)—*Hermodesworde.*

> 1 miles holds 2 hides.
> 2 villani hold 1 hide each.
> 2 „ of 1 hide (*i.e.* ½ hide each).
> 14 „ each of 1 virgate.
> 6 „ „ ½ „
> 6 bordarii each of 5 acres.
> 7 cotarii.
> 6 servi.

And so on throughout the survey for the county.

As might be expected, most of the villani held virgates and half-virgates, but there are a sufficient number of cases of hides and half-hides to show conclusively the relation to each other of the four grades in the regular hierarchy of villenage.

Another local and solitary exception occurs in the record for *Sawbridgeworth*, in Hertfordshire. The holdings in this case were as follows :— Examples in Herts.

(F. 139 *b*.)—*Sabrixteworde.*

> The præpositus holds a ½ hide.
> The priest holds 1 hide.
> 14 villani hold each 1½ virgate.
> 35 villani hold each ½ virgate, and among them
>   1½ virgate with 9 acres, paying 17*s*. 4½*d*.
> 46 bordarii hold each 8 acres.
> 2 bordarii hold 10 acres (*i.e.* 5 acres each).
> 20 cotarii hold 26 acres (*i.e.* among them).

A few other exceptional cases occur in the *Liber*

Eliensis. The abbey had three manors in Hertfordshire, and in these the holdings were as follows:

(P. 509–10.)—IN OEDWINESTREU HUNDRED.

Hadam. 1 'villanus' of 1 virgate.
   18 'villani,' each of ½ virgate.
   7 'cotarii' of ½ virgate (*i.e.* together).

IN THE TWO HUNDREDS OF BRADEUTRE.

Hatfield. 18 'villani' each of 1 virgate.
   The priest of ½ hide.
   4 'homines' of 4 hides (*i.e.* a hide each).

IN ODESEIE HUNDRED.

Chyllessella. 2 villani of ½ hide (*i.e.* 1 virgate each).
   10 villani of 5 virgates (*i.e.* ½ virgate each).
   9 bordarii of 1 virgate (*i.e* together).
   7 servi.

In the Fen Country.

The monks of Ely also had several manors in the Fen country, but the holdings in this district seem to have been peculiar. Instead of being 'each of a virgate,' or 'each of a half-virgate,' they are 'each of so many acres,' as was also found to be the case in some districts of Cambridgeshire in the Hundred Rolls. The Fen district seems to have had its own local peculiarities, both in the eleventh and in the fourteenth centuries, just as Kent also had. But here was no exception to the rule that the villani were classed in grades, each grade with equal holdings.

These accidental instances in the Domesday Survey in which the required information is given are numerous enough to make it clear that at the date of the Survey the holdings of the villani were generally

The yardland the normal holding of the villanus.

hides, half-hides, virgates, and half-virgates. The virgate or yard-land was the normal holding, as it was afterwards. And this being so, it may reasonably be concluded also that the virgates and half-virgates were themselves what they were afterwards—bundles of strips scattered over the open fields, and having some connexion not yet fully explained, but clearly indicated, with the number of oxen allotted to their holders or contributed by them to the manorial plough team of eight oxen.

VI. THE HOLDINGS OF THE BORDARII OR COTTIERS.

It has already been noticed that in the *Inquisitio Eliensis* the particulars to be recorded as regards the tenants were—

    1. Quot villani.
    2. Quot *cottarii*.
    3. Quot servi, &c.

And that with few exceptions throughout the Survey the three classes actually found in the Survey were—

    1. Villani.
    2. *Bordarii*.
    3. Servi.

From this fact alone it would not be wrong to conclude that to a great extent the words *bordarii* and *cottarii* were interchangeable.

This inference gains much weight from the fact that a great many bordarii as well as cottarii are found even in the *Inquisitio Eliensis* itself. The facts, however, when collected together are some-

CHAP. III.

Cottiers
and bor-
darii very
much alike.

what curious, as a reference to the note below will show.[1]

In a few cases there are both bordarii and cottarii mentioned, which would lead to the conclusion that they were distinct classes. But in most cases there are either one or the other of the two classes mentioned, but not both. Examining their holdings there seems to be no difference between them.

There are bordarii holding so many acres each, generally *five*, but varying sometimes from one to ten. There are cottarii with all these variations of holdings. There are ' bordarii with their gardens,' and there are likewise ' cottarii with their gardens.' There are both bordarii and cottarii who, as their holdings are not described at all, may, for anything we know, have held cottages only, and no land or gardens.

Comparing these Cambridgeshire examples with those in Hertfordshire, and others in the Domesday Survey for Middlesex, we may conclude that for all

---

[1] In the *Inquisitio Eliensis* the instances of bordarii and cottarii in Cambridgeshire are as follows :—

iii. cot.	iiii. bor.	xii. bor. et ix. cot.
iii. bor.	viii. bor.	ix. cot. de ortis suis.
ii. bor.	iv. bor.	viii. cot.
iiii. bor.	iiii. bor.	i.
vi. bor.	xv. bor. cum suis ortis.	iiii. cot.
ii. bor.	xv. bor. et iii. cot.	viii. cot.
xiiii. bor. de suis ortis.	x. bor. et iii. cot.	ii. cot.
ii. bor.	ix. bor. et iii. cot.	viii. cot. de i. a.
v. bor.	xviii. bor. et x. cot.	v. cot.
v. bor. de v. acris.	iii. bor. de xv. ac.	iiii. cot.
v. bor. de v. ac.	(*i.e.* 5 a. each).	x. cot. quisq. de i. a.
vii. bor.	viii. cot.	x. cot.
iii. bor. de iii. ac.	iii. cot. de ortis.	ix. cot.
iiii. bor.	iv. quisq. de v. ac.	iiii. cot.
xii. bor. de x. ac. quisque.	ii. bor. et iv. cot. quisq.	vi. cot. et iiii. bor. quisq.
v. bor.	de x. a.	de v. a.

practical purposes the *bordarius* was a *cottier*—sometimes with no land, sometimes with a garden, sometimes with one solitary acre strip in the open fields, sometimes with more, even up to 10 acres, but that the typical bordarius was a cottager who held, in addition to his cottage, 5 acres in the open fields. His was, therefore, a subordinate position to that of the villanus proper in the village hierarchy, and he differed from the villanus probably most clearly in this, that he put no oxen into the village plough teams, and took no part in the common ploughing.

His services were no less servile than those of the villanus, but of a more trivial kind. He was above the *servus*, or slave, but his was the class which most easily would slide into that of the modern labourer, and in which the *servus* himself in his turn might most easily merge. The word ' bordarius ' was noticed in the *Liber Niger* of Peterborough, but though so universal in the Domesday Survey it soon slipped out of use ; and as ' bord ' gave place to ' cottage ' in the common speech, so the whole class below the villani came to be known as cottagers.

VII. THE DOMESDAY SURVEY OF THE VILLA OF WESTMINSTER.

It may be worth while to test the value of the key which the results of this inquiry have put into our hand by applying it to the Domesday description of a particular manor.

For this purpose the survey of the manor of

H

Westminster may be chosen as one of great national and historical interest.   It is as follows : [1]—

> In the villa where is situated the church of St. Peter [*i.e.* the abbey] the abbot of the same place holds 13½ hides [*i.e.* land rated at so much]. There is land for 11 plough teams.
>
> To the *demesne* belong 9 hides and 1 virgate, and there are 4 plough teams.
>
> The *villeins* have 6 plough teams, and one more might be made.
>
> There are 9 villani with a virgate each.
>
> >   1 villanus with a hide.
> >   9 villani with a half-virgate each.
> >   1 cottier with 5 acres.
> >   41 cottiers rendering a shilling each yearly for their gardens.
>
> There is meadow for 11 plough teams,
>
> >   Pasture for the cattle of the village,
> >   Wood for 100 pigs.
>
> There are 25 houses of the abbot's soldiers and of other men, who render 8*s.* per annum or 10*l.* in all ; when he received them, the same ; in the time of King Edward, 12*l.*
>
> This manor was and is in the demesne of the Church of St. Peter of Westminster.
>
> In the same villa *Bainiardus* holds 3 hides of the abbot.   There is land for 2 plough teams, and they are there, in demesne, and one cottier.   Wood for 100 pigs.   Pasture for cattle.   Four arpents of vineyard newly planted.   All these are worth 60*s.* ; when he received them, 20*s.* ; in the time of King Edward, 6*l.*   This land belonged, and belongs, to the Church of St. Peter.

It is clear from this description that the village which nestled round the new minster just completed by Edward the Confessor, was on a manor of the abbot.   It consisted of 25 houses of the abbot's immediate followers, 19 homesteads of villani, 42 cottages with their little gardens, and one of them with 5 acres of land.   There was also the larger homestead of the sub-manor of the abbot's under-tenant, with a single cottage and a vineyard of 4 half-acres newly planted.   There was meadow enough by the river side to make hay for the herd of oxen

---

[1] F. 128 *a.*

belonging to the dozen plough teams of the village, and pasture for them and other cattle. Further round the village in open fields were about 1,000 acres of arable land mostly in the acre strips, lying no doubt in their shots or furlongs, and divided by green turf balks and field-ways. Lastly, surrounding the whole on the land side were the woods where the swineherd found mast for the 200 pigs of the place. On every one of these points we have the certain evidence of sworn eye-witnesses.

And so with little variation must have been the condition of things in all material points twenty years earlier,[1] when King Edward lay on his death-bed and wandered in his mind, and saw in his delirium two holy monks whom he remembered in Normandy, who foretold to him the coming disasters to the realm, which should only be ended when 'the green tree, after severance from its trunk and removal for the space of three acres (*trium jugerum spatio*), should return to its parent stem, and again bear leaf and fruit and flower.' It may be that the delirious king as 'he sat up in bed' dreamily gazed through the window of his chamber upon the open fields, and the turf balks dividing the acres. The green tree may have been suggested to his mind by an actual tree growing out of one of the balks. The uneven glass of his window-panes would be just as likely as not as he rose in his bed to sever the stem from the root to his eye, moving it apparently three acres' breadth higher up the open field, restoring it again to its root as he sank back on his pillow. The very delirium of

---

[1] The value of the rentals had decreased since T.R.E., so that the village had not increased in the interval.

CHAP. III. the dying king thus becomes the most natural thing in the world when we know that all round were the open fields, and balks, and acres. Without this knowledge even the learned and graphic historian of the Norman Conquest can make nothing of the ' trium jugerum spatio, and casts about for other renderings instead of the perfectly intelligible right one.[1]

Further incidental evidence.

Once more; the contemporary biographer of Edward the Confessor, with the accuracy of one to whom Westminster was no doubt familiar, tells us that ' the devout king destined to God that place, both ' for that it was near unto the famous and wealthy city ' of London, and also had a pleasant situation *amongst* ' *fruitful fields lying round about it*, with the principal ' river running hard by, bringing in from all parts of ' the world great variety of wares and merchandise of ' all sorts to the city adjoining; but chiefly for the ' love of the apostle, whom he reverenced with a ' special and singular affection.'[2] Even the delicate historical insight of the late historian of the abbey, to whom all its picturesque surroundings were so dear, failed to catch the full meaning of this passage. Whilst referred to in a note it becomes paraphrased thus in the text:—' By this time also the wilderness of ' Thorney was cleared ; and the crowded river with ' *its green meadows*, and the sunny aspect of the island, ' may have had a charm for the king whose choice ' had hitherto lain in the rustic fields of Islip and ' Windsor.'[3]   Yes, ' meadows of Thorney ' there were,

---

[1] Freeman's *Norman Conquest*, iii. 12.

[2] Contemporary Life of Edward the Confessor in the Harleian MSS.,

pp. 980, 985.

[3] *Memorials of Westminster Abbey*, p. 15.

on which the oxen of a dozen plough teams were grazing, but the contemporary writer's '*fruitful fields lying round about the place*' were the 1,000 acres of corn land of which Dean Stanley was unconscious. No blame to him, for what economic student had sufficiently understood the Domesday Survey to tell him that every virgate of the villani of the '*villa ubi sedet Æcclesia Sancti Petri*' was a bundle of strips of arable land scattered all over the three great fields stretching away from the village, and the river, and the ' meadows of Thorney' for a mile or two round ?

VIII. THE EXTENT OF THE CULTIVATED LAND OF ENGLAND, AND HOW MUCH WAS INCLUDED IN THE YARD-LANDS OF THE VILLANI.

Knowing now that the virgate or yard-land was the normal holding of the villanus, though some villani held hides and half-hides, *i.e.* more virgates than one, and others half-virgates ; and knowing that the normal holding of the villanus, whether called a yard-land or a husband-land, or by any other name, was a bundle of scattered strips, containing normally thirty acres ; and knowing also the number of villani in the several counties embraced in the Survey, it becomes perfectly possible to estimate, roughly no doubt, but with remarkable certainty, the total area contained in their holdings.

The total number of villani in these counties was 108,407.[1] If each villanus held a yard-land or virgate of 30 acres, then about 3,250,000 acres were con-

---

[1] See Ellis's *Introduction*, vol. ii. p. 514.

tained in their holdings.   The number of villani
holding half-virgates was, however, probably greater
than the number holding half-hides and hides; so
that the average holding would perhaps hardly be
equal in acreage to the normal holding of 30 acres.
Taking the average holding at 20 acres instead of 30,
we should probably under-estimate the acreage.   It
would even then amount to 2,168,000.   We shall be
safe if we say that the villani held in their bundles of
strips 2¼ millions of acres.[1]

We must add the holdings of the 82,000 bordarii
and of the 6,000 or 7,000 cottier tenants.[2]   If these
lesser holdings averaged three acres each, we must add
another quarter of a million acres for them.   The
total of two and a half millions of acres can thus hardly
be an over-estimate of the acreage of the arable
strips in the open fields held by the villani and
bordarii in villenage.   What proportion did this bear
to the whole cultivated area of these counties?

To include the total acreage under the plough,
the holdings of the *sochmanni* and *liberi homines* of
the Danish district must be added, and also the
arable land (ploughed mainly by the villani) on the
lord's demesne.   The 23,000 *sochmanni*[3] can hardly
have held as little as a similar number of villani—
say half a million acres.   The 12,000 *liberi homines*
may have held another half-million.   And one or two
million acres can hardly be an excessive estimate for
the arable portion of the lord's demesne.

Putting all these figures together, the evidence of
the Domesday Survey seems therefore to show that

Ellis, ii. p. 511.   [2] *Id.*   [3] *Ibid.* p. 514.

at its date about five million acres were under the
plough, *i.e.* from one-third to one-half of the acreage
now in arable cultivation in the same counties of
England.[1]
This is not mere conjecture. It rests upon facts
recorded in detail in the Survey for each manor
upon the oath of the villani themselves ; with no
chance of exaggeration, because upon the result was
to be founded a tax ; with little chance of omission,
because the men of the hundred, who also were sworn,
would take care in their own interests that one place
was not assessed more lightly than others. The
general opinion was that ' not a single hide or yard-
land was omitted.'

The acreage under arable cultivation at the time
of the Survey, and twenty years earlier in the time
of Edward the Confessor, was thus really very large.
And the villani in their yard-lands held nearly half of
it, and together with the bordarii fully half of it, in
villenage. It must be borne in mind also that by their
services they tilled the greater part of the rest.

This was the economic condition in which England
was left by the Saxons as the result of the 500 years
of their rule. The agriculture of England, *as they left
it*, was carried on under the open field system by village
communities in villenage. It was under the system
of Saxon serfdom, with some little help from the
actual slaves on the lord's demesne, that the land was
tilled throughout all those counties which the Saxons
had thoroughly conquered, with some partial excep-

---

[1] The arable acreage in these counties in 1879 was about twelve
million acres.

tion as regards the Danish districts, where the *sochmanni* and *liberi homines* were settled.

This is the solid foundation of fact firmly vouched for by the Domesday Survey, read in the light of the evidence leading up to it.

From this firm basis the inquiry must proceed, carefully following the same lines as before—working still from the known to the unknown—tracing the open field system, its villani, and their yard-lands still farther back into the earlier periods of Saxon rule.

The question to be answered is, how far back into the earlier Saxon times the open field system and its yard-lands can be followed, and whether the serfdom connected with them was more or was less complete and servile in its character in the earlier than in the later period.

CHAPTER IV.

*THE OPEN FIELD SYSTEM TRACED IN SAXON TIMES
—THE SCATTERING OF THE STRIPS ORIGINATED IN
THE METHODS OF CO-ARATION.*

I. THE VILLAGE FIELDS UNDER SAXON RULE WERE OPEN FIELDS.

WE have learned from a long line of evidence, leading backwards to the date of the Domesday Survey, that the community in villenage fitted into the open field system as a snail fits into a shell. Let us now, following the same method, and beginning again with the shell, inquire whether its distinctive features can be traced on English fields in early Saxon times from the date of the Domesday Survey, and of Edward the Confessor, backwards.

And first it will be convenient to find out whether traces can be found of the ' strips,' and the ' furlongs,' ' headlands,' ' linches,' ' gored acres,' ' butts,' and odds and ends of ' no-man's-land,' the remains of which are still to be seen wherever the open fields are unenclosed.

It will be remembered that the strips upon examination were found to be *acres* laid out for ploughing on the open fields.   They were, in fact, the original actual divisions, from the general dimensions of which the statute acre, with its four roods, was derived.

In the Saxon translation of the Gospels.   Bearing this in mind, the Anglo-Saxon translation of the Gospels may be quoted in proof that the fields round a Saxon village were open fields, and generally divided into acre strips in the tenth century, just as the vision of *Piers Plowman* was quoted in proof that it was so in the fourteenth century.

The Saxon translator of the story of the disciples walking through the corn-fields describes them as walking over the ' *œcera.*'

Obviously the translator's notion of the corn-fields round a village was that of the open fields of his own country.   They were divided into 'acres,' and he who walked over them walked over the ' acres.'

In Saxon charters.   But by far the best evidence occurs in the multitudes of charters, from the eighth century downwards, so many of which are contained in the cartularies of the various abbeys, and more than 1,300 of which are collected in Kemble's *Codex Diplomaticus.*

These charters are generally in Latin.   They most often relate to the grant of a whole manor or estate with the village upon it.   And to the charters is generally added in Saxon a description of the boundaries as known to the inhabitants.   These descriptions are in precisely the same form as the description of the boundaries on the Hitchin manor rolls as presented by the homage in 1819.[1]

The boundary is always described as starting at

---

[1] The boundaries of the charters contained in first two volumes of the *Codex Dip.* are collected in the Appendix to vol. iii.   After this they are given with the charters.

some well-known point—perhaps a road or stream— as passing on from it to some other, and so on, from point to point, till the starting-place is reached again. The chance of finding out from these boundaries whether they contained within them open fields lies simply in the possibility that some one or another of the distinctive features of the system may happen to occur at the edge of the estate or township, and so to be mentioned among the links in the chain of objects making up the boundary.

The fact is that this happens very often.

By way of example, the boundaries of *Hordwell* in Hampshire may be taken. They are appended to a charter [1] by which King Edward, the son of King Alfred, gave the estate to the Abbey of Abingdon, and they are as follows :—

Metæ de Hordwella.

An Swinbroc ærest, thæt up of Swinebroce in on riscslæd, of thæs riscslædes byge foran ongean Hord-wylles weg, thæt andlang thæs weges oth hit cymth to Iecenhilde wege, thonne of thæm wege, up on thone ealdan wude weg, thonne of thæn wude waga be eastan Telles-byrg on ænne garan, thonne of thæm garan on næne garæcer, thæt andlangs thære furh to anum and-heafdum to anre forierthe, and sio forierth gæth in to tham lande, thanne on gerihte to tham stane on hricg weg, thanon west on anne goran, andlanges thære furh to anum anheafdum, thanon of dune on fearnhylles slæd, thæt thanon on

On Swinbroc first, thence up from Swinbroc on to rush-slade, from this rush-slade's corner fore-against Hordwell-way, thence along this way until it comes to the Icknild way, then from these ways upon the old wood-way, then from that wood-way by east Tellesburg to a corner, then from that corner to a *goreacre*, thence along its fur-row to the head of a *headland*, and which headland goes into the land, then right on to the stone on ridge way, then on west to a *gore* along the furrow to its head, then adown to fernhills slade, thence on a furrow in the acre nearer the *lince*, then on that lince at fernhills slade south-

---

[1] *Hist. Monasterii de Abingdon*, vol. i. p. 57.

ane furh an æcer near thæm hlince, thonne on thæt hlinc æt fearnhylles slæde suthewearde, of thæm hlince on anon heafde, forth thær on ane furh, on ane stanræwe, thanon on gerihte on bricgweg thæt thanone on ane garæcer on anon heafde, and se garæcer in on thæt land, thanone andlanges anre furh oth hit cymth to anum byg, thanone of thæm byge forth on ane furh oth hit cymth to anre forierthe, and sio forierth into tham lande, thonne on Icenhilde weg be Tellesburh westan, thanone north ofer Icenhilde weg on sican wylle, thæt hthweres ofer an furlang on gerihte on an ælrbed on hæghylles broces byge, anlang thæs broces oth hit cymth to twam garæcer, and than garæceras in on thæt land, thanon on ane forierthe on anon heafde, thanon on gerihte on readan clif on Swinbroc, thonne andlang thæs broces on thæt riscslæd.

ward from that lince to its head, forward then on a furrow to a stonerow, then right on to the ridge-way, thence thereon to a *goreacre* at its head, the goreacre being within that land, thence along a furrow till it comes to a corner, thence from that corner forward on a furrow till it comes to a *headland*, which headland is within the land, then on the Ickenild way by Tellesburg west, thence north over the Ickenild way to Sican-well, thence . . . over a *furlong* right on to an elder-bed at hedgehill's brook corner, along this brook till it comes to two *goreacres*, which goreacres are within that land, thence on a *headland* to its head, then right on to Redcliffe on Swin-brook, then along this brook on that rush-slade.

In this single instance there is mention of *acres* or strips, of *gores* or *gored-acres*, of *headlands*, of *furlongs*, and of *linches*.

Scores of similar instances might be given from the Abingdon charters, ' Liber de Hyda,' and the ' Codex Diplomaticus,' showing that the boundaries constantly make mention of one or another of the distinctive marks by which the open field system may be recognised.[1]

---

[1] *Codex Dip.* cclxxii. ' *grenan hlinc*,' cccliii. ' *hlinces*,' ccclxxvii. ' ealde gare quod indigenæ *nane monnes land* vocant.' (See also dlxx. ' *nane mannes land* '), cccxcix. ' *furlang*,' ccccvii. ' *forlang*,' ' *heued lande*,' ccccxiii. ' *furlang*,' ' *hlinces*,' ccccxiv. ' *mær hlinces*,' ccccxvii, ' *forerth akere*,' ccccxviii. ' *furlanges*,' ccccxix. and xx. ' *foryrthe*,' ' *greatan hlinces*,' and so on. Instances are equally numerous in the Abing-

There can, therefore, be no doubt that the fields of Saxon manors or villages were open fields divided into furlongs and strips, and having their headlands and linches. Even the little odds and ends of '*no man's land*' are incidentally found to have their place in the Saxon open fields 1,000 years ago.

But how far back can these Saxon open fields be traced? The answer is, as far back as the laws of King Ine can be held to reach into the past.

These laws were republished by King Alfred as 'The Dooms of Ine,' who came to the throne in A.D. 688. In their first clause they claim to have been recorded by King Ine with the counsel and teaching of his father *Cenred*, and of *Hedde*, his bishop (who was Bishop of Winchester from A.D. 676 to 705), and of *Eorcenwold*, his bishop (who obtained the see of London in 675); and so, if genuine, they seem to represent what was settled customary law in Wessex during the last half of the seventh century—the century after the conquest of the greater part of Wessex.

In these laws there occurs a section which so clearly refers to open common fields divided into acres, and to common meadows also divided into strips or doles, that it would have been perfectly intelligible and reasonable if it had been included word for word in the record of the customs of the Hitchin manor as regards the three common fields and the green commons and Lammas land :—

---

don charters and those of the *Liber de Hyda*. For linces, see *Hist. Abingdon*, i. pp. 111, 147, 158, 188, 259, 284, 315, 341, 404. *Liber de Hyda*, pp. 86, 103, 107, 176, 235, 239.

Be Ceorles Gærs-tune.[1]	*Of a Ceorle's grass-tun (meadow).*
(xlii.) Gɪꝼ ceoꝓlaꝛ ᵹæꝓꝛ-ᴄun hæbben ᵹemænne. oꝓꝓe oðeꝓ ᵹeðál-lanð ᴄo ᴄýnanne.⁊ hæbben ꝛume ᵹeᴄýneð hɪoꝓa ðæl. ꝛume næbban.⁊ . . . eᴄᴄen hɪoꝓa ᵹemænan æceꝓaꝛ oꝓꝓe ᵹæꝓꝛ, ᵹán ꝓa ꝓonne ꝓe ꝥ ᵹeaᴄ aᵹan. ⁊ ᵹebeᴄe[n] ꝓam oðꝓum ꝓe hɪoꝓa ðæl ᵹeᴄýneðne. . . .	(42) If ceorls have common meadow or other *land divided into strips* [2] to fence, and some have fenced their strip, some have not, and . . . [stray cattle (?)] eat their common acres or grass, let those go who own the gap, and compensate the others who have fenced their strip. . . .

There is here in the smallest possible compass the most complete evidence that in the seventh century the fields of Wessex were common open fields, the arable being divided into *acres* and the meadows into *doles* [2]; and as the system is incidentally mentioned as a thing existing as a matter of course, it is not likely to have been suddenly or recently introduced. The evidence throws it back, therefore, at least to the earliest period of Saxon rule.

II. THE HOLDINGS WERE COMPOSED OF SCATTERED STRIPS.

The holdings were *hides* and *yard-lands.*

Let us next ask whether there are traces of the *scattered ownership*—the scattering all over the open fields of the strips included in the holdings—which was so essential a characteristic of the system; and, further, whether in tracing it back into early Saxon

---

[1] Laws of King Ine. *Ancient Laws, &c., of England*, Thorpe, p. 55.

[2] It will be remembered that Lammas land is divided into strips for the hay crop. In the Winslow Rolls, in the list of strips included in the virgate of John Moldeson were some strips or *doles* of meadow —hence *dǽl* and *gedál-land.* That gedal-land = open fields divided into strips, see *Hist. Abingdon* (p. 304), where there is a charter, A.D. 961, making a grant of '9 mansas' and 'thas nigon hida licggead on gemang othran *gedal-lande,* feldes gemane and mæda gemane and yrthland gemane.'

times any clue to its original meaning and intention
can be found.

First, it may be stated generally that, when the nature and incidents of the holdings are examined hereafter, it will be found that throughout the period of Saxon rule, from the time of Edward the Confessor backward to the date of the laws of King Ine, 300 years earlier, the holdings were mainly the same as those with which we have become familiar, viz. *hides*, *half-hides*, and *yard-lands*, and that, generally speaking, there were no other kinds of holdings the names of which are mentioned.

That these Saxon hides and yard-lands were com-posed of scattered strips in the open fields, as they were afterwards, might well be inferred from the mere fact that they bore the same names as those used after the Conquest. It would be strange indeed if the same names at the two dates meant entirely different things —if the virgate or yard-land before the Conquest was a thing wholly different from what it was after it.

Holdings composed of scattered strips.

But there is other evidence than the mere names of the holdings.

There is a general characteristic of the numerous Saxon charters of all periods, which, when carefully considered, can hardly have any other explanation than the fact that the holdings were composed not of contiguous blocks of land, but of scattered strips.

It is this—that whatever be the subject of the grant made by the charter, *i.e.* whether it be a whole manor or township that is granted, or only some of the holdings in it, the boundaries appended are the boundaries of the *whole* manor or township. No doubt the royal gifts to the monastic houses generally did consist of whole manors, and thus the boundaries in most cases naturally were the boundaries of the whole, and could not be otherwise. But it was not always so. Thus, among the Abingdon charters there are two of Edward the Martyr, one of vii. hides (cassatos), in ' Cingestune,' and another of xiii. ' mansas' in ' Cyngestun,' one to the Church of St. Mary at Abingdon, the other to a person named *Ælfstan*;[1] and to both charters are appended *the same boundaries* in substantially the same words. And these are the boundaries of the *whole township*.[2]

There can hardly be any other explanation of this peculiarity than the fact that the holdings were not blocks of land, the boundaries of which could be easily given, but, in fact, like the hides and virgates after the Conquest, bundles of strips scattered over the open fields, and intermixed with strips belonging to other holdings. Indeed, there is in a charter of King Ethelred (A.D. 982) among the Abingdon series relating to five hides at ' *Cheorletun*,' a direct confession of the reason why in this case all boundaries are omitted. Instead of the usual boundaries of the whole township there is the statement that the estate is ' the less distinctly defined by boundaries, *quia jugera altrinsecus copulata adjacent* '—because the acres are intermixed.[3]

On the hypothesis already suggested that the hides, half-hides, virgates, and bovates were the shares in the results of the ploughing of the village plough teams

---

[1] Vol. i. pp. 349–352.

[2] So also see *Codex Diplomaticus*, dii. and dxvi., and cccclxvii. and cccxxxv.

[3] Vol. i. p. 384. Compare also the boundaries of Draitune, ' *æcer under æcer*,' p. 248. Also the same expression, pp. 350 and 353.

—in other words, the number of strips allotted to each holder in respect of the oxen contributed by him to the plough team of eight oxen—it is perfectly natural that in a grant of *some* only of the holdings the boundaries given should be those of the whole township, viz. of the whole area, an intermixed share in which constituted the holding.

There is another fact, which has, perhaps, never yet been explained, but which is nevertheless perfectly intelligible on the same hypothesis.

It will be remembered that there was observed in the Winslow example of a virgate a certain regular turn or rotation in the order of the strips in the virgates—that John Moldeson's strips almost always came next after the strips of one, and were followed by those of another, particular neighbour. Now this fact strongly suggests that originally the holdings had not always and permanently consisted of the same actual strips, but that once upon a time the strips were perhaps allotted afresh each year in the ploughing according to a certain order of rotation, the turn of the contributor of two oxen coming twice as often as that of the contributor of one ox, and so making the virgate contain twice as many strips as the bovate. This, and this alone, would give the requisite elasticity to the system so as to allow, if necessary, of the admission of new-comers into the village community, and new virgates into the village fields.

So long as the limits of the land were not reached a fresh tenant would rob no one by adding his oxen to the village plough teams, and receiving in regular turn the strips allotted in the ploughing to his oxen. In the working of the system the strips of a new holding would be intermixed with the others by a perfectly natural process.

Now, that something like this process did actually happen in Saxon times is clear from the way in which the Church was provided for under the Saxon laws.

The mode in which *tithes* were taken.
In the light which is given by the knowledge of what the open field system really was, there is nothing intrinsically impossible even in the alleged but doubtful donation by King Ethelwulf of one-tenth of the whole land of England by one stroke of the pen to the Church. It has been said that he could not do it except on the royal domains without robbing the landowners and their tenants of their holdings. It would be so if the holdings were blocks. But there is nothing impossible in the supposition that a Saxon king should enact a law that every tenth strip ploughed by the common ploughs throughout the villages of England should be devoted to the Church. It would create no confusion or dislocation anywhere. And it would have meant just the same thing if Ethelwulf had enacted that every tenth virgate, or every tenth holding, should be devoted to the Church. For the sum of every tenth strip ploughed by the villagers, when the strips were tied, as it were, together into the bundles called virgates or hides, would amount to every tenth virgate, or hide, as the case might be. Nor would there be anything strange in his freeing the strips thus granted to the Church from all secular services.[1]

The alleged donation may be spurious, the documents relating to it may be forgeries, but there is

---

[1] See, with regard to this donation, Kemble's *Saxons in England,* c. x. ; and Stubbs' *Const. Hist.* i. pp. 262-71.

nothing impossible or unlikely in the thing itself.
And the very fact of the forgery of such a grant is
evidence of its intrinsic possibility. And, whatever
may be said as to the donation of Ethelwulf, whether
it be spurious or not, there are other proofs that
something of the kind was afterwards effected.

In No. XXV.[1] of the 'Excerptiones' of Archbishop *Priests often have yard-lands.*
Egbert (A.D. 735–766) it is ordained that 'to every
' church shall be allotted one complete holding
' (mansa), and that this shall be free from all but
' ecclesiastical services.' This was simply putting the
priest in the position of a recognised village official,
like the *præpositus* or the *faber*. They held their virgates free of service, and perhaps their strips were
ploughed by the common ploughs in return for their
services without their contributing oxen to the
manorial plough team. The Domesday Survey proves
that, in a great number of instances at least, room
had in fact been made in the village community for
the priest and his *virgate*.[2]

The following passages in the Saxon laws also *Tithe taken in acres, i.e. every tenth strip.*
show that for some time, at all events, the tithes were
actually taken, not in the shape of every tenth sheaf,
but exactly in accordance with the plan suggested by
the spurious grant of Ethelwulf, by every tenth strip
being set aside for the Church in the ploughing.

In the laws of King Ethelred[3] (A.D. 978–1016)

---

[1] Thorpe, p. 328. 'Item—
Ut unicuique æcclesiæ vel una
mansa integra absque alio servitio
adtribuatur, et presbiteri in eis con-
stituti non de decimis, neque de ob-
lationibus fidelium, nec de domibus,
neque de atriis vel ortis juxta æc-
clesiam positis, neque de præscripta

mansa, aliquod servitium faciant
præter æcclesiasticum; et si aliquid
amplius habuerint, inde senioribus
suis secundum patriæ morem, de-
bitum servitium impendant.'

[2] See especially the Survey for
Middlesex, and *supra* pp. 92–95.

[3] Thorpe, p. 146.

there is a command that every Christian man shall
' pay his tithe justly, *always as the plough traverses*
' *the tenth " œcer."* '

VII. Ánd pice cpiycenpa manna ʒehpilc. ꝥ he hir Dpih-cene hir ceoðunʒe. á rpa reó rulh þone ceoðan æcep ʒeʒá. pihclice ʒelæyce.be Loþey milcre.[1]	And be it known to every Christian man that he pay to his lord his tithe rightly always *as the plough traverses the tenth acre*, on peril of God's mercy.

Further, in a Latin law of King Ethelred there is
the following direction :—

Et præcipimus, ut omnis homo . . . det cyricsceattum et rectam decimam suam, . . . hoc est, sicut aratrum peragrabit decimam ac-ram.[2]	And we command, that every man . . . give his *churchshot* and just *tithe,* . . . that is, *as the plough traverses the tenth acre.*

And that this applied to land in villenage as well
as to land in demesne is clear from a still earlier law
of King Edgar (A.D. 959, 975) : ' That every tithe be
' rendered to the old minster to which the district
ʾ belongs, and that it be then so paid both from a
' *thane's in-land and from geneat-land, so as the plough*
' *traverses it.*'

1. Ðæc rynðon þonne æpeyc. ꝥ Loþey cýpican rýn ælcey pihcey þýpðe. ꞃ man aʒíre ælce ceo-ðunʒe co þam ealðan mýnycpe þe reo hypney co-hýpð. ꞃ ꝥ rý þonne rpa ʒelæyc. æʒðep ʒe or þeʒney in-lanðe ʒe or ʒeneac-lanðe. rpa rpa hic reo rulh ʒe-ʒanʒe.[3]	1. These then are first: that God's churches be entitled to every right ; and that every tithe be ren-dered to the old minster to which the district belongs ; and that it be then so paid, both from a thane's *in-land,* and from *geneat-land, so as the plough traverses it.*

There is very little reference in the Domesday
Survey to the churches and their tithes, but there
happens to be one entry at least in which there seems

---

[1] Thorpe, p. 146.
[2] *Ibid.* p. 144. So also in the Laws of Cnut, ' The tenth acre as
the plough traverses it.' Thorpe, p. 156.
[3] *Ibid.* p. 111.

to be a clear reference to this practice of the tithes
being taken in actual strips and acres. It relates to
the church at *Wallop*, in Hampshire (the place from
which the family name of the Earls of Portsmouth is
derived), and it states that ' to the church there per-
' tains one hide, also half of the tithes of the manor,
' also the whole kirkshot. And of the tithes of the
' villani xlvi. pence and *half of the acres.* There is in
' addition a little church to which pertain *viii. acres*
' *of the tithes.*' [1]

It may be taken then as certain that the holdings
in villenage in the open fields of the Saxon ' hams '
and ' tuns ' were composed, like the virgate of John
Moldeson, in the manor of Winslow, centuries afterwards, of strips scattered, one in this furlong and
another in that, all over the village fields ; and it may
be taken as already almost certain that the scattering
of the strips was in some way connected with the order
in which the strips were allotted in respect of the
oxen contributed to the village plough teams.

III. THE OPEN FIELD SYSTEM OF CO-ARATION DESCRIBED IN THE ANCIENT LAWS OF WALES.

The law that every tenth strip as it was traversed
by the plough was to be set apart for the tithe is
certainly the clearest hint that has yet been discovered
of the perhaps annual redistribution of the strips
among the holdings in a certain order of rotation,

---

[1] *D.* i. 38 *b.* Wallope (Hants).
' Ibi æcclesia cui pertinet una hida
' et medietas decimæ manerii et
totum Cirset, et de decima villa-
' norum XLVI. denarii et medietas
' agrorum.'
   ' Ibi est adhuc æcclesiola, ad quam
' pertinent viii. acræ de decima.'

though it is possible of course that a redistribution being once made, to make room for the acres set apart for the tithe, the same strips might always thereafter be assigned to the tithe and to each particular yard-land year after year without alteration.

What is still wanted to lift the explanation already offered of the connexion of the grades of holdings in the open fields and the scattering of the strips in each holding, with the team of 8 oxen, out of the region of hypothesis into that of ascertained fact is the discovery if possible somewhere actually at work of the system of common ploughing with eight oxen, and according to the oxen contributed. the assignment of the strips in respect of the oxen to their several owners. Were it possible to watch such an example of the actual process going on, there probably would be disclosed by some little detail of its working the reason and method of the scattering of the strips, and of the order of rotation in which they seem to have been allotted.

Now it happens that such an instance is at hand, affording every opportunity for examination under The system at work under the ancient laws of Wales. the most favourable circumstances possible. We find it in the ancient Welsh laws, representing to a large extent ancient Welsh traditions collected and codified in the tenth century, but somewhat modified afterwards, and coming down to us in a text of the fourteenth century. In these laws is much trustworthy evidence from which might be drawn a very graphic picture of the social and economic condition of the unconquered Welsh people, at a time parallel to the centuries of Saxon rule in England. And amongst other things fortunately there is an almost perfect picture of the method of ploughing. Nor is it too

much to say that in this picture we have a key which
completely fits the lock, and explains the riddle of
the English open field system.

For the ancient Welsh laws describe a simple form
of the open field system at an earlier stage than that
in which we have yet seen it—at a time, in fact, when
it was a living system at work, and everything about
it had a present and obvious meaning, and its details
were consistent and intelligible.

Let us examine this Welsh evidence.

Precisely as the modern statute acre had its origin
in the Saxon *æcer*, which was an actual division of the
fields, so that the Saxon *æcera* were the strips divided
by balks—the *seliones*—of the open field system ; so
the modern Welsh word for *acre* as a quantity of land
is ' *erw*,' and the same word in its ancient meaning in
the Welsh laws was the actual strip in the open fields.
This is placed beyond a doubt by the fact that
its measurements are carefully given over and over
again, and that it was divided from its neighbours by
an unploughed balk of turf two furrows wide.[1]

The Welsh laws describe the primitive way in
which the erw was to be measured. In one province
this was to be done by a man holding a rod of a certain length and stretching it on both sides of him to
fix the width, while the length is to be a certain multiple of its breadth.[2] In other provinces of Wales the
width was to be fixed by a rod equal in length to the

The Welsh erws, or acre strips.

Divided by turf balks.

Measured by a rod.

---

[1] (5) The breadth of a boundary
(*fin*) between two trevs, if it be of
land, is a fathom and a half. . . .

(7) Between two erws, two
furrows (*Ancient Laws, &c., of
Wales*, p. 373). ' The boundary
(tervyn) between two erws, two
furrows, and that is called a *balk*
(synach).' (P. 525.)

[2] *Ancient Laws : Venedotian
Code*, pp. 81 and 90. *Leges Wal-
licæ*, p. 831.

long yoke used in ploughing with four oxen abreast.[1] The erw thus ascertained closely resembled in shape the English strips, though it varied in size in different districts, and was less than the modern acre in its contents.

Next there was, according to the Welsh laws, a certain regulated rotation of ownership in the erws ' *as they were traversed by the plough*,' resulting from a well-ordered system of co-operative ploughing. In the *Venedotian* Code especially are elaborate rules as to the ' *cyvar* ' or *co-aration*, and these expose the system in its ancient form actually at work, with great vividness of detail.

The chief of these rules are given below,[2] from

---

[1] *Ancient Laws*, p. 263 (*Dimetian Code*); p. 374 (*Gwentian Code*).

[2] *Ancient Laws*, p. 153. (*Venedotian Code.*)

XXIV. *Of Co-tillage this treats.*

1. Whoever shall engage in co-tillage with another, it is right for them to give surety for performance, and mutually join hands; and, after they have done that, to keep it until the tye be completed: the tye is twelve erws.

2. The measure of the erw, has it not been before set forth?

3. The first erw belongs to the ploughman ; the second to the irons; the third to the exterior sod ox; the fourth to the exterior sward ox, lest the yoke should be broken; and the fifth to the driver: and so the erws are appropriated, from best to best, to the oxen, thence onward, unless the yoke be stopped between them, unto the last; and after that the plough erw,

which is called the plough-bote cyvar ; and that once in the year.

. . . . . .

10. Every one is to bring his requisites to the ploughing, whether ox, or irons, or other things pertaining to him ; and after everything is brought to them, the ploughman and the driver are to keep the whole safely, and use them as well as they would their own.

The driver is to yoke in the oxen carefully, so that they be not too tight, nor too loose; and drive them so as not to break their hearts: and if damage happen to them on that occasion, he is to make it good; or else swear that he used them not worse than his own.

12. The ploughman is not to pay for the oxen, unless they be bruised by him; and if he bruise either one or the whole, let him pay,

which it will be seen that in the co-tillage the team,
as in England and Scotland, was assumed to be of
eight oxen. And those who join in co-ploughing
must bring a proper contribution, whether oxen or
plough irons, handing them over during the common
ploughing to the charge of the common ploughman
and the driver, who together are bound to keep and
use everything as well as they would do their own,
till, the co-ploughing being done, the owners take their
own property away.

So the common ploughing was arranged But
how was the produce of the partnership to be divided ?
This, too, is settled by the law, representing no
doubt immemorial custom. The first erw ploughed
was to go to the ploughman, the second to the irons,
the third to the outside sod ox, the fourth to the outside sward ox, the fifth to the driver, the sixth,
seventh, eighth, ninth, tenth, and eleventh to the other
six oxen in order of worth ; and lastly, the twelfth was
the plough erw, for ploughbote, *i.e.* for the maintenance of the woodwork of the plough ; and so, it is
stated, ' the tie of 12 erws was completed.' Further,

---

or exonerate himself. The ploughman is to assist the driver in yoking
the oxen; but he is to loosen only
the two short-yoked.

13. After the co-tillage shall be
completed, every one is to take his
requisites with him home.

.   .   .   .   .

16. If there should be a dispute
about bad tillage between two co-
tillers, let the erw of the ploughman be examined as to the depth,
length, and breadth of the furrow,

and let every one's be completed
alike.

.   .   .   .   .

28. Whoever shall own the
irons is to keep them in order, that
the ploughman and driver be not
impeded ; and they are to have no
assistance.

The driver is to furnish the
bows of the yokes with wythes ;
and, if it be a long team, the small
rings, and pegs of the bows.

See also *Gwentian Code*, p. 354 ;
and the *Leges Wallice*, p. 801.

if any dispute should arise between the co-tillers as to the fairness of the ploughing, the common-sense rule was to be followed that the erw which fell to the ploughman should be examined as to the depth, length, and breadth of the furrows and every one's erw must be ploughed equally well.

Here, then, in the Welsh laws is the clearest evidence not only of the division of the common fields by turf balks two furrows wide into the long narrow strips called *erws*, or acres, and roughly corresponding in shape, though not in area, with those on English fields, but also of the very rules and methods by which their size and shape, as well as the order of their ownership, were fixed in Wales.

It is the method of division of the results of co-tillage.
And this order in the allotment of the erws turns out to be an ingenious system for equitably dividing year by year the produce of the co-operative ploughing between the contributors to it.

Now, without entering at present into the question of its connexion with the tribal system in Wales, which will require careful consideration hereafter, several interesting and useful flashes of light may be drawn from this glimpse into the methods and rules of the ancient Welsh system of co-operative ploughing.

The size of the team necessitates co-operation,
In the first place, ancient Welsh ploughing was evidently not like the classical ploughing of the sunny south, a mere scratching of the ground with a light plough, which one or two horses or oxen could draw. In the Welsh laws a team of eight oxen, as already said, is assumed to be necessary. And hence the necessity of co-operative ploughing. The plough was evidently heavy and the ploughing deep, just as was the case in

the twelfth century, and probably from still earlier to quite modern times in Scotland, where, as we have seen, the plough was of the same heavy kind, and the team of eight or of twelve oxen. And it is curious to observe that the Welsh, like the Scotch oxen in modern times, were driven four abreast, *i.e.* yoked four to a yoke. So that, as already suggested, the plough was aptly described by the monks in their mediæval Latin as a ' caruca,' and the ploughed land as a 'carucate.'

But the most interesting point about the ancient Welsh co-operative ploughing was the fact that the key to a share in the produce was the contribution of one or more oxen to the team. He who contributed one ox was entitled to one erw in the twelve. He who contributed two oxen was entitled to two erws. He who contributed a whole yoke of four oxen would receive four erws, while only the *owner* of the full team of eight oxen could possibly do without the co-operation of others in ploughing. Surely this Welsh evidence satisfactorily verifies the hypothesis already suggested by the term *bovate*, and by the allotment of two oxen as outfit to the yard-land or virgate, and by the taking of tithes in the shape of every tenth strip as it was traversed by the plough, and lastly by the order of rotation in the strips disclosed by the Winslow example.

It explains how the possession of the oxen came to be in Saxon, as probably in still earlier British or Roman times, the key to the position of the holder, and his rank in the hierarchy of the village community. And it points to the Saxon system of hides and yard-lands having possibly sprung naturally out of pre-existing British or Roman arrangements, rather than as having been a purely Saxon importation.

Hence the yard-land became a bundle of scattered strips.

It also suggests a ready explanation of how when the common tillage died out, and the strips included in a hide, yard-land, or virgate, instead of varying with each year's arrangements of the plough teams, became occupied by the villein tenant year after year in permanent possession, there would naturally be left, as a survival of the ancient system, that now meaningless and inconvenient scattering of the strips forming a holding all over the open fields which in modern times so incensed Arthur Young, and made the Enclosure Acts necessary.

There is, lastly, another point in which the Welsh laws of co-aration suggest a clue to the reason and origin of a widely spread trait of the open field system. Why were the strips in the open field system uniformly so small? The acre or *erw* was obviously a furrow-long for the convenience of the ploughing. But what fixed its breadth and its area? This, too, is explained. According to the Welsh laws it was the measure of a *day's co-ploughing*. This is clear from two passages in the laws where it is called a ' *cyvar*,' or a ' co-ploughing.'[1] And it would seem that a day's ploughing ended at midday, because in the legal description of a complete ox it is required to plough only to midday.[2] The Gallic word for the acre or strip, '*journel*,' in the Latin of the monks '*jurnalis*,' and

The strip the day's ploughing.

---

[1] *Ancient Laws, &c.,* p. 150, *Venedotian Code.* The worth of ' winter tilth of a *cyvar* two legal pence ;' and so p. 286, *Dimetian Code.*

P. 153. ' The plough erw, which is called the ploughbot cyvar.'

P. 354, *Gwentian Code.* ' The worth of one day's ploughing is two legal pence.'

[2] *Ancient Laws, &c.,* p. 134.

sometimes *diurnalis*,[1] also points to a day's ploughing ;
while the German word ' morgen ' for the same strips
in the German open fields still more clearly points to
a day's work which ended, like the Welsh ' cyvar,' at
noon.

---

[1] See Du Cange under ' *Diurnalis,*' who quotes a passage of A.D. 704.

CHAPTER V.

MANORS AND SERFDOM UNDER SAXON RULE.

I. THE SAXON 'HAMS' AND 'TUNS' WERE MANORS WITH
VILLAGE COMMUNITIES IN SERFDOM UPON THEM.

HAVING now ascertained that the open field system
was prevalent during Saxon, and probably pre-
Saxon times, we have next to inquire whether the
'hams' and 'tuns' to which the common fields belonged were manors—*i.e.* estates with a village community in serfdom upon them—or whether, on the
contrary, there once dwelt within them a free village
community holding their yard-lands by freehold or
allodial tenure.

Let us at once dismiss from the question the word
'manor.' It was the *name* generally used in the
Domesday Survey, for a *thing* described in the Survey
as already existing at the time of Edward the Confessor. The estate called a manor was certainly as
much a Saxon institution under the Confessor as it
was a *Norman* one afterwards.

The Domesday book itself does not always adhere
to this single word '*manor*' throughout its pages.

The word *manerium* gives place in the Exeter Survey to the word *villa* for the whole manor, and *mansio* for the manor-house ; and the same words, *villa* and *mansio*, are also used in the instructions[1] given at the commencement of the *Inquisitio Eliensis.* It is perfectly clear, then, that what was called a *manor* or *villa*, both in the west and in the east of England, was in fact the estate of a lord with a village community in villenage upon it.

In the Boldon Book also the word *villa* is used instead of manor.

So in Saxon documents the whole manor or estate was called by various names, generally ' ham ' or ' tun.'

In King Alfred's will[2] estates in the south-east of King England, including the villages upon them, which by Alfred's will. Norman scribes would have been called manors, are described as *hams* (the *ham* at such a place). In the old English version of the will given in the ' Liber de Hyda '[3] the word ' *twune* ' is used to translate ' ham,' and in the Latin version the word ' villa.'[4]

In the Saxon translation of the parable of the Parable of prodigal son, the country estate of the citizen—the the prodigal son. ' *burh-sittenden man* '—to which the prodigal was sent to feed swine, and where he starved upon the ' bean-cods ' that the swine did eat, was the citizen's ' *tune.*'[5]

So that the ' *hams* ' and ' *tuns* ' of Saxon times were in fact commonly private estates with villages upon them, *i.e.* manors.

This fact is fully borne out by the series of Saxon

[1] ' — *villani uniuscujusque villæ.* Deinde quomodo vocatur *mansio* ' (f. 497).

[2] *Liber de Hyda,* p. 63.
[3] *Id.* p. 68.   [4] *Id.* p. 72.
[5] Luke xv. 16.

Grants of whole manors.

Saxon words.

charters from first to last. They generally, as already said, contain grants of *whole* manors in this sense, including the villages upon them, with all the village fields, pastures, meadows, &c., embraced within the boundaries given. And these boundaries are the boundaries of the *whole village or township —i.e.* of the whole estate.

Further, a careful examination of Anglo-Saxon documents will show that the Saxon manors, not only at the time of Edward the Confessor, as shown by the Domesday Survey, but also long previously, were divided into the land of the lord's *demesne* and the land *in villenage*, though the Norman phraseology was not yet used. The lord of the manor was a *thane* or ' *hlaford.*' The demesne land was the *thane's inland*. All classes of villeins were called *geneats*. The land in villenage was the *geneat-land*, or the *gesettes-land*, or sometimes the *gafol-land*. And further, this *geneat-*, or *gesettes-*, or *gafol-land* was composed, like the later land in villenage, of hides and yard-lands, whilst the villein tenants of it, as in the Domesday Survey, were divided mainly into two classes: (1) the *geburs* (villani proper), or holders of yard-lands ; and (2) the *cottiers* with their smaller holdings. Beneath these two classes of holders of *geneat* land were the *theows* or slaves, answering to the *servi* of the Survey. Lastly, there is clear evidence that this was so as early as the date of the laws of King Ine, which claim to represent the customs of the seventh century.

To the proof of these points attention must now be directed.

II. THE RECTITUDINES SINGULARUM PERSONARUM.

In order to make these points clear, attention must be turned to a remarkable document, the Saxon version of which dates probably from the tenth, and the Latin translation from the twelfth century.[1]

It is entitled the ' *Rectitudines Singularum Person-arum,*' which may be translated ' *the services due from various persons.*'

The ' *Rectitudines,*' tenth century.

It commences with two general sections, the first relating to the services of the ' *thane,*' and the second to those of the ' *geneat.*'

ÐEGENES LAGU.	TAINI LEX.	THANE'S LAW.
Ðeᵹeneꞃ laᵹu iꞃ þ he ꞃy hiꞃ boc-ꞃihteꞃ ꝥyꞃðe. Ᵹ þ he ðꞃeo ðinc oꝼ hiꞃ lanðe ðo. ꝼꝝꞃð-ꝼæꞃelð. Ᵹ buꞃh-boꞇe Ᵹ bꞃyc-ᵹeꞃeoꞃc. Eac oꝼ maneᵹum lanðum maꞃe lanð-ꞃiht aꞃiꞃꞇ ꞇo cýniᵹeꞃ ᵹebanne. ꞃꝝilce iꞃ ðeoꞃheᵹe ꞇo cýniᵹeꞃ hame. Ᵹ ꞃcoꞃp ꞇo ꝼꞃið-ꞃciꞃe. Ᵹ ꞃæ-peanð. Ᵹ heaꝼoð-peaꞃð. Ᵹ ꝼꝝꞃð-peaꞃð. ælmeꞃ-ꝼeoh. Ᵹ cýꞃic-ꞃceaꞇ. Ᵹ mæniᵹe oðeꞃe iniꞃꞇlice ðinᵹc :	Taini lex est, ut sit dignus rectitudine testamenti sui, et ut ita faciat pro terra sua, scilicet, expeditionem, burh-botam et brig-botam. Et de multis terris majus landirectum exurgit ad bannum regis, sic-ut est deorhege ad mansionem regiam et scorpum in hosticum, et custodiam maris et capitis, et pacis, et elmesfeoh, id est pecunia elemosine et ciricsceatum, et alie res multimode.	*The thane's law is that he be worthy of his* boc-*rights, and that he do three things for his land,* fyrd-færeld, burh-bot, *and* brig-bot. *Also from many lands more land-services are due at the king's bann, as deer-hedging at the king's* ham, *and apparel for the guard, and* sea-ward *and* head-ward *and* fyrd-ward *and* almsfee *and* kirkshot, *and many other various things.*

Thane's services.

[1] See *Ancient Laws and Institutes of England,* Thorpe, p. 185. This document was the subject of a special treatise by Dr. Heinrich Leo, Halle, 1842.

K

ᵹENEᴁTES RIHT.	VILLANI RECTUM.	GENEAT'S SERVICES.
Ᵹeneat-piht iſ miſtlic be ðam ðe on lanðe ſtænt. On ſumon he ſceal lanðᵹaſol ſẏllan ⁊ ᵹæpſⷧſpẏn on ᵹeape. ⁊ piðan ⁊ aueſian ⁊ laðe læðan. pẏpcan ⁊ hlaſoþð ſeoſuman. ⁊ piðan ⁊ maþan. ðeoſheᵹe heaþan. ⁊ ſæte halðan. bẏʈhan. ⁊ buþh heᵹeᵹian niᵹe ſaþan ʈo ʈune ſeccan. cẏpic-ſceaʈ ſẏllan ⁊ ælmeſ-ſeoh. heaſoð-peaþðe healðan ⁊ hoþſ-þeaþðe. æpenðian. ſẏp ſſa nẏp. ſſa hſẏðeþ ſſa him mon ʈo-ʈæcð :.	Villani rectum est varium et multiplex, secundum quod in terra statutum est. In quibusdam terris debet dare landgablum et gærsspin, id est, porcum herbagii, et equitare vel averiare, et summagium ducere, operari, et dominum suum firmare, metere et falcare, deorhege cedere, et stabilitatem observare, edificare et circumsepire, novam faram adducere, ciricsceatum dare et almesfeoh, id est, pecuniam elemosine, heafod-wardam custodire et horswardam, in nuncium ire, longe vel prope, quocunque dicetur ei.	*The geneat's services are various as on the land is fixed. On some he shall* pay land-gafol *and* grass-swine *yearly, and ride, and carry, and lead loads; work and support his lord, and reap and mow, cut deerhedge and keep it up, build, and hedge the* burh, *make new roads for the* tun: *pay* kirkshot *and* almsfee: *keep* headward *and* horseward: *go errands far or near wherever he is directed.*

Then follow what really are sub-sections of the latter clause, and they describe the services of the various classes of *geneats*; first of the cottiers.

KOT-SETLAN RIHT.	COTSETLE RECTUM.	COTTIER'S SERVICES.
Koʈe-ſeʈlan piht. be ðam ðe on lanðe ſʈenʈ. On ſumon he ſceal ælce Ⲙon-ðæᵹe oſeþ ᵹeapeſ ſẏpſʈ hiſ laſoþðe pẏpcan. oðð .iii. ⁊ aᵹaſ ælcþe pucan on hæpſeſʈ.	Cotsetle rectum est juxta quod in terra constitutum est. Apud quosdam debet omni die Lune per anni spatium operari domino suo, et tribus diebus unaquaque septimana in Augusto. Apud quosdam operatur per totum Augustum, omni die, et	*The cottier's services are what on the land is fixed. On some he shall each Monday in the year work for his lord, and three days a week in harvest.*

KOT-ʃETLÆN RIHT.

ne ðeapf he lanð-ȝafol
ȝyllan. Þım ȝe-bý-
pıað [.v.] æcepaf co
habbanne. maþe ȝýf
hıc on lanðe ðeap ȝý.
ꝺ co lýcel hıc bıð beo
hıc a læffe. fopðan
hıf peopc fceal beon
oft-pæðe. fýlle hıf
heopð-pænıȝ on hal-
ȝan Þunpef-bæȝ. eal
fpa alcan ffıȝean
men ȝebýpeð. ꝺ pe-
pıȝe hıf hlafopðef ın-
lanð. ȝıf hım man
beoðe. æc fæ-peaþðe ꝺ
æc cýnıȝef ðeop-heȝe.
ꝺ æc fpılcan ðınȝan
fpılc hıf mæð ȝý. ꝺ
fýlle hıf cýpıc-fceac
co Mapcınuf mæf-
fan :·

COTSETLE RECTUM.

unam acram avene
metit pro diurnale
opere. Et habeat gar-
bam suam quam præ-
positus vel minister
domini dabit ei. Non
dabit landgablum.
Debet habere quinque
acras ad perhaben-
dum, plus si consue-
tudo sit ibi, et parum
nimis est si minus
sit quod deservit, quia
sepius est operi illius.
Det super heorðpe-
nig in sancto die
Jovis, sicut omnis li-
ber facere debet, et
adquietet inland do-
mini sui, si submo-
nitio fiat de sewarde,
id est de custodia
maris, vel de regis
deorhege, et ceteris
rebus que sue men-
sure sunt ; et det
suum cyricsceatum in
festo Scī Martini.

COTTIER'S SER-VICES.

*He ought not to
pay land-gafol. He
ought to have five
acres in his holding,
more if it be the
custom on the land,
and too little it is if
it be less: because
his work is often
required. He pays
hearth-penny on
Holy Thursday, as
pertains to every
freeman, and de-
fends his lord's in-
land, if he is re-
quired, from sea-
ward and from
king's deer-hedge,
and from such things
as befit his degree.
And he pays his kirk-
shot at Martinmas.*

Then the services of the *gebur* or holder of a
yard-land are described as follows:—

ȠEBUReſ ȠeRIHTe.

Ȝebup-ȝepıhca fýn
mıflıce. ȝehpaþ hý
fýn hefıȝe. ȝehpaþ eac
meðeme. on fumen
lanðe ıf þ he fceal
pýpcan co pıc-peopce
.ıı. baȝaf. fpılc peopc
fpılc hım man cæcð
o, eþ ȝeapef fýpıc.
ælcpe pucan. ꝺ on
hæpfefc .ııı. baȝaf co

GEBURI CONSUE-TUDINES.

Geburi consuetu-
dines inveniuntur
multimode, et ubi
sunt onerose et ubi
sunt leviores aut me-
die. In quibusdam
terris operatur opus
septimane, II. dies,
sic opus sicut ei dici-
tur per anni spatium,
omni septimana; et

GEBUR'S SER-VICES.

*The Gebur's ser-
vices are various, in
some places heavy,
in others moderate.
On some land he
must work at* week-
work *two days at
such work as he is
required through the
year every week,
and at harvest three*

Gebur's
services.

K 2

ᏞEBUREꟅ ᏞERIHTE.	GEBURI CONSUE-TUDINES.	GEBUR'S SER-VICES.

Week-work.

pic-peopce.] oᚱ Ꝇan-
belmæᚱᚱe oð Eaᚱcpan
.iii. ʒiᚱ he aᚱepað ne
ðeapᚱ he pýpcan ða
hᚱile ðe hiᚱ hoᚱᚱ uce
bið. þe ᚱceal ᚱýllan
on Ϻichaeleᚱ mæᚱᚱe-

Gafol.

bæiʒ .x. ʒaᚱol-p̄.] on
Ϻaᚱcinuᚱ mæᚱᚱe-bæʒ
.xxiii. ᚱýᚱcᚱa bepeᚱ.
]. ii. henᚱuʒelaᚱ. on
Eaᚱcpan an ʒeonʒ
ᚱceap. oððe .ii. p̄.]
he ᚱceal liʒan oᚱ
Ϻaᚱcinuᚱ mæᚱᚱan oð
Eaᚱcpan æc hlaᚱopbeᚱ
ᚱalbe. ᚱpa oᚱc ᚱpa him
co-beʒæð.] oᚱ ðam
ciman ðe man æpeᚱc
epeð oð Ϻaᚱcinuᚱ
mæᚱᚱan he ᚱceal
ælcpe pucan epian .i.
æcep.] pæban ᚱýlᚱ
þ ᚱæb on . hlaᚱopbeᚱ
bepne. co-eacan ðam
.iii. æcepaᚱ co bene.

Bene-work.

] .ii. co ʒæpᚱ-ýpðe.
ʒýᚱ he mapan ʒæpᚱeᚱ
beð ypᚱe ðohne eapniʒe
[epiʒe ?] ðæᚱ ᚱpa him
man ðaᚱiʒe. Þiᚱ
ʒauol-ýpðe .iii. æcepaᚱ

Gafol-yrthe.

epiʒe] ᚱape oᚱ hiᚱ
aʒanum bepne.] ᚱylle
hiᚱ heopð-pæniʒ. cpe-
ʒen] cpeʒen ᚱeban
ænne heaðop-hunð.
] ælc ʒebup ᚱýlle .vi.
hlaᚱaᚱ ðam in-ᚱpane
ðonne he hiᚱ heopbe
co mæᚱ-cene bᚱiᚱe.
On ðam ᚱýlᚱum lanbe
ðe ðeoᚱ pæben on-
ᚱcænc ʒel upe ʒebýpeð
þ him man co lanb-

---

in Augusto iii. dies
pro septimanali opera-
tione, et a festo Can-
delarum ad usque
Pascha iii. Si ave-
riat, non cogitur ope-
rari quamdiu equus
ejus foris moratur.
Dare debet in festo
Scī Michaelis x. đ. de
gablo, et Scī Martini
die xxiii., et sesta-
rium ordei, et ii. gal-
linas. Ad Pascha i.
ovem juvenem vel
ii. đ. Et jacebit a
festo Scī Martini
usque ad Pascha ad
faldam domini sui,
quotiens ei pertinebit.
Et a termino quo
primitus arabitur
usque ad festum Scī
Martini arabit una-
quaque septimana i.
acram, et ipse parabit
semen domini sui in
horreo. Ad hæc iii.
acras precum, et duas
de herbagio. Si plus
indigeat herbagio, ara-
bit proinde sicut ei
permittatur. De ara-
tura gabli sui arabit
iii. acras, et semina-
bit de horreo suo et
dabit suum heorðpe-
nig; et duo et duo
pascant unum molos-
sum. Et omnis ge-
burus det vi. panes
porcario curie quando
gregem suum minabit
in pastinagium. In
ipsa terra ubi hec

---

days for week-work,
and from Candle-
mas to Easter three.
If he do carrying
he has not to work
while his horse is
out. He shall pay
on Michaelmas Day
x. *gafol-pence, and*
on Martinmas Day
xxiii. *sesters of bar-*
ley and two hens;
at Easter a young
sheep or two pence;
and he shall lie
from Martinmas to
Easter at his lord's
fold as often as he
is told. And from
the time that they
first plough to Mar-
tinmas he shall each
week plough one
acre, and prepare
himself the seed in
his lord's barn. Also
iii. *acres* bene-work,
and ii. *to grass-*
yrth. If he needs
more grass then he
ploughs for it as
he is allowed. For
his gafol-yrthe *he*
ploughs iii. *acres,*
and sows it from
his own barn. And
he pays his hearth-
penny. *Two and*
two feed one hound,
and each gebur gives
vi. *loaves to the*
swineherd when he
drives his herd to
mast. On that land
where this custom

ᵹeBures ᵹeriHte.	GEBURI CONSUE-TUDINES.	GEBUR'S SER-VICES.	Chap. V.

<table>
<tr><td>

ꞅeꞇene ꞃ́ylle .ii. oxan
] .i. cu.] .vi ꞃceap.
] .vii. æceꞗaꞃ ʒeꞃa-
pene on hiꞃ ʒýꞗꝺe
lanꝺeꞃ. ꞃoꞗꝺiʒe oꞃeꝺ þ
ʒeaꝺ ealle ʒeꝺihꞇu ꝺe
him ꞇo-ʒebýꞗiʒean.]
ꞃylle him man ꞇol ꞇo
hiꞃ ꝺeoꝛce] anꝺla-
nian ꞇo hiꞃ huꞃe.
Ꝺonne him ꞃoꞗꝺ-ꞃiꝺ
ʒebýꞗiʒe ʒýme hiꞃ
hlaꞃoꝛꝺ ꝺæꞃ he læꞃe .

Deoꞃ lanꝺ-laʒu
ꞅꞇænꞇ on ꞃuman
lanꝺe. ʒehꝺaꞗ hiꞇ iꞃ ꞃa
ic æꝺ cꝛæꝺ heꞃiʒne ʒeh-
ꝺaꝺ eac leohꞇꝛe. ꞃoꞗ-
ꝺam ealle lanꝺ-ꞃiꝺa ne
ꞃýn ʒeliꞇe. On ꞃuman
lanꝺe ʒebuꞗ ꞃceal
ꞃýllan huniʒ-ʒaꞃol. on
ꞃuman-meꞇe-ʒaꞃol. on
ꞃuman ealu - ʒaꞃol.
Ꝺebeꞃeꝺe ꞃciꞗe healꝺe
þ he ꝏꞇe á hꝛæꞇ
ealꝺ lanꝺ-ꞃ.æꝺen ꞃy.
] hꝛæꞇ ꝺeoꝺe ꝺeaꝛ ·.

</td><td>

consuetudo stat, moris
est ut ad terram assi-
dendam dentur ei ii.
boves et l. vacca, et
vi. oves, et vii. acre
seminate, in sua vir-
gata terra. Post il-
lum annum faciat
omnes rectitudines
que ad eum attinent;
et committantur ei
tela ad opus suum et
suppollex ad domum
suam. Si mortem
obeat, rehabeat do-
minus suus omnia.
Hæc consuetudo
stat in quibusdam
locis, et alicubi est,
sicut prediximus, gra-
vior, et alicubi levior;
quia omnium terra-
rum instituta non
sunt equalia. In qui-
busdam locis gebur
dabit hunigablum, in
quibusdam metega-
blum, in quibusdam
ealagablum. Videat
qui scyram tenet, ut
semper sciat que sit
antiqua terrarum in-
stitutio, vel populi
consuetudo.

</td><td>

holds it pertains to
the gebur that he
shall have given to
him for his outfit ii.
oxen and i. *cow and*
vi. *sheep, and* vii.
acres sown on his
yard-land. *Where-*
fore after that year
he must perform all
services which per-
tain to him. And
he must have given
to him tools for his
work, and utensils
for his house. Then
when he dies his lord
takes back what he
leaves.

This land-law
holds on some lands,
but here and there,
as I have said, it is
heavier or lighter, for
all land services are
not alike. On some
land the gebur shall
pay honey-gafol, *on*
some meat-gafol, *on*
some ale-gafol. *Let*
him who is over the
district take care
that he knows what
the old land-customs
are, and what are
the customs of the
people.

</td><td>

Outfit of
two oxen
to yard-
land.

</td></tr>
</table>

Then follow the special services of the beekeeper,
oxherd, cowherd, shepherd, goatherd, &c., upon which
we need not dwell here; and the document concludes
with another declaration that the services vary according to the custom of each district.

This important document is therefore a general description of the services due from the thane to the king, and from the classes in villenage to their manorial lord. And it might be the very model from which the form of the Domesday Survey was taken. Both, in fact, first speak of the lord of the manor, and then of the villein tenants; the latter being in both cases divided into the two main classes of villani and cottiers; for, as already stated, the Saxon *thane* answered to the Norman *lord*, the Saxon *gebur* answered to the *villanus* of the Survey, and the *cotsetle* to the cottier or *bordarius* of the Survey. But these various classes require separate consideration.

III. THE THANE AND HIS SERVICES.

The ' *Rectitudines* ' begins with the thane or lord of the manor; and informs us that he owed his military and other services (for his manor) to the king—always including the three great needs—the *trinoda necessitas*; viz. (1) to accompany the king in his military expeditions, or *fyrd*; (2) to aid in the building of his castles, or *burhbote* ; (3) to maintain the bridges, or *brigbote.*

The lord's demesne land was called in the Exon Domesday for Cornwall the ' thane's inland.' So, too, in a law of King Edgar's already quoted, the tithes are ordered to be paid ' as well on the *thane's inland* as on *geneat land*,' showing that this distinction between the two was exhaustive.

So also in Scotland, where the old Saxon words were not so soon displaced by Norman terms as in

England, the lord of a manor was long called the
thane of such and such a place. In the chronicler
Wintoun's story of Macbeth, as well as in Shakespeare's
version of it, there are the ' thane of Fyfe ', and the
' thane of Cawdor.'

And the circumstance which, according to Win- Scotch
toun, gave rise to Macbeth's hatred of Macduff is burhbote.
itself a graphic illustration of the ' burhbote,' or aid
in castle-building due from the thane to his king :—

> And in Scotland than as kyng
> This Makbeth mad gret steryng
> And set hym than in hys powere
> A gret hows for to mak off were
> Upon the hycht off Dwnsynane.
> Tymbyr thare-till to draw and stane
> Off Fyfe and off Angws he
> Gert mony oxin gadryd be.
> Sa on a day in thare traivaile
> A yhok off oxyn Makbeth saw fayle,
> Than speryt Makbeth quha that awcht
> The yhoke that fayled in that drawcht.
> Thai awnsweryd till Makbeth agayne,
> And sayd, ' Makduff off Fyffe the Thane
> That ilk yhoke off oxyn awcht
> That he saw fayle in to the drawcht.'
> Than spak Makbeth dyspytusly,
> And to the Thane sayd angryly,
> Lyk all wythyn in hys skin,
> Hys awyn nek he suld put in
> The yhoke and gev hym drawchtis drawe.[1]

But the military service was by far the most im- The thane
portant of ' the three needs ' or services due from the as a soldier.
thane to the king. The thane was a *soldier* first
of all things. The very word *thane* implies this.
In translating the story of the centurion who had
soldiers under him, the Saxon Gospel makes the

---

[1] *The Cronykil of Scotland*, B. VI. c. xviii.

'Hundredes ealdor' say, '*I have thanes* under me' (ic hæbbe þegnas under me).[1] And though the text of the translation may not be earlier than the tenth century, yet, as the meaning of words does not change suddenly, it shows that the military service of the thane dated from a still earlier period.

And just as in Norman times the barons and their Norman followers (*Francigenæ eorum*) were marked off from the population in villenage as companions or associates of the king or some great earl, or as they might now be called 'county men,' so the Saxon thanes 400 years before the Norman Conquest were 'Gesithcundmen,' in respect of their obligation to 'do fyrd-færeld,' *i.e.* to accompany the king in his royal expeditions. But this association with the king did not break the bond of *service.* By the laws of King Ine[2] the *gesithcundmen* were fined and forfeited their land if they neglected their 'fyrd:'—

LI. Ᵹɪf ᵹeɲðcunb mon lanb-aᵹenbe ɸoɲɲɪᴄᴄe ɸýɲbe ᵹeɲelle .c.xx. ɲcɪll. ꞇ þolɪe hɪɲ lanbeɲ.	51. If a gesithcund man owning land neglect the *fyrd*, let him pay cxx. shillings and forfeit his land.

As a
landlord. But the 'gesithcund' thanes were landlords as well as soldiers. And King Ine found it needful to enact laws to secure that they performed their landlord's duties. They must not absent themselves from their manors without provision for the cultivation of the land. When he *færes*, *i.e.* goes on long expeditions, a gesithcundman may take with him on his journey his reeve, his smith to forge his weapons, and his child's fosterer, or nurse.[3] But if he have xx. hides of land, he must show xii. hides at least of

---

[1] Matt. viii. 9.   [2] *Ines Domas,* s. 51.   Thorpe, p. 58.
[3] *Id.* s. 63.   Thorpe, p. 62.

gesettes land on his manor ; if he have x. hides, vi.
hides of gesettes land ; and if he have iii. hides, one and
a half hides of gesettes land before he absents himself
from his manor.[1]

That ' gesettes land ' was a general and rather The
geneat,
gesettes, or
gafol land.
loose term meaning the same thing as ' geneat land '
is clear from a charter of A.D. 950, which will be referred to hereafter, wherein a manor is described as
containing xxx. hides, ix. of inland and xxi. of ' gesettes
land,' and the latter is said to contain so many yard-
lands (' gyrda gafol-landes '). This instance also helps
us to understand how *gafol land,* and *gesettes land,*
and *geneat land* were all interchangeable terms—all,
in fact, meaning ' land in villenage,' to the tenants on
which we must now turn our attention.

IV. THE GENEATS AND THEIR SERVICES.

It has been shown that the Saxon thane's estate *Geneat*
land was
land in
villenage.
or manor was divided into *thane's inland* or demesne
land, and *geneat land* or *gesettes land,* answering to the
land in villenage of the Domesday Survey. Let us
now examine into the nature of the villenage on the
geneat land under Saxon rule.

' Gesettes land ' etymologically seems to mean
simply land set or let out to tenants. In the parable
of the vineyard, the Saxon translation makes the
wingeardes hlaford[2] *gesette*' it out to husbandmen
(gesette þone myd eorð-tylion) before he takes his
journey into a far country, and the husbandmen are
to pay him as tribute a portion of the annual fruits.

---

[1] *Id.* s. 63–6. Thorpe, pp. 62–3.   [2] Matt. xxi. 33.

Need of
husband-
men.

In early times, when population was scanty, there was a lack of husbandmen.

King Alfred, in his Saxon translation of Boethius, into which he often puts observations of his own, expresses in one of the most often quoted of these interpolations what doubtless his own experience had shown him, viz., that ' a king must have his tools to ' reign with—his realm must be well peopled—full ' manned.' Unless there are priests, soldiers, and workmen—' *gebedmen, fyrdmen,* and *weorcmen* '—no king, he says, can show his craft.[1]

We are to take it, then, that population was still scanty, that a thane's manor was not always as well stocked with husbandmen as the necessities of agriculture required. The nation must be fed as well as defended, and both these economic needs were imperative. How, then, was a thane to plant new settlers on his ' gesettes-land ' ?

*Settene
stuht,* or
outfit of
geburs.

We have seen the Kelso monks furnishing their tenants with their outfit or ' *stuht* '—the two oxen needful to till the husbandland of two bovates ; also a horse, and enough of oats, barley, and wheat for seed. The ' *Rectitudines* ' shows that in the tenth century this custom had long been followed by Saxon landlords. It further shows that the new tenants so created were settled on *yard-lands*, and called *geburs*.

Two oxen
to yard-
land.

It states that in some places it is the custom that in settling the *gebur* on the land, there shall be given to him ' to *land setene* ' (*i.e.* as ' stuht ' or outfit) two oxen, one cow, six sheep, and seven acres sown on his *yard-land* or virgate. Then after the first year

---

[1] Boethius, c. xvii.

he performs the usual services. Having been supplied by his lord, not only with his stuht, but also even with tools for his work and utensils for his house, it is not surprising that on his death everything reverted to his lord.

The gebur here answers exactly to the villanus of post-Domesday times.[1] His normal holding is the *yard-land* or virgate. His *stuht*, which goes with the yard land ' to setene,' or for outfit, is two oxen, one cow, &c.; *i.e.* one ox for each of the two bovates which made up the yard-land.

That this was the usual outfit of the yard-land, and that the yard-land at the same time was the one-fourth part of the *sulung* or full plough-land, in still earlier times than the date of the ' *Rectitudines*,' receives clear confirmation from an Anglo-Saxon will dated A.D. 835, in which there is a gift of ' *an half swulung*,' and ' to ꝥem londe iiii oxan & ii cy & 1 scepa,' &c.[2] The *half-sulung* being the double of the yard-land, it is natural that the allowance for outfit in

---

[1] In the *Codex Diplomaticus,* No. MCCCLIV., there is an interesting document early in the eleventh century, the original of which is in the British Museum (*MS. Cott. Tib.* B. v. f. 76 *b*), written on the back of a much older copy of the Gospels, and containing particulars respecting the *geburs* on the Hatfield estate in Hertfordshire—their *pedigrees*, in fact—showing that they had intermarried with others of the following manors in Hertfordshire, viz. : —*Tæccingawyrde* (Datchworth), *Wealaden* (King's or Paul's Walden), *Welugun* (Welwyn), *Wad-* *tune* (Watton), *Munddene* (Mundon), *Wilmundeslea* (Wymondley), and *Eslingadene* (Essenden). The fact that it was worth while to preserve a record of the pedigree of the *geburs* shows that they were *adscripti glebæ.* And there can be no doubt of the identity of the *geburs* of this document with the *villani* of the Domesday Survey of these various places. The pedigrees of *villani* or *nativi* were carefully kept in some manors even after the *Black Death.*

[2] Cotton MS. *Augustus*, ii. 64. Fac-similes of Ancient Charters in the British Museum, Part II.

the bequest of oxen and cows should be just double the outfit assigned by custom to the yard-land. It is obvious that the allotment to the whole *sulung* would be a full team of eight oxen.

Services.　The gebur, then, having been 'set' upon his yard-land by his lord, and supplied with his *setene* or 'stuht,' had to perform his services.

What were these services?

An examination of them as stated in the ' *Recti-tudines*' will show at once their close resemblance to those of the holders of virgates in villenage in post-Domesday times.

They may be classified in the same way as these were classified.

Gafol.　Some of them are called *gafol*; *i.e.* they were *tributes* in money and in kind, and in work at plough-ing, &c., in the nature rather of rent, rates, and taxes than anything else. They were as follows :

At *Michaelmas* x. gafol-pence.

At *Martinmas* xxiii. sesters of barley and ii. hens.[1]

At *Easter* a young sheep, or ii.*d.*

Gafol-yrthe.　Of gafol-ploughing (*gafol*-yrðe) to plough three acres, and sow it from his barn.

The hearth-penny.

With another gebur to feed a hound.

Six loaves to the swineherd of the manor, when he takes the flock to pasture.

In some places the gebur gives *honey-gafol*, in some *mete-gafol*, and in some *ale-gafol*.

*Bene-*work.　Next there were the *precariæ* or *bene-work*, extra special services :

To plough three acres 'to bene' (*ad precem*), and two to 'gærsyrðe.'[2]

---

[1] This may be read 23*d.* and a sester of barley; or, perhaps, 20*d* and three sestras of barley. But the best reading seems to be that in the text.

[2] This is a word often used in

Lastly, the chief services were the regular *week* CHAP. V.
work (wic-weorce), generally limited to certain days a Week-
week according to the season. work.

'He shall work for week-work two days at such work as he is bid
'throughout the year, each week; and in August three days' week-
'work, and from Candlemas to Easter three days.'

These were the services of the *gebur* or *villanus*, Thirty
and we may gather that his yard-land embraced the yard-land;
usual thirty acres or strips, *i.e.* ten strips in each of field.
the three common fields of his village. This seems to
follow from the fact that his outfit included *seven
acres sown.*' These seven acres were no doubt on the
wheat-field which had to be sown before winter. It
was seven acres, and not ten, because the crop on
the other three counted as ' gafolyrðe ' to his lord,
and this was not due the first season. The oats or
beans on the second or spring-sown field he could
sow for himself. The third field was in fallow. The
only start he required was therefore the seven acres
of wheat which must be sown before winter.

So much for the *gebur*; now as to the *cottier*.

The cottier tenant, in respect of his five acres Cottier's
(more or less), rendered similar services on an humbler holding of
scale. His week-work was on Mondays each week and his
throughout the year, three days a week at harvest. services.
He was free from land-gafol, but paid hearth-penny
and church-scot at Martinmas. The nature of his
work was the ordinary service of the geneat as re-

---

later documents, and seems to mean | *gafol* for the share in the *Lammas*
a certain amount of ploughing done | *meadows,* and the *gafol-yrthe* for the
as an equivalent for an allowance | arable in the *yard-land.*
of grass. *Grass-yrthe* may be the |

CHAP. V.

quired by his lord from time to time; only, having no oxen, he was exempt from ploughing, as he was also after the Norman Conquest.

V. THE DOUBLE AND ANCIENT CHARACTER OF THE SERVICES OF THE GEBUR—GAFOL AND WEEK-WORK.

Returning to the services of the gebur, stress must be laid upon their double character. Like the later *villanus* he paid a double debt to his lord in respect of his yard-land and outfit, or '*setene*'—(1) *gafol*; (2) week-work.

Laws of King Ine.

This is a point of great importance at this stage of the inquiry; for it gives us the key to the meaning of an otherwise almost unintelligible passage in the laws of King Ine, which bears directly upon the matter in hand.

Gesettes land.

This passage immediately follows those already quoted, requiring one-half or more of the land of the absentee landlord to be 'gesettes land.'

It follows in natural order after this requirement, because it evidently relates to the process of increasing the number of tenants on the gesettes land, so introducing new geburs or villani, with new yard-lands or virgates, into the village community. The clause is as follows:

Yard-land. *Gafol* and *weorce.*

BE GYRDE LONDES.	OF A YARD OF LAND.
Gif mon geþingað gýrde landes oþþe mære to ræde-gafole. ⁊ geereð. gif se hlaford him wile ꝥ land aræran to weorce ⁊ to gafole. ne þearf he him onfón gif he him nan botl ne seleð. . . .	If a man agree for a yard-land or more at a fixed *gafol* and plough it, if the lord desire to raise the land to him *to work and to gafol*, he need not take it upon him, if the lord do not give him a dwelling. . . .

[1] *Laws of Ine*, s. 67. Thorpe, p. 63.

The meaning of it apparently is that if a man agree for a yard land or more to ' ræde-gafol' (*i.e.* at such gafol payments as have been described), and plough it, still the lord cannot put the new holding ' *to weorce* and *to gafole,*' that is, make the holder completely into a *gebur* or villanus, owing both gafol and week-work to his lord, unless the lord also supply the homestead (' botl ').

That the ' botl' or homestead was looked upon as the essential part of a man's holding is shown by another law of King Ine :—

LXVIII. Ᵹif mon ᵹeþiðcunðne monnan aðþiᵹe. ᵹoþðþiᵹe þȳ boᵹle. næþ þæþe þeᵹene ⸱·	68. If a gesithcund man be driven off, it must be from the *botl*, not the *setene.*

Now the importance of these passages can hardly be exaggerated ; for, if we may trust the genuineness of the laws of King Ine,[1] they show more clearly than anything else could do, that in the seventh century —400 years before the Domesday Survey—the manor was already to all intents and purposes what it was afterwards. They show that at that early date part of the land was in the lord's demesne and part let out to tenants, who when supplied by the lord with everything—their homestead and their yard-land— owed, not only customary tribute or *gafol*, but also ' *weorce*' or service to the lord ; and how otherwise could this ' weorce' be given then or afterwards

---

[1] The opening clause of Ine's laws, as republished by King Alfred with his own, states that they were recorded under the counsel and teaching of his father *Cenred,* who resigned his kingship to Ine in A.D. 688.

except in the shape of labour on the lord's demesne, as is described in the ' *Rectitudines* ' ?

It is worth while to notice that while the double debt of both gafol and week-work was due from the *gebur* or *villanus* proper, and the week-work was the most servile service, yet even the mere payment of gafol was the sign of a submission to an overlordship. It had a servile taint about it, as well it might, being paid apparently part in kind and part in work.   As the class of free hired labourers had not yet been born into existence under these early Saxon economic conditions, in times when the *theows* were the servants, so the modern class of farmers or free tenants at a rent of another's land had not yet come into being. It was the ' ceorl' who lived on ' gafol land,' [1] and to pay gafol was to do service, though of a limited kind.

Gafol a servile tribute.   The Saxon translators of the Gospels rendered the question, ' Doth your master pay tribute? ' [2] by the words ' *gylt he gafol?* '   And they used the same word *gafol* also in translating the counter question, ' Of whom do kings take *tribute,* of their own people or of aliens ? '

Bede.   So when Bede described the northern conquest of Ethelfred, king of the Northumbrians, over the Britons in A.D. 603, and spoke of the inhabitants as being either exterminated or subjugated, and their lands as either cleared for new settlers or *made tributary* to the English, King Alfred in his translation expressed

---

[1] *Alfred and Guthrum's Peace,* Thorpe, p. 66. ' We hold all equally dear, English and Danish, at viii. half marks of pure gold, except the " ceorle þe on *gafol-lande sit,* and heora *liesingum* " (*lysingon*); they also are equally dear at cc. shillings,' *i.e.* they are ' *twihinde men.*'

[2] Matt. xvii. 25.

the latter alternative by the words 'set to gafol'—*to* *gafulgyldum gesette.*[1]

No doubt the Teutonic notion of a subjugated people was that of a people reduced to serfdom or villenage. *They*—the conquerors—were the nation, the freemen. The conquered race were the aliens, subjected to *gafol* and servitude.

Thus, recurring to the Saxon translation of the parable of 'the unjust steward,' one may recognise how perfectly naturally everything seemed to the translators to transfer itself to a Saxon thane's estate, and to translate itself into Saxon terms.[2]

The '*hlaford*' of the '*tun*' or manor had his '*tun-* '*gerefan*' or reeve, just as the Saxon thane had. The land in villenage was occupied not by mere trade debtors of the lord, as our version has it, but by '*gafol-gyldan*'—tenants to whom land and goods of the lord had been entrusted, as Saxon tenants were entrusted with their 'setene,' and who, therefore, paid *gafol* or tribute in kind. The natural *gafol* of the tenant of an olive-garden would be so many ' sesters ' of oil. The tenant of corn land would pay for *gafol*, like the English tenant of a yard-land *inter alia* so

---

[1] *Beda*, i. c. 34 :—

Nemo enim in tribunis, nemo in regibus plures eorum terras, exterminatis vel subjugatis indigenis, aut tributarias genti Anglorum, aut habitabiles fecit.	Ne þær æþþe æniȝ cýninȝ ne ealdoþman þ̵ ma heoþa lanða uce amæþðe ꞇ hım co ȝeþealðe unðeþþeoðbe þoþþon ðe he hı co ȝaþulȝýlðum ȝeþecce on Ænȝel ðeoðbe. oþþe oþ heoþa lanðe aðþaþ.	Never was there ever any king nor ealdorman that more their lands exterminated, and to his power subjected, for that he them to gafol set to the English people, or else off their land drove.

[2] Luke xvi.

many ' mittena' of wheat ; and it was the duty of the
unrighteous ' tun-gerefan,' or reeve of the manor, to
collect the *gafol* from these tenants, as it was the
duty of the Saxon thane's reeve to gather the dues
from his servile tenants.

How many otherwise free tenants hired yard-lands
without becoming *geburs*, and rendering the full *week-
work* as well as *gafol*, we do not know. Except in the
Danish district they seem to have left, as we have
seen, no trace behind them on most manors in the
Domesday Survey.   The fact already mentioned, that
the yard-lands of *geburs*, who owed both gafol and
services, were sometimes called ' *gyrda gafollandes*,'
shows how completely the *gafol* and the services had
become united as coincidents of a common villein
tenure.   All villein tenants were apparently ' geneats '
and paid ' gafol,' and there is a passage in the laws of
King Edgar which states that if a *geneat-man* after
notice should persist in neglecting to pay his lord's
gafol, he must expect that his lord in his anger will
spare *neither his goods nor his life*.[1]

Complete-
ness of the
evidence
to the
seventh
century.   On the whole, leaving out of notice doubtful
and exceptional tenants, as well we may, we are now
in a position to state generally what were the main
classes of villein tenants in early Saxon times, and
what were their holdings on the land in villenage,
whether it were known as *geneat*, or *gesettes*, or *gafol*
land.

First, the ' *Rectitudines*,' of the tenth century, describes, as we have seen, these tenants as all *geneats*
or villeins, and records their services in general terms.

---

[1] *Supplement to Edgar's Laws*, i.   Thorpe, p. 115.

It then divides them into classes, just as the Domesday Survey does. And the two chief classes of the geneats are the *geburs* and the cottiers. These two classes are evidently the *villani* and the *bordarii* or cottiers of the Domesday Survey.

Secondly, the same document describes the holdings of these two classes. It speaks of the cottiers as holding mostly five acres each—sometimes more and sometimes less—in singular coincidence with the Domesday Survey and later evidence. And it describes the *gebur*, as we have seen, as holding a *yard-land* or *virgate*, the typical holding of the Domesday villanus, and as having allotted to him as ' outfit ' two oxen, just as was the case with the Kelso husbandmen.

Thirdly, the laws of King Ine bring back the evidence to the seventh century by their incidental mention of the *yard-land* as a typical holding on *gesettes-land* ; and also of *half-hides*[1] and *hides*, as well as of *geneats*[2] and *geburs*,[3] with their *gafol* and *weorce*.

When this concurrence of the evidence of the tenth and the seventh century is duly considered, it will be seen how complete is the proof that in the seventh century the West Saxon estate, though called a ' *tun* ' or a ' *ham*,' was in reality a *manor* in the Norman sense of the term—an estate with a village community in villenage upon it under a lord's jurisdiction.

---

[1] Thorpe, p. 53, where they are mentioned as sometimes held by even *Wiliscmen*,' *i.e.* tenants not of Saxon blood.

[2] Thorpe, p. 50.

[3] *Ibid.* p. 46.

VI. SERFDOM ON A MANOR OF KING EDWY.

The evidence hitherto given on the nature of the serfdom on Anglo-Saxon manors has been of a general character.

We are fortunately able to confirm and illustrate it by reference to actual local instances.

Manor of
Tidênham,

The first example is that of the manor of *Tidenham*, and it derives a more than ordinary value from its peculiar geographical position.

The parish of Tidenham comprises the wedge-shaped corner of Gloucestershire, shut in between the Wye and the Severn, where they join and widen into the Bristol Channel; while to the north-east, on its land side, it was surrounded by the Forest of Dean.

In the belief of local antiquaries, the Roman road from Gloucester to Caerleon-upon-Usk—the key to South Wales—passed through it as well as the western continuation of the old British road of Akeman Street from the landing-place of the Severn, opposite Aust (where St. Augustine is said to have met the Welsh Christians) to the further crossing-place on the Wye. Lastly, upon it was the southern end of *Offa's Dyke*, the mysterious rampart which, commencing thus at the mouth of the Wye, extended to the mouth of the Dee.[1]

Saxon
since A.D.
577,

The manor probably has been in English hands ever since about the time when, according to the Saxon Chronicle, after Deorham battle in A.D. 577, Bath, Gloucester, and Cirencester were wrested from

---

[1] For the archæology of Tidenham see *Proceedings of the Cotteswold Naturalists' Field Club*, 1874-5, and Mr. Ormerod's *Archæological* | *Memoirs* relating to the district adjacent to the confluence of the Severn and the Wye. London, 1861 (not published).

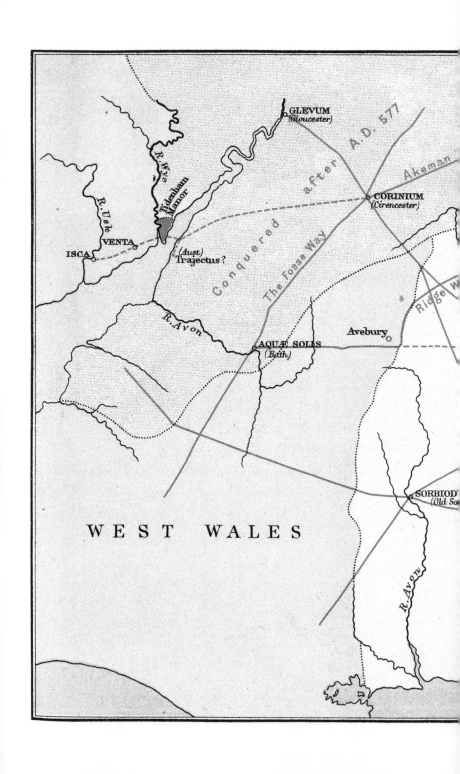

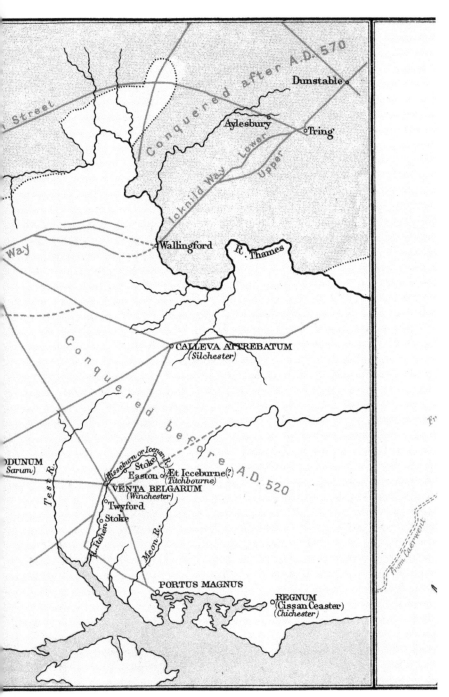

London: Longmans & Co.

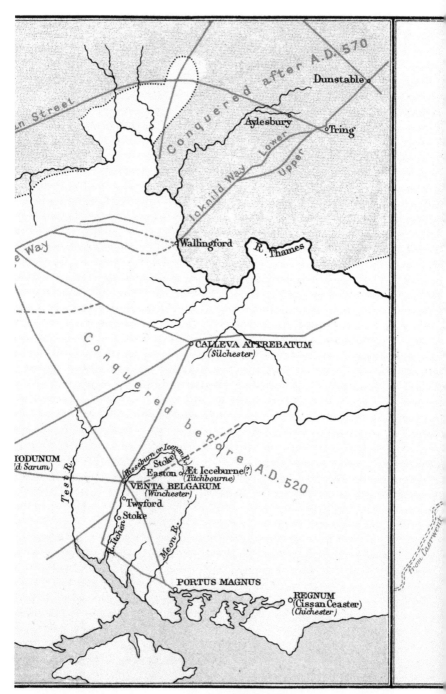

London: Longmans & C?

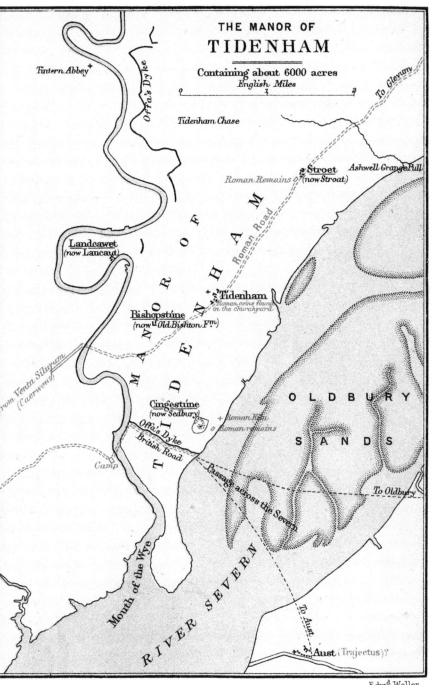

THE MANOR OF
TIDENHAM

Containing about 6000 acres
English Miles

To Glevum

Tidenham Chase

Tintern Abbey

Offa's Dyke

Stroet
(now Stroat)

Ashwell Grange Pill

Roman Remains

Roman Road

Landcawet
(now Lancaut)

MANOR OF

Tidenham
Roman coins found
in the churchyard

Bishopstúne
(now Old Bishton Fᵐ)

From Venta Silurum
(Caerwent)

TIDENHAM

OLDBURY

Cingestúne
(now Sedbury)

Roman Fan
Roman remains

SANDS

Offa's Dyke

British Road

Camp

Passage across the Severn

To Oldbury

Mouth of the Wye

To Aust

RIVER SEVERN

To Aust

Aust (Trajectus)?

Edwᵈ Weller

the Welsh by Ceawlin, king of the West Saxons. CHAP. V.
According to the Welsh legends of the *Liber Landavensis* [1] this was about the time when the diocese
of Llandaff was curtailed by the Wye instead of the
Severn becoming the boundary between the two king-
doms. It may therefore have been for nearly five
centuries before the Norman Conquest the extreme
corner of West Saxon England on the side of South
Wales.

Conquered probably by Ceawlin, or soon after
the year 577, the manor of Tidenham seems to have
remained folkland or *terra regis* of the West Saxon
kings, till Offa conquered it from them and gave his
name to the dyke upon it. One of its hamlets bore,
as we shall find, the name of *Cinges tune*, and Tidenham Chase remained a royal chase till after the
Norman Conquest. was a
royal
manor,

The manor itself was granted by King Edwy in
A.D. 956 by charter [2] to the Abbot of Bath, under
whose name it is registered in the Domesday Survey.
It is in this charter of King Edwy that the description of the manor and of the services of the tenants
is contained. The services must be regarded, therefore, as those of a royal manor before it was handed
over to ecclesiastical hands. given by
KingEdwy,
A.D. 956, to
the Abbey
of Bath.

The boundaries as appended to the charter are
given below,[3] and may still, with slight exceptions, be
traced on the Ordnance Survey. The boun-
daries still
to be
traced.

---

[1] Pp. 374–6.

[2] Kemble's *Cod. Dip.* CCCCLII.
(vol. ii. p. 327).

[3] *Codex Dip.* iii. p. 444; App.
CCCCLII. 'Ðis synd ða landge-
mæra tó Dyddenháme. Of Wæge-
mūðan to iwes héafdan; of iwes

héafden on Stánræwe; of Stánræwe on hwítan heal; of hwítan
heale on iwdene; of iwdene on
brádan mór; of brádan mór on
Twyfyrd; of Twyfyrd on astege pul
ut innan Sæfern.'

The northern limit on the Severn is described
as *Astege pul*, now, after a thousand years, known as
Ashwell Grange Pill, the *puls* of 1,000 years ago and
the present *pills* being the little streams which wear
away a sort of miniature tidal estuary in the mud-
banks as they empty themselves into the Severn and
the Wye. Numbers of pills are marked in the Ordnance map, and as many ' puls ' are mentioned in the
boundaries of Saxon charters and those inserted in
the *Liber Landavensis.*

After the boundaries, under the heading ' *Divi-*
' *siones et consuetudines in Dyddanhamme,*'[1] the document proceeds to state that ' at Dyddanhamme are

Inland and *gesettes* land.
' xxx. hides, ix. of *inland* and xxi. of *gesettes land.*'
The manor was therefore in the tenth century divided
into demesne land and land in villenage.

Next are stated separately the contents of each
hamlet on the manor, as follows :—

Yard-lands.
At *Stræt* are xii. hides—xxvii. gyrda gafollandes, and on the Severn
xxx. cytweras.

At *Middeltune* are v. hides—xiiii. gyrda gafollandes, xiiii. cytweras
on the Severn, and ii. hæcweras on the Wye.

Hæc- and *cyt*- weirs.
At the *Cinges túne* are v. hides—xiii. gyrda gafollandes, and i. hide
above the dyke, which is now also gafolland; and that outside the
hamme is still part inland and part gesett to gafol to ' scipwealan.'
At the Cinges túne on the Severn are xxi. cytweras, and on the
Wye xii.

At the *Bishop's túne* are iii. hides, and xv. cytweras on the Wye.

At *Landcawet* are iii. hides and ii. hæcweras on the Wye, and ix.
cytweras.

Thus this manor, like the Winslow manor, had
hamlets or small dependencies upon it, and these are

---

[1] *Cod. Dip.* iii. p. 450, where they are evidently misplaced.

still traceable on the map. *Street* is still *Stroat* on the old Roman street—the *Via Julia* (?)—from Gloucester to Caerleon. The *Cinges túne*, now *Sudbury*, lay on the high wedge-shaped southern promontory above the cliffs, between the Wye and Severn where they join; and it lies as it did then, part on one side and part on the other side of Offa's Dyke, as if the dyke had been cut through its open fields. Its fisheries were naturally some on the Severn and some on the Wye. The ' *Bishop's túne* ' is still traceable in *Bishton* farm. Lastly, *Llancaut*, the only hamlet on this Saxon manor 900 years ago with a Welsh name, bears its old name still. This hamlet is surrounded almost entirely by a bend of the Wye, and its situation backed by its woods (*coit=wood*) may well have protected it from destruction at the time of the Saxon conquest.

Next, it is clear that the *gesettes land* in the open fields round each ' túne ' or hamlet, except at *Llancaut* and *Bishop's tune*, was divided, as usual, into yard-lands—*gyrda gafollandes*. These yard-lands and the open fields have long since been swept away by the enclosure of the parish.

Besides the yard-lands there were belonging to each hamlet the numerous fisheries—*cytweras* and *hœcweras*—some on the Severn and some on the Wye. What were these ' *cyt* ' and ' *hœc* ' weirs?

They certainly were not the ancient dams or banks across the river which are now called ' weirs,' over which the tidal wave sweeps, thus—

' Hushing half the babbling Wye.'

It is impossible that there can have been so many of these as there were *cytweras* and *hœcweras* 900 years ago—as many as thirty together at Street, fourteen at Middletune, and twenty-one at Cingestune. The fact is that the old Saxon word *wera* meant any structure for entrapping fish or aiding their capture. And no doubt arrangements which would not be called ' weirs' now were so called then. The words *cyt* and *hæc* weras seem to point rather to wattled basket and hedge weirs than to the solid structures now called weirs.

But the best illustration of what they were may be derived from the arrangements now at work for catching salmon in the Wye and Severn.

Cytweras. The stranger who visits this locality will find here and there across the muddy shore of the Severn structures which at a distance look like breakwaters ; but on nearer inspection he will find them to be built up of rows two or three deep of long tapering baskets arranged between upright stakes at regular distances. These baskets are called *putts* or *butts* or *kypes*, and are made of long rods wattled together by smaller ones, with a wide mouth, and gradually tapering almost to a point at the smaller or butt end. These *putts* are placed in groups of six or nine between each pair of stakes, with their mouths set against the outrunning stream ; and each group of them between its two stakes is called a ' puttcher.' The word ' puttcher' can hardly be other than a rapidly pronounced *putts weir*, *i.e.* a weir made of *putts*. If the baskets had been called ' cyts ' instead of ' putts,' the group would be a *cytweir*. So, *e.g.*, the thirty *cytweras* at Street would represent a breakwater such as may be seen there now, consisting of as many puttchers. This use of what may be called basket weirs

Group of Putchers on the Severn near Tidenham.

Edw.ᵈ Weller

London. Longmans & Cᵒ.

is peculiar to the Wye and the Severn, and has been
adopted to meet the difficulty presented by the unusual volume and rapidity of the tidal current.

Then as to the *hæcweras* there is nothing unusual
in the use of barriers or fences of wattle, or, as it is
still called, *hackle*, to produce an eddy, or to entrap
the fish. Thus a statute (1 Geo. I. c. 18, s. 14)
relating to the fisheries on the Severn and the Wye
uses the following words : ' If any person shall make,
' erect, or set any bank, dam, *hedge*, stank, or net
' across the same,' &c.

These wattled hedges or hackle-weirs are sometimes used to guide the fish into the puttchers, but
generally in the same way as more permanent structures on the Wye, now called *cribs*, to make an eddy
in which the fish are caught from a boat in what is
called a *stop-net*.

This mode of fishing is also peculiar to the Wye
and Severn. The boat is fixed by two long stakes
sideways across the eddy, and a wide net, like a bag
with its open end stretched between two poles, is let
down so as to offer a wide open mouth to the stream
which carries the closed end of the bag-net under the
boat. When a salmon strikes the net the open end is
raised out of the water, and the fish is taken out
behind. This clumsy process of catching salmon is
the ancient traditional method used in the Wye and
Severn fisheries, and so tenaciously is it adhered to
that the fishermen can hardly be induced to substitute more efficient modern improvements.

So much for the *cytweras* and the *hæcweras*.

The fisheries are now almost exclusively devoted
to salmon. About the date of the Norman Conquest

the manor of Tidenham was let on lease by the Bishop of Bath to Stigand, Archbishop of Canterbury,[1] and as a portion of the rent reserved was 6 porpoises (merswin) and 30,000 herrings, it would seem at first sight that the main fisheries there were for herrings rather than salmon, but it is more probable that the lease was a mutual arrangement whereby the arch-bishop's table was provided with salmon from the west, and the monks of Bath with herrings from the east.

Turning from the fisheries to the services, they are described as follows :[2]—

General services of *geneats.*

Of Dyddanhamme gebyreð micel weorcrǽden.

Se geneát sceal wyrcan swá on lande, swá of lande, hweðer swá him man byt, and ridan and aue-rian, and láde lǽdan, dráfe drífan, and fela óðra þinga dón.

To Tidenham belong many services.

The geneat shall work as well on land as off land, whichever he is bid ; and ride, and carry and lead loads, and drive droves, and do other things.

And after thus stating, to begin with, the general services of all *geneats,* the document proceeds, like the ' *Rectitudines,*' to describe the special services of the *gebur,* or holder of a yard-land.

Services of *geburs.*

Se gebúr sceal his riht dón.

He sceal erian healfne æcer tó wíceworce, and ræcan sylf ðæt sǽd on hláfordes berne gehálne tó cyrcscette, sá hweðere of his ágenum berne.

The gebur shall do his ' *riht.*'

He shall plough a half-acre as week-work, and himself prepare the seed in the lord's barn ready for kirkshot, or else from his own barn.

Week-work.

Tó werbolde xl. mǽra oððe án foðer gyrda ; oððe viii. geocu byld. iii. ebban tyne. Æcertyninge xv. gyrda, oððe díche fiftyne ; and dície i. gyrde burhheges, ripe óðer healfne æcer, máwe healfné ; on oðran weorcan wyrce, á be weorces mǽðe.

For weir-building 40 large rods or 1 load of small rods, or build 8 yokes and wattle 3 ebbs. Of acre-fencing 15 yards, or ditch 15 ; and ditch 1 yard of burh-hedge, reap 1 acre and a half, mow half an acre. At other work, work as the work requires.

---

[1] *Cod. Dip.* DCCC., XXII.   [2] *Cod. Dip.* iii. p. 450.

These are the various details of his *week-work*.
Then follow the *gafol*-payments.

Sylle **vi.** penegas ofer éstre, healfne sester hunies tó Hláfmæssan. **vi.** systres mealtes tó Martines mæsse, an cliwen gódes nettgernes. On ðam sylfum lande stent seðe vii. swýn hæbbe ðæt he sylle iii. and swá forð á ðæt teoðe, and ðæs naðulæs mæstenrǽdene ðonne mæsten beó.	Pay 6*d.* after Easter, half a sester of honey (or mead ?) at Lammas. 6 sesters of malt at Martinmas, 1 clew of good net-yarn. On the same land, if he has 7 swine, he pays 3, and so forth at that rate, and nevertheless give mast dues if there be mast.

Gafol. (margin)

It will be observed that in their *week-work* the geburs of Tidenham, in addition to strictly agricultural services, had to provide the materials for the puttchers and hedge-weirs, as well as other requisites for the fisheries.

What the eight *geocu* to be built may have been is doubtful ; but the tyning or wattling of three ebbs was at once explained on the spot by the lessee of the fisheries, who pointed out that when hackle weirs were used, three separate wattled hedges would always be needed, as, owing to the very various heights of the tide, the hedge must be differently placed for the spring tides, the middle tides, and the neap tides respectively.

The ' *week-work* ' was shown by the ' *Rectitudines* ' to be the chief service of the gebur, and this *work*, added to the *gafol*, made the holder of the yard-land into a *gebur*, according to the laws of Ine.

Two things are very striking about the week-work on the manor of Tidenham. (1) There is no limit to three days a week more or less, as in the ' *Rectitudines.*' (2) There is a clear adaptation of the week-

No limitation of week-work to three days. (margin)

work to local circumstances. In particular the fisheries have a prominent regard in its arrangement. As described in the ' *Rectitudines*,' the work varied according to the customs of each place.

So much for the ' week-work.'

No bene-work. Next, there were at Tidenham no ' *precariæ*,' or ' *bene*' works, which formed so prominent a feature in the later services. When the week-work was not limited to some days only, clearly there was no need or room for these additional services.

Lastly, as to the *gafol*—this formed a prominent feature of the *weork-ræden* of the Tidenham yard-land.

Gafol chiefly in produce : honey, &c. It consisted mainly of the produce of the land, like the gafol of the *gafolgylders* in the Saxon translation of the parable of ' the unjust steward.' Honey and malt, or ale, and yarn and pork—these, as we shall see by-and-by, were the chief products of this and the adjoining districts of Wales.

These, then, were the services of the geburs of Tidenham in respect of their yard-lands in A.D. 950, while the manor was still in royal hands just before it was handed over to the Abbot of Bath.

Comparison of services in the thirteenth century. Now let us compare these services with the services on the same manor 350 years afterwards, in the time of Edward I. An *Inquisitio post mortem* of the 35th year of Edward I. enables us to make this comparison.[1]

The following is an abstract of the services of a tenant who held a messuage and xviii. acres of land in villenage (probably a half-virgate).

---

[1] Record Office, *Chancery Inquisitions post mortem*, Anno 35 Edw. I. No. 46 *b*. Gloucestria, § *Manerium de Tudenham*.

His *week-work* was—

5 days in every other week for xxxv. weeks in the year from Michaelmas to Midsummer, except the festival weeks of Christmas, Easter, and Pentecost ; 87½ works.

2½ days every week for 6 weeks from Midsummer to Gules of August ; 15 works.

3 days every week for 8 weeks from Gules of August to Michaelmas ; 24 works.

And of this week-work between Michaelmas and Christmas, 1 day's work every other week was to be ploughing and harrowing a half-acre. Each ploughing was accounted for a day's work.

Then as to his *precariæ*,—

He made 1 *precaria* called 'cherched,' and he ploughed and harrowed a half-acre for corn, and sowed it with 1 bushel of corn from his own seed ; and in the time of harvest he had to reap and bind and stack the produce, receiving one sheaf for himself on account of the half-acre, ' as much as can be bound with a binding of the same corn, cut near the land.'

And he had to plough 1 acre for oats, and this was accounted for 2 days' manual work.

And he made another *precaria*, ploughing a half-acre with his own plough for winter sowing with as many oxen as he possessed, so that there should be a team of 8 oxen. But if he had no oxen he did not plough.

And he made [several other *precariæ* of various kinds].

Lastly came his *gafol*, &c.

He gave i. hen, which was called ' wodehen,' at Christmas.

And 5 eggs at Easter.

And 1*d.* for every yearling pig, and ½*d.* for those only of half-year, by way of pannage.

He paid . . . for every horse or mare sold.

And viii. gallons of beer at every brewing.

And he could not marry his daughter without licence.

Now, comparing the services on the manor of Tidenham at these dates 300 years apart, at which period was the service most complete serfdom ? at the later date, when the week-work of the villeins was limited to two and a half or three days a week, and in addition he made *precariæ* or extra works ; or at the earlier date, *when his week-work was unlimited* as to the days, and therefore there was no room for the extra work?

Surely the unlimited week-work marked the most complete serfdom. Surely the later services, limited in their amount and commutable into money payments, were clearly a mitigated service fast growing into a fixed money rent. In fact, the *gebur* or *villanus* was fast growing into a mere customary tenant in the time of Edward I. Indeed, he is not called in the 'Inquisition' a '*villanus*,' but a '*custumarius*,' and such he was. He was halfway on the road to freedom. Another sign of the times was this, that at the later date, side by side with the customary tenants on the land in villenage, a whole host of *libere tenentes* had already grown up upon the lord's demesne, not, as we have more than once observed, necessarily *liberi homines* at all, but some of them villein tenants or *custumarii* holding additional pieces of free land of the lord's demesne. Of these free tenants there were none at the earlier period. So that the *gebur*, with his *weork-ræden* 100 years and more before the Norman Conquest, was much more clearly a serf, and rendered far more complete and servile services than his successor in the thirteenth century, with the Black Death and Wat Tyler's rebellion in the near future before him.

Finally, let us look backward and ask how long this more complete serfdom had lasted on the manor of Tidenham.

If in the laws of King Ine are found, as we have seen, the '*gesettes land*' and '*gyrd lands*,' and the '*gafol*,' and the '*weork*,' and the '*geneat*,' and the '*gebur*,' and the obligation not to leave the lord's land ; and if all these were incidents of what in the *'Rectitudines'* and in the charter of King Edwy just examined was in fact serfdom—if the laws of Ine are good evidence that this serfdom existed in full force in the seventh century *anywhere*—they must surely be good evidence that it existed on the manor of Tidenham. For it was, as we have seen, a royal manor of King Edwy, and most probably he had received it through a succession of royal holders from King Ine. There is no evidence of its having ceased to be folcland, and so to be in the royal demesne of the kings of Wessex or of Mercia, from Ine's time to Edwy's. And if it was a royal manor of King Ine's, surely the laws of King Ine may be taken to interpret the serfdom on his own estate. Lastly, looking further back still, as King Ine probably held the manor in direct succession from Ceawlin, or whoever conquered it from the Welsh, and cut it from the diocese of Llandaff in A.D. 577 or thereabouts, the inference is very strong indeed that the *weork-ræden* had remained much the same ever since, 100 years before the date of King Ine's laws, it first fell under Saxon rule.

The lesson to be learned from a careful tracing back of the customs of such a manor as Tidenham, and we might add also the methods of fishing, and the construction of the '*cyt*' and '*hæcweras*,' surely is, that in those early times changes in custom and habit were slow, and not easily made. It would be as unlikely that between the days of King Ceawlin and those of King Ine great changes should have been made in the internal economic structure of a Saxon manor, as that in the same period bees should have changed the shape of their hexagonal cells.

Changes in local customs very slow.

VII. SERFDOM ON A MANOR OF KING ALFRED.

Manor of Hysseburne, which had belonged to Egbert, Ethelwulf, and Alfred.

The second example of a Saxon manor is that of 'Stoke-by-Hysseburne' on the river Itchin in Hampshire.[1] It had belonged in succession to King Egbert, King Ethelwulf, and King Alfred, and was by his son Edward given over to the monks of the 'old minster' at Winchester under the following curious circumstances.

King Alfred, towards the close of his reign, in his anxiety for the better education of the children of his nobles, called to his aid the monk Grimbald, from the monastery of St. Bertin, near St. Omer in Picardy, in which he himself had spent some time in his childhood on his way to Rome. It was the plan of Grimbald and King Alfred to build a new monastery (the 'new minster') at Winchester where Grimbald should carry out the royal object. But King Alfred died before this wish was fully accomplished. He had bought the land for the chapel and dormitory in

---

[1] Mr. Kemble identifies this place with Stoke near Hurstbourne Priors, near Whitechurch; but it seems rather to be one of the Stokes on the Itchin River near Winchester.

That the upper part of the Itchin was called 'Hysseburne' and 'Ticceburne,' see *Cod. Dip.* MLXXVII., CCCXLII., MXXXIX. & CLVIII. The boundaries in MLXXVII. of 'Hysseburna' (beginning at Twyford) correspond at a few points with those of 'Hisseburne' in Abingdon, i. p. 318, and of Eastune appended thereto, and of Eastune

in *Cod. Dip.* MCCXXX. The position of Twyford and Easton fixes the locality on the Itchin. The parishes of Itchin Stoke and Titchbourne ('æt Hisseburne') still nearly adjoin those of Twyford and Easton, but the parishes here are intermixed, and the 'Hysseburne' of the charters may have been a district with different boundaries. Compare Domesday Survey, i. 40, where *Twyford, Eastune,* and *Stoches* occur together among the '*Terra Wintonensis Episcopi.*' See the map in the last section.

the city, but the building and endowment of the monastery was left for his son King Edward to complete. Grimbald, then eighty-two years old, was the first abbot, but within a year died and was canonised. The body of King Alfred lay enshrined in Winchester Cathedral, in the ' old minster ' of the bishop ; but the canons of the old foundation having, according to the Abbey Chronicle, conceived ' delirious fancies' that the royal ghost, roaming by night about their cloisters, could not rest in peace, the remains of Alfred and his queen were removed to the ' new minster.'[1]

Now, King Ethelwolf, when dying, having left to King Alfred his son certain lands at ' *Cyseldene*' and elsewhere, with instructions when he died to give them over to the refectory of the old minster, King Alfred in his will gave his land at that place to the proper official at Winchester accordingly. In other words, the body of King Alfred lay in the ' new minster,' and this land given for the good of his soul belonged to the ' old minster.' So it came to pass— whether this time the ' delirious fancies' of the super- stitious canons had anything to do with it or not cannot be told—that this property at Cyseldene, like the royal donor's body, could not rest in the hands of the ' old minster,' but must be transferred to the ' new minster.' So King Edward in the year 900 made an arrangement with the monks, whereby the lands at Cyseldene were transferred to the ' new minster,' and by charter he gave instead of them to the ' old minster ' ten holdings (*manentes*) at *Stoke-*

Granted to the ' old minster' at Winchester.

---

[1] See *Liber de Hyda,* Mr. Edwards' Introduction.

M

CHAP. V.

be-*Hisseburne*, with all the men who were thereon, and those at ' *Hisseburne*,' when King Alfred died.

It is in the charter [1] effecting this object that the services are described. ' Here are written the *gerihte* ' that the ceorls shall do at Hysseburne.' From every ' *hiwisce* ' such and such services. The *hiwisce* or *family holding* seems from the services to have been a yard-land of 30 acres. The services were as follows :—

The ' *hiwisce*,' or family holding, equal here to yard-land.

Services.

Gafol and gafol-*yrthe*.

Hér synd gewriten ða gerihta ðæ ða ceorlas sculan dón tó Hysse-burnan. Ærest æt hilcan hiwisce feor-werti penega tó herfestes emnihte : and vi. ciricmittan ealað ; and iii. sesðlar hláfhwétes : and iii. æceras ge-erian on heora ægenre hwíle, and mid heora ágenan sæda gesá-wan, and on hyra ágenre [h]wíle on bærene gebringan : and þréo pund gauolbæres and healfne æcer gauol-mæde on hiora ágienre hwíle, and ðæt on hreace gebringan : and iiii. fóðera áclofenas gauolwyda tó scidhræce on hiora ágenre hwíle : and xvi. gyrda gauoltininga eác on hiora ágenre hwíle : and tó Eástran twó ewe mid twam lam-ban, and we [talað] twó geong sceap tó eald sceapan : and hí scu-lan waxan sceap and scíran on hiora ágenre hwíle.	Here are written the services that the ceorls shall do at Hysse-burne. From each *hiwisc* (family) 40*d.* at harvest equinox, and 6 church-mittans of ale, and 3 sesters of bread-wheat : and plough 3 acres in their own time, and sow it with their own seed, and in their own time bring it to the barn : and 3 pounds of gafol-barley, and a half-acre of gafol-mowing in their own time, and to bring it to the rick : and split 4 fothers (loads) of gafol-wood and stack it in their own time, and 16 yards of gafol-fencing in their own time ; and at Easter two ewes with two lambs, and two young sheep may be taken for one old one : and they shall wash sheep and shear them in their own time.

Here we have clearly, as in the ' *Rectitudines*,' the *gafol*, including the three acres of *gafol-yrth* or plough-ing, as well as other gafol-work and payments in

---

[1] *Codex Dip.* MLXXVII. ; and Dugdale, Winchester Monastery, Num. X. This charter is preserved in a copy of the twelfth century in the Winchester Cartulary (St. Swithin's) now in the British Museum. Add. MSS. 15350, f. 69*b.*

kind. And if the services had stopped here, we might
have concluded that the ' ceorls ' of Hysseburne were
gafolgelders, and not serfs. But there is another
clause which forbids such a conclusion—which shows
that, in the words of the laws of King Ine, they were
' set to *work* as well as to *gafol*.' It is this :—

And ǽlce wucan wircen ðæt hí man háte bútan þrim, án tó middan-wintra, oðeru tó Eástran, þridde to Gangdagan.	And every week do what work they are bid, except three weeks— one at midwinter, the second at Easter, and the third at ' Gang days.'

Week-work.

Comparing these services with the other examples,
they do not seem to be any more the services of freemen, or any less those of serfs. They seem to plainly
bear the ordinary characteristics of what is meant by
serfdom wherever it is found. There is the *gafol* and
there is the *week-work* ; and the latter is not limited *Unlimited.*
to certain days each week, as in the ' *Rectitudines*,' but
' *each week, except three in the year, they are* TO WORK
AS THEY ARE BID.'

And these are the services—this is the serfdom—
on a manor which was part of the royal domain of
King Alfred, which for three successive reigns at least,
and probably for generations earlier, had been royal
domain, and now by the last royal holder is handed
over, with the men that were upon it, to the perpetual,
never-dying lordship of a monastery, as an eternal
inheritance.

Finally, the evidence of these Saxon documents— *The chain*
the ' *Rectitudines* ' and the charters of Tidenham and *of evidence*
Hysseburne—read in the light of the later evidence *complete.*
and of the earlier laws of King Ine, is so clear that it
seems needful to explain how it has happened that

CHAP. V.
there has ever been any doubt as to the servile nature
of the services of the holders of yard-lands in Saxon
times.   The explanation is simple.   Mr. Kemble
quotes from all these documents in his chapter on
'*Lænland*;'[1] but for want of the clear knowledge what
a yard-land was, it never seems to have occurred to
him that in these services of the *geburs* or holders of
yard-lands we have the services of the later *villani* of
the Domesday Survey—the services of the holdings
embracing by far the greater part of the arable land
of England.   Dr. Leo, in his work on the '*Rectitudines*,' confesses that he does not know what is meant
by the yard-land of the gebur.[2]   It is only when, proceeding from the known to the unknown, we get a
firm grasp of the fact that the yard-land was the
normal holding of the *gebur* or *villanus*, that it was a
bundle of normally thirty scattered acres in the open
fields, that it was held in villenage, and that these
were the services under which it was held of the
manorial lord of the *ham* or *tun* to which it belonged—it is only when these facts are known and
their importance realised, that these documents become intelligible, and take their proper place as links
in what really is an unbroken chain of evidence.

VIII. THE THEOWS OR SLAVES ON THE LORD'S DEMESNE.

The *theows*,
or slave
class.
One word must be said of the *theows* or slaves on
the lord's demesne—the thane's *inland*—lest we should

---

[1] *Saxons in England*, pp. 319
et seq.
[2] H. Leo, *Rectitudines*.   Halle,
1842, p. 231.   'Wenigstens weisz
ich "on his gyrde landes" (auf seiner
rute des gutes, oder des landes) an
dieser stelle nicht anders zu er-
klären.'

forget the existence of this lowest class of all, in contrast with whose slavery the *geburs* and cottiers on the *geneat* land, notwithstanding their serfdom, were '*free.*' These latter were prædial serfs 'adscripti glebæ,' but not slaves. The *theows* were slaves, bought and sold in the market, and exported from English ports across the seas as part of the commercial produce of the island. Some of the *theows* were slaves by birth. But it seems to have been a not uncommon thing for freemen to sell themselves into slavery under the pressure of want.[1]

The 'servi' of the Domesday Survey were no doubt the successors of the Saxon *theows*. And as in the Survey the *servi* are mostly found on the demesne land of the lord, so probably in Saxon times the *theows* were chiefly the slaves of the manor-house. Most of the farm work on the thane's *inland*, especially the ploughing, was done no doubt by the services of the villein tenants ; but as, in addition to the villein ploughs, there were the great manorial plough teams, so also there were *theows* doing slave labour of various kinds on the home farm of the lord, and maintained at the lord's expense.

The servi of the Domesday Survey.

In the bilingual dialogue of Ælfric,[2] written in Saxon and Latin late in the tenth century as an educational lesson, in the reply of the '*yrthling*' or ploughman to the question put as to the nature of his daily work, a touching picture is given of the work of a theow conscious of his thraldom :—

---

[1] See Kemble's *Saxons in England,* i. p. 196.

[2] *British Museum* Cotton MS.

Tib. A. III. f. 58 *b*. For the text of this passage I am indebted to Mr. Thompson of the British Museum.

Hwæt sægest þu yrþlinge ?
Hu begæst þu weorc þin ?
Eala leof hlaford þearle ic
deorfe ic ga ut on dægræd þywende oxon to felda and iugie hig
to syl. Nys hyt swa stearc winter
þæt ic durre lutian æt ham for
ege hlafordes mines ac geiukodan
oxan and gefæstnodon sceare and
cultre mit þære syl ælce dæg ic
sceal erian fulne æþer (æcer) oþþe
mare.

Hæfst þu ænigne geferan ?

Ic hæbbe sumne cnapan þywende
oxan mid gad isene þe eacswilce nu
has ys for cylde and hreame.

Hwæt mare dest þu on dæg ?

Gewyslice þænne mare ic do.
Ic sceal fyllan binnan oxan mid
hig and wæterian hig and sceasn
(scearn) heora beran ut. hig hig
micel gedeorf ys hyt geleof micel
gedeorf hit ys forþam ic neom
freoh.

What sayest thou, plowman ?
How dost thou do thy work ?
Oh, my lord, hard do I work.
I go out at daybreak driving the
oxen to field, and I yoke them to
the plough. Nor is it ever so hard
winter that I dare loiter at home,
for fear of my lord, but the oxen
yoked, and the ploughshare and
coulter fastened to the plough,
every day must I plough a full
acre, or more.

Hast thou any comrade ?

I have a boy driving the oxen
with an iron goad, who also is
hoarse with cold and shouting.

What more dost thou in the
day ?

Verily then I do more. I must
fill the bin of the oxen with hay,
and water them, and carry out the
dung. Ha! ha! hard work it is,
hard work it is! because *I am not
free.*

Perhaps some day his lord will provide him with
an outfit of oxen, give him a yard-land, and make
him into a *gebur* instead of a *theow*. This at least
seems to be his yearning.

IX. THE CREATION OF NEW MANORS.

We have hitherto spoken only of the manors.
Are we therefore to conclude that there was no land
extra-manorial?

Folkland,
or *terra
regis*, in-
cluded
royal *hams*
or manors.

It may be asked whether ' folkland ' was not extra-
manorial.

Now in one sense all that belonged to the ancient
demesne of the Crown was folkland and extra-manorial. All estates with the villages and towns upon
them, which had no manorial lord but the king,

were in the demesne of the Crown, as also were the
royal forests.

Formerly, while there were many petty kings in
England, and before the kingship had attained its
unity and its full growth, *i.e.* before it had, as we are
told by historians, absorbed in itself exclusively the
sole representation of the nation, the term *folkland*
was apparently applied to all that was afterwards
included in the royal demesne. All that had not
become the *boc-land* or private property either of
members of the royal house or of a monastery or of a
private person was still folkland. And it has been
supposed that the kings had originally no power to
alienate this folkland without the consent of the
great men of their witan.

But inasmuch as the royal demesne or folkland
included an endless number of manors as well as
forest, it cannot properly be said that it was necessarily extra-manorial. More correctly it was in the
manor of the king. The king was its manorial lord,
and the *geburs* and cottiers upon it were *geneats* or
villani of the king. The Tidenham and Hysseburne
manors were both of them manors of the royal demesne until they were granted by charter to their
new monastic owners.

Now, it is clear that in the course of time, after
that in a similar way grant after grant had been
made of ' ham ' after ' ham,' with its little territory—
its *ager*, or *agellus*, or *agellulus*, as the ecclesiastical
writers were wont to describe it in the charters—to
the king's thanes or to monasteries, as *boc-land* or
private estate, the number of ' hams ' still remaining
folkland would grow less and less.

These were
granted as
lænland to
thanes in
reward for
services.

In the meantime the royal forests were managed
by royal foresters under separate laws and regulations
of great severity, whilst the royal *hams* or manors
were put under the management of a resident steward,
præpositus or *villicus*—in Saxon ' *tun-gerefan*,'—or
were let out for life as *lænland* to neighbouring great
men or their sons, or to thanes in the royal service.

This granting of life-leases of folkland or *hams*
on the royal demesne seems to have been a usual mode
of rewarding special military services, and Bede
bitterly complained that the profuse and illegitimate
grants which were wheedled out of the king for pre-
tended monastic purposes had already in his time
seriously weakened the king's power of using the
royal estates legitimately as a means of keeping up
his army and maintaining the national defences.[1] To
be able to provide some adequate maintenance for
the thanes, on whose services he relied, was a king's
necessity; for well might King Alfred enforce the
truth of the philosophy of his favourite Boethius by
exclaiming that every one may know how ' full miser-
able and full unmighty' kings must be who cannot
count upon the support of their thanes.[2]

Tendency
for them to
pass into
private
hands.

But from the nature of the case it was inevitable
that the area of folkland or royal demesne must constantly be lessened as each succeeding grant increased
the area of the *boc-land*. In other words, to use the
later phrase, the tendency was not only for new

---

[1] Bede's letter to Bishop Egbert.
Smith, p. 309. ' Quod enim turpe est
dicere, tot sub nomine monasterio-
rum loca hi qui-monachicæ vitæ
prorsus sunt expertes in suam ditionem acceperunt, sicut ipsi melius
nostis, *ut omnino desit locus, ubi filii
nobilium aut emeritorum militum
possessionem accipere possint*,' &c.

[2] King Alfred's Boethius, c.
xxix. s. 10.

manors to be created out of the royal forests and wastes, but also for more and more of the royal manors to pass from the royal demesne into private hands.

Now there is a remarkable passage in one of King Alfred's treatises[1] which incidentally throws some light upon this process, and explains the way in which new manors may have been created. He describes how the forest or a great wood provided every

---

[1] Alfred's *Blossom Gatherings out of St. Augustine.* British Museum, Vit. A. xv. f. 1:—Gaderode me þonne kiȝclas ꝺ stupan sceaftas ꝺ lohsceaftas ꝺ hylfa to ælcum þara tola þe ic mid pircan cuðe ꝺ bohtimbru ꝺ bolt timbru ꝺ to ælcum þara peorca þe ic pyrcan cuðe þa pliteȝostan treopo be þam dele ðe ic aberan meihte. ne com ic naþer mid anre byrðene ham þe me ne lyste ealne þane pude ham brenȝan ȝif ic hyne ealne aberan meihte. on ælcum treopo ic ȝeseah hpæt hpuȝu þæs þe ic æt ham beþorfte. For þam ic lære ælcne ðara þe maȝa si ꝺ ma[nigne] pæn hæbbe þ he meniȝe to þam ilcan puda þar ic ðas stuðan sceaftas cearf. Fetiȝe hym þar ma ꝺ ȝefeðriȝe hys pænas mid feȝrum gerdum þat he maȝe pindan maniȝne smicerne pan ꝺ maniȝ ænlic hus settan ꝺ feȝerne tun timbrian ꝺ þara ꝺ þær murȝe ꝺ softe mid mæȝe oneardian æȝðer ȝe pintras ȝe sumeras spa spa ic nu ne ȝyt ne dyde. Ac se þe me lærde þam se pudu licode se mæȝ ȝedon þ ic softor eardian æȝðer ȝe on þisum lænan stoclife be þis pæȝe ða phile þe ic on þisse peorulde beo ȝe eac on þam hecan hame ðe he us ȝehaten hefð þurh scanctus augustinus ꝺ sēs ȝreȝorius ꝺ scanctus Ieronimus ꝺ þurh maneȝe oððre halie fædras spa ic ȝelyfe. eac þ he ȝedo for heora ealra earnum ȝe æȝðer ȝe þisne peiȝ ȝelimpfulran ȝedo þonne he ær þissum pes ȝe hure mines modes eaȝan to þam onȝelihte þ ic maȝe rihtne peiȝ aredian to þam ecan hame ꝺ to þam ecan are ꝺ to þare ecan reste þe us ȝehaten is þurh þa halȝan fæderas sie spa. Nis hit nan pundor þeah m[an] sp[ylce] on timber ȝepirce ꝺ eac on þæ[re] lade ꝺ eac on þære bytlinȝe. ac ælcne man lyst siððan he æniȝ cotlyf on his hlafordes læne myd his fultume ȝetimbred hæfð þ he hine mote hpilum þar onȝerestan. ꝺ huntiȝan. ꝺ fulian. ꝺ fiscian. ꝺ his on ȝehpilce pisan to þære lænan tilian æȝþær ȝe on se ȝe on lande oð oð þone fyrst þe he bocland ꝺ æce yrfe þurh his hlafordes miltse ȝeearniȝe. spa ȝedo se pile ȝa ȝidfola seðe eȝðer pilt ȝe þissa lænena stoclife ȝe þara ecena hama. Seðe æȝþer ȝescop ꝺ æȝðeres pilt forȝife me þ me to æȝðrum onhaȝiȝe ȝe her nytpyrde to beonne ȝe huru þider to cumane.—For the text of this passage I am indebted to Mr. Thompson.

requisite of building, shafts and handles for tools, bay timbers and bolt timbers for house-building, fair rods (*gerda*) with which many a house (*hus*) may be constructed, and many a fair *tun* timbered, wherein men may dwell permanently in peace and quiet, summer and winter, which, writes the king with a sigh, ' is more than I have yet done ! ' There was, he said, an eternal ' *ham* ' above, but He that had promised it through the holy fathers might in the meantime make him, so long as he was in this world, to dwell softly in a log-hut on *lænland* (' *lænan stoclif* ' [1]), waiting patiently for his eternal inheritance. So we wonder not, he continued, that men should work in timber-felling and in carrying and in building,[2] for a man hopes that if he has built a cottage on lænland of his lord, with his lord's help, he may be allowed to lie there awhile, and hunt and fowl and fish, and occupy the *læn* as he likes on sea and land, until through his lord's grace he may perhaps some day obtain *boc-land* and permanent inheritance. Then finally he completes his parable by reverting once more to the contrast between ' thissa lænena stoclife ' and ' *thara ecena hama* '—between the log hut on lænland and the permanent freehold ' *ham* ' on the *boc-land*, or hereditary manorial estate.

It is true that in this passage King Alfred does not suggest distinctly that the lord would make the actual holding of lænland into boc-land, thus converting a clearing in his forest into a new manor for his thane; but, on the other hand, there was a good reason

---

[1] ' *Stoc-lif*,' literally *stake-hut*. The logs were put upright, as in the case of the Saxon church at *Green*- stead in Essex.

[2] ' Bytlinge ; ' hence the house was a ' *botl*.'

for this omission, seeing that such a suggestion would
have just overreached the point of his parable.

Be this as it may, the vivid little glimpse we get
into the *modus operandi* of the possible growth of a
Saxon manorial estate, out of folkland granted first as
lænland, and then as *boc-land*, or out of the woods
or waste of an ealdorman's domain, may well be
made use of to illustrate the matter in hand.

The typical importance in so many ways of the
gyrd, or *rod*, or *virga* in the origin and growth of the
Saxon ' tun ' or ' ham ' is worth at least a moment's
notice.

The *rod,
gyrd,* or
virga in
the growth
of a new
ham.

The typical site for a new settlement was a clearing in a wood or forest, because of the ' fair rods '
which there abound. The clearing was measured
out by rods. An allusion to this occurs in Notker's
paraphrase of Psa. lxxviii. 55—' He cast out the
' heathen before them, and divided them an inherit-
' ance by line.' The Vulgate which Notker had
before him was ' Et sorte divisit eis terram in funi-
' culo distributionis ;' and he translated the last clause
thus—' teilta er daz lant mit mazseile,'—to which he
added, ' *also man nu tuot mit* RUOTO,' as they now do
it with *rods, i.e.* at St. Gall in the tenth or eleventh
century.[1]

So in England the typical holding in the cleared
land of the open fields was called a *yard*-land, or
in earlier Saxon a *gyrd* landes, or in Latin a *virgata*
terra ; *yard, gyrd,* and *virga* all meaning *rod,* and all
meaning also in a secondary sense a yard measure.
The holdings in the open fields were of *yarded* or

---

[1] *Schilteri Thesaur. Antiq. Teut.* i. p. 158. Ulm, 1728.

rooded land—land measured out with a rod into acres four rods wide, each *rod* in width being there-fore a *rood*, as we have seen.

Again, the whole homestead was called a *tun* or a *worth*, because it was *tyn*ed or *gird*ed with a wattled fence of *gyrds* or rods. And so, too, in the Gothic of Ulfilas the homestead was a ' *gard*.' So that in the evident connexion of these words we seem to get confirmation of the hint given by King Alfred of the process of the growth of new manors.

It begins with a clearing in the forest.

The young thane, with his lord's permission, makes a clearing in a forest, building his log hut and then other log huts for his servants. At first it is forest game on which he lives. By-and-by the cluster of huts becomes a little hamlet of homesteads. He provides his servants with their outfits of oxen, and they become his *geburs*. The cleared land is measured out by rods into acres. The acres ploughed by the common plough are allotted in rotation to the yard-lands. A new hamlet has grown up in the royal forest, or in the outlying woods of an old *ham* or manor. In the meantime the king perhaps rewards his industrious thane, who has made the clearing in his forest, with a grant of the estate with the village upon it, as his boc-land for ever, and it becomes a manor, or the lord of the old manor of which it is a hamlet grants to him the inheritance, and the hamlet becomes a subject manor held of the higher lord

So we seem now to see clearly how new *tuns* and *hams* or manors were always growing up century after century, on the royal demesne and on private estates or manors, as in a former chapter it became

clear incidentally how new geburs with fresh yard-
lands could be added to the village community, and
the strips which made up the yard-lands intermixed
with those of their neighbours in the village fields.

X. THE LAWS OF KING ETHELBERT—THERE WERE MANORS IN THE SIXTH CENTURY.

We have seen that not only the general descrip- *Tuns* and
tion of serfdom contained in the ' *Rectitudines*,' but *hams* in the
time of
also the two examples we have been able to examine Ethelbert,
of serfdom upon particular manors in Saxon times,
testify clearly to the existence of a serfdom upon
Saxon manors as complete and onerous as the later
serfdom upon Norman manors. And we have seen
that, connecting this evidence with that of the laws of
King Ine, the proof is clear of the existence of manors
and serfdom in the seventh century, *i.e.* 400 years
before the Norman Conquest. There remains to be
quoted the still earlier though scanty evidence of the
laws of King Ethelbert, A.D. 597–616 ; which, if
genuine, bring us back to the date of the mission of
St. Augustine to England.

The evidence of these laws is accidental and indirect, but taken in connexion with that already considered, it seems to show conclusively that the ' hams '
and ' tuns ' of that early period were already manors.
Upon one point at least it is clear. It goes so far in single
as to indicate that they were in the ownership of ownership,
individuals, and not of free village communities.

The following passages occur :—

III. Ꝺⁱꝼ cÿnⁱnᵹ æꞇ manneꞃ ham ꞇ·ꞃⁱncæꝺ, &c.	3. If the king drink at a man's *ham,* &c.
v. Ꝺⁱꝼ ⁱn cÿnⁱnᵹeꞃ ꞇúne man mannan oꝼꝼlea, &c.	5. If in the king's *tun* a man slay another, &c.
XIII. Ꝺⁱꝼ on eopleꞃ ꞇúne man mannan oꝼꝼlæhꝺ, &c.	13. If in an earl's *tun* a man slay another, &c.
XVII. Ꝺⁱꝼ man ⁱn manneꞃ ꞇun æꝥeꞃꞇ ᵹeⁱꝥneꝺ, &c.	17. If a man into a man's *tun* enter, &c.

If there be any doubt as to the manorial character of these ' hams ' and ' tuns,' it lies not in the point
of the single ownership of them, but in other points,
whether they were worked and tilled by the owners'
slaves, or by a village community in serfdom.

The only classes of tenants which are mentioned
in the laws of King Ethelbert are the three grades of
læts referred to in the following passage :

XXVI. Ꝺⁱꝼ [man] læꞇ oꝼꝼlæhꝺ ꝥone ꞃeleꞃꞇan. lxxx. ꞃcⁱll. ꝼoꝥᵹelꝺe. Ꝺⁱꝼ ꝥane oꝺeꝥne oꝼꝼlæhꝺ. lx. ꞃcⁱllⁱnᵹum ꝼoꝥᵹelꝺe. ꝥane ꝥꞃⁱꝺ-ꝺan. xl. ꞃcⁱllⁱnᵹum ꝼoꝥᵹelꝺen.	26. If [a man] slay a *læt* of the best [class], let him pay lxxx. shil-lings : if he slay one of the second, let him pay lx. shillings : of the third, let him pay xl. shillings.

The word *læt* is of doubtful meaning in this passage. It might have reference to the Roman *læti,* or
people of conquered tribes deported into Roman
provinces at the end of a war ; or it might refer to
the *liti* or *lidi*—the servile tenants mentioned in so
many of the early Continental codes. We are not
yet in a position to decide. But in any case these
læts of King Ethelbert's laws were clearly of a semi-
servile class here in Kent, as were the *lidi* in Frankish
Gaul,[1] for their ' wergild ' was distinctly less than that
of the Kentish freemen.[2]   Whether they were a dif-

---

[1] See M. Guérard's *Introduction to the Polyptyque de l'Abbé Irminon,*

pp. 250–75.

[2] The *leod-geld* or *wer-gild* of a

ferent class from the *geburs* or *villani*, or identical Chap. V.
with them, it is not easy to decide.

XI. RESULT OF THE SAXON EVIDENCE.

The evidence of the earliest Saxon or Jutish laws
thus leaves us with a strong presumption, if not actual
certainty, that the Saxon *ham* or *tun* was the estate of
a lord, and not of a free village community, and that
it was so when the laws of the Kentish men were first
codified a few years after the mission of St. Augustine.

It becomes, therefore, all but impossible that the The manorial
manorial character of English *hams* and *tuns* can have system not
had an ecclesiastical origin. The codification of the of ecclesiastical
laws was possibly indeed the direct result of eccle- origin.
siastical influence no less than in the case of the Alamannic, and Bavarian, and Visigothic, and Burgundian,
and Lombardic codes. In all these cases the codification partook, to some extent, of the character of a
compact between the king and the Church. Room
had to be made, so to speak, for the new ecclesiastical
authority. A recognised status and protection had
to be given to the Church for the first time, and this
introduction of a new element into national arrangements was perhaps in some cases the occasion of the
codification. This may be so; but at the same time
it is impossible that a new system of land tenure can
have been suddenly introduced with the new reli-

'man' was 200 shillings (see mention of the half leod-geld of c. shillings, s. 21). As regards the three
grades of *læts*, there were also three
grades of female *theows* of the king

(see s. 10-11), the *cup-bearer*, the
grinding-theow, and the *lowest class.*
See also s. 16, where again there is
mention of three classes of *theows*,
each with its value.

gion.   The property granted to the Church from the first was already manorial.   A *ham* or a *tun* could not be granted to the Church by the king, or an earl, unless it already existed as a manorial estate.   The monasteries became, by the grants which now were showered down upon them, lords of manors which were already existing estates, or they could not have been transferred.

Further, looking within the manor, whether on the royal demesne or in private hands, it seems to be

The hold- clear that as far back as the evidence extends, *i.e.* the
ings in
yard-lands time of King Ine, the holdings—the yard-lands—were
implied
serfdom, held in villenage, and were bundles of a recognised number of acre or half-acre strips in the open field, handed down from one generation to another in single succession without alteration.

Now let it be fully understood what is involved in this indivisible character of the holding, in its devolution from one holder to another without division among heirs.   We have seen that the theory was that as the land and homestead, and also the *setene*, or outfit, were provided by the lord, they returned to the lord on the death of the holder.   The lord granted the holding afresh, most often, no doubt, to the eldest son or nearest relation of the landholder on his payment of an ox or other relief in recognition of the servile nature of the tenure, and thus a custom of primogeniture, no doubt, grew up, which, in the course of generations—how early we do not know— being sanctioned by custom, could not be departed from by the lord.   The very possibility of this permanent succession, generation after generation, of a single holder to the indivisible bundle of strips

called a yard-land or virgate, thus seems to have
implied the servile nature of the holding. The lord
put in his servant as tenant of the yard-land, and put
in a successor when the previous one died. This
seems to be the theory of it. It was probably precisely the same course of things which ultimately produced primogeniture in the holding of whole manors.
The king put in a *thane* or *servant* of his (sometimes
called the '*king's geneat*'), or a monastery put in a
steward or *villicus* to manage a manor. When he
died his son may have naturally succeeded to the
office or *service*, until by long custom the office became
hereditary, and a succession or inheritance by primogeniture under feudal law was the result. The benefice, or *læn*, or office was probably not at first generally
hereditary; though of course there were many cases
of the creation of estates of inheritance, or *boc-land*,
by direct grant of the king. As we have seen from
the passage quoted from Bede, the *læn* of an estate
for life was the recognised way in which the king's
thanes were rewarded for their services.

Thus it seems that in the very nature of things
the permanent equality of the holdings in yard-lands
(or double, or half yard-lands), on a manor, was a
proof that the tenure was servile, and that the community was not a free village community. For imagine
a free village community taking equal lots, and holding
these lots, as land of inheritance, by allodial tenure,
and with (what seems to have been the universal custom of Teutonic nations as regards land of inheritance)
equal division among heirs, how could the *equality*
be possibly maintained? One holder of a yard-land
would have seven sons, and another two, and another

one. How could equality be maintained generation after generation? What could prevent the multiplication of intricate subdivisions among heirs, breaking up the yard-lands into smaller bundles of all imaginable sizes? Even if a certain equality could be restored, which is very unlikely, at intervals, by a *re-division*, which should reverse the inequality produced by the rule of inheritance, what would become of the *yard-lands*? How could the contents of the yard-land remain the same on the same estate for hundreds of years, notwithstanding the increase in the number of sharers in the land of the free village community?

We may take it, then, as inherently certain that the system of yard-lands is a system involving in its continuance a *servile origin*. The community of holders of yard-lands we may regard as a community of servile tenants, without any strict rights of inheritance—in theory tenants at the will of their lord, becoming by custom *adscripti glebæ*, and therefore tenants for life, and by still longer custom gaining a right of single undivided succession by primogeniture, or something very much like it.

Result of the Saxon evidence. Now we know that the holdings were *yard-lands* and the holders *geburs*, rendering the customary *gafol* and *week-work* to their lords, in the time of King Ine, if we may trust the genuineness of his 'laws.' There was but an interval of 100 years between Ine and Ethelbert; whilst Ine lived as near to the first conquest of large portions of the middle districts of England as Ethelbert did to the conquest of Kent.

The laws of Ethelbert, taken in connexion with the subsequent laws of Ine, and the later actual in-

stances of Saxon manors which have been examined,
form a connected chain, and bring back the links of
the evidence of the manorial character of Saxon
estates to the very century in which the greater part
of the West Saxon conquests took place. The existence of earl's and king's and men's *hams* and *tuns*
in the year of the codification of the Kentish laws,
A.D. 602 or thereabouts, means their existence as a
manorial type of estate in the sixth century ; and with
the exception of the southern districts, the West
Saxon conquests were not made till late in the sixth
century. Surely there is too short an interval left
unaccounted for to allow of great economic changes
—to admit of the degeneracy of an original free village community if a widely spread institution, into a
community in serfdom. So that the evidence strongly
points to the *hams* and *tuns* having been manorial in
their type from the first conquest. In other words,
so far as this evidence goes, the Saxons seem either
to have introduced the manorial system into England themselves, founding *hams* and *tuns* on the
manorial type, or to have found them already existing
on their arrival in Britain. There seems no room for
the theory that the Saxons introduced everywhere
free village communities on the system of the German
'mark,' which afterwards sank into serfdom under
manorial lords.

But before we can be in a position to understand
what probably happened we must turn our attention
to those portions of Britain *which were not manorial*,
and where village communities did not generally exist.
They form an integral part of our present England,
and English economic history has to do with the

Chap. V.

The tribal
system
must be
investi-
gated.

economic growth of the whole people. It cannot, therefore, confine itself to facts relating to one element only of the nation, and to one set of influences, merely because they became in the long run the paramount and overruling ones. And, moreover, the history of the manorial system itself cannot be properly understood without an understanding also of the parallel, and perhaps older, *tribal system,* which in the course of many centuries it was destined in some districts to overrule and supplant ; in others, after centuries of effort, to fail in supplanting.

CHAPTER VI.

THE TRIBAL SYSTEM (IN WALES).

I. EVIDENCE OF THE DOMESDAY SURVEY.

THE Saxon land system has now been examined. No feature has been found to be more marked and general than its universally manorial character; that is to say, the Saxon 'ham' or 'tun' was an estate or manor with a village community in villenage upon it. And the services of the villein tenants were of a uniform and clearly defined type; they consisted of the combination of two distinct things—fixed *gafol* payments in money, in kind, or in labour, and the more servile *week-work*.

It is needful now to examine the land system beyond the border of Saxon conquest.

A good opportunity of doing this occurs in the Domesday Survey.

The Tidenham manor has already been examined. It afforded a singularly useful example of the Saxon system. Its geographical position, at the extreme south-west corner of England, on the side of Wales, enabled us to trace its history from its probable conquest in 577, or soon after, and to conclude that it remained Saxon from that time to the date of the Survey; and distinctly manorial was found to be the character of its holdings and services.

Now, the neighbouring land, on the west side of the Wye, was equally remarkable in its geographical position. For as long as Tidenham had been the extreme south-west corner of England, so long had the neighbouring land between the Wye and the Usk been the extreme south-east corner of unconquered Wales.

It was part of the district of *Gwent,* and it seems to have remained in the hands of the Welsh till Harold conquered it from the Welsh king Gruffydd, a few years only before the Norman Conquest.

Harold seems to have annexed whatever he conquered between the Wye and the Usk—*i.e.* in Gwent—to his earldom of Hereford; and after the Norman Conquest it fell into the hands of William FitzOsborn, created by William the Conqueror Earl of Hereford and Lord of Gwent.[1]

It was he[2] who built at Chepstow the Castle of *Estrighoiel,* the ruins of which still stand on the west bank of the Wye, opposite Tidenham. His son, Roger FitzOsbern, succeeded to the earldom of Hereford and the lordship of Gwent; and, upon his rebellion

---

[1] *Liber Landavensis,* p. 545. *Ordericus Vitalis,* ii. 190. It may have been conquered in 1049, after Gruffydd and Irish pirates had, according to Florence, crossed the Wye and burned 'Dymedham' (see Freeman's *Norman Conquest,* ii. App. P); but most likely shortly before A.D. 1065, under which date is the following entry in the Saxon Chronicle:—

'A. 1065. In this year before

Lammas, Harold the Eorl ordered a building to be erected in Wales at Portskewith *after he had subdued it,* and there he gathered much goods and thought to have King Edward there for the purpose of hunting; but when it was all ready, then went Cradock, Griffin's son, with the whole force which he could procure, and slew almost all the people who there had been building.'

[2] *Domesday,* i. 162 *a.*

and imprisonment, this region of Wales became *terra*
regis, and as such is described in the Domesday Survey, mostly as a sort of annexe to Gloucestershire,[1] but partly as belonging to the county of Hereford.[2]

Nor is *Gwent* the only district very near to Tidenham whose Welsh history can be traced down to the time of the Domesday Survey. There was another part of ancient Wales, the district of *Ergyng,* or *Archenfield,*—which included the ' Golden Valley ' of the *Dour.* It lay, like Gwent—but further north— between the unmistakable boundaries of the Wye and the Usk, and it remained Welsh till conquered by Harold ; and this is confirmed by the fact that the district of '*Arcenefelde*' is brought within the limits of the Domesday Survey[3] as an irregular addition to Herefordshire, just as Gwent was an annexe to Gloucestershire.

Here, then, we have two districts, one to the west and the other to the north of Tidenham, both of which clearly remained Welsh till conquered by Harold a few years before the Norman Conquest, and both of them are described in the Domesday Survey. Further, it so happens that because they had been but recently conquered, and had not yet been added to any English county, and because also their customs differed from those of the neighbouring English manors, the services of their tenants, quite out of ordinary course, are described.

So that, by a convenient chance, we are able to bring together upon the evidence of the Domesday

---

[1] *Ibid.* 162 *a et seq.*

[2] 185*b.*   See also Freeman's

Norman Conquest, ii. App. SS, p. 685.

[3] *Domesday,* i. 179 *a.*

CHAP. VI.

Survey the *land systems* of a district which for five hundred years before the Norman Conquest had been the extreme south-east edge of Wales, and of a district which for the same five hundred years had been the extreme south-west corner of Saxon England, beyond the Severn.

We have seen what was the Saxon land system on one side of the Wye, which divided the two districts; let us now see what was the Welsh land system on the other side of the river, so far as it is disclosed in the Survey.

Gwent.

Part of the Welsh district of Gwent is thus described in the Domesday annexe to Gloucestershire :—

'Under Waswic, the præpositus, are xiii. villæ ; under [another præpositus] xiiii. villæ, under [another præpositus] xiii., under [another præpositus] xiiii. (*i.e.* 54 in all). These render xlvii. sextars of honey, and xl. pigs, and xli. cows, and xxviii. shillings for hawks.[1] . . .

'Under the same præpositi are four villæ wasted by King Caraduech.'[2]

Again, a little further on, this entry occurs :—

'The same A. has in Wales *vii. villæ* which were in the demesne of Count William and Roger his son (*i.e.* Fitz-Osbern, Earl of Hereford and Lord of Gwent). These render *vi. sextars of honey*, vi. pigs, and x. shillings.'[3]

Passing to the Domesday description of the district of *Archenfield*, we find a similar record.

Archenfield.

The heading of the survey for Herefordshire[4] is as follows : 'Hic annotantur terras tenentes in Here-

---

[1] See *Leges Wallice*, p. 812. 'De qualibet villa rusticana debet habere ovem fetam vel 4 denarios in cibos accipitrum.' The 54 villæ at 4*d.* each would make xviii. *s.*

(? whether xxviii. by an extra x. in error).

[2] *Domesday*, i. 162 *a*.

[3] *Domesday*, i. 162 *a* (last entry).

[4] F. 179 *a*.

fordscire et in Arcenefelde et in Walis.' And further
on [1] we learn that—

'In *Arcenefelde* the king has 100 men less 4, who with their men have 73 teams, and give of custom 41 sextars of honey and 20s. instead of the sheep which they used to give, and 10s. for *fumagium*; nor do they give *geld* or other custom, except that they march in the king's army if it is so ordered to them. If a *liber homo* dies there, the king has his horse, with arms. From a *villanus* when he dies the king has one ox. King Grifin and Blein devastated this land in the time of King Edward, and so what it was then is not known.' *Lagademar* pertained to Arcenefelde in the time of King Edward, &c. There is a manor [at Arcenefelde] in which 4 *liberi homines* with 4 teams render 4 sextars of honey and 16d. of custom. Also a villa with its men and 6 teams, and a forest, rendering a half sextar of honey and 6d.

There are other instances of similar honey rents, *e.g.*—

In *Chipeete* 57 men with xix. teams render xv. sextars of honey and x. shillings.

In *Cape* v. Welshmen having v. teams render v. sextars of honey, and v. sheep with lambs, and xd.

In *Mainaure* one under-tenant having iv. teams renders vi. sextars of honey and x. s.

In *Penebecdoc* one under-tenant having iv. teams render vi. sextars of honey and x. s.

In *Hulla* xii. villani and xii. bordarii with xi. teams render xviii. sextars of honey.

The distinctive points in these descriptions of the Food rents and clusters of villas under a præpositus. recently Welsh districts west and north of Tidenham are obviously (1) the prevalence of produce or food rents—honey, cows, sheep, pigs, &c.—*honey* being the most prominent item; (2) the absence of the word ' manor,' used everywhere else in the survey of Gloucestershire and Herefordshire; (3) the remarkable grouping in the district of *Gwent* of the ' villas ' *in batches of thirteen or fourteen*, each batch under a separate *præpositus*.

---

[1] F. 181 a.

It is clear that on the Welsh side of the Wye Welsh instead of Saxon customs prevailed, and that these were some of them.[1] So much we learn from these irregular additions of newly conquered Welsh ground to the area of the Domesday Survey.

The meaning of the peculiarities thus indicated will become apparent when the Welsh system has been examined upon its own independent evidence.

II. THE WELSH LAND SYSTEM IN THE TWELFTH CENTURY.

There is no reason why, in trying to learn the nature of the Welsh land system, the method followed throughout, of proceeding backwards from the known to the unknown, should not be followed.

Open-field system in Wales.

It has already been shown that such arable fields as there are in Wales, like the Saxon arable fields, were *open* fields. They were shown to be divided by turf balks, two furrows wide,[2] into strips called erws —representing a day's work in ploughing. The Welsh laws were also found to supply the simplest and clearest solution given anywhere of the reason of the scattering of the strips in the holdings, as well as of the relations of the grades of holdings to the number of oxen contributed by the holders to the common plough team of eight oxen.

In fact, the Welsh codes clearly prove that, as regards arable husbandry, the open field system was the system prevalent throughout all the three districts of Wales.

---

[1] So f. 185 *b*: 'In Castellaria de *Carlion* . . . iii. Walenses *lege Walensi viventes* cum iii. car. et ii. bord. cum dim. car. et reddunt iiii. sextar. mellis.'

[2] *Ancient Laws of Wales*, p. 373.

But partly from the mountainous nature of the country, and partly from the peculiar stage of economic development through which the Welsh were passing, long after the Norman Conquest they were still a *pastoral* people. Cattle rather than corn claimed the first consideration, and ruled their habits ; and hence the Welsh land system, even in later times, was very different from that of the Saxons.

In fact, the two land systems, though both using an open-field husbandry, were in their main features radically distinct. In those parts of Wales which were unconquered, and therefore uncivilised, till the conquest of Edward I., we look in vain in the early surveys for the manor or estate with the village community in villenage upon it.

The Welsh system was not manorial. Its unit was not a village community on a lord's estate.

As late as the twelfth century *Giraldus Cambrensis*[1] described the houses of the Welsh as not built either in towns or even in villages, but as scattered along the edges of the woods. To his eye they seemed mere huts made of boughs of trees twisted together, easily constructed, and lasting scarcely more than a season. They consisted of one room, and the whole family, guests and all, slept on rushes laid along the wall, with their feet to the fire, the smoke of which found its way through a hole in the roof.[2] The Welsh, in fact, being a *pastoral* people, had two sets of homesteads. In summer their herds fed on the higher ranges of the hills, and in winter in the valleys. So they themselves, following their cattle, had separate

---

[1] *Description of Wales,* chap. cxvii.   [2] C. x.

Chap. VI. huts for summer and for winter use, as was also the custom in the Highlands of Scotland, and is still the case in the higher Alpine valleys. Giraldus Cambrensis describes the greater part of the land as in pasture and very little as arable; and accordingly the food of the Welsh he describes, just as Cæsar had described it eleven centuries earlier, as being chiefly the produce of their herds—milk, cheese and butter, and flesh in larger proportions than bread.[1] The latter was mostly of oats.

Welsh ploughing.

The Welsh ploughed for their oats in March and April, and for wheat in summer and winter, yoking to their ploughs seldom fewer than four oxen; and he mentions as a peculiarity that the driver walked backward in front of the oxen, as we found was the custom in Scotland.[2]

Love of war.

Another marked peculiarity of the Welsh was their hereditary liking and universal training for warlike enterprise. They were soldiers as well as herdsmen; even husbandmen eagerly rushed to arms from the plough.[3] Long settlement and the law of division of labour had not yet brought about the separation of the military from the agricultural population of Wales even so late as the twelfth century. And here we come upon traces of their old tribal economy. For the facts that they had not yet attained to settled villages and townships, that they had not yet passed from the pastoral to the agricultural stage, that they were still craving after warfare and wild enterprise—all

---

[1] C. viii. The district of Snowdon afforded the best pasturage and Anglesey the best corn-growing land.

[2] C. viii. and xvii. In the Isle of Man four oxen were yoked abreast to the plough, Train's *Isle of Man*, ii. p. 241. [3] C. viii.

these are traces of tribal habits still remaining. And
a still clearer mark of the same thing was the stress
they laid upon their genealogy. Even the common
people (he says) keep their genealogies, and can not
only readily recount the names of their grandfathers
and great-grandfathers, but even refer back to the
sixth or *seventh* generation, or beyond them, in this
manner : *Rhys*, son of *Gruffydh*, son of *Rhys*, son of
Theodor, son of *Eineon*, son of *Owen*, son of *Howel*,
son of *Cadelh*, son of *Roderic Mawr*, and so on.[1]

Thus in the twelfth century there were in Wales
distinct survivals of a tribal economy. Instead of a
system like the Saxons, of village communities and
townships, the Welsh system was evidently a tribal
system in the later stages of gradual disintegration,
tenaciously preserving within it arrangements and
customs pointing back to a period when its rules had
been in full force.

But the Welsh codes must be further examined
before the significance of the Domesday entries can be
fully appreciated.

III. THE WELSH LAND SYSTEM ACCORDING TO THE WELSH LAWS.

The Welsh version of the ancient laws of Wales
contains three several codes : The Venedotian of North
Wales, the Dimetian and Gwentian of South Wales.
They profess to date substantially from *Howel dda*,
who codified the local customs about the middle of
the tenth century. They contain, however, later

---

[1] C. xvii.

Chap. VI. additions, and the MSS. are not earlier than the end
of the thirteenth century. There is a Latin version
of the Dimetian code in MS. of the early part of the
thirteenth century, which is especially valuable as
giving the received Latin equivalent of the Welsh
terms used in the laws. And there are also, apart
from these codes, triads of doubtful date, but profess-
ing to preserve traditional customs and laws of the
Welsh nation before the time of the Saxon conquest
of Britain.[1]

For the present purpose the actual date of a law
or custom is not so important as its own intrinsic
character. We seek to gain a true notion of the
tribal system, and an economically early trait may
well be preserved in a document of later date.

Saxon and
Welsh
systems
contempo-
rary.

There is no reason why we should be even tempted
to exaggerate the antiquity of the evidence. The
later the survival of the system the more valuable for
our purpose. The Saxon and Welsh systems were
contemporary systems, and it is best to compare them
as such.

It would appear that under this tribal system a
district was occupied by a tribe (*cenedl*) under a petty
king (*brenhin*) or chief.

Free
tribesmen
of tribal
blood.

The tribe was composed of households of free
Welshmen, all blood relations ; and the homesteads of
these households were scattered about on the country
side, as they were found to be in the time of Giraldus
Cambrensis. They seem to have been grouped into
artificial clusters mainly, as we shall see, for purposes
of tribute or legal jurisdiction.

---

[1] *Ancient Laws and Institutes of Wales.* Record Commission, 1841.
See preface by *Aneurin Owen*.

But all the inhabitants of Wales were not members Chap. VI. of the tribes. Besides the households of tribesmen of blood relations and pure descent, there were hanging on to the tribes or their chiefs, and under the over-lordship of the latter, or sometimes of tribesmen, strangers in blood who were not free Welshmen; Taeogs also Welshmen illegitimately born, or degraded for without tribal crime. And these classes, being without tribal or blood. family rights, were placed in groups of households and homesteads by themselves. If there were any approach to the Saxon village community in villenage upon a lord's estate under Welsh arrangements, it was to be found in this subordinate class, who were not Welshmen, and had no rights of kindred, and were known as *aillts* and *taeogs* of the chief on whose land they were settled. Further, as there was this marked distinction between tribesmen and non-tribesmen, so also there was a marked and essential distinction between the free tribe land occupied by the families of free Welsh tribesmen, called '*tir gwelyawg*,' or *family land*, and the '*caeth land*' or *bond land* of the taeogs and aillts, which latter was also called '*tir-cyfrif*' or *register land*, and sometimes '*tir-kyllydus*' or *geldable land* (gafol-land?).[1]

The main significance of the Welsh system, both as regards individual rights and land usages, turns

---

[1] *Venedotian Code. Ancient Laws of Wales*, pp. 81-2, and see pp. 644-6 (*Welsh Laws*). Mr. Skene, in his chapter on *The Tribe in Wales* in his *Celtic Scotland*, iii. pp. 200, 201, does not seem to have grasped fully the distinction between the *free tribesmen* and their *family* land on the one hand and the Aillts and Taeogs with their *geldable* or *register* land on the other. Everything, however, turns upon this. Compare *Welsh Laws*, xiv. s. 31 and s. 32 (pp. 739-741), where the distinction is again clearly stated.

on this distinction between the two different classes of persons and the two different kinds of land occupied by them. They will require separate examination.

Let us first take the free tribesmen (' Uchelwyrs ' or ' Breyrs ') and their ' family land.'

The free tribesmen. If the professed triads of *Dyvnwal Moelmud* may be taken to represent, as they claim to do, the condition of things in earlier centuries, the essential to membership in the *cenedl,* or tribe, was *birth* within it of Welsh parents.

Free-born Welshmen were ' tied ' together in a ' social state' by the three ties of—

(1) Common defence (cyvnawdd).
(2) Common tillage (cyvar).
(3) Common law   (chyvraith).[1]

Every free Welshman was entitled to three things :—

(1) Five free *erws* (or acre strips).
(2) Co-tillage of the waste (cyvar gobaith).
(3) Hunting.[2]

The homestead or tyddyn. The free tribesman's homestead, or *tyddyn,* consisted of three things :—

(1) His house   (ty).
(2) „ cattle-yard (bu-arth).
(3) „ corn-yard (yd-arth).[3]

And the five free strips, afterwards apparently

---

[1] *Ancient Laws of Wales,* p. 638 (s. 45).   [2] *Id.* 651 (s. 83).   [3] P. 639 (s. 51).

reduced to four, of each head of a house—free, CHAP. VI. possibly, in the sense of their having been freed from the common rights of others over them, as well as being free from charges or tribute—we may probably regard as contained in the *tyddyn*, or as lying in croft near the homesteads.

The *Gwentian, Dimetian,* and *Venedotian* codes all represent the homestead or tyddyn and land of the free Welshman as a *family holding.* So long as the head of the family lived, all his descendants lived with him, apparently in the same homestead, unless new ones had already been built for them on the family land. In any case, they still formed part of the joint household of which he was the head.[1]

The holding that of a household or family.

When a free tribesman, the head of a household, died, his holding was not broken up. It was held by his heirs for three generations as one joint holding; it was known as the holding of ‘ the heirs of So-and-so.’[2] But within the holding there was equality of division between his sons; the younger son, however, retaining the original *tyddyn* or homestead, and others having tyddyns found for them on the family land. All the sons had equal rights in the scattered strips and pasture belonging to the holding.[3]

Thus, in the first generation there was equality between brothers; they were co-tenants in equal

Equality within the family

---

[1] Pp. 81–2.

[2] See the surveys in the *Record of Carnarvon* (14th century), where the holdings are sometimes called ‘ *Weles*,’ thus :—‘ In eadem villa sunt tria *Wele* libera, viz. *Wele* Yarthur ap Ruwon Wele Joz. ap Ruwon and *Wele* Keneth ap Ru-won. Et sunt heredes predicte Wele de Yarthur ap Ruwon, Eign. ap Griffiri and Hoell. ap Griffri et alii coheredes sui;’ and so on of the other Weles (p. 11). This is the common form of the survey *passim.*

[3] *Ancient Laws, &c., of Wales,* p. 741.

O

Chap. VI. shares of the family holding of which they were co-heirs.

When all the brothers were dead there was, if desired, a re-division, so as to make equality between the co-heirs, who were now first cousins.

When all the first cousins were dead there might be still another re-division, to make equality between the co-heirs, who were now second cousins.

to second cousins. But no one beyond second cousins could claim equality; and if a man died without heirs of his body, and there were no kindred within the degree of second cousins, the land reverted to the chief who represented the tribe.[1]

Great-grandfather the common ancestor. The great-grandfather was thus always looked back to as the common ancestor, whose name was still given to the family holding of his co-heirs. The family tie reached from him to his great-grandchildren, and then ceased to bind together further generations.[2]

The Gwely or family couch. We have seen that even in the twelfth century the household all used one couch, extending round the wall of the single room of the house; this couch was called the 'gwely.' The 'tir gwelyawg' was thus the land of the family using the same couch; and the descendants of one ancestor living together were a 'gweli-gordd.'[3] As late as the fourteenth century, in the *Record of Carnarvon*, the holdings

---

[1] *Id.* pp. 82 and 740.

[2] The fullest description of the rules of '*family land*' are those in the *Venedotian Code*, c. xii., *The Law of Brothers for Land*, pp. 81 et seq. See also *Welsh Laws*, Book IX. xxxi. p. 536; also Book XIV. xxxi. pp. 739 et seq.

[3] *Ancient Laws, &c., of Wales*, Glossary, p. 1001.

are still called ' Weles' and ' Gavells.' They are CHAP. VI.
essentially ' family' or tribal holdings.[1]

And now as to the tenure upon which these holdings of the free tribesmen were held.

It was a free tenure, subject to the obligation to The
Gwestva
or food
rent.
pay *Gwestva*, or 'food rent,' to the chief, and to some
incidents which marked an almost feudal relationship
to the chief, viz. :—

(1) The *Amobr*, or marriage fee of a female.

(2) The *Ebediw*,[2] or death payment (heriot).

(3) Aid in building the king's castles.

(4) Joining his host in his enterprises *in* the
country whenever required, *out* of the country six
weeks only in the year.[3]

These were the usual accompaniments of free
tenure everywhere, and are no special marks of
serfdom.

Several homesteads were grouped together in The *tunc*
pound in
lieu of it.
' maenols' or ' trevs' for the purpose of the payment of
the *Gwestva*, as we shall see by-and-by. This consisted
in *Gwent*, of a horse-load of wheat-flour, an ox, seven
threaves of oats, a vat of honey, and 24 pence of
silver.[4] And as the money value of the *Gwestva* was
always one pound, so that its money equivalent was
known as ' the tunc pound,' holdings of family land
were spoken of, as late as the fourteenth century, as
' paying tunc'[5]—the *gwestva*, or *tunc pound* in lieu

---

[1] The *Record of Carnarvon, passim.* Thus 'the *Wele* of So-and-so, the son of So-and-so, and the heirs of this Wele are So-and-so.'

[2] This was not payable if an investiture fee had been paid by the person dying.

[3] *Ancient Laws, &c.,* p. 92 and 93.

[4] *Id.* p. 375.

[5] *Book of Carnarvon, passim.*

of it, being the distinctive tribute of the free tribes-men.

Such was the tenure of the family land, and these were the services of the free tribesmen.

A free tribal tenure.

There is no trace here of villenage, or of the servile *week-work* of the Saxon serf. The tribesmen had no manorial lord over them but their chief, and he was their natural and elected tribal head. So, when Wales was finally conquered, the *tunc* was paid to the Prince of Wales, and no mesne lord was inter-posed between the tribesman and the Prince.

Thus the freedom of the free tribesman was guarded at every point.

The *aillts* or *taeogs*.

Turning now to the other class, the *aillts* or *taeogs*—who in the Latin translations of the laws are called *villani*—the key to their position was their non-possession of tribal blood, and therefore of the rights of kindred. They were not free-born Welsh-men; though, on the other hand, by no means to be confounded with *caeths*, or slaves. They must be sworn men of some chieftain or lord, on whose land they were placed, and at whose will and pleasure they

Their tyddyns and ploughs.

were deemed to remain.[1] Each of these taeogs had his *tyddyn*—his homestead, with corn and cattle yard. In his tyddyn he had cattle of his own. In South Wales several of these taeogs' homesteads were grouped together into what was called a *taeog-trev*. Further, the arable fields of the 'taeog-trev' were ploughed on the open-field system by the taeogs'

---

[1] Sometimes an '*uchelwr*' or tribesman had taeogs under him. *Ancient Laws, &c.*, pp. 88, 339, and 573. See also *Id.* p. 646. *Welsh Laws*.

common plough team, to which each contributed oxen.

But the distinctive feature of the taeog-trev was that an *absolute equality* ruled, not between brothers or cousins of one household, as in the case of the family land of the free tribesmen, but *throughout the whole trev*. Family relationships were ignored. All adults in the trev—fathers and sons, and strangers in blood—took equal shares, with the single exception of *youngest sons*, who lived with their fathers, and had no tyddyn of their own till the parent's death. This principle of equality ruled everything.[1] The common ploughing must not begin till every taeog in the trev had his place appointed in the co-tillage.[2] Nor could there be any escheat of land in the taeog-trev to the lord on failure of heirs ; for there was nothing heredi- tary about the holdings. Succession always fell (except in the case of the youngest son, who took his father's tyddyn) to the whole trev.[3] When there was a death there was a re-division of the whole land, care, how- ever, being taken to disturb the occupation of the actual tyddyns only when absolutely needful.[4]

The principle upon which the taeog's rights rested was simply this : where there was no true Welsh blood no family rights were recognised. In the ab- sence of these, equality ruled between individuals ; they shared ' per capita,' and not ' per stirpes.'

The land of a taeog-trev was, as already said, called ' register land '[5]—*tir cyfrif*.

Equality in the taeog-trev.

Per capita no account of blood relation- ship.

Their register land.

---

[1] *Id.* pp. 82 and 536. *Welsh Laws*, s. xxxii.

[2] *Id.* p. 376.

[3] *Id.* p. 82.

[4] *Id.* p. 82.

[5] It was sometimes called ' tir kyllidin,' or geldable land, as before stated.

CHAP. VI.   There were other incidents marking off the taeog
from the free Welshman. He might not bear arms;[1]
he might not, without his lord's consent, become a
scholar, a smith, or a bard, nor sell his swine, honey,
or horse.[2] Even if he were to marry a free Welsh
woman, his descendants till the fourth, and in some
cases the ninth degree, remained taeogs. But the
fourth or ninth descendant of the free Welsh woman,
as the case might be, might at last claim his five free
strips, and become the head of a new kindred.[3]

Incidents
to their
tenures.   Even the taeog was, however, under these laws,
hardly a serf. With the exception of his duty to
assist the lord in the erection of buildings, and to
submit to *kylch*, *i.e.* to the lord's followers, being
quartered upon him when making a ' progress,' and to
dovraith, or maintenance of the chief's dogs and servants, there seems to have been no exaction of menial
personal services.[4]

Food-
rents.   The taeogs' dues, like those of free Welshmen,
consisted of fixed summer and winter contributions
of food for the chief's table. In *Gwent* they had to
provide in winter a sow, a salted flitch, threescore
loaves of wheat bread, a tub of ale, twenty sheaves
of oats, and pence for the servants. In summer, a
tub of butter and twelve cheeses and bread.[5]

These tributes of food were called ' dawnbwyds,'
gifts of food, or ' board-gifts,' and from these the
taeog or register land is in one place in the Welsh
laws called *tir bwrdd*, or ' board-land ' (*terra mensalia*,

---

[1] *Ancient Laws, &c.*, p. 673.
[2] Pp. 36–7 and 212–13.
[3] *Id.* pp. 88 and 646.

[4] Pp. 93 and 376.
[5] P. 375–6. *Gwentian Code*, 11,
xxxv.

or ' mensal land ' [1]), a term which we shall find again Chap. VI.
when we come to examine the Irish tribal system.

Lastly, it must not be forgotten that beneath the The caeth,
taeogs, as beneath the Saxon *geneat* and *gebur*, were or slave.
the ' caeths,' or bondmen, the property of their
owners,[2] without tyddyn and without land, unless
such were assigned to them by their lord. These
caeths were, therefore, not settled in separate trevs,
but scattered about as household slaves in the tyddyns
of their masters.

IV. LAND DIVISIONS UNDER THE WELSH CODES.

There were, then, these two kinds of holdings—
those of the free tribesmen, of ' family land,' and those
of the taeogs, of ' register land.' There remains to
be considered the system on which the holdings were
clustered together.

The principle of this it is not very easy at first to The
understand, and the difficulty is increased by a con- holdings
grouped
fusion of terms between the codes. But there is one for pay-
ment of
fact, by keeping hold of which the system becomes the food-
rent or
intelligible, viz., that the grouping seems to have been tunc
based upon the collective amount of the *food-rent*. pound.
The homesteads, or tyddyns, each containing its four
free erws, were scattered over the country side. But
they were artificially grouped together for the purpose
of the payment of the food-rent, or *tunc pound* in lieu
of it. And by following the group which pays the

---

[1] *Ancient Laws, &c.*, p. 697.
[2] P. 294 (Dimetian Code). ' The
caeth—there is no *galanas* (death-

fine) for him, only payment of his
" werth " to his master *like the
" werth " of a beast.'

'tunc pound' as the unit of comparison, the at first conflicting evidence falls into its proper place.

In the Venedotian Code the *maenol* is this unit. In the Dimetian and Gwentian Codes this unit is the *trev.*

According to the Venedotian Code of North Wales,[1]

4 erws	= 1 tyddyn.
4 tyddyns	= 1 randir
4 randirs	= 1 gavael.
4 gavaels	= 1 trev.
4 trevs	= 1 maenol.
12 maenols and 2 supernumerary trevs	= 1 cymwd (or comote).
2 cymwds	= 1 cantrev (100 trevs).

The *cymwd* was thus a half-hundred, and each cymwd had its court, and so was the unit of legal jurisdiction. At its head was a *maer* and a *canghellor*, the two officers of the chief who had jurisdiction over it.

The twelve maenols in the cymwd were thus disposed :—

> 1 free maenol for the support of the office of maer.
> 1 free maenol for the support of the office of canghellor.
> 6 occupied by '*uchelwrs*,' or tribesmen.

> ———

> Making 8 free maenols of 'family land,' from each of which a gwestva or *tunc pound* was paid.
> The other 4 maenols were 'register land' occupied by aillts or taeogs, paying 'dawn bwyds.'

> ———

> 12 in the 'cymwd.'[2]

Now, it must be admitted that all this singular system, arranged according to strict arithmetical rules, *looks* very much like a merely theoretical arrangement, plausible on paper but impossible in practice.

It will be found, however, that there is more

---

[1] *Ancient Laws, &c.*, pp. 90–1.   [2] *Id.* p. 91, s. 14.

probability, as well as reason and meaning in it, than
at first sight appears.

In the first place, as regards the twelve maenols making up the *cymwd*, there is no difficulty ; four of them were taeog maenols and eight were free maenols. But there is an obvious difficulty in the description of the contents of each maenol. Taken literally, the description in the Venedotian Code seems to imply that every maenol was composed of four trevs, each of which contained four gavaels composed of four randirs, each of which contained four tyddyns composed of four erws. But in this case the maenol would contain nothing but tyddyns—nothing but homesteads!—there would be no arable and no pasture. This cannot be the true reading. A clue to the real meaning is found in a clause which, after repeating that from each of the eight free maenols in the cymwd the chief has a *gwestva* yearly, ' that is a pound yearly from each of them,' goes on to say, ' Threescore pence is charged on each trev of the four that are in a maenol, and so subdivided into quarters in succession until each erw of the tyddyn be assessed.' [1]

Threescore pence of the tunc pound to each trev.

Now, from this statement it may be assumed that there must be some correspondence between the number of pence in the tunc pound and the number of erws in the maenol, otherwise why speak of each erw being assessed ? But, according to the foregoing figures, there would be 1,024 erws in the maenol.[2]

---

[1] *Id.* p. 91, s. 15. In *Leges Wallice*, p. 825, ' score pence' or ' score of silver' is translated ' uncia argenti ;' ∴ 3 *uncie agri* should equal a ' *trev.*' See *Liber Landavensis*, pp. 70 and 317.

[2]
4 erw	= tyddyn.
16 ,,	= randir.
64 ,,	= gavael.
256 ,,	= trev.
1024 ,,	= maenol.

Each trev, which thus contains 256 erws, is to pay threescore pence. How can 256 erws be divided into quarters till each erw is assessed? Dividing the trev by four we get the gavael of sixty-four erws, and threescore pence divided by four is sixty farthings. It is evident that sixty farthings cannot be divided between sixty-four erws. But if we suppose each trev to contain four homesteads or tyddyns, then the *gavael*[1] of sixty-four erws would be the single holding belonging to a tyddyn or homestead, and the four erws in the actual tyddyn (which are to be *free* erws) being deducted, then the sixty farthings exactly correspond with the remaining sixty erws forming the holding of land appendant to the tyddyn, and each erw would pay one farthing. We may take it then as possible that each Venedotian maenol contained four trevs, paying sixty pence each, and that each trev was a cluster of four holdings of sixty erws each, in respect of which the holders paid sixty farthings each to the *gwestva*, holding their actual tyddyns free.

A group of
sixteen
home-
steads
paid the
tunc
pound.

In other words, each of the eight free maenols contained sixteen homesteads, which sixteen homesteads were first classified in groups of four called trevs. Or, to put the case the other way, the eight free maenols, were divided into quarters or trevs, and these trevs again each contained four homesteads.

It is evidently a tribal arrangement, clustering the homesteads numerically for purposes of the payment of gwestva, and probably the discharge of other

---

[1] The word *Gabail* still in Scotch Gaelic retains its meaning of *a farm.* The word is pronounced '*găv'-ul.*'

public duties, and not a natural territorial arrangement
on the basis of the village or township.

Turning now to the Dimetian and Gwentian Codes, according to which the free *trev* instead of the maenol is the gwestva-paying unit :[1] there is first the group of twelve trevs (instead of twelve maenols) under a single maer, and under the name of *maenol* instead of *cymwd* ; but apparently all the trevs in the group of twelve [2] are free trevs. There are other groups of seven taeog trevs making a taeog-maenol, and the maenol (instead of the cymwd) has its court, and becomes the unit of legal jurisdiction.[3]

Confining attention to the free maenol, the first thing to notice is that each of the twelve free trevs of which it was composed paid its gwestva, or tunc pound in lieu of it. The trev, therefore, was the gwestva-paying unit.

And as to the interior of the trev we read,—

‘ There are to be four randirs in the trev, from which the king's gwestva shall be paid.’

‘ 312 erws are to be in the randir between clear and brake, wood and field, and wet and dry, except a supernumerary trev [the upland has in addition].’[4]

In this case the ‘ tunc pound ’ of 240d. was paid by each trev of 4 randirs, each randir containing 312 erws, and the trev 1,248 erws in all. The *trev* in South Wales is, therefore, slightly larger than the

---

[1] *Ancient Laws*, pp. 261. ‘ Four randirs are to be in the trev from which the king's gwestva is to be paid ’ (s. 5).

[2] In upland districts there were 13 trevs in the maenol, p. 375.

[3] There were seven taeog-trevs in taeog-maenols, and each contained three randirs, in two of which there were three taeog-tyddyns to each, the third being pasture for the other two. There were therefore six taeog holdings in each taeog-trev. *Ancient Laws, &c.*, pp. 375 and 829.

[4] Pp. 374–5.

Venedotian *maenol.* Here we are bound by no law that the pence in the gwestva should exactly correspond with the number of erws. But in the other versions the 12 odd erws in the randir are stated to be for ' domicilia,' [1] or buildings, and 12 erws would allow of 3 tyddyns of the requisite 4 erws each.

This fixes for us the number of homesteads or tyddyns in the trev. There were 3 tyddyns to each randir, and 4 randirs to the trev, and so there were 12 tyddyns in each trev, and to each tyddyn there were appendant 100 erws in the arable, pasture, and waste.

The trev which paid its tunc pound of 240*d.* was thus made up of 12 holdings, each paying a score pence. And as in the Latin version of the Dimetian Laws (p. 825) a score pence is translated *uncia argenti,* the connexion is at once made clear between the system of grouping the holdings so as to pay the tunc pound, and the monetary system which prevailed in Wales, viz., that according to which 20*d.* made an ounce, and 12 ounces one pound. The 12 holdings each paying a score of pence, or ounce of silver, made up between them the tunc pound of the trev.

This curious geometrical arrangement or classification of tyddyns and trevs, with an equal area of land to each, is at first sight entirely inconsistent with the division of the family land among the heirs of the holder, inasmuch as the great grandchildren when they divided the original family holding must, one would suppose, have held smaller shares than their great

---

[1] P. 829. ' In randir continentur ccc. et xii. acre : ut in ccc. acris, araturam, et pascua et focalia possessor habeat ; inde xii. domicilia.'

See also p. 790. ' Id est xii. domicilia.' The Dimetian Code has it ' space for buildings on the 12 erws ' (p. 263).

grandfather. And there is only one answer to this. It would have been so if the tribe, and the families composing it, were permanently fixed and settled on the same land, and pursuing a regular agriculture, with an increasing population within certain boundaries. But the Welsh were still a *pastoral* people, and, as we shall see when we come to examine the Irish tribal system, while the homesteads and land divisions were fixed, the occupants were shifted about by the chiefs from time to time, each sept, or clan, or family receiving at each rearrangement a certain number of tyddyns or homesteads, according to certain tribal rules of blood relationship of a very intricate character.

The tribal households shifted among the holdings.

This permanence of the geographical divisions and homesteads, and shifting of the tribal households whenever occasion required it, was only possible with a pastoral and scanty population. Long before the fourteenth century the households were settled in their homesteads, geometrical regularity had ceased, and the land was divided and subdivided into irregular fractions. This is the state of things disclosed in the *Record of Carnarvon.* But in the tenth century, according to the Welsh laws, the old tribal rules were apparently still in force.

Without pretending to have mastered all the details of these obscure tribal arrangements, the point to be noted is that the scattering of the tyddyns all over the country side, and the clustering of them by fours and sixteens, or twelves, into the group which was the unit paying the gwestva or tunc pound, and again into clusters of twelve or thirteen[1] under a

The clustering of households the distinctive mark of the tribal system.

---

[1] 'There are to be thirteen trevs in every maenol, and the thirteenth | of these is the supernumerary trev.' *Gwentian Code,* p. 375.

maer, as the unit of civil jurisdiction, were obviously distinctive features arising from the tribal holding of land, and that the system was adopted apparently to facilitate the division of the land among the families in the tribe somewhat in the same way as in the open field system the division of the arable land by turf balks into actual erws facilitated the division of the ploughed land among the contributors to the plough team.

Bearing this in mind we may now turn back to the Domesday Survey, and compare its description of the land system of *Gwent* and *Archenfield* with the results obtained from the Welsh laws.

In order, however, to make this comparison the Welsh terms must be translated into Latin, otherwise it will be difficult to recognise the trev, and maer, and maenol, and gwestva in the Domesday description.

The before-mentioned Latin version of the Dimetian Code, the MS. of which dates from the early thirteenth century, will do this for us.[1]

It translates *trev*, the unit of the tunc pound, by *villa*. It takes the Welsh word 'maenol' as equivalent to *manor*, and indeed it did resemble the Saxon and Norman manor in this, that it was the unit of the jurisdiction of each single steward or *villicus* of the chief. This officer was called in Welsh the *maer*, which was translated into the Latin *præpositus*. He did to some extent resemble the English præpositus, but he differed in this—that instead of being set over the 'trev' or 'villata' of a single manor,

---

[1] *Leges Wallice, Ancient Laws, &c.,* p. 771 *et seq.*

the Welsh maer was, as we have seen, set over a
number of 'villas' or trevs—thirteen free trevs or
seven taeog-trevs, in Gwent—each free trev of which
rendered its 'tunc pound' or 'gwestva,' and each
taeog or villein-trev its 'dawn-bwyd' of food.

Now, this is precisely what is described in the
Domesday Survey of Gwent.

There are four groups of thirteen or fourteen The
clusters of
villas
under a
præpositus
paying
food-rent.
'villas' or trevs, each group under a 'præpositus' or
maer; and these four groups, which were in fact
Gwentian 'maenols,' rendered as gwesta a food-rent
amounting to 47 sextars of honey, 40 pigs, 41 cows,
and 28 shillings for hawks.

In the district of *Archenfield* the clusters of trevs
do not appear, but the food-rents were similar—*honey*
being a marked item throughout.

In the Welsh gwestva, also, *honey* was an important Honey
rents.
element. It is mentioned as such in the Welsh codes,
and it is conspicuous also in the Domesday Survey
both of Gwent and Archenfield.

Its importance is shown by the fact that in the Import-
ance of
honey.
Gwentian Code a separate section was devoted to
'The Law of Bees.' It begins as follows :—'The
origin of bees is from Paradise, and on account of
the sin of man they came from thence, and they were
blessed by God, and, therefore, the mass cannot be
without the wax.' [1]

The price of a swarm of bees in August was equal
to the price of an ox ready for the yoke, *i.e.* ten or
fifteen times its present value, in proportion to the ox.

Honey had, in fact, two uses, besides its being the

---

[1] *Ancient Laws, &c.,* p. 360.

substitute for the modern sugar—one for the making of mead, which was three times the price of beer ; the other for the wax for candles used in the chief's household, and on the altar of the mass.[1]　The lord of a taeog had the right of buying up all his honey;[2] and in North Wales, according to the Venedotian Code, *all* the honey of the king's aillts or taeogs was reserved for the court.[3]　The mead brewer was also an important royal officer in all the three divisions of Wales.

It is not surprising, then, that the tribute of honey, which formed so important a part of the Welsh gwestva, should be retained as an item in the tribute of the trevs of Gwent after their conquest by Harold.

V. EARLIER EVIDENCE OF THE PAYMENT OF WELSH GWESTVA, OR FOOD-RENT.

From the combined evidence of the Domesday Survey and the 'Ancient Laws of Wales,' the fact has now been learned that in the eleventh century, as it had done previously probably for 400 years, the river Wye separated by a sharp line the Saxon land, on which the manorial land system prevailed, from the Welsh land, on which the Welsh tribal land system prevailed. On the one side of the river, at the date of the Survey, clusters of scattered homesteads of free Welshmen contributed food-rents in the form of gwestva to the conqueror of their chief, and taeogs their dawnbwyds. On the other side the *villata* of geneats and geburs, besides paying gafol, performed servile week-work upon the demesne lands of the lord of the

---

[1] *Ancient Laws, &c.,* p. 325.　　[2] *Id.* p. 213.　　[3] *Id.* p. 92 (s. 5).

village or manor. It may be well, however, to seek for some earlier evidence of the payment of gwestva on the Welsh side of the river.

Documentary evidence of the manorial system on the Saxon side was forthcoming as early as the seventh century, in the laws of King Ine. How far back can documentary evidence be traced of the Welsh system?

In the possession of the church of Llandaff there was long preserved an ancient MS. of the Gospels in Latin, called the Book of St. Chad.[1] This MS. appears to date back to the eighth century. And it was for long the custom to enter on its margin a record of solemn compacts sworn upon it, as in the similar case of the Book of Deer. It thus happens to contain (*inter alia*) two short records of grants to the church of St. Teilo (or Llandaff). One of these gifts is as follows :[2]—

The Book of St. Chad. Charters of the eighth century mention food-rent.

' This writing showeth that Ris and the family of
' Grethi gave to God and St. Teilo, *Treb guidauc.* . . .
' and this is its census : 40 loaves and a wether sheep
' in summer ; and in winter, 40 loaves, a hog, and 40
' dishes of butter. . . .'

Another is in these words :—

' This writing showeth that Ris and Hirv . . . .
' gave Bracma as far as *Hirmain Guidauc*, from the
' desert of Gelli Irlath as far as Camdubr, its " hichet "
' [food-rent ?], 3 score loaves and a wether sheep,

---

[1] *Liber Landavensis*, p. 271, App., and p. 615.

[2] For the translation see p. 616. For the original, p. 272, as follows : ' Ostendit ista scriptio quod dederunt Ris et luith Grethi *Treb* guidauc i malitiduck Cimarguich, et hic est census ejus, douceint torth hamaharuin in irham, haduceint torth in irgaem, ha huch, ha douceint mannudenn deo et sancto elindo. . . .

' and a vessel of butter. And then follow the wit-
' nesses.' [1]

Evidently
of Taeog-
trevs.

Rhys ap Ithael, the donor in these two cases, was
king of the district of Glewyssig in the middle of the
ninth century, about the time of Alfred the Great.
Now, a king or chief would hardly be likely to transfer
to the church of Llandaff a free trev and the gwestva
paid therefrom. This would have involved the severance of free members of the tribe from the tribe, to put
them under an ecclesiastical lordship. We should expect then to find that the Trev ' Guidauc ' was a *taeog-
trev* on the chief's own land, and according to the
description given in the grants, the census corresponds
not with the gwestva of a free trev under the Welsh
laws, but with the ' dawn-bwyd ' of the taeog-trev.

The food tribute in these grants was divided into
summer and winter payments, and so, as we have seen,
were the dawn-bwyds of the taeogs in the Welsh laws ;
the scores of loaves, the sow, the wether sheep, and
the tubs of butter, correspond also with the food-gifts
from the taeog-trevs, as described in the laws, though
with varying quantities.[2]

These grants in the margin of the Book of St.
Chad may, therefore, be taken as evidence that the
system of food-rents was prevalent in Wales in the
middle of the ninth century.

Survival
of Welsh
customs in
Wessex.

There is still earlier evidence of the prevalence
of the system of food-rents where we should little
expect to find it, viz., in the laws of King Ine. Ine
being King of Wessex, and Wessex shading off as it

---

[1] For the translation see p. 617 ;
for the original, p. 272.

[2] See *Leges Wallice,* ii. 14,

' *De Daunbwyt* '[Dono Cibi]. *Ancient Laws, &c., of Wales,* p. 790.

were into the old British districts both south and east
of the Severn, it was but natural that some old Welsh
or British customs should have survived in certain
places ; as *Walisc* men here and there survived
amongst the conquering English. These Welshmen
were allowed under Ine's laws to hold half-hides and
hides of land. We have only to examine the Domesday
Survey for Gloucestershire and Herefordshire to find
traces even at that date of survivals of Welsh and
Saxon customs in exceptional cases, even outside
those districts which had only just been conquered.

In some places where Saxon customs had long
prevailed a little community of Welshmen remained
under Welsh customs. In other places the customs
were partly Welsh and partly English.[1]

---

[1] Fol. 162 *b*. ' In *Cirencester*
hundred King Edward had five
hides of land. In demesne v.
ploughs and xxxi. villani with x.
ploughs. xiii. servi and x. bordarii,
&c. The Queen has the wool of the
sheep. T. R. E. : this manor rendered iii.½ modii of corn, and of
barley iii. modii, and of honey vi.½
sextars, and ix.*l.* and v.*s.*, and 3,000
loaves for dogs.'

This is very much like a survival of the Welsh food-rents at
one of the cities conquered by the
Saxons in 577.

In some other places out of
Archenfield there was a mixture of
Welsh and English customs.

The manor of *Westwode* (f. 181)
was held by the St. Peter of Gloucester. It contained vi. hides, ' one
of which had Welsh custom, the
others English.' A Welshman in
this manor had half a carucate, and
rendered i. sextar of honey.

And at *Clive* (f. 179 *b*), 8 Welshmen had 8 teams, and rendered x.½
sextars of honey and vi.*s.* v.*d.*, and
in the forest of the king was land
of this manor, which T. R. E. had
rendered vi. -sextars of honey, and
vi. sheep with lambs.

These instances are sufficient to
show that in Herefordshire, as in
Gloucestershire, in the newly conquered districts, the old Welsh dues
of honey, sheep, &c., remained undisturbed ; while in the districts
which had long been under Saxon
rule, in some few cases there was a
mixture of services, and in others
the Saxon services of ploughing on
the lord's demesne had become
general.

It may be assumed that when
the services were thus described

Chap. VI.

Food-rents mentioned in the laws of Ine in the seventh century.

In precisely the same way survivals such as these must have existed in King Ine's time. There must have been then, as 400 years afterwards, at the date of the Survey, places in Wessex where Welshmen predominated and Welsh customs survived. There must have been, in other words, manors which paid Welsh gwestva instead of Saxon services. There is a remarkable passage in King Ine's laws which can only be thus explained. On the same page, and in the next paragraph but two to the law about the yard-land set to '*gafol*' and to '*weork*,'[1] there is a clause apparently out of place, which begins abruptly with this heading : ' *Æt x. hidum* ꞇo ꝼoꞃꞇꝛe.'[2] In the Latin version this is rendered ' De x. hides ad corredium.'[3] Now, there is a passage in a charter of Louis VII. of France, anno 1157, given by Du Cange under the word ' *Corredium*,' in which certain ' villas ' are freed from the exaction of ' quædam convivia, quæ vulgo Coreede vel *Giste* vocantur.' This definition of corredium and of ' giste,' as a contribution of food exacted from tenants, corresponds exactly to the Welsh ' gwestva.' And the Saxon word *fostre* also means food. So that this heading to the passage in question may be translated—' from x. hides paying gwestva.' And so interpreted the following list be-

---

contrary to the usual routine of the Domesday surveyors, it was because there was something unusual about them ; and that in the majority of instances where Saxon customs prevailed, no description was deemed needful. Compare the Domesday survey of Dorsetshire—a portion of the ' West Wales '—where the manors in the royal demesne are grouped so that each group renders a ' firma unius noctis,' or a ' firma dimidiæ noctis.'

[1] *Laws of Ine*, No. 67. Thorpe, p. 63.

[2] *Id.* No. 70. Thorpe. p. 63.

[3] *Id.* p. 504.

comes perfectly intelligible, for it describes what the gwestva consisted of.

From 10 *hides—*
  x. dolia of honey.
  ccc. loaves.
  xii. amphora of Welsh ale.
  xxx. of clear [do.]
  ii. oxen or x. wethers.
  x. geese.
  xx. hens.
  x. cheeses.
  A full amphora of butter.
  v. salmons of xx. pounds weight.
  c. eels.

Now, if the system of gwestva payment or food-rent described in this passage of the laws of King Ine be evidence of the survival of the Welsh custom after the Saxon conquest, it is at the same time equally clear documentary evidence of the seventh century that the system of gwestva or food-rents was prevalent outside Wales in the west of Britain before the Saxon conquest.[1]

---

[1] For much curious information respecting the Welsh system of tenures, see Taylor's *History of Gavel-kind.* London. 1663.

CHAPTER VII.

THE TRIBAL SYSTEM (*continued*).

I. THE TRIBAL SYSTEM IN IRELAND AND SCOTLAND.

THE Welsh evidence brings us back to a period parallel with the Saxon era marking the date of King Ine's laws. The Welsh land system was then clearly distinguished from the Saxon by the absence of the manor with its village community in serfdom, and by the presence instead of it of the scattered homesteads (*tyddyns*) of the tribesmen and taeogs, grouped together for the purpose of the payment to the chief of the food-rents, or their money equivalents.

Further light may possibly be obtained from observation of the tribal system in a still earlier economic stage, though at a much later date, in Ireland.

Irish land divisions closely resemble the Welsh. Now, first—without going out of our depth as we might easily do in the Irish evidence—it may readily be shown, sufficiently for the present purpose, that the system of land divisions, or rather of the grouping of homesteads into artificial clusters with arithmetical precision, was prevalent in Ireland outside the Pale as late as the times of Queen Elizabeth and

James I., when an effort was made to substitute CHAP. VII. English for Irish customs and laws.

There are extant several surveys of parts of Ireland of that date in which are to be recognised arrangements of homesteads almost precisely similar to those of the Welsh Codes. And further, the names of the tenants being given, we can see that they were *blood relations* like the Welsh tribesmen, with a carefully preserved genealogy guarding the fact of their relationship and consequent position in the tribe.

The best way to realise this fact may be to turn to actual examples.

According to an inquisition [1] made of the county of *Fermanagh* in 1 James I. (1603), the county was found to be divided into seven equal baronies, the description of one of which may be taken as a sample.

'The temporal land within this barony is all equally divided into Clusters of 7½ *ballybetaghes* [literally *victuallers'* towns,[2] or units for purposes of the *taths* or food-rents like the Welsh *trevs*], each containing 4 quarters, each of *tyddyns*. those quarters containing 4 tathes [corresponding with the Welsh *tyddyns*], and each of those tathes aforesaid to be 30 acres country measure.'

Of ' *spiritual* lands ' there are two parish churches, one having 4 quarters, the other 1 quarter.

Also there are ' other small freedoms containing small parcels of land, some belonging to the spiritualty, and others being part of the *mensal* lands allotted to Macgwire (the chief).'

This exactly corresponds with the arrangement for the purposes of the gwestva of the Welsh *tyddyns* in groups of 4 and 16, as in the Venedotian Code.

---

[1] *Inquisitiones Cancellariæ Hiberniæ*, ii. xxx. iii.

[2] *Proceedings of the Royal Irish Academy*, vii. p. xiv., p. 474. Paper by the Rev. W. Reeves, D.D.

There is also a *Survey of County Monaghan* in 33 Elizabeth [1] (1591), in which the names of the holders of the *tates* in each *bailebiatagh*, or group of 16, are given. Thus, again, to take a single example,—

Example in Co. Monaghan.

Balleclonangre, a ballibeatach containing xvi. *tates.*

To Breine McCabe Fitz Alexander	.	5 tates.
„ Edmond McCabe Fitz Alexander	.	1 tate.
„ Cormocke McCabe . . .	.	2 tates.
„ Breine Kiagh McCabe .	.	2 „
„ Edmond boy, McCabe . .	.	1 tate.
„ Rosse McCabe McMelaghen .	.	1 „
„ Gilpatric McCowla McCabe .	.	1 „
„ Toole McAlexander McCabe .	.	1 „
„ James McTirlogh McCabe .	.	1 „
„ Arte McMelaghlin Dale McMahon .		1 „
		16

A fresh survey of the same district was made by Sir John Davies in 1607 ; [2] the record for this same bailebiatagh is as follows :—

Patrick M'Brian M'Cabe being found by a jury the legitimate son of Brian M'Cabe Fitz-Alexander, in demesne, 5 tates . . .	1. Lissenarte. 2. Cremoyle. 3. Sharaghanadan. 4. Nealoste. 5. Tirehannely.
Patrick M'Edmond M'Cabe Fitz-Alexander, in demesne, 1 tate	6. Curleighe.
Cormock M'Cabe, in demesne, 2 tates .	7. Aghenelogh. 8. Derraghlin.
Rosse M'Arte Moyle, in demesne, 2 tates .	9. Benage. 10. Cowlerasack.
James M'Edmond boy M'Cabe, in demesne, 1 tate	11. Tollagheisce.
Colloe M'Art Oge M'Mahowne, in demesne, 1 tate	12. Dromegeryne.

---

[1] *Inquisitiones Cancellariæ Hiberniæ,* ii. p. xxi.

[2] *Calendar of State Papers, Irelund,* 1606–8, p. 170.

Patrick M'Art Oge M'Mahowne, in regard there is good hope of his honest deserts, and that the first patentee disclaimeth, in demesne, 1 tate . . . . } 13. Corevanane.

Toole M'Toole M'Alexander M'Cabe, in demesne, 1 tate . . . . } 14. Turrgher.

James M'Tirleogh M'Cabe, in demesne, 1 tate . 15.

Brian M'Art Oge M'Mahowne, in demesne, 1 tate . . . . } 16.

Now, by comparison it will be seen that at both dates there were sixteen *tates* in the bailebiatagh, and that the holders were evidently blood relations. In some cases the name of a son takes the place of his father (the genealogy being kept up), and in others new tenants appear.

The tribesmen blood relations.

There is also reason to suppose that these *tates* were family homesteads (like the *tyddyns* of the Welsh ' family land '), with smaller internal divisions, and embracing a considerable number of lesser households. The fact that one person only is named as holding the tate, or the two tates, as the case may be, suggests that he is so named as the common ancestor or head of the chief household representing all the belongings to the tate. *Within* the tate the subdivision of land seems to have been carried to an indefinite extent. The following extract from Sir John Davies' report will probably give the best account of the actual and, to his eye, somewhat confused condition of things within the tates, as he found them. It relates to the county of Fermanagh, and is in the form of a letter to the Earl of Salisbury, dated 1607 : [1]—

The tates family holdings.

---

[1] Appended to Sir John Davies' *Discovery of Ireland,* in some of the early editions.

CHAP. VII.

Sir John
Davies'
description
of the
septs.

For the several possessions of all these lands we took this course to find them out, and set them down for his lordship's information. We called unto us the inhabitants of every barony severally. . . . We had present certain of the clerks or scholars of the country, who know all the *septs* and *families,* and all their branches, and *the dignity*[1] *of one sept above another,* and what families or persons *were chief of every sept,* and who were *next,* and who were of *a third rank,* and so forth, till they descended to the most inferior man in all the baronies; moreover, they took upon them to tell what quantity of land every man ought to have by the custom of their country, which is of the nature of gavelkind. Whereby, as their septs or families did multiply, their possessions have been from time to time divided and subdivided and broken into so many small parcels as almost every acre of land hath a several owner, which termeth himself a lord, and his portion of land his country: notwithstanding, as McGuyre himself had a chiefry over all the country, and some demesnes that did ever pass to him only who carried that title; so was there a chief of every sept who had certain services, duties, or demesnes, that ever passed to the tannist of that sept, and never was subject to division. When this was understood, we first inquired whether one or more septs did possess that barony which we had in hand. That being set down, we took the names of the chief parties of the sept or septs that did possess the baronies, and also the names of such as were second in them, and so of others that were inferior unto them again in rank and in possessions. Then, whereas every barony containeth seven ballibetaghs and a half, we caused the name of every ballibetagh to be written down; and thereupon we made inquiry what portion of land or services every man held in every ballibetagh, beginning with such first as had land and services; and after naming such as had the greatest quantity of land, and so descending unto such as possess only two taths; then we stayed, for lower we could not go,[2] because we knew the purpose of the State was only to establish such freeholders as are fit to serve on juries; at least, we had found by experience in the county of Monaghan that such as had less than two taths allotted to them had not 40s. freehold per annum *ultra reprisalem*; and therefore were not of competent ability for that service; and yet the number of freeholders named in the county was above 200.

Sir John Davies, in the same report, also gives a graphic description of the difficulty he had in ob-

---

[1] Compare the words of Tacitus, ' Agri pro numero cultorum ab universis vicis occupantur, quos mox inter se *secundum dignationem* partiuntur. *Germania,* xxvi.

[2] In Monaghan Sir J. Davies had found tates with 60 acres each. Here there were only 30 acres in a tate, so he kept to his old rule, and took 2 tates as his lowest unit.

taining from the aged Brehon of the district the roll on which were inscribed the particulars of the various holdings, including those on the demesne or mensal land of the chief.[1]

It is difficult to form a clear conception of what the tribes, septs, and families were, and what were their relations to one another. But for the present purpose it is sufficient to understand that a sept consisted of a number of actual or reputed *blood relations*, bearing the same family names, and bound together by other and probably more artificial ties, such as common liability for the payment of *eric*, or blood fines.

A curious example of what is virtually an actual sept is found in the State Papers of James I.

In 1606 a sept of the 'Grames,' under their chief 'Walter, the gude man of Netherby,' being troublesome on the Scottish border, were transplanted from Cumberland to Roscommon ; and in the schedule to the articles arranging for this transfer, it appears that the sept consisted of 124 persons, nearly all bearing the surname of *Grame*. They were divided into families, seventeen of which were set down as possessed of 20*l.* and upwards, four of 10*l.* and upwards, six of the poorer sort, six of no abilities, while as dependants there were four servants of the name of Grame, and about a dozen of irregular hangers on to the sept.[2]

The sept was a human swarm. The chief was the Queen Bee round whom they clustered. The territory occupied by a whole sept was divided

---

[1] This may be found also in *Ancient Laws of Ireland,* iii. Preface, xxxv. 6.

[2] *Calendar of State Papers, Ireland,* 1603-6, p. 554; and 1606-8, p. 492.

among the ınferior septs which had swarmed off it. And a sort of feudal relation prevailed between the parent and the inferior septs.

There can probably, on the whole, be no more correct view of the Irish tribal system in its essence and spirit than the simple generalisation made by Sir John Davies himself, from the various and, in some sense, inconsistent and entangled facts which bewildered him in detail.[1]

The chiefs and tl e tanists.

First, as regards the chiefs, whether of tribes or septs, and their demesne lands, he writes :[2]—

'1. By the Irish custom of tanistry the chieftains of every country and the chief of every sept had no longer estate than for life in their chieferies, the inheritance whereof did rest in no man. And these chieferies, though they had some portions of land allotted unto them, did consist chiefly in cuttings and coscheries and other Irish exactions, whereby they did spoil and impoverish the people at their pleasure. And when their chieftains were dead their sons or next heirs did not succeed them, but their *tanists,* who were elective, and purchased their elections by show of hands.'

Division of holdings among tribesmen.

Next, as to tribesmen and their inferior tenancies :—

'2. And by the Irish custom of gavelkind the inferior tenancies were partible amongst all the males of the sept; and after partition made, if any one of the sept had died his portion was not divided among his sons, but the chief of the sept made a new partition of all the lands belonging to that sept, and gave every one his part according to his antiquity.'

The shuffling and chang-ing' and frequent redistribu-tions.

These two Irish customs (Sir John Davies con-tinues) made all their possessions uncertain, being shuffled and changed and removed so often from one to another, by new elections and partitions, 'which uncertainty of estates hath been the true cause of desolation and barbarism in this land.'

---

[1] The evidence by which he was gradually informed may be traced in detail in the above-men- tioned *Calendars.*

[2] Sir John Davies' *Discovery of Ireland,* 1612, pp. 167 *et seq.*

These were obviously the main features of an earlier stage of the tribal system than we have seen in Wales. It was the system which fitted easily into the artificial land divisions and clusters of homesteads. And this method of clustering homesteads, in its turn, not only facilitated, but even made possible those frequent redistributions which mark this early stage of the tribal system.

The method of artificial clustering was apparently widely spread through Ireland, as we found it in the various divisions of Wales.

It also was ancient; for according to an early The system ancient poem, supposed by Dr. Sullivan [1] to belong ' in substance though not in language to the sixth or seventh century,' Ireland was anciently divided into 184 ' Tricha Céds ' (30 hundreds [of cows]), each of which contained 30 *bailes* (or townlands) ; 5,520 *bailes* in all.

The *baile* or townland is thus described :—

> ' A baile sustains 300 cows,
> Four full herds therein may roam.'

The poem describes the *bailes* (or townlands) as and pastoral. divided into 4 quarters, *i.e.* a quarter for each of the 4 herds of 75 cows each.

The poem further explains that the *baile* or town-Ballys and quarters. land was equal to 12 ' seisrighs ' (by some translated ' plough-lands '), and that the latter land measure is 120 acres,[2] making the quarter equal to three ' seisrighs '

---

[1] *Manners and Customs of the Ancient Irish*, E. O'Curry. Dr. Sullivan's Introduction, p. xcvi. See also Skene's *Celtic Scotland*, iii. 154.

[2] Skene, iii. 155. Sullivan, p. xcii.

Chap. VII. or 360 acres. But this latter mode of measurement is probably a later innovation introduced with the growth of arable farms. The old system was division into quarters, and founded on the prevalent pastoral habits of the people. In the earliest records Connaught is found to be divided into *ballys*, and the ballys into *quarters*, which were generally distinguished by certain mears and bounds.[1] The quarters were sometimes called 'cartrons,' but in other cases the cartron was the quarter of a quarter, *i.e.* a 'tate.' O'Kelly's county in 1589 was found to contain $665\frac{1}{2}$ *quarters* of 120 acres each.[2]

Lastly, it may be mentioned that in the re-allotment of the lands in Roscommon to the sept of the *Grames* on their removal from Cumberland each family of the better class was to receive a *quarter* of land containing 120 acres.[3]

The system in Scotland   The evidence as regards Scotland is scanty, but Mr. Skene, in his interesting chapter on 'the tribe in ' Scotland,' has collected together sufficient evidence to show that the tribal organisation in the Gaelic districts was closely analogous to that in Ireland.[4]

and in the Isle of Man.   There are also indications that the Isle of Man was anciently divided into ballys and quarters.[5]

---

[1] Skene, iii. 158, quoting a tract published in the appendix to *Tribes and Customs* of Hy Fiachraich, p. 453.

[2] *Id.* p. 160, quoting the *Tribes and Customs* of Hy Many.

[3] *Calendars of State Papers*, Ireland, 1606–8, pp. 491–2.

[4] Skene's *Celtic Scotland*, iii. c. vi.

[5] In a poem of the sixteenth century (1507–22), in Manks, given in Train's *Isle of Man*, i. p. 50, occur the lines—

'Ayns dagh treen *Balley* ren eh unnane
D'an sleih shen ayn dy heet dy ghuee,'

alluding to St. Germain; translated thus by Mr. Train:—

The old tribal division of the ballys into ' quarters ' and ' tates ' has left distinct and numerous traces
in the names of the present townlands in Ireland.

Annexed is an example of an ancient bally divided
into quarters. It is taken from the Ordnance Survey
of county Galway. Two of the quarters, now townlands, still bear the names of ' Cartron ' and ' Carrow,'
or ' Quarter,' as do more than 600 townlands in
various parts of Ireland.[1] This example will show
that the quarters were actual divisions.

Scattered over the bally were the sixteen ' tates '
or homesteads, four in each quarter ; and in some
counties—Monaghan especially—they are still to be
traced as the centres of modern townlands, which bear
the names borne by the ' tates ' three hundred years
ago, as registered in Sir John Davies' survey. There
is still often to be found in the centre of the modern
townland the circular and partly fortified enclosure [2]
where the old ' tate ' stood, and the lines of the present divisions of the fields often wind themselves
round it in a way which proves that it was once their
natural centre.

Moreover, the names of the ' tates ' still preserved
in the present townlands bear indirect witness to the

' For each four *quarterlands* he
made a chapel
For people of them to meet in
prayer.'

For the ' quarterlands ' see Statute
of the Tinwald Court, 1645. Also
Feltham's Tour, *Manx Society*, p.
41, &c.

[1] That in many cases the quar-
ters had become townlands as early
as the year 1683, see *Tribes and
Customs of Hy Many*, Introd. p. 454.
See also Dr. Reeve's paper ' On the
Townland Distribution of Ireland,'
*Proceedings of the Royal Irish
Academy*, 1861, vol. vii. p. 483.

[2] Many thousands of these circular enclosures are marked on the
Ordnance Map of Ireland.

reality of the old tribal redistributions and shiftings of the households from one ' tate' to another. They seldom are compounded of personal names. They generally are taken from some local natural feature. The homestead was permanent. The occupants were shifting.

Again, an example taken from the Ordnance Survey—from county Monaghan—will most clearly illustrate these points, and help the reader to appreciate the reality of the tribal arrangements.

In the survey of the barony of ' Monoughan '[1] made in 1607, the ' *half ballibetogh called Correskallie* ' is described as containing eight ' tates,' the Irish names of which are recorded. They are given below, and an English translation of the names is added[2] in brackets to illustrate their peculiar and generally non-personal character.

In the half ballibetogh called Correskallie (Round Hill of the Story-tellers)—

4 tates
{
Corneskelfee (? Correskallie).
Correvolen (Round Hill of the Mill).
Corredull (Round Hill of the Black Fort).
Aghelick (Field of the Badger).
}

4 tates
{
Dromore (the Great Ridge).
Killagharnane (Wood of the Heap).
Fedowe (Black Wood).
Clonelolane (Lonan's Meadow).
}

A reduced map of this ancient ' half-ballibetogh,' as it appears now on the large Ordnance Survey, is appended, in which the names of the old ' tates' appear, with but little change, in the modern townlands. The remains of the circular enclosures mark-

---

[1] *Calendars of State Papers, Ireland,* 1607, p. 170.

[2] Taken from Shirley's *Hist. of Monaghan,* part iv. pp. 480–482.

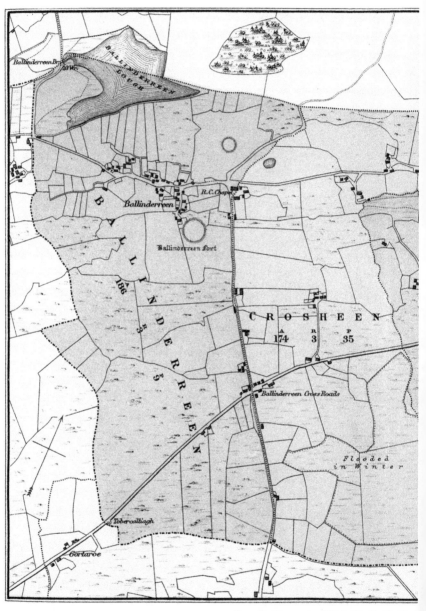

Example of an ancient 'Bally' or 'Townland' still
'Townlands', taken from sheet 103 of the Ordnance

London: Longmans & Co.

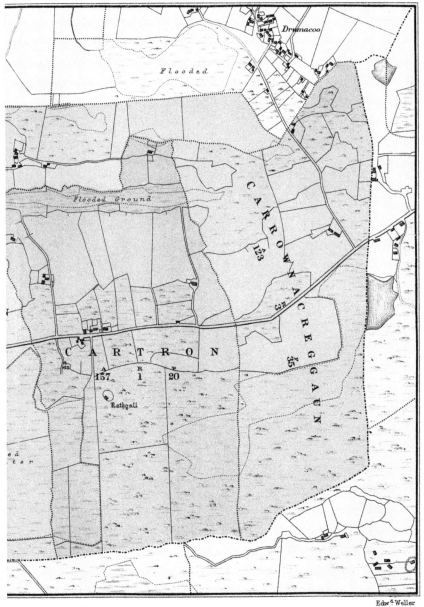

Drumacoo

Flooded

Flooded Ground

CARROWNACREGGAUN

123

35

35

C A R T R O N

65

A   R   P
157   1   20

Rathgall

ed
ter

divided into 'Quarters' which are now called
Survey of Co.Galway. Scale 6 inches to the Mile.

Edw.ᵈ Weller

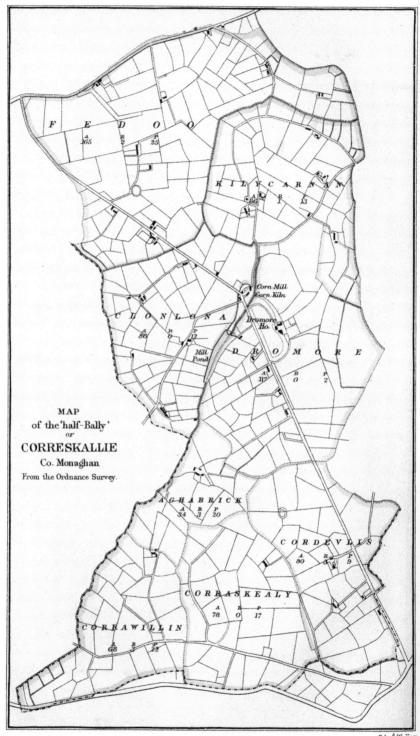

MAP
of the 'half-Bally'
OF
CORRESKALLIE
Co. Monaghan
From the Ordnance Survey.

London: Longmans & Co.

Edw.d Weller

ing the sites of the old 'tates' are still to be traced in one or two cases. The acreage of each townland is given on the map in English measures. It will be remembered that in Monaghan 60 Irish acres were allotted to each tate instead of the usual 30.

This evidence will be sufficient to prove that the arithmetical clustering of the homesteads was real, and that, as in Wales, so in Ireland, under the tribal system the homesteads were scattered over the country, and not grouped together in villages and towns.[1]

Passing to the methods of agriculture, it is obvious, that, even in a pastoral state, the growth of corn cannot be wholly neglected. We have seen that in Wales there was agriculture, and that, so far as it extended, the ploughing was conducted on an open-field system, and by joint-ploughing.

It was precisely so also in Ireland, and it had been from time immemorial.

It is stated in the 'Book of the Dun Cow' (*Lebor* Openfields. *na Huidre*), compiled in the *seventh* century by the Abbot of Clanmacnois, known to us in an Irish MS. of the year 1100, that 'there was not a ditch, nor fence, 'nor stone wall round land till came the period of the 'sons of Aed Slane [in the seventh century], but only 'smooth fields.' Add to this the passage pointed out by Sir H. S. Maine[2] in the 'Liber Hymnorum' (a MS. probably of the eleventh century), viz.—

---

[1] 'Neither did any of them in all this time plant any gardens or orchards, enclose or improve their lands, live together in settled villages or towns.'—*Discovery of Ireland*, p. 170. Compare this with the description of the Germans by Tacitus. It was, as Sir John Davies remarks, a condition of things 'to be imputed to those [tribal] customs which made their estates so uncertain and transitory in their possessions' (*id.*).

[2] *Early History of Institutions*, p. 113.

'Very numerous were the inhabitants of Ireland at this time [the time of the sons of Aed Slane in the seventh century], and their number was so great that they only received in the partition 3 *lots of 9 ridges* [immaire] *of land,* namely 9 ridges of bog land, 9 of forest, and 9 of arable land.'

The *run-rig* or *Rundale* system in Ireland and Scotland.

Taking these two passages together, and noting that the word for ' ridges' *(immaire)* is the same word *(imire,* or *iomair* [1]) now used in Gaelic for a ridge of land, and that the recently remaining system of strips and balks in Ireland and Scotland is still known as the ' run-rig ' system, it becomes clear that whatever there was of arable land in any particular year lay in open fields divided into ridges or strips.

There are, further, some passages in the *Brehon Laws* which show that at least among the lower grades of tribesmen there was joint-ploughing. And this arose not simply from ' joint-tenancy ' of un-divided land by co-heirs,[2] but from the fact that the tribesmen of lower rank only possessed *portions* of the requisites of a plough,[3] just as was the case with Welsh tribesmen and the Saxon holders of yard-lands.

There can be little doubt, therefore, that we must picture the households of tribesmen occupying the four ' tates' in each ' quarter ' as often combining to produce the plough team, and as engaged to some extent in joint-ploughing.

---

[1] Skene's *Celtic Scotland,* iii. p. 381.

[2] As to joint-tenancy between co-heirs, see tract called ' Judgments of Co-tenancy.' *Brehon Laws,* iv. pp. 69 *et seq.*

[3] See the tract ' Crith Gablach.' *Brehon Laws,* iv. pp. 300 *et seq.* One grade has ' a fourth part of a ploughing apparatus, *i.e.* an ox, a plough-straw, a goad, and a bridle '

(p. 307) ; another ' half the means of ploughing ' (p. 309) ; another ' a perfect plough ' (p. 311) ; and so on. And the size of their respective houses and the amount of their food-rent is graduated also according to their rank in the tribal hierarchy. There is a reference to ' tillage in common in the ' Senchus Mor.' *Brehon Laws,* iii. p. 17.

At first, what little agriculture was needful would be, like the Welsh 'coaration of the waste,' the joint-ploughing of grass land, which after the year's crop, or perhaps three or four years' crop, would go back into grass.[1] But it would seem from the passage quoted above, that the whole quarter of normally 120 Irish acres was at first divided into 'ridges'—possibly Irish acres—to facilitate the allotment among the households not only of that portion which was arable for the year, but also of the shares in the bog and the forest. No doubt originally there was plenty of mountain pasture besides the thirty, or sometimes sixty scattered acres or ridges allotted in

---

[1] The following appeared in the *Athenæum,* March 3, 1883, under the signature of Mr. G. L. Gomme: —'The 312 acres in possession of the Corporation of Kells (co. Meath) are divided into six fields, and thus used. The fields are broken up in rotation one at a time, and tilled during four years. Before the field is broken the members of the Corporation repair to it with a surveyor, and it is marked out into equal lots, according to the existing number of resident members of the body. Each resident freeman gets one lot, each portreeve and burgess two lots, and the deputy sovereign five lots. A portion of the field, generally five or six acres, is set apart for letting, and the rent obtained for it is applied to pay the tithes and taxes of the entire. The members hold their lots in severalty for four years and cultivate them as they please, and at the expiration of the fourth year the field is laid down with grass and a new one is broken, when a similar process of partition takes place. The other five fields are in the interim in pasture, and the right of depasturing them is enjoyed by the members of the Corporation in the same proportion as they hold the arable land; that is to say, the deputy sovereign grasses five heads of cattle (called " bolls ") for every two grazed by the portreeves and burgesses, and for every one grazed by the freemen ; with this modification, however, that the widow of a burgess enjoys a right of grazing to the same extent as a freeman, and the widow of a freeman to half that extent. The widows do not obtain any portions of the field in tillage. I should note that the first charter of incorporation to Kells dates from Richard I.'

' run-rig ' to each ' tate ' or household. In the seventh century, as we have seen, the complaint was made that the pressure of population had reduced the shares to twenty-seven ridges instead of thirty.

Finally, when we examine in the Highlands of Scotland as well as in Ireland the still remaining custom known as the ' *Rundale* ' or ' run-rig ' system, whereby a whole townland or smaller area is held in common by the people of the village, and shared among them in rough equality by dividing it up into a large number of small pieces, of which each holder takes one here and another there ; we see before us in Scotland as in Ireland a survival of that custom of scattered ownership which belonged to the open-field system all the world over ; whilst we mark again the absence of the yard-land, which was so constant a feature of the English system. The method is even applied to potato ground, where the spade takes the place of the plough ; and thus instead of the strip, or acre laid out for ploughing, there is the ' patch ' which so often marks the untidy Celtic townland.

Existing maps of townlands, whilst showing very clearly the practice still in vogue of subdividing a holding by giving to each sharer a strip in each of the scattered parcels of which the old holding con- sisted, hardly retain traces of the ancient division of the whole ' quarter ' into equal ridges or acres. But they show very clearly the scattered ownership which has been so tenaciously adhered to, along with the old tribal practice of equal division among male heirs. An example of a modern townland is annexed, which will illustrate these interesting points. The confusion it presents will also illustrate the inherent incompati-

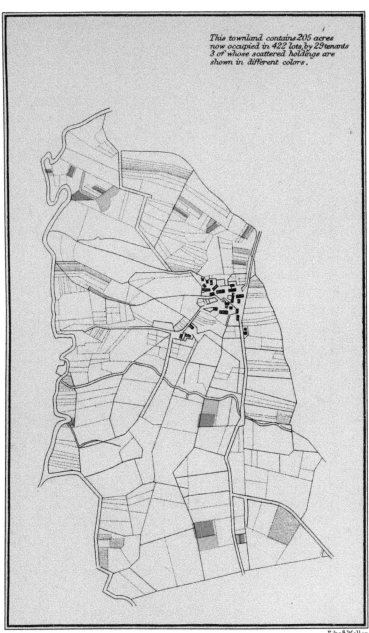

This townland contains 205 acres
now occupied in 422 lots, by 29 tenants
3 of whose scattered holdings are
shown in different colors.

Edw.d Weller

Example of divisions and holdings in a Townland on the 'Run-rig' system, Extracted
from Report of Devon Commission, see Lord Dufferin's 'Irish Emigration & Tenure'.

London: Longmans & C.º

bility in a settled district of equal division among
heirs with anything like the yard-land, or bundle of
equal strips handed down unchanged from generation
to generation.

Mr. Skene, in his interesting chapter on the ' Land
Tenure in the Highlands and Islands,'[1] has brought
together many interesting facts, and has drawn a
vivid picture of local survivals of farming communities pursuing their agriculture on the *run-rig* system,
and holding their pasture land in common. And the
traveller on the west coast of Scotland cannot fail to
find among the crofters many examples of modified
forms of joint occupation in which the methods of the
run-rig system are more or less applied even to newly
leased land at the present time.

Thus whilst the tribal system seems to be the
result mainly of the long-continued habits of a pastoral people, it could and did adapt itself to arable
agriculture, and it did so on the lines of the open
field system in a very simple form, extemporised
wherever occasion required, becoming permanent
when the tribe became settled on a particular territory.

Returning now to the main object of the inquiry
we seem, in the perhaps to some extent superficial and
too simple view taken by Sir John Davies of the Irish
tribal arrangements, to have found what we sought—
to have got a glimpse in the sixteenth and seventeenth
centuries of an earlier stage in the working of the
tribal system than we get in Wales nearly 1,000
years earlier. In this stage the land in theory was still
in tribal ownership, its redistribution among the tribes-

The Irish tribal system in an earlier stage than the Welsh.

---

[1] *Celtic Scotland,* iii. c. x. See the Estate of *Sutherland.*' By James
also ' Account of Improvements on Loch. London, 1820.

men was still frequent, and arable agriculture was still subordinate to pasture. Lastly, the arithmetical clustering of the homesteads was the natural method by which the frequent redistributions of the land were made easy ; while the run-rig form of the open-field system was the natural mode of conducting a co-operative and shifting agriculture.

But whilst gaining this step, and resting upon it for our present purpose, we must not be blind to the fact that in another way the Irish system had become more developed and more complex than the Welsh.

Sir John Davies sometimes dwells upon the fact that the chief was in no true sense the lord of the county, and the tribesmen in no true sense the free-holders of the land. The land belonged to the tribe. But, as we have seen, he found also that, as in Wales, the chiefs and sub-chiefs had, as a matter of fact, rightly or wrongly, gradually acquired a permanent occupation of a certain portion of land—so many townlands—which, using the English manorial phrase, he speaks of as ' *in demesne.*' Upon these the chief's immediate followers, and probably bondservants, lived, like the Welsh taeogs, paying him food-rents or tribute very much resembling those of the taeogs.

The complications described in the *Brehon Laws.* This land, as we have seen, he calls ' *mensal land,*' probably translating an Irish term ; and we are reminded at once of the Welsh *taeog-land* in the *Register trevs*, which also, from the gifts of food, was called in one of the Welsh laws ' *mensal land.*'

Further, besides these innovations upon the ancient simplicity of the tribal system, there had evidently, and perhaps from early times, grown up artificial relationships, founded upon contract, or even fiction, which, so to speak, ran across and complicated very greatly the tribal arrangements resting upon blood relationship. This probably is what makes the *Brehon laws* so bewildering and apparently inconsistent with the simplicity of the tribal system as in its main features it presented itself to Sir John Davies.

The loan of cattle by those tribesmen (Boaires) who had more than enough to stock their proper share of the tribe land to other tribesmen who had not cattle enough to stock theirs, in itself introduced a sort of semi-feudal, or perhaps semi-*commercial* dependence of one tribesman upon another. Tribal equality, or rather gradation of rank according to blood relationship, thus became no doubt overlaid or crossed by an actual inequality, which earlier or later developed in some sense into an irregular form of lordship and service. Hence the complicated rules of ' *Saer* ' and ' *Daer* ' tenancy. There were perhaps also artificial modes of introducing new tribesmen into a sept without the blood relationship on which the tribal system was originally built. These complications may be studied in the Brehon laws, as they have been studied by Sir Henry Maine and Mr. Skene, and the learned editors of the 'Laws' themselves; but, however ancient may be the state of things which they describe, they need not detain us here, or prevent our recognising in the actual conditions described by Sir John Davies the main features of an earlier stage of the system than is described in the ancient Welsh laws.

II. THE TRIBAL SYSTEM IN ITS EARLIER STAGES.

The comparison of the Gaelic and Cymric tribal systems has shown resemblances so close in leading principles, that we may safely seek to obtain from some of the differences between them a glimpse into earlier stages of the tribal system than the Welsh evidence, taken alone, would have opened to our view.

Outside influences: Rome, Christianity, and the ecclesiastical system.   Two powerful influences had evidently already partially arrested the tribal system in Wales, and turned it as it were against its natural bent into fixed and hardened grooves, before it assumed the shape in which it appears in the Welsh laws. These two powerful influences were (1) Roman rule and (2) Christianity. Their first action was to some extent exercised singly and apart, though concurrently in point of time. But their separate influences were afterwards surpassed and consolidated by the remarkable combination of them both which was presented in the ecclesiastical system.

The influences of Christianity, and of the later ecclesiastical system, were powerfully exerted in Ireland also ; but the Irish tribal system differed from the Welsh in its never having passed directly under Roman imperial rule.

The Brehon laws of Ireland perhaps owe their form and origin to the necessity of moulding the old traditional customs to the new Christian standard of the ecclesiastics, under whose eye the codification was made. So, also, the Welsh laws of Howell the Good, and the Saxon laws of Ine and his successors, all reflect and bear witness to this influence, and had been no doubt moulded by it into softer forms than had once prevailed. At least the harshest thorns which grew, we may guess, even rankly upon the tribal system, must, we may be sure, have been already removed before our first view of it.

In fact, nearly all the early codes, whether those of Chap. VII. Ireland, Wales, or England, or those of German tribes on the Continent, bear marks of a Christian influence, either directly impressed upon them by ecclesiastical authorship and authority, or indirectly through contact with the Roman law, which itself in the later edicts contained in the Codes of Theodosius and Justinian had undergone evident modification in a Christian sense.

So far as the Welsh tribal system is concerned, it is quite clear that whatever had been the influence upon it of direct Roman imperial rule and early Christianity, it submitted to a second and fresh influence in the tenth century.

This appears when we consider the avowed motives and object of Howell the Good in making his code. Its preface recites that he 'found the Cymry perverting the laws and customs, and therefore summoned from every *cymwd* of his kingdom six men practised in authority and jurisprudence; and also the archbishop, bishops, abbots, and priors, imploring grace and discernment for the king to amend the laws and customs of Cymru.' It goes on to say that, 'by the advice of these wise men, the king retained some of the old laws, others he amended, others he abolished entirely, establishing new laws in their place;' special pains being taken to guard against doing anything 'in opposition to *the law of the Church* or *the law of the Emperor*.' [1]

Finally, it is stated in the same preface that Howell the Good went to Rome to confirm his laws by papal

---

[1] *Ancient Laws, &c., of Wales,* p. 165.

authority, A.D. 914, and died A.D. 940. It may be added that the reference to the ' law of the Emperor' was no fiction, for ' *Blegewryd*, Archdeacon of Llandav, ' was the clerk, and he was a doctor in the law of the ' Emperor and in the law of the Church.'

The tribal division among male heirs survives these influences.

In connexion with this ecclesiastical influence there is a curious exception which proves the rule, in the refusal of Howell the Good to give up the tribal rule of equal division among sons, which lay at the root of the tribal system, and to introduce in its place the law of primogeniture.

> ' The ecclesiastical law says that no son is to have the patrimony but the eldest born to the father by the married wife: the law of Howell, however, adjudges it to the youngest son as well as to the oldest, [i.e. all the sons] and decides that sin of the father or his illegal act is not to be brought against a son as to his patrimony.'[1]

And so tenaciously was this tribal rule adhered to that even Edward I., after his conquest of Wales, was obliged for the sake of peace to concede its continuance to the Welsh, insisting only that none but lawful sons should share in the inheritance.[2]

The fixing of the gwestva dues, and their commutation into the *tunc pound* from every free trev, may well have been one of the emendations needful to bring the Welsh laws into correspondence with the ' law of the Emperor,' if it was not indeed the result of direct Roman rule, under which the chiefs paid a fixed *tributum* to the Roman State, possibly founded on the tribal food-rent.[3]

---

[1] The *Venedotian Code. Ancient Laws, &c.*, p. 86.

[2] See the last clause in the ' *Statuta de Rothelan.*' *Record of Carnarvon*, pp. 128-9, and *Ancient*

Laws, p. 872.

[3] The pound of 12 ounces of 20 pence used in codes of South Wales seems to have been the pound used in Gaul in Roman

The special Welsh laws which relieve the free trevs of ' family land ' from being under the *maer* (or villicus) and *canchellor*, and from *kylch* (or progress), and from *dovraeth* (or having the king's officers quartered upon them), and even limit the right of the *maer* and *canchellor* to quarter on the taeogs to three times a year with three followers, and their share in the royal dues from the taeogs to one-third of the *dawnbwyds*,[1] look very much like restrictions of old and oppressive customs resembling those prevalent in Ireland in later times, made with the intention of bringing the tribesmen and even the taeogs within the protection of rules similar to those in the Theodosian Code protecting the coloni on Roman estates.

The probability, therefore, is that the picture drawn by Sir John Davies of the lawless exactions of the Irish chieftain from the tribesmen of his sept would apply also to early Welsh and British chieftains before the influence of Christianity and later Roman law, through the Church, had restrained their harshness, and limited their originally wild and lawless exactions from the tribesmen. The legends of the *Liber Landavensis* contain stories of as wild and unbridled license and cruelty on the part of Welsh chieftains as are recorded in the ancient stories of the Irish tribes. And Cæsar records that the chiefs of Gallic tribes had so oppressively exacted their dues (probably food-rents), that they had reduced the smaller people almost into the condition of slaves.

---

times. ' Juxta Gallos vigesima pars unciæ denarius est et duodecim denarii solidum reddunt . . . duodecim unciæ libram xx. solidos continentem efficiunt. Sed veteres *solidum* qui nunc *aureus* dicitur nuncupabunt.' *De mensuris excerpta. Gromatici Veteres.* Lachmann, i. pp. 373–4.

[1] *Ancient Laws, &c.,* p. 781.

The close resemblance of the Welsh system of clustering the homesteads and trevs in groups of four and twelve or sixteen, to that prevalent in Ireland, points to the common origin of both. It confirms the inference that both in Wales and in Ireland this curious practice found its *raison d'être* in a stage of tribal life when the families of free tribesmen did not as yet always occupy the same tyddyn, but were shifted from one to another whenever the dying out of a family rendered needful a redistribution to ensure the fair and equal division of the tribal lands among the tribesmen, ' according to their antiquity' and their rank under the tribal rules.

Redivisions and shifting of holdings.   This occasional shifting of tribal occupation within the tribe-land was still going on in Ireland under the eyes of Sir John Davies, and it seems to have survived the Roman rule in Wales, though it was there probably confined within very narrow limits.

It seems, however, to have been itself a survival of the originally more or less nomad habits of pastoral tribes.

Semi-nomadic habits stopped by the Roman rule.   So, also, the frailty of the slightly constructed homesteads of the Welsh of the thirteenth century, which seemed to *Giraldus Cambrensis* as built only to last for a year, may be a survival of a state of tribal life when the tribes were nomadic, and driven to move from place to place by the pressure of warlike neighbours, or the necessity of seeking new pastures for their flocks and herds. But the nomadic stage of Welsh tribal life had probably come to an end during the period of Roman rule.

Putting together the Irish and Welsh evidence in

a variety of smaller points, a clearer conception may perhaps be gained than before of the character and relations to each other of the three or four orders into which tribal life seems to have separated peoples —the *chiefs*, the *tribesmen*, the *taeogs*, and under all these, and classed among chattels, the *slaves*.

The *chief* evidently corresponds less with the later lord of a manor than with the modern king. He is the head and chosen chief of the tribesmen. His office is not hereditary. His successor, his *tanist* or *edling*, is chosen in his lifetime, and is not necessarily his son.[1] The chieftains of Ireland are spoken of in mediæval records and laws as *reguli*—little kings. When Wales (or such part of it as had not been before conquered and made manorial) was conquered by Edward I. the chieftainship did not fall into the hands of manorial lords, but was vested directly in the Prince of Wales.[2]

The *tribesmen* are men of the tribal blood, *i.e.* of equal blood with the chief. They, therefore, do not at all resemble serfs. They are more like manorial lords of lordships split up and divided by inheritance, than serfs. They are not truly allodial holders, for they hold tribal land ; but they have no manorial lord over them. Their chief is their elected chief, not their manorial lord. When Irish chieftains claim to be owners of the tribal land in the English sense, and set up manorial claims over the tribesmen, they are disallowed by Sir John Davies. When Wales is con-

---

[1] This presents a curious analogy to the method followed by ' adoptive' Roman emperors.

[2] See the surveys in the *Record of Carnarvon,* and compare the Statute of Rothelan.

CHAP. VII.

quered, the *tunc pound* is paid by the free tribesmen direct to the Prince of Wales, the substituted chieftain of the tribe, and the tribesmen remain freeholders, with no mesne lord between him and them.[1] So it would have been also in Ireland if the plans of Sir John Davies had been permanently carried out.[2]

The taeogs.

The *taeogs* are not generally the serfs of the free tribesmen, but, if serfs at all, of the chief. They are more like Roman *coloni* than mediæval serfs. But they are easily changed into serfs. In Ireland the *mensal land* on which they live is allowed by Sir John Davies to be (by a rough analogy) called the chief's *demesne land.* In Wales they are called in Latin documents *villani*; but they become after the Conquest the villani, not of manorial lords, but of the Prince of Wales, and they still live in separate trevs from the tribesmen.[3]

The slaves.

These, then, are the three orders in tribal life; while the slaves in household or field service, and more or less numerous, are, like the cattle, bought and sold, and reckoned as chattels alike under the tribal and the manorial systems.

And we may go still further. These three tribal orders of men, with their large households and cattle in the more or less nomadic stage of the tribal system, move about from place to place, and wherever they

---

[1] See the surveys in the *Record of Carnarvon.* The *tunc pound* in some districts of Wales is still collected for the Prince of Wales. *Id.* Introduction, p. xvii.

[2] See Sir John Davies' *Discovery,* &c., the concluding paragraphs.

And for further information on this point, see my articles in the *Fortnightly Review,* 1870, and the *Nineteenth Century,* January 1881, ' On the Irish Land Question.'

[3] See the surveys in the *Record of Carnarvon.*

go, what may be called tribal houses must be erected for them.

The tribal house is in itself typical of their tribal and nomadic life. It is of the same type and pattern for all their orders, but varying in size according to the gradation in rank of the occupier.

It is built, like the houses observed by Giraldus The tribal house. Cambrensis, of trees newly cut from the forest.[1] A long straight pole is selected for the roof-tree. Six well-grown trees, with suitable branches apparently reaching over to meet one another, and of about the same size as the roof-tree, are stuck upright in the ground at even distances in two parallel rows—three in each row. Their extremities bending over make a Gothic arch, and crossing one another at the top each pair makes a fork, upon which the roof-tree is fixed. These trees supporting the roof-tree are called *gavaels*, *forks*, or *columns*,[2] and they form the nave of the tribal house. Then, at some distance back from these rows of *columns* or *forks*, low walls of stakes and wattle shut in the *aisles* of the house, and over all is the roof of branches and rough thatch, while at the ends are the wattle doors of entrance. All along the aisles, behind the pillars, are placed beds of rushes,

---

[1] To make a royal house more pretentious the bark is peeled off, and it is called ' the *White House.*' See *Ancient Laws, &c.*, pp. 164 and 303.

[2] See *Ancient Laws, &c.*, p. 142. —Hall of the *chief.* 40*d.* for each *gavael* supporting the roof, *i.e.* six *kolonon*, 80*d.* for roof. Hall of *uchelwe* or tribesman, 20*d.* each *gavael* supporting the roof, *i.e.* six *colonen*, 40*d.* the roof. House of *aillt* or *taeog*, 10*d.* for each *gavael* supporting the roof, *i.e.* six *kolovyn.* P. 351.—Worth of winter house, 30*d.* the roof-tree, 30*d.* each *forck* supporting the roof-tree. P. 676.— Three indispensables of the summer bothy (*bwd havodwr*)—a roof-tree (nen bren), roof-supporting forks (nen fyrch), and wattling (bangor). See also p. 288.

called *gwelys* (*lecti*), on which the inmates sleep. The footboards of the beds, between the columns, form their seats in the daytime. The fire is lighted on an open hearth in the centre of the nave, between the middle columns, and in the chieftain's hall a screen runs between these central pillars and either wall, so partially dividing off the upper portion where the chief, the edling, and his principal officers have their own appointed places, from the lower end of the hall where the humbler members of the household are ranged in order.[1] The columns, like those in Homeric houses and Solomon's temple, are sometimes cased in metal, and the silentiary, to call attention, strikes one of them with his staff. The bed or seat of the chieftain is also sometimes covered by a metal canopy.[2] In his hand he holds a sceptre or wand of gold, equal in length to himself, and as thick as his little finger. He eats from a golden plate as wide as his face, and as thick as the thumb-nail of a ploughman who has handled the plough for seven years.[3]

The kitchen and other outbuildings are ranged round the hall, and beyond these again are the corn and the cattle-yard included in the *tyddyn*.

The chieftain's hall is twice the size and value of the free tribesman's, and the free tribesman's is twice

---

[1] Compare description of Irish houses in Dr. Sullivan's *Introduction*, cccxlv. *et seq.*, with the *Venedotian Code. Ancient Laws, &c., of Wales*, p. 5, s. vi.—'Of Appropriate Places.' Compare also the curious resemblances in the structure of stone huts in the Scotch islands where trees could not be used, and especially the position of the beds in the walls or in the rough aisles.—Mitchell's *Past in the Present*, Lecture III. Compare Dr. Guest's description of the Celtic houses. *Origines Celticæ*, ii. 70–83.

[2] *Id.*

[3] *Ancient Laws, &c.*, p. 3.

that of the taeog. But the plan is the same. They
are all built with similar green timber forks and roof-
tree and wattle,[1] with the fireplace in the nave and
the rush beds in the aisles. One might almost conjecture that as the tabernacle was the type which
grew into Solomon's temple, so the tribal house built
of green timber and wattle, with its high nave and
lower aisles, when imitated in stone, grew into the
Gothic cathedral. Certainly the Gothic cathedral,   *Likeness*
simplified and reduced in size and materials to a   *of the
tribal*
rough and rapidly erected structure of green timber   *house to
the Gothic*
and wattle, would give no bad idea of the tribal   *cathedral.*
house of Wales or Ireland. It has been noticed in a
former chapter that the Bishop of Durham had his
episcopal bothy, or hunting hall, erected for him
every year by his villeins, in the forest, as late as the
time of the Boldon Book. This also was possibly a
survival of the tribal house.[2]

In this tribal house the undivided household of   *The tribal
household.*
free tribesmen, comprising several generations down
to the great-grandchildren of a common ancestor,
lived together ; and, as already mentioned, even the
structure of the house was typical of the tribal family
arrangement.

In the aisles were the *gwelys* of rushes, and the
whole household was bound as it were together in
one *gwellygord.* The *gwelys* were divided by the

---

[1] See *Ancient Laws, &c.*, p. 142.
[2] Compare Strabo's description
of the *Gallic* houses, 'great houses,
arched, constructed of planks and
wicker and covered with a heavy
thatched roof' (iv. c. iv. s. 3). Also
for the early stake and wattle *Ger-*
man houses, see Tacitus (*Germania,*
xvi.), and the interesting section
(Bk. i. s. 4) on the subject in Dr.
Karl von Inama-Sternegg's *Deutsche Wirthschaftsgeschichte.* Leipzig,
1879.

Chap. VII. central columns, or *gavaels* (Welsh for 'fork'), into four separate divisions; so there were four *gavaels* in a trev, and four randirs in a gavael. And so in after times, long after the tribal life was broken up, the original holding of an ancient tribesman became divided in the hands of his descendants into *gavells* and *gwelys*, or *weles*.[1]

Another point has been noticed. In the old times, when the tribesmen shifted about from place to place, their personal names by necessity could not be given to the places or tyddyns they lived in. The local names in a country where the tribal system prevailed were taken from natural characteristics—the streams, the woods, the hills, which marked the site. This was the case, for instance, with the townlands and *tates* of Ireland. Most of them bear witness, as we have seen, by their impersonal names, to the shifting and inconstant tenancy of successive tribesmen.[2]

It was probably not till the tribes became stationary, and, after many generations, the same families became permanent holders of the same homesteads, that the Welsh *gwelys* and *gavells* became permanent family possessions, known by the personal name of their occupants, as we find them in the extents of the fourteenth century.[3]

The tribal blood-money. Another characteristic of the tribal system in its early stages was the purely natural and tribal character of the system of *blood-money*, answering to the

---

[1] See the *Record of Carnarvon*, Introduction, p. vii. *Wele, Gwele, or Gwely* in Welsh signifies a bed, and accordingly in these extents it is often called in Latin *Lectus*. See pp. 90, 95–99, 101.

[2] See *supra*, and the lists given of the names of townlands and their meanings in Shirley's *Hist. of Co. Monaghan*, pp. 392–542.

[3] *Record of Carnarvon, passim.*

Wergelt of the Germans. It was not an artificial
bundling together of persons in tens or tithings, like
the later Saxon and Norman system of *frankpledge*,
but strictly ruled by actual family relationship. The
murderer of a man, or his relations of a certain degree,
and in a certain order and proportion, according to
their nearness of blood, owed the fixed amount of
blood-money to the family of the murdered person,
who shared it in the same order and proportions on
their side.[1] The same principle held good for insults
and injuries, between not only individuals, but tribes.
For an insult done by the tribesman of another tribe
to a chief, the latter could claim one hundred cows
for every cantrev in his dominion (*i.e.* a cow for
every trev), and a golden rod.[2]

The tribesmen and the tribes were thus bound Tenacity
together by the closest ties, all springing, in the first of tribal
instance, from their common blood-relationship. As habits.
this ruled the extent of their liability one for another,
so it fixed both the nearness of the neighbourhood of
their tyddyns, and the closeness of the relationships of
their common life. And these ties were so close, and
the rules of the system so firmly fixed by custom and
by tribal instinct, that Roman or Saxon conquest,
and centuries of Christian influence, while they modified and hardened it in some points, and stopped its
actual nomadic tendencies, left its main features and
spirit, in Ireland and Wales and Western Scotland,
unbroken. It would seem that tribal life might well
go on repeating itself, generation after generation,
for a thousand years, with little variation, without

[1] See *Dimetian Code*, B. II., c. i. *Ancient Laws, &c.*, pp. 197 *et seq.*
[2] *Id.* p. 3.

really passing out of its early stages, unless in the meantime some uncontrollable force from outside of it should break its strength and force its life into other grooves.

Nor was the tenacity of the tribal system more remarkable than its universality. As an economic stage in a people's growth it seems to be well-nigh universal. It is confined to no race, to no continent, and to no quarter of the globe. Almost every people in historic or prehistoric times has passed or is passing through its stages.

Lastly, this wide prevalence and extreme tenacity of the tribal system may perhaps make it the more easy to understand the almost equally wide prevalence of that open-field system, by the simplest forms of which nomadic and pastoral tribes, forced by circumstances into a simple and common agriculture, have everywhere apparently provided themselves with corn. It is not the system of a single people or a single race, but, in its simplest form, a system belonging to the tribal stage of economic progress. And as that tribal stage may itself take a thousand years, as in Ireland, to wear itself out, so the open field system also may linger as long, adapting itself meanwhile to other economic conditions; in England becoming for centuries, under the manorial system, in a more complex form, the shell of serfdom, and leaving its *débris* on the fields centuries after the stage of serfdom has been passed ; in Ireland following the vicissitudes of a poor and wretched peasantry, whose tribal system, running its course till suddenly arrested under other and economically sadder phases than serfdom, leaves a people swarming on the subdivided

land, with scattered patches of potato ground, held in
' run-rig ' or ' rundale,' and clinging to the ' grazing '
on the mountain side for their single cow or pig,
with a pastoral and tribal instinct ingrained in their
nature as the inheritance of a thousand years.

Such in its main features seems to have been the
tribal system as revealed by the earliest Irish and
Welsh evidence taken together.

There remains the question, What was the relation of this tribal system to the manorial system in
the south-east of England and on the continent of
Europe?

III. THE DISTINCTION BETWEEN THE TRIBAL AND AGRI-
CULTURAL ECONOMY OF THE WEST AND SOUTH-EAST
OF BRITAIN WAS PRE-ROMAN, AND SO ALSO WAS THE
OPEN-FIELD SYSTEM.

The manorial system of the east and the tribal *The south*
system of the west of Britain have now been traced *and east of Britain*
back, in turn, upon British ground, as far as the *not tribal but mainly*
direct evidence extends, *i.e.* to within a very few *agricul-*
generations of the time of the Saxon conquest ; and *tural before the*
in neither system is any indication discernible of a *Saxon conquest.*
recent origin.

So far as the evidence has hitherto gone, the two
systems were, and had long been, historically distinct. The tribal system probably once extended as
far into Wessex as the eastern limits of the district
long known as West Wales, *i.e.* as far east as Wiltshire ; and within this district of England the
manorial system was evidently imposed upon the
conquered country, as it was later in portions of

Chap. VII. Wales, leaving only here and there, as we have found, small and mainly local survivals of the earlier tribal system.

But no evidence has yet been adduced leading to the inference that before the Saxon invasion the Welsh tribal system extended all over Britain.

Indeed, the evidence of Cæsar is clear upon the point that the economic condition of the south-east of Britain was quite distinct from that of the interior and west of Britain even in pre-Roman times.

Evidence of Cæsar. Cæsar describes the south and east of Britain, which he calls the maritime portion, as inhabited by those who had passed over from the country of the Belgæ for the purpose of plunder and war, almost all of whom, he says, retain the name of the states (*civitates*) from which they came to Britain, where after the war they remained, and began to cultivate the fields. Their buildings he describes as exceedingly numerous, and very like those of the Gauls.[1] The most civilised of all these nations, he says, are those who inhabit Kent, which is entirely a maritime district; nor do they differ much from Gallic customs.[2]

He speaks, on the other hand, of the inland inhabitants as aborigines who mostly did not sow corn, but fed upon flesh and milk.[3]

Now, we have seen that the main distinctive mark of the tribal system was the absence of towns and villages, and the preponderance of cattle over corn.

When corn becomes the ruling item in economic arrangements, there grows up the settled homestead and the *village*, with its open fields around it.

---

[1] Lib. v. c. 12. [2] C. 14. [3] C. 14.

Cæsar, therefore, in describing the agriculture and CHAP. VII.
buildings of the Belgic portion of England, and the
non-agricultural but pastoral habits of the interior,
exactly hit upon the distinctive differences between
the already settled and agricultural character of the
south-east and the pastoral and tribal polity of the
interior and west of Britain.

Nor was this statement one resting merely upon A corn-growing country before and during Roman rule.
hearsay evidence. Cæsar himself found corn crops
ripening on the fields, and relied upon them for the
maintenance of his army. Nay, the reason which
led him to invade the island was in part the fact
that the Britons had given aid to the Gauls. Further,
he obtained his information about Britain from the
merchants, and the news of his approach was carried
by the *merchants* into Britain, thus making it evident
that there was a commerce going on between the
two coasts, even in pre-Roman times.[1]

We know that throughout the period of Roman
occupation Britain was a corn-growing country.

Zosimus represents Julian as sending 800 vessels, Evidence of Zosimus.
larger than mere boats, backwards and forwards to
Britain for corn to supply the granaries of the cities
on the Rhine.[2]

Eumenius, in his ' Panegyric of Constantine ' (A.D. Eumenius.
310), also describes Britain as remarkable for the
richness of its corn crops and the multitude of its
cattle.[3]

Pliny further describes the inhabitants of Britain Pliny.
as being so far advanced in agriculture as to plough

[1] Book iv. c. xx. and xxi.
[2] Book iii. c. v. *Mon. Brit.*
p. lxxvi., A.D. 358.
[3] *Mon. Brit.* p. lxix.

CHAP VII. in *marl* in order to increase the fertility of the
fields.[1]

Tacitus.   *Tacitus,*[2] in the same way (A.D. *circa* 90), speaks
of the soil of Britain as fertile and bearing heavy
crops (*patiens frugum*), and describes the tricks of
the tax gatherers in collecting the *tributum*, which was
exacted in corn.[3]

Strabo.   *Strabo*[4] (B.C. 30) mentions the export from Britain
of '*corn*, cattle, gold, silver, iron, skins, slaves, and
dogs.'

Diodorus   *Diodorus Siculus*[5] (B.C. 44) describes the manner
Siculus.   of reaping and storing corn in England thus:—

> They have mean habitations constructed for the most part of reeds
> or of wood, and they gather in the harvest by cutting off the ears of corn
> and storing them in subterraneous repositories; they cull therefrom
> daily such as are old, and dressing them, have thence their sustenance.
> . . . The island is thickly inhabited.

Pytheas.   Lastly, we have been recently reminded by Mr.
Elton that *Pytheas*, 'the Humboldt of antiquity,' who
visited Britain in the fourth century B.C., saw in the
southern districts abundance of wheat in the fields,

---

[1] Pliny (*Monument. Hist. Brit.,*
pp. viii. ix.): ' Alia est ratio, quam
Britannia et Gallia invenere alendi
eam (terram) ipsa: quod genus
vocant "*margam.*" . . . Omnis
autem marga aratro injicienda est.'
    Pugh's *Welsh Dict.*, p. 328:
' *Marl*, earth deposited by water, a
rich kind of clay (with many com-
pounds).'
    See *Chron. Monas. Abingdon.*
II. xxx. P. 147, ' *on tha lam-
pyttes*;' p. 402, '*on thone lampyt*'
('*lam*,' loam, mud, clay.—Bos-
worth, p. 41 *b*). Pp. 150 and

404, '*on tha cealc seathas*' (*chalk-
pits*).
    See *Liber de Hyda*, p. 88,
' caelcgrafan ' (chalk-pits).
    Compare Pliny (*ubi supra*) with
Abingdon, ii. p. 294: 'Totam terram quæ nimis pessima et infruc-
tifera erat tam citra aquam quam
ultra compositione terræ quæ vulgo
" *Marla* " dicitur, ipse optimam et
fructiferam fecit.' (*Colne* in Essex.)
    [2] In his *Agricola*, xii.
    [3] *Agricola*, xix.
    [4] Strabo, Bk. IV. c. v. s. 2.
    [5] *Mon. Brit.* Excerpta, ii.

and observed the necessity of threshing it out in covered barns, instead of using the unroofed threshing-floors to which he was accustomed in Marseilles. 'The natives,' he says, 'collect the sheaves in great 'barns, and thresh out the corn there, because they 'have so little sunshine that our open threshing-places 'would be of little use in that land of clouds and 'rain.' [1]

It is clear, then, that in the south-east of Britain a considerable quantity of corn was grown all through the period of Roman rule and centuries before the Roman conquest of the island. And if so, that difference between the pastoral tribal districts of the interior and the more settled agricultural districts of the south and east, noticed by Cæsar, was one of long standing.

The tribal system of Wales furnishes us, therefore, with no direct key to the economic condition of South-eastern Britain.

But, on the other hand, the continuous and long-continued growth of corn in Britain from century to century adds great interest to the further question, Upon what system was it grown ?

Upon what other system can it have been grown than the *open-field system* ? The universal prevalence of this system makes it almost certain that the fields found by Cæsar waving with ripening corn were *open* fields. The open-field system was hardly first introduced by the Saxons, because we find it also in Wales and Scotland. It was hardly introduced by the Romans, because its division lines and measure-

The corn probably grown on the open-field system.

---

[1] Elton's *Origins of English History*, p. 3 .

ments are evidently not those of the Roman *agrimensores*. The methods of these latter are well known from their own writings. Their rules were clear and definite, and wherever they went they either *adopted the previous divisions of the land*, or set to work on *their own system of straight lines and rectangular divisions*. We may thus guess what an open field would have been if laid out, *de novo*, by the Roman *agrimensores*; and conclude that the irregular network or spider's web of furlongs and strips in the actual open fields of England with which we have become familiar is as great a contrast as could well be imagined to what the open field would have been if laid out directly under Roman rules.

We happen to know also, from passages which we shall have occasion to quote hereafter, that the Roman *agrimensores* did find in other provinces—we have no direct evidence for Britain—an open-field system, with its irregular boundaries, its joint occupation, its holdings of scattered pieces, and its common rights of way and of pasture, existing in many districts—*in multis regionibus*—where the red tape rules of their craft had not been consulted, and the land was not occupied by regularly settled Roman colonies.[1]

The open-field system in some form or other we may understand, then, to have preceded in Britain even the Roman occupation. And perhaps we may go one step further. If the practice of ploughing marl into the ground mentioned by Pliny was an early and local peculiarity of Britain and of Gaul, as it seems to have been from his description, then clearly

---

[1] Siculus Flaccus, *De Conditionibus Agrorum. Gromatici veteres.* | Lachmann. P. 152. The passage will be given in full hereafter

it indicates a more advanced stage of the system than the early Welsh co-aration of portions of the waste. The marling of land implies a settled arable farming of the same land year after year, and not a ploughing up of new ground each year. It does not follow that there was yet a regular rotation of crops in three courses, and so the fully organised three-field system ; but evidently there were permanent arable fields devoted to the growth of corn, and separate from the grass land and waste, before Roman improvements were made upon British agriculture.

But the prevalence of an open-field husbandry in its simpler forms was, as we have been taught by the investigation into the tribal systems of Wales and Ireland, no evidence of the prevalence of that particular form of the open-field husbandry which was connected with the *manorial* system, and of which the yard-land was an essential feature. In order to ascertain the probability of the manorial system having been introduced by the Saxons, or having preceded the Saxon conquest in the south and east of Britain, it becomes necessary to examine the manorial system in its Continental history, so as if possible, working once more from the known to the unknown —this time from the better known Roman and German side of the question—to find some stepping-stones at least over the chasm in the English evidence.

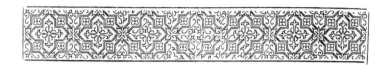

CHAPTER VIII.

CONNEXION BETWEEN THE ROMAN LAND SYSTEM AND THE LATER MANORIAL SYSTEM.

I. IMPORTANCE OF THE CONTINENTAL EVIDENCE.

CHAP.
VIII.
———
The ques-
tion a
complex
one.

IN now returning to the question of the origin of the English manorial system it is needful to widen the range of the inquiry, and to seek for further light in Continental evidence.

The question itself has become a complex one. There may have been manors in the south-eastern districts of Britain before the Saxon conquest, while Britain was a Roman province, or the Saxons may have introduced the manorial system when they conquered the country. These remain the alternatives now that we have seen that the tribal system in Britain was evidently not its parent. But even if the Saxons introduced the manorial system, the further question arises whether it was a natural growth from their own tribal system, or whether they had themselves adopted it from the Romans? It is obvious, therefore, that no adequate. result can be obtained without a sufficiently careful study (1) of the Roman provincial land system and (2) of the

German tribal system. Not till both these have been examined can it be possible to judge which of the two factors contributed most to the manorial system, and to what extent it was their joint product.

The question must needs be complicated by the fact that during the whole period of the later empire a large portion of Germany was included within the lines of the Roman provinces ; or, to state the point more exactly, that a large proportion of the inhabitants of these Roman provinces were Germans. It will be seen in the course of the inquiry how much depends upon the full recognition of this fact. Indeed, the very first step taken will bring it into prominence, and put us, so to speak, on right geographical lines, by showing that the nearest analogies to the English manor were to be found in those districts precisely which were both Roman and German under the later empire.

The two factors, the Roman land system and the German tribal system.

In studying, therefore, the land system in Roman provinces, we must not forget that we are studying what, though Roman, may have been subject to barbarian influences. In studying, on the other hand, the German tribal system, it is no less important to remember that some German customs may betray the results of centuries of contact with Roman rule.

II. THE CONNEXION BETWEEN THE SAXON 'HAM,' THE GERMAN 'HEIM,' AND THE FRANKISH 'VILLA.'

It would be unwise to build too much upon a mere resemblance in terms, but we have seen that the Saxon words generally used for manor were '*ham*' and '*tun*.'

The Saxon ham and the Latin villa.

We have seen how King Alfred, in the remarkable passage quoted in an earlier chapter, put in contrast the temporary log hut on lænland with the permanent hereditary possession—the '*ham*' or manor. This latter was, as we have seen, the estate of a manorial lord, with a community of dependants or serfs upon it, and not a village of coequal freemen. Hence the word *ham* did not properly describe the clusters of scattered homesteads in the Welsh district. In King Alfred's time Cornwall, Devon, Somerset, and even parts of Wiltshire were still, as already mentioned, regarded as Welsh. They formed what was known as West Wales. The manorial system had encroached far into them, but it would seem that the phraseology of the earlier system had not yet wholly disappeared. King Alfred in his will carefully abstained from applying the word *ham* to his numerous possessions in these districts.

He disposed in his will of more than thirty separately named estates in this West Welsh district, but he invariably used, in describing them, the word '*land*'—the *land* or the *landes* at such and such a place;—and he concluded this part of his will with the statement, 'These are all that I have in *Wealcyne*, except in *Truconstirie*' (Cornwall). Then in the rest of his will King Alfred disposed of nearly as many estates in the south-east or manorial districts of England, and here he immediately changed his style. It was no more the *land* at this place and that, but the *ham* at such and such a place.[1] In the old English translation of the will given in the *Liber de Hyda*

---

[1] *Liber de Hyda*, p. 63.

'land' is rendered by 'lond' and 'ham' invariably by '*twune*.'[1] Thus without saying that the words *ham* and *tun* always were used in this sense, and could be used in no other, they were generally at least synonymous with *manor*.

As late as the time of Bede, the suffix 'ham' or 'tun' was not yet so fully embodied with the names of places as to form a part of them. In the Cambridge MS. of his works 'ham' is still written as a separate word.

It is a curious fact that the suffix 'ton' or 'tun' was practically used nowhere on the Continent in the names of places; but the other manorial suffix, 'ham,' in one or other of its forms—'hem,' 'heim,' or 'haim' —was widely spread. And as in those districts where it was found most abundantly, it translated itself, as in England, into the Latin *villa*, its early geographical distribution may have an important significance.

On the annexed map is marked for each county the per-centage of the names of places mentioned in the Domesday Survey ending in *ham*.[2] This will give a fair view of their distribution in Saxon England. It will be seen that the 'hams' of England were most numerous in the south-eastern counties, from Lincolnshire and Norfolk to Sussex, finding their densest centre in Essex.[3]

Passing on to the Continent, very similar evidence, but of earlier date, is afforded for a small district surrounding St. Omer, in Picardy, by a survey of the

[1] *Liber de Hyda*, pp. 67 *et seq.*
[2] The per-centage is under-estimated, owing to the repetition of various forms of the same name having been excluded in counting those ending in *ham*, but not in counting the *total* number of places.
[3] In Essex the *h* is often dropped, and the suffix becomes '*am*.'

estates of the Abbey of St. Bertin, taken about the year 850. The 'villas' there mentioned as '*ad fratrum usus pertinentes*,' and which were distinctly manors, are twenty-five in number, and the names of fifteen of them ended in ' hem.' [1]

Similar evidence is given for various districts in Germany in the list of donations to the abbeys, the abbots· of which possessed estates in different parts of Germany—sometimes whole manors or villages, sometimes only one or two holdings in this or that place.

In the various abbey cartularies.

On the accompanying map are marked the sites of places mentioned in the cartularies of the Abbeys of Fulda,[2] Corvey,[3] St. Gall,[4] Frising,[5] Wizenburg,[6] Lorsch,[7] and in other early records, ending in *heim* in the various districts of Germany. The result is re-

Heims most numerous in the Roman province of Germa- nia Prima.

markable. It shows that these *heims* were most numerous in what was once the Roman province of *Germania Prima*, on the left bank of the upper Rhine, the present Elsass, and on both sides of the Rhine around Mayence—districts conquered by the Frankish and Alamannic tribes in the fifth century, but in- habited by Germans from the time of Tacitus, and perhaps of Cæsar, and so districts in which German populations had come very early and continued long under Roman rule. In this district the *heims* rose in

---

[1] *Chartularium Sithiense*, p. 97.

[2] *Traditiones et Antiquitates Fuldenses.* Dronke, Fulda, 1844.

[3] *Traditiones Corbeienses.* Wi- gand, 1843.

[4] *Urkundenbuch der Abtei St. Gallen*, A.D. 700–840. Wartmann,

Zurich, 1863.

[5] *Historia Frisingensis*, Mei- chelbeck, 1729.

[6] *Traditiones possessionesque Wizenburgenses.* Spiræ, 1842.

[7] *Codex Laureshamensis Diplo- maticus*, 1768.

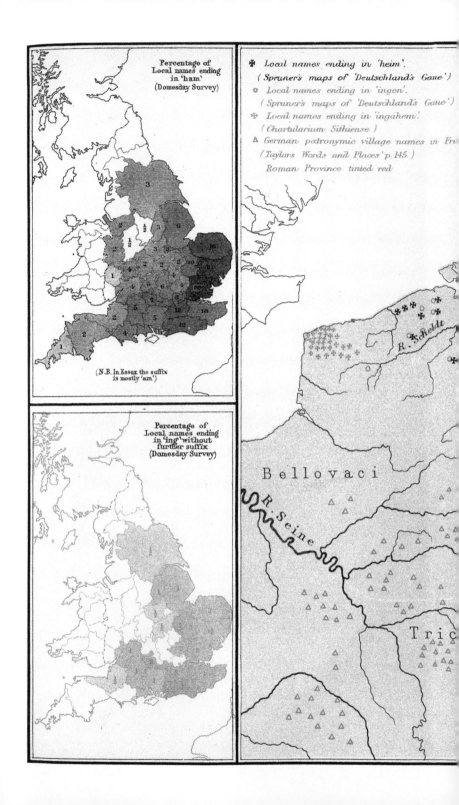

Percentage of
Local names ending
in 'ham'
(Domesday Survey)

(N.B. In Essex the suffix
is mostly 'am')

Percentage of
Local names ending
in 'ing' without
further suffix
(Domesday Survey)

✠ Local names ending in 'heim'.
    (Spruner's maps of 'Deutschland's Gaue')
○ Local names ending in 'ingen'.
    (Spruner's maps of 'Deutschland's Gaue')
✳ Local names ending in 'ingahem'.
    (Chartularium Sithiense)
△ German patronymic village names in Fr[...]
    (Taylor's 'Words and Places' p. 145.)
    Roman Province tinted red

R. Scheldt

Bellovaci

R. Seine

Tric[...]

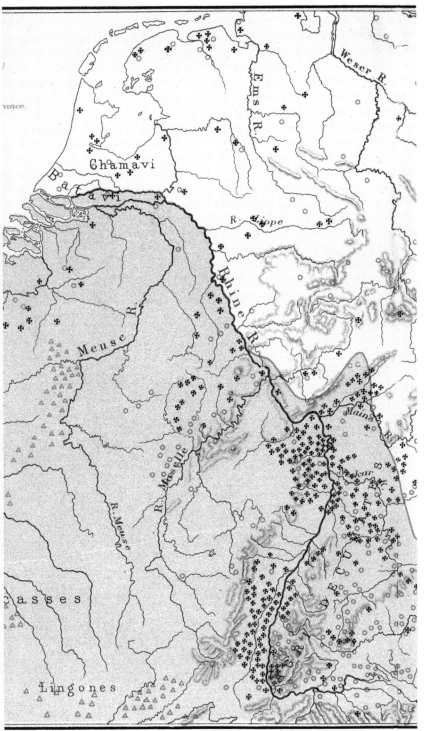

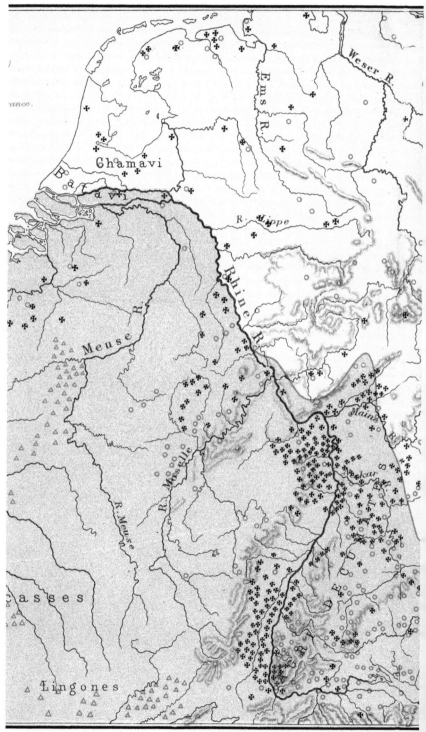

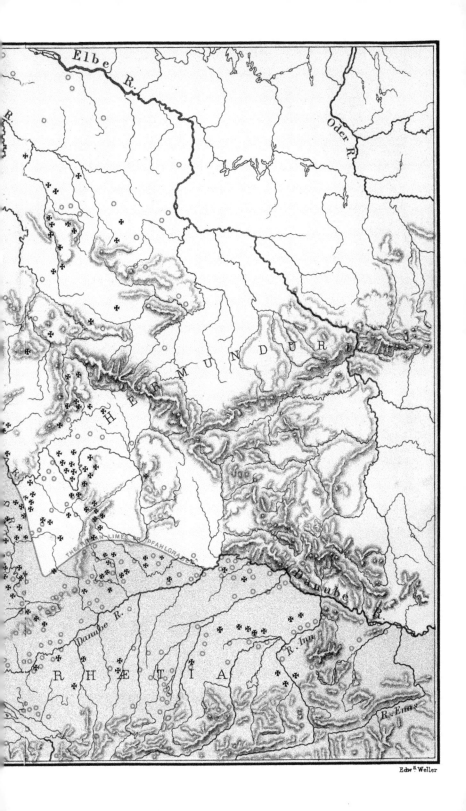

Edwᵈ Weller

number to 80 per cent. of the places mentioned in the charters.

There were many, but not so many, *heims* in the valley of the Neckar ; but everywhere (with small local exceptions) they faded away in districts outside the Roman boundary, except in Frisia, where the proportion was large.

Now, the question is, what do these *heims* represent ?

We have already said that they interchange like the English ' ham' with the Latin ' villa.' The districts where they occur most thickly, where they formed 80 per cent. of the names of places in the time of the monastic grants, and which had formed for several centuries the Roman province of Upper Germany, shade off into districts which abounded with local names ending in *villa*.

Heim and *villa* interchange.

They did so a thousand years ago, and they do so now. It is only needful to examine the Ordnance Survey of any part of these districts to see how, even now, the places with names ending in ' heim' are mixed with others ending in ' villa,' or ' wilare,' or the Germanised form of the word, ' weiler,' or ' wyl ; ' and further, how the region abounding with ' heims' shades off into a district abounding with names ending in ' villa,' or ' wilare,' and we may add the equally manorial Latin or Romance termination *curtis*, or ' court,' and its German equivalent ' hof,' or ' hoven.' And such was the case also at the date of the earliest monastic charters.

Wilare, weiler, and *wyl.*

This fact in itself at least suggests very strongly that here, as in England, ' ham' and ' villa' were synonyms for the same thing, sometimes called by its

s

Latin and sometimes by its German name. Indeed, actual instances may be found in the charters of these districts in which the name of the same place has sometimes the suffix *villa* or *wilare* and sometimes *heim*.[1]

Moreover, these places which are thus called 'villas' or 'heims' in the monastic charters were to all intents and purposes *manors* as far back as the records allow us to trace them.

The earliest surveys of the possessions of the abbeys leave no doubt as to their manorial character.[2]

And the earliest charters prove that they were often at least manorial estates before they were handed over to the monks.

Indeed, a careful examination of the Wizenburg and Lorsch charters and donations leads to the result that these 'heims' and 'villas' were often royal manors, '*villæ fiscales*' on the royal domains, just as Tidenham and Hysseburne were in England. They seem to have often been held as benefices by a *dux*

---

[1] The following are examples of the interchange of villa and heim in the names of places mentioned in the charters of the Abbey of Wizenburg in the district of Spires. The numbers refer to the charters in the *Traditiones Wizenburgenses*.

Batanandouilla (9).
Batanantesheim (28).

Hariolfesuilla (4).
Hariolueshaim (55).

Lorencenheim (141).
Lorenzenuillare (275).

Modenesheim (2).
Moduinouilare (52).

Moresuuilari (189).
Moresheim (181).

Munifridesheim (118).
Munifridouilla (52).

Radolfeshamomarca (90).
Ratolfesham, p. 241.
Radolfouuilari, Radulfo villa (71 and 73). So also, among the manors of the Abbey of St. Bertin, 'Tattinga Villa' granted to the abbey in A.D. 648 (*Chart. Sithiense*, p. 18), called afterwards 'Tattingaheim' (p. 158). See also *Codex Dip.* ii. p. 227, 'Oswaldingvillare' interchangeable with 'Oswaldingtune,' in England. See also *Codex Laureshamensis*, iii. preface.

[2] See *Traditiones Wizenburgenses*, pp. 269 *et seq.* *Codex Laureshamensis*, iii. pp. 175 *et seq.*

or a *comes*, or other beneficiary of the king, just as Saxon royal manors were held by the king's thanes as ' læn-land.' [1]

Thus the royal domains of Frankish kings were apparently under manorial management, and practically divided up into manors. The boundaries or 'marchæ' of one manor often divided it from the next manor; [2] while one 'villa' or 'heim' often had sub-manors upon it, as in the case of Tidenham.[3]

Thus the 'villa,' 'heim,' or 'manor,' seems to have been the usual fiscal and judicial territorial unit under Frankish rule, as the manor once was and the parish now is in England. And this alone seems to afford a satisfactory explanation of the use of the word 'villa' in the early Frankish capitularies, and in the Salic laws. It is there used apparently for both private estates and the smallest usual territorial unit for judicial or fiscal purposes.[4]

When a law speaks of a person attacking or taking possession of the 'villa' of another, the 'villa' is clearly a private estate. But when it speaks of a

---

[1] See among the Lorsch charters that of *Hephenheim* (A.D. 773). 'Hanc villam cum sylva habuerunt in beneficio Wegelenzo, pater Warini, et post eum Warinus Comes filius ejus in ministerium habuit ad opus regis et post eum Bougolfus Comes quousque eam Carolus rex Sancto Nazario tradidit' (I. p. 16).

[2] See again the case of *Hephenheim*. 'Limites. Inprimis incipit a loco ubi Gernesheim marcha adjungitur ad Hephenheim marcham,' &c.

[3] 'Villam aliquam nuncupatam Hephenheim sitam in Pago Renense, cum omni merito et solidi-

tate sua, et quicquid ad eandem villam legitime aspicere vel pertinere videtur.' See also the case of the Manor of 'Sitdiu,' with its twelve sub-estates upon it, granted to the Abbot of St. Bertin A.D. 648. *Chartularium Sithiense*, p. 18.

[4] *Lex Salica*, xxxix. (cod. ii.), 4. 'Nomina hominum et *villarum* semper debeat nominare.'

xlv. (De Migrantibus). When any one wants to move from one 'villa' to another, he cannot do so without the licence of those 'qui in villa consistunt;' but if he has removed and stayed in another 'villa'

crime committed ' between two villas,' the word seems
to be used for a judicial jurisdiction, just as if we
should say ' between two parishes.'

This double use of the word becomes intelligible
if ' villa ' may be used as ' manor,' and if the whole
country—the *terra regis* with the rest—were divided
in the fifth century into ' villas' or ' manors,' but
hardly otherwise.

The remarkable passage in the Salic laws ' *De
Migrantibus*,' which provides that no one can move
into and settle in another ' villa ' without the license
of those ' qui in villa consistunt,' but that after
a twelvemonth's stay unmolested he shall remain
secure, ' sicut et alii vicini,' seems at first sight to
imply a *free village*.[1] But another clause which per-
mits the emigrant to settle if he has the royal ' præ-
ceptum ' to do so,[2] suggests that the ' villa ' in question was one of the royal ' villas'—a ' villa fiscalis '
in the demesne of the Crown.[3]

Ham and
villa in the
Salic laws,

The Salic laws are in Latin, but in the Malberg
glosses they contain some indications that the word
villa was translated by variations of the word *ham*,
then applied by the Franks to both kinds of *villas* in
the manorial sense.

The old tradition recorded in the prologue to the

---

twelve months, ' securus sicut et *alii
vicini* maneat.'

xiv. ' Si quis *villa* aliena adsa-
lierit. . . .'

xlii. v. ' Si quis *villam* alienam
expugnaverit. . . .'

Capitulare Ludovici Primi, viii.
' De eo qui villam alterius occu-
paverit ' (Hessels and Kern's edition,
p. 419).

Chlodovechi Regis Capitula.
Pertz, iv. 4. A.D. 500–1. ' De
hominem inter duas *villas* occisum.'

[1] *Lex Salica*, xlv.

[2] *Id.* xiv.

[3] This inference is drawn by Dr.
P. Roth, *Geschichte des Beneficialwe-
sens*, p. 74. See also *Waitz*, V. G.
ii. 31.

later versions of the Salic laws, whatever it be worth, attributes their first compilation to four chosen men, whose names and residences are as follows :—Uuisogastis, Bodogastis, Salegastis, Uuidogastis, *in loca nominancium*, Bodochamæ, Salchamæ, Uuidochamæ.

In another version of the prologue instead of the words ' *in loca nominancium*,' the reading is ' *in villis*,' and the termination of the names is ' chem,' ' hem,' and ' em.'[1]

Dr. Kern, in editing the Malberg glosses, points out that the gloss in Title xlii. shows that ' *ham* ' might be used by the Franks in the sense of ' court ' —king's court,'—just as in some parts of the Netherlands, especially in the Betuwe, ' *ham* ' is even now a common name for ancient mansions, such as in mediæval Latin were termed ' *curtes*.' Thus he shows that the Frankish words ' *chami theuto* ' (the bull of the ham) were translated in Latin as ' *taurum regis*,' *cham* being taken to mean king's court.[2] Possibly the lord of a *villa* provided the ' village bull,' just as till recent times in the Hitchin manor, as we have seen, the village bull was under the manorial customs provided for the commoners by the rectorial sub-manor.

So in another place the word ' *chamestalia* ' seems to be used in the Malberg gloss for ' in truste *dominica*,'[3] the ' cham' again being taken in a thoroughly *manorial* sense.

That there were manorial lords with *lidi* and tributarii—semi-servile tenants—as well as *servi*, or slaves, under them, is clear from other passages of the Salic laws.[4]

---

[1] Hessels and Kern's edition, pp. 422–3.

[2] By the authors of the *Lex*

Emendata. Note 39, p. 451.

[3] Note 216, p. 528.

[4] Tit. xxvi. (1) ' Si quis lidum

But the 'ham' of the Malberg glosses seems to have had sometimes at least the *king* for its lord. And this brings us again to the double use in the Salic laws of the word 'villa.' It seems, as we have said, to have been used not only for a 'villa' in private hands, but also in a wider sense for the usual fiscal or judicial territorial unit, whether under the jurisdiction of a manorial lord, or of the 'villicus' or 'judex,' or beneficiary of the king.

Lastly, the early date of the Salic laws bringing the Frankish and Roman provincial rule into such close proximity, irresistibly raises the question [1] whether there may not have been an actual continuity, first between the Roman and Frankish villa, and secondly, between the Roman system of management of the imperial provincial domains during the later empire, and the Frankish system of manorial management of the 'terra regis' or 'villæ fiscales' after the Frankish conquest. If this should turn out to have been the case, then the further question will arise whether under the tribal system of the Germans the beginnings of manorial tendencies can be so far traced as to explain the ease with which Frankish and Saxon conquerors of the old Roman provinces fell into manorial ways, and adopted the manor as the normal type of estate.

This is the line of inquiry which it is now proposed to follow.

---

alienum extra consilium domini sui ante Regem per denarium ingenuum dimiserit IIIIM. den. qui faciunt sol. c. culp. judicetur, et capitate domino ipsius restituat. (2) Res vero ipsius lidi legitimo domino restituantur. (3) Si quis servum alie- num,' &c. &c. (H. and K. 136–144).

There were also Roman tributarii, Tit. xli. 'Si quis Romanum tributarium occiderit,' &c. (s. 7).

[1] See on this point Roth, pp. 83 *et seq.*

III. THE ROMAN 'VILLA,' ITS EASY TRANSITION INTO THE
LATER MANOR, AND ITS TENDENCY TO BECOME THE
PREDOMINANT TYPE OF ESTATE.

The Roman *villa* was, in fact, exceedingly like The Roman villa like a manor.
a manor, and, moreover, becoming more and more
so in the Gallic and German provinces, at least under
the later empire as time went on.

The villa, as described by Varro and Columella, An estate.
before and shortly after the Christian era, was a farm
—a *fundus.* It was not a mere residence, but, like
the villa of the present day in Italy, a territory or
estate in land.

The lord's homestead on the villa was surrounded The *curtis.*
by two enclosed 'cohortes,' or courts, from which
was derived the word '*curtis*,' so often applied to the
later manor-house.[1]

At the entrance of the outer court was the abode The *villicus* and slaves.
of the '*villicus*'—a strictly manorial officer, as we have
seen—generally a slave chosen for his good qualities.[2]
Near this was the common kitchen, where not only
the food was cooked, but also the slaves performed
their indoor work. Here also were cellars and
granaries for the storing of produce, the cells in which
were the night quarters of the slaves, and the under-
ground '*ergastulum*,' with its narrow windows, high
and out of reach, where those slaves who were kept
in chains lived, worked, and were tormented; for

---

[1] Varro, i. 13.

[2] Cato, *R. R.* 2. Columella, *R.
R.* i. 6–8. M. Guerard says of the
' villicus,' ' Cet officier est le même
que nous retrouvons au moyen âge
sous son ancien nom de *villicus*, ou
sous le nom nouveau de *major*.'
Polyptique d'Irminon, i. 442.

in the *ergastulum* was revealed the cruel side of the system of slave labour under Roman law. Columella says that the cleverest slaves must oftenest be kept in chains.[1] Cato, according to Plutarch, advised that slaves should be incited to quarrel amongst themselves, lest they should conspire against their master, and considered it to be cheaper to work them to death than to let them grow old and useless.[2]

In the inner 'cohort' were the stalls and stables for the oxen, horses, and other live stock; and all around was the land to be tilled.

Thus the Roman villa, if not at first a complete manor, was already an estate of a lord (dominus) *worked by slaves* under a *villicus*.

Sometimes the whole work of the estate was done by slaves; and though the estimates of historians have varied very much, there is no reason to doubt that in the first and second centuries the proportion of slaves to the whole population of the empire was enormous.

The *decuriæ* of slaves.

But even the management of slaves required organisation. The anciently approved Roman method of managing the slaves on a villa was to form them into groups of *tens*, called *decuriæ*, each under an overseer or *decurio*.[3]

The *villicus*, or general steward of the manor, was sometimes a *freedman*. And there was a strong reason why a freedman was often put in a position of trust, viz. that if he should be dishonest, or show

---

[1] Columella, *De Re Rustica*, i. 8.
[2] Plutarch, *Cato*, c. 21. See *Cod. Theod.* IX. xii.
[3] 'Classes etiam non majores quam denum hominum faciundæ, quas *decurias* appellaverunt antiqui et maxime probaverunt.'—Columella, i. 9.

ingratitude to his patron, he was liable to be degraded again into slavery. There is an interesting fragment of Roman law which suggests that the decurio of a gang of slaves was sometimes a *freedman*, and that it was a common practice to assign to the freedman a portion of land and a *decuria* of slaves, and no doubt oxen also to work it, thus putting him very much in the position of a colonus with slaves under him. The result of his betrayal of trust, in the case mentioned in the fragment, was his degradation, and the resumption by his patron of the *decuria* of slaves.[1] Thus we learn that the lord of a villa might, in addition to his home farm worked by the slaves in his own homestead, have portions of the land of his estate let out, as it were, to farm to *freedmen*, each with his *decuria* of slaves, and paying rent in produce.

There was nothing very peculiarly Roman in this system of classification in *tens*. The fact that men everywhere have ten fingers makes such a classification all but universal. But the Romans certainly did use it for a variety of purposes—for taxation and military organisation as well as in the management of the slaves of a villa. And *M. Guerard*, probably with reason, connects these *decuriæ* of the Roman villa with the *decaniæ*, or groups of originally ten servile holdings, under a villicus or *decanus*, which are described on the estates of the Abbey of St. Germain in the Survey of the Abbot Irminon about A.D. 850.[2] So possibly a survival of a similar system may be traced also in the much earlier instances mentioned by Bede under date A.D. 655, in one of which

Chap. VIII.

Groups of tens.

---

[1] Fragment Jur. Rom. Vatic. 272. Huschke, p. 774.

[2] *Polyptique d'Irminon*, i. pp. 45 and 456.

King Oswy grants to the monastery at Hartlepool twelve *possessiunculæ, each of ' ten families ;'* and in the other of which the abbess Hilda, having obtained a *'possession of ten families,'* proceeds to build Whitby Abbey.[1] In all these cases of the Roman freedman and his *decuria*, the Gallic decanus and his *decania*, and the Saxon *possessiuncula* of ten families, there is the bundle of ten slaves or semi-servile tenants with their holdings, treated as the smallest usual territorial division.[2]

But to return to the Roman villa. The organisation of *decuriæ* of slaves was not the only resource of the lord in the management of his estate.

The coloni, on a villa.

Varro speaks of its being an open point, to be decided according to the circumstances of each farm, whether it were better to till the land by slaves or by freemen, or by *both*.[3] And Columella, speaking of the families or ' hands ' upon a farm, says 'they ' are either slaves or *coloni* ;'[4] and he goes on to say, ' It is pleasanter to deal with coloni, and easier to get ' out of them *work* than *payments*. . . . They will ' sooner ask to be let off the one than the other. The ' best *coloni*,' he says, ' are those which are *indigeni*, ' born on the estate and bound by hereditary ties ' to it.' Especially distant corn farms, he considers. are cultivated with less trouble by free coloni than by slaves under a villicus, because slaves are dishonest and lazy, neglect the cattle, and waste the produce ;

---

[1] Bede, III. c. xxiv. ' Singulæ possessiones decem erant familiarum.'

[2] See also the Anglo-Saxon Chronicle, anno 777, where mention is made of ' 10 bonde lands ' given to the monks at Medeshampstede.

[3] Varro, i. xvii.

[4] Columella, i. vii.

whilst *coloni*, sharing in the produce, have a joint interest with their lord.

That the *coloni* sometimes were *indigeni* upon the estate, and were sometimes called *originarii*, shows the beginning at least of a tendency to treat them as *adscripti glebæ*, like the mediæval ' nativi.' Indeed, we find it laid down in the later laws of the empire that *coloni* leaving their lord's estate could be reclaimed at any time within thirty years.[1] And nothing could more clearly indicate the growth of the semiservile condition of the colonus, as time went on, than the declaration (A.D. 531) that the son of a colonus who had done no service to the ' dominus terræ ' during his father's lifetime, and had been absent more than thirty or forty years, could be recalled upon his father's death and obliged to continue the services due from the holding.[2]

We know from Tacitus that the typical colonus had his own homestead and land allotted to his use, and paid tribute to his lord in corn or cattle, or other produce. And there is a clause in the Justinian Code prohibiting the arbitrary increase of these tributes, another point in which the *coloni* resembled the later *villani*.[3]

A villa under a villicus, with servi under him living within the ' curtis ' of the villa, and with a little group of coloni in their *vicus* also upon the estate, but outside the court, would thus be very much like a later manor indeed. And Frontinus,[4] describing

---

[1] ' Si quis colonus *originalis vel inquilinus* ante hos triginta annos de possessione discessit,' &c. —*Cod. Theod.* v. tit. x. 1.

[2] *Cod. Just.* xi. tit. xlvii. 22.

[3] *Cod. Just.* xi. tit. xlix. 1.

[4] Frontini, Lib. ii. *De controversiis Agrorum.* Lachmann, p. 53.

Village
round a
villa.

the great extent of the *latifundia*, especially of provincial landowners, expressly says that on some of
these private estates there was quite a population
of rustics, and that often there were *villages* surrounding the *villa* like fortifications. It would seem
then that the villas in the provinces were still more
like manors than those in Italy.

The villa
becoming
the preva-
lent type
of estate.

It is now generally admitted that indirectly, at
least, the Roman conquest of German territory—the
extension of the Roman province beyond the Rhine
and along the Danube—added greatly to the number
of semi-servile tenants upon the Roman provincial
estates, and so tended more and more to increase
during the later empire the manorial character of
the 'villa;' whilst at the same time the pressure
of Roman taxation within the old province of Gaul,
and beyond it, was so great as steadily to force more
and more of the free tenants on the *Ager Publicus* to
surrender their freedom and swell the numbers of
the semi-servile class on the greater estates; so that
not only was the villa becoming more and more
manorial itself, but also it was becoming more and
more the prevalent type of estate.

As regards the first point, during the later empire there was direct encouragement given to landowners to introduce barbarians taken from recently
conquered districts, and to settle them on their estates
as *coloni*, and not as slaves. These foreign coloni
became very numerous under the name of *tributarii*
and perhaps ' læti ;' so that the proportion of coloni to

' Frequenter in provinciis . . . .
habent autem in saltibus privati
non exiguum populum plebeium et
vicos circa villam in modum muni-
tionum.'

slaves was probably, during the later period of Roman rule, always increasing, and the Roman villa under its *villicus* was becoming more and more like a later manor, with a semi-servile village community of *coloni* or *tributarii* upon it in addition to the slaves.[1]

As regards the second point, the evidence will be given at a later stage of the inquiry.

Confining our attention at present to the Roman villa, and the slaves and semi-servile tenants upon it, we have finally to add to the fact of close resemblance to the later manor and manorial tenants proof of actual historical connexion and continuity in districts where the evidence is most complete.

A clear and continuous connexion can be traced in many cases, at all events in Gaul, between the Roman villa and the later manor.

In the letters of Sidonius Apollinaris the Visigothic and Burgundian invaders are described as adapting themselves roughly and coarsely to Roman habits in many respects. He speaks of their being put into the 'villas' as 'hospites.' Indeed, it is well known that these Teutonic invaders settled as invited guests, being called *hospites* or *gasti* ;[2] that they shared the villas and lands of the Romans on the same system as that which was adopted when Roman legions—often of German soldiers—were quartered on a district, according to a well-known

German lords of villas.

---

[1] *Cod. Theod.* v. tit. iv. 3, A.D. 409. By this edict liberty is given for landowners to settle upon their property, as free *coloni*, people of the recently conquered 'Scyras' (a tribe inhabiting the present 'Moravia').

[2] Sid. Apol. *Epist.* ii. xii. He complains that a governor partial to barbarians '*implet villas hospitibus.*'

passage of the ' Codex Theodosianus.'[1] They took their *sortes*, or fixed proportions of houses and lands and slaves, and, sharing the lordship of these with their Roman ' *consortes*,' they must have sanctioned and adapted themselves to the manorial character of the villas whose occupation they shared, ultimately becoming themselves lords of villas probably as manorial as any Roman villas could be.[2]

Dr. P. Roth has shown that in Frankish districts many of the wealthy provincials remained, under Frankish rule, in unbroken possession of their former estates—their numerous ' villæ.' Amongst these the bishops and abbots were conspicuous examples. He shows that thousands of ' villæ' thus remained unchanged upon the widely extended ecclesiastical estates.[3]

Gregory of Tours speaks of the restitution by King Hildebert of the ' villas ' unjustly seized under the lawless regime of Hilperic.[4] He also relates how bishops and monasteries were endowed by the transfer to them of villas with the slaves and coloni upon them.

Villas
given to
the
Church.
Under the year 582, he mentions the death of a certain *Chrodinus*, also the subject of a poem by Fortunatus, a great benefactor of the clergy, and describes him as ' founding villas, setting vineyards, ' building houses [*domos*], making fields [*culturas*],' and then, having invited bishops of slender means to

---

[1] *Cod. Theod.* lib. vii. tit. viii. 5. Compare as regards the *Burgundian* settlement the passages in the *Burgundian Laws,* carefully commented upon in Binding's ' *Das Burgundisch-Romanische König-reich, von* 443 *bis* 532 A.D.,' 1, c. i.

s. ii. *et seq.*

[2] Binding, p. 36. And they called them *villas. Leges Burg.* T. 38-9.

[3] Roth's *Geschichte des Benefi-cialwesens,* p. 81.

[4] *Hist. Francorum,* f. 344.

his table, after dinner 'kindly distributing these
'*houses, with the cultivators and the fields, with the*
'*furniture, and male and female servants and house-*
'*hold slaves* [*ministris et famulis*], saying, "These are
' "given to the Church, and whilst with these the
' "poor will be fed, they will secure to me favour
' "with God." '[1]

Here, then, after the Frankish conquest, we have
the word *villa* still used for the typical estate; and the
estate consists of the *domus*, with the vineyards and
the fields, and their cultivators.

Turning to the earliest monastic records we have
seen that the 'villas' or 'heims' of the abbeys of
Wizenburg and Lorsch were in fact manors.

The donations to the Abbot of St. Germain-des-
Prés,[2] in the neighbourhood of Paris, commenced in
the year 558, and in the survey of the estates of the
Abbey made in the year 820, there are described
villas still cultivated by *coloni, leti*, &c.—villas which
grew into villages which now bear the names of the
villas out of which they sprang :—

> *Levaci Villa*, now *Levaville* (p. 90).
> *Landulfi Villa*, now *Landonville* (p. 94).
> *Aneis Villa*, now *Anville*.
> *Gaudeni Villa*, now *Grinville* (p. 99).
> *Sonani Villa*, now *Senainville* (p. 100).
> *Villa Alleni*, now *Allainville* (p. 102).
> *Ledi Villa*, now *Laideville* (p. 102).
> *Disboth Villa*, now *Bouville* (p. 104).
> *Mornane Villare*, now *Mainvilliers* (p. 112).
> And so on in numbers of instances.

The chartulary of the Abbey of St. Bertin also

---

[1] *Hist. Francorum*, f. 295.

[2] *Polyptique d'Irminon.* Large
donations were made to the abbey
as early as A.D. 558 by the Frankish King Hildebert. See M. Guerard's Introduction, p. 35.

contains instructive examples. By the earliest charter
of A.D. 648 the founder of the abbey granted to the
monks his villa called ' *Sitdiu*,' and it included within
it twelve sub-estates, one of them, the *Tattinga Villa*,
which later is called in the cartulary *Tattingaheim*.[1]

The chief villa with these sub-estates was granted
to the abbey ' *cum domibus, ædificiis, terris cultis et
' incultis, mansiones cum silvis pratis pascuis, aquis
' aquarumve decursibus, seu farinariis, mancipiis, acco-
' labus, greges cum pastoribus*,' &c. &c., and therefore
was a manor with both slaves (*mancipia*) and *coloni*,
or other semi-servile tenants (*accolæ*) upon it, as indeed
were the generality of villas handed over to the
monasteries.

There seems, therefore, to be conclusive evidence
not only of a remarkable resemblance, but also in
many cases of a real historical continuity between
the Roman ' *villa* ' and the later Frankish manor.

IV. THE SMALLER TENANTS ON THE AGER PUBLICUS IN
ROMAN PROVINCES—THE VETERANS.

Passing from that part of the land in Roman
provinces included in the villas, or *latifundia*, of the
richer Romans, and so placed under private lordship,
we must now turn our attention to the wide tracts of
' *Ager Publicus*,' and try to discover the position and
social economy of the tenants, so to speak, on the
great provincial manor of the Roman Emperor.

Care must be taken to discriminate between the

---

[1] *Chartularium Sithiense*, pp. 18 and 158.

different classes of these tenants, some of them being of a free and some of them of a semi-servile kind.

First, there were the veterans of the legions, who, according to Roman custom, were settled on the public lands at the close of a war, by way of pay for their services.

For the settlement of these, sometimes regularly constituted military *coloniæ* were founded ; and in this case, where everything had to be started *de novo*; a large tract of land was divided for the purpose by straight roads and lanes—pointing north, and south, and east, and west—into *centuriæ* of mostly 200 or 240 *jugera*, which were then sub-divided into equal rectangular divisions, according to the elaborate rules of the *Agrimensores*,[1] the odds and ends of land, chiefly woods and marshes, being alone left to be used in common by the ' vicini,' or body of settlers.

But in other cases the settlement was much more irregular and haphazard in its character.

Sometimes the veteran received his pay and his outfit, and was left to settle wherever he could find un-occupied land—' *vacantes terræ* —to his mind. Under the later empire, owing to the constant ravages of German tribes, there was no lack of land ready for cultivators, without the appliance of the red-tape rules of the *Agrimensores*. The veterans settled upon this and occupied it pretty much as they liked, taking what they wanted according to their present or prospective means of cultivating it. Lands thus taken were called ' *agri occupatorii*,' and were irre-

---

[1] Mr. Coote has pointed out many remains of this centuriation in Britain; and the inscriptions on many centurial stones are given in *Hübner's* collection.

gular in their boundaries and divisions, instead of being divided into the rectangular *centuriæ.*[1]

It is to these more irregular occupations of territory that the chief interest attaches.

Outfit of oxen and seed of two kinds.
When, under the later empire, veterans were allowed to settle upon ' *vacantes terræ,*' they had assigned to them an outfit of oxen and seed closely resembling the Saxon ' setene ' and the Northumbrian ' stuht.'

Those of the upper grade, whether so considered from military rank or special service rendered by them to the State, were provided, according to the edicts of A.D. 320 and 364, with an outfit of *two pairs of oxen* and 100 modii of each of two kinds of seed. Those of lower rank received as outfit one pair of oxen and fifty modii of each of the two kinds of

Single or double *juga.*
seed.[2] And the land they cultivated with these single or double yokes of oxen was perhaps called their single or double *jugum.* Cicero, in his oration

---

[1] Siculus Flaccus, Lachmann and Rudorff, i. pp. 136-8.

[2] *Cod. Theod.* lib. vii. tit. xx. 3. A.D. 320. 'Constantinus ad universos veteranos.' 'Let veterans according to our command receive vacant lands, and hold them "immunes" for ever; and for the needful improvement of the country let them have also 25 thousand *folles,* a pair of oxen (*boum quoque par*), and 100 modii of different kinds of grain, &c. (*frugum*).'

Ib. s. 8. 'Valentinianus et Valens ad universos provinciales,' A.D. 364. 'To all deserving veterans we give what dwelling-place (*patriam*) they wish, and promise perpetual "immunity."

'Let them have vacant or other lands where they chose, free from stipendium and annual " præstatio." Further, we grant them for the cultivation of these lands both animals and seed, so that those who have been protectores (body-guards) should receive two pairs of oxen (*duo boum paria*) and 100 modii, of each of the two kinds of corn (*fruges*)—others after faithful service a single pair of oxen (*singula paria boum*) and 50 modii of each of the two kinds of corn, &c. If they bring male or female slaves on to the land, let them ossess them "immunes" for ever

against Verres, speaks of the Sicilian peasants as
mostly cultivating '*in singulis jugis*.'[1] During the
later empire the typical holding of land—the hypothetical unit for purposes of taxation—as we shall
see, came to be the *jugum*, but the assessment no
longer always corresponded with the actual holdings.

But to return to the holding of the Roman veteran.
It is not impossible to ascertain roughly its normal
acreage from the amount of seed allotted in the outfit, as well as from the number of oxen.

A single pair of oxen was, as we have seen, allotted
under Saxon rules as outfit to the yard-land of
thirty acres, of which, under the three-field or three-
course system, ten acres would be in wheat, ten in
oats or pulse, and ten in fallow. With the single
pair of oxen was allotted to the veteran fifty modii
of wheat seed, and fifty of oats or pulse. Five
modii of wheat seed, according to the Roman writers
on agriculture, commonly went to the jugerum;[2] so
that the veteran with a single yoke of oxen had seed
for ten jugera of wheat, and thus was apparently assumed to be able to cultivate, if farming on the
three-course system, about thirty jugera in all, like
the holder of the Saxon yard-land. The veteran to
whom was assigned the double yoke of four oxen
and 200 modii of seed—100 modii of each kind—
would have about 60 jugera in his double holding.

Of course, too much stress should not be placed
upon any close correspondence in the number of
jugera; but it is, on the other hand, perfectly natural

---

[1] *In Verrem*, Actio 2, lib. iii. 27. | Columella, ii. 9. Guerard, *Irminon*,
[2] Varro, *De Re Rustica*, i. 44. | i. 1.

that, in the theory of these outfits, seed should be given for a definite area, and that this should be some actual division of the centuria of the *Agrimensores*.

Siculus Flaccus, who wrote about A.D. 100, and chiefly of Italy, describes how, in the regular allotments by the *Agrimensores*, one settler, according to his military rank, would receive a single modus, another one and a half, and another two modii, whilst sometimes a single allotment was given *to several people jointly*. He mentions also that the *centuriæ* varied in size, being sometimes 200 jugera and sometimes 240 ; the smaller lots also sometimes varying in size, even in the same centuria, according to the fertility or otherwise of the land.[1]

Normal
centuria,
200 and
240 jugera.

All we can say is that the centuria of 240 jugera would be divisible into single and double holdings of thirty and sixty jugera respectively, just as the English double hide of 240 acres, or single hide of 120 acres, was divisible into yard lands of thirty acres. The centuria of 200 jugera would be divisible into holdings of fifty and twenty-five jugera respectively.[2]

Passing from the outfit and the holdings, it may

---

[1] Siculus Flaccus, *De Condicionibus Agrorum*. Lachmann and Rudorff, i. pp. 154–6.

[2] In the division of the land between the Romans and Visigoths the amount allotted '*per singula aratra*' was to be 50 aripennes (i.e. 25 jugera). *Lex Visigothorum*, x. 1, 14 (A.D. 650 or thereabouts).

The *Liber Coloniarum I.* describes the 'ager *jugarius*' as 'in

quinquagenis jugeribus,' the 'ager *meridianus* in xxv. jugeribus.' Lachmann, i. 247. Here we have the normal divisions of the centuria of 200 jugera into holdings of 25 and 50 jugera. On the other hand, the *Lex Thoria*, B.C. 111, fixed 30 jugera as the largest holding to be recognised on the public lands. Rudorff, p. 213 (*Corp. Jur. Lat.* 200, l. 14).

be asked, what was the system of cultivation? was it an open field husbandry?

It is obvious that formal centuriation in straight lines and rectangular divisions, by the *Agrimensores*, produced something entirely different from the open field system as we have found it in England. But Siculus Flaccus records that in some cases, when vacant districts were occupied by settlers without this formal centuriation, as ' *agri occupatorii*'—the settlers taking such tracts of land as they had the means or expectation of cultivating—the boundaries were irregular, and followed no rules but those of common sense and the custom of the country.[1] And he gives as an instance of such a common-sense rule the custom about ' *supercilia*,' or *linches*, the sloping surface of which, where they formed boundaries between the land of two owners, should be kept the same number of feet in width, the slope always belonging to the upper owner, because otherwise it would be in the power of the lower owner, by ploughing into the slope, to jeopardise the upper owner's land.[2] This, he says, is the reason of the rule that the land of the owner of the upper terrace generally descends to the bottom of the slope.[3]

Traces of an open-field husbandry in some cases.

Supercilia or linches.

Here, in this mention of *linches* and irregular boundaries, traces seem to turn up of an open-field husbandry; and a few pages further on the same writer makes another observation which shows clearly that frequently the holding, like the yard-land, was

The holdings sometimes composed of scattered pieces.

---

[1] P. 142. ' Quam maxime secundum consuetudinem regionum omnia intuenda sunt.'

[2] P. 143. See also Frontinus,

p. 43, and Hyginus, p. 115, and p. 128 on the same point.

[3] P. 152.

composed of *scattered pieces* in open fields, and that this scattered ownership, as in England, was the result of an original joint occupation, and probably of a system of co-operative ploughing.

He says[1] that in many districts were to be found *possessores* whose lands were not contiguous, but made up of little pieces scattered in different places, and intermixed with those of the others, the several owners having common rights of way over one another's land to their scattered pieces, and also to the common woods, in which the *vicini* only have common rights of cutting timber and feeding stock.

This reference to the common woods and rights of way belonging only to the ' vicini ' seems to show that the scattering of the pieces in the holdings had arisen as in the later open-field system, from an original co-operation of ploughing or other cultivation.

The result of joint occupation.
Connecting these statements with the previous one, that sometimes land was assigned to *a number of settlers jointly*, and that sometimes settlers took possession, without centuriation, of so much land as they could cultivate, and transferring these same methods from Italy, where Flaccus observed them, to transalpine provinces, where larger teams were

---

[1] Siculus Flaccus, Lachmann, p. 152. ' Præterea et in multis regionibus comperimus quosdam possessores non continuas habere terras, sed particulas quasdam in diversis locis, intervenientibus complurium possessionibus : propter quod etiam complures vicinales viæ sint, ut unusquisque possit ad particulas suas jure pervenire. Sed et de viarum conditionibus locuti sumus. Quorundam agri servitutem possessoribus ad particulas suas eundi redeundique præstant. Quorundam etiam vicinorum aliquas silvas quasi publicas, immo proprias quasi vicinorum, esse comperimus, nec quemquam in eis cedendi pascendique jus habere nisi vicinos quorum sint : ad quas itinera sæpe, ut supra diximus, per alienos agros dantur.'

needful for ploughing, it would seem that we may
rightly picture bodies of free settlers on the 'ager
publicus' as frequently joining their yokes of oxen
together to plough their allotments on the open-
field system. And if this was done by retired
veterans on public land, they were probably only
following the common method adopted by the *coloni*
on the villas of the richer Roman landowners in the
provinces. If they did so, they probably simply
adopted the custom of the country in which they
settled, and followed a method common not only to
Gaul and Germany, but also to Europe and Asia.[1]

Even in the case of the regular centuriation, there
was an *opportunity*, apparently, for joint occupation,
and probably often a necessity for joint ploughing.

The method of centuriation.

Hyginus, describing the mode of centuriation,
speaks first of the two broad roads running north
and south and east and west; and then he says the
'*sortes*' were divided, and the names recorded in tens
(*per decurias, i.e. per homines denos*), the subdivision
among the ten being left till afterwards.[2] It does
not follow, perhaps, that the subdivision was always
made in regular squares. There may sometimes
have been a common occupation and joint ploughing; but of this we know nothing.

The retired veterans were a privileged class, and
specially exempted from many public burdens;[3] but
in other respects there is no reason to suppose that
in their methods of settlement and agriculture, and

The veterans a privileged class.

---

[1] Teams of six and of eight oxen in the plough are mentioned in the Vedas. '*Altindisches Leben*,' H. Zimmer. Berlin, 1879, p. 237.

[2] Hyginus, Lachmann and Rudorff, i. 113.

[3] See *Codex Theodosianus*, vii. tit. xx. s. 9, A.D. 366.

———
in the size of their holdings proportioned to their single or double yokes, they differed from other free settlers or ancient original tenants on the *ager publicus*. We may add that, following the usual Roman custom, these settlers probably as a rule lived in towns and villages, and not on their farms. We may assume that, having single or double yokes of oxen and outfits of two kinds of seed, they were arable and not pasture farmers, with their home-steads in the village and their land in the fields around it—in some places under the three-field system, in others with a rectangular block of land on which they followed the three-course or other rotation of crops for themselves.

Groups of settlers may therefore be regarded as sometimes forming something very much like a free village community upon the public land of the Empire, with no lord over it except the fiscal and judicial officers of the Emperor.

V. THE SMALLER TENANTS ON THE 'AGER PUBLICUS' (*continued*)—THE LÆTI.

The *Læti* a semi-servile class, like the Welsh *taeogs*.

In the second place, there were settlers of quite another grade—families of the conquered tribes of Germany, who were forcibly settled within the *limes* of the Roman provinces, in order that they might repeople desolated districts or replace the other-wise dwindling provincial population—in order that they might bear the public burdens and minister to the public needs, *i.e.* till the public land, pay the public tribute, and also provide for the defence of the empire. They formed a semi-servile class, partly agricultural and partly military ; they furnished corn for the granaries and soldiers for the cohorts of the empire, and were generally known in later times by the name of '*Læti*,' or '*Liti*.'[1] They were somewhat in the same position as the Welsh '*taeogs*' or '*aillts*.' They were foreigners, without Roman blood, and hence a semi-servile class of occupiers distinct from, and without the full rights of, Roman citizens[2]—a class, in short, upon whom the full burden of taxation and military service could be laid.

Probably this system had been followed from the time of Augustus, as a substitute for the earlier and more cruel course of sending tens of thousands of vanquished foes to the Roman slave market for sale ; but it became a more and more important part of the imperial defensive policy of Rome during the later empire, as the inroads of barbarians became more and more frequent.

There is clear evidence, from the third century, of the extension of this kind of colonisation over a wide district. It is important to realise both its extent and locality.

In order fully to comprehend the meaning and consequences of this German colonisation of Roman provinces, it must be borne in mind that the rich lands on the left bank of the Rhine, between the Vosges mountains and the river, had been settled

---

[1] In *Cod. Theod.* vii. xx. s. 10, A.D. 369,' læti ' are mentioned ; and in s. 12, A.D. 400, ' lætus Alamannus Sarmata, vagus, vel filius veterani,' are mentioned together.

[2] Compare the Welsh *aillt*, or *alltud* (Saxon *althud*, foreigner), and the *Aldiones* of the Lombardic laws, with the *Læti*.

CHAP.
VIII.

A German
population
already in
Rhætia,
the *Agri
Decumates,*
and in
Elsass.

by Germans before the time of Tacitus. Strabo [1] distinctly says that the Suevic tribes, who in his day dwelt on the east bank of the Rhine, had driven out the former German inhabitants, and that the latter had taken refuge on the west bank. Tacitus describes three German tribes as settled in this district (now Elsass). [2] Further, the large extent of country to the east of the Rhine, within the Roman lines, reaching from Mayence to Regensburg, included in the *Agri Decumates* and the old province of Rhætia (*i.e.* what is now Baden, Wirtemberg, and Bavaria), had by the third century become filled with straggling offshoots from various German and mostly Suevic tribes who had crossed the ' Limes '—a mixed population of Hermunduri, Thuringi, Marcomanni, and Juthungi, with a sprinkling of Franks, Vandals, Longobards, and Burgundians,—some of them friendly, some of them hostile to the empire and gradually becoming absorbed in the greater group of the ' Alamanni.'

Further, it should be remembered that in the third century offshoots from the Alamanni and the Franks attempted to spread themselves over the country on the Gallic side of the Rhine, assuming, during periods of Roman weakness, a certain independence and even over-lordship, so that Probus found sixty cities under their control. Probus completely reduced them once more into obedience, and again made the Roman authority supreme over the ' Agri Decumates,' and Rhætia as far as the ' Limes.' [3]

---

[1] B. iv. c. iii. s. 4.
[2] *Germania,* 28.
[3] The importance of the *Limes* | or *Pfahlgraben* as marking the extent of Roman rule to the east of the Rhine, has recently been fully

A few years before, Marcus Antoninus, after he had conquered the Marcomanni in this district, had deported many of them into Britain.[1]

Probus followed his example, and deported also into Britain such of the Burgundians and Vandals from the ' Agri Decumates ' as he could secure alive as prisoners, ' in order that they might be useful as security against revolts in Britain.' [2]

He also colonised large numbers of Germans in the Rhine valley (where he introduced, it is said, the vine culture), and some of them in Belgic Gaul. In his report to the Senate he described his victory as the reconquest of all Germany. He boasted of the subjection of the numerous petty kings, and declared that the Germans now ploughed, and sowed, and fought for the Romans. And, as he himself had deported Germans into Britain, his words cover the British as well as the Gallic and German provinces.[3] This victory over the Alamannic tribes and colonisation of them in Britain and Gaul, by Probus, was in A.D. 277.

Very soon afterwards the same policy was again followed in dealing with the Franks, who were plundering and depopulating the Belgic provinces of Gaul further to the north, and ravaging the coasts of Britain.

Chap. VIII.

Forced colonisation in Britain and Belgic Gaul.

Of *Læti* in Belgic Gaul and the Moselle Valley.

---

realised. See Wilhelm Arnold's *Deutsche Urzeit*, c. iii. ' *Der Pfahlgraben und seine Bedeutung.*' See also ' *Allgemeine Geschichte in Einzeldarstellungen* ' (Berlin, 1882), Abth. 48, c. viii. And Mr. Hodgkin's interesting paper on ' The Pfahlgraben' in *Archæologia Æliana*, pt. 25, vol. ix. new series.

Newcastle-on-Tyne, 1882.

[1] Gibbon, c. ix., quoting *Dion. Cas.*, lxxi. and lxxii.

[2] Zosimus, i. p. 68. Excerpta, *Mon. Brit.* lxxv.

[3] Wietersheim's *Geschichte der Völkerwanderung* (Dahn), i. 245. Guerard's *Polypt. d'Irminon*, i. p. 252.

In 286, Carausius, who was put in charge of the Roman fleet, and whose business it was to guard the Gallic and British shores infested by the Saxons and Franks, revolted and proclaimed himself Emperor, defending himself successfully against the Emperor Maximian, and leaguing himself with the Franks and Saxons. In 291, Maximian, after directing his arms against the Franks, deported a number of them and settled them as læti on the vacant lands of the Nervii and Treviri, in Belgic Gaul and in the valley of the Moselle.[1]

The further steps taken by his co-Cæsar Constantius to put an end to the revolt of Carausius are very instructive. He first recovered the haven of Gesoriacum (Boulogne), and cut off the connexion of the British fleet with Gaul. Then he turned northward again upon the districts from whence the Frankish and Saxon pirates had been accustomed to make their ravages upon Britain and Gaul. They were, as has been said, in league with the British usurper, but succumbed to the arms of Constantius. The first use he made of his victory over them was to repeat the policy of his predecessors—to deport a great multitude into those very Belgic districts which they had depopulated by their ravages. This was the time when the districts around Amiens and Beauvais, once inhabited by the Bellovaci, and further south around Troyes and Langres, where the Tricassi and Lingones had dwelt, were colonised by Franks,

Further deportations of Franks, Frisians, and Chamavi.

----

[1] 'Tuo, Maximiane Auguste, nutu, Nerviorum et Treverorum arva jacentia Lætus postliminio restitutus et receptus in leges Francus ex- coluit.' *Eumen. Panegyr. Constantio Cæs.*, c. 21. Guerard, i. 250.

Chamavi, and Frisians; and Eumenius,[1] in his Panegyric, represented them, as Probus had described the
Alamanni, as now tilling the fields they had once
plundered, and supplying recruits to the Roman
legions. A '*pagus Chamavorum*' existed in the ninth
century in this district, and so bore witness to the
extent and permanence of this colony of *Chamavi*,[2]
Similar evidence for the other districts, as we
shall have occasion to see hereafter, is possibly to be
found in the names of places with a Teutonic termination remaining to this day, though the language
spoken is French.

A recent German writer, in a sketch of the reign
of Diocletian, makes the pregnant remark that when
account is taken of all the masses of Germans thus
brought into the Roman provinces, partly as colonists
and partly as soldiers, it becomes clear that the
northern districts of Gaul were already half German
before the Frankish invasion. These German settlers
were valuable at the time as tillers of the land, payers
of tribute, and as furnishing recruits to the legions; but
in history they were more than this, for they were,
partly against their will, the pioneers of the German
' *Völkerwanderung.*'[3]

We have seen that Probus had deported Alamanni into Britain in pursuance of this continuous

---

[1] *Eumen. Paneg. Constantio,* 9.
Guerard, i. 252.

[2] Zeuss, *Die Deutschen und die
Nachbarstämme,* pp. 582-4, quoting
the will of *St. Widrad,* Abbot of
Flavigny in the eighth century:
'In pago *Commavorum,*' 'in pago
'*Ammaviorum.*' In the *Notitia*

Occidentis, cxl., there is mention of
Læti from this district—*Præfectus
Lætorum Lingonensium.* Boeking,
p. 120.

[3] *Kaiser Diocletian und seine
Zeit,* von Theodor Preuss. Leipzig, 1869 (pp. 54-5).

policy. It is curious to observe that when Constantius soon after (in A.D. 306) died at York, and Constantine was proclaimed Emperor in Britain, one of
his supporters was Crocus or Erocus,[1] a king of the
Alamanni, proving that there were Alamannic soldiers
in Britain under their own king—probably, more
properly speaking, a sept or clan under its own chief
—at that date.

But it was not long before both the Alamanni
and the Franks again became troublesome in the
Rhine valley. Under the year 357, in the history of
Ammianus Marcellinus, there is a vivid description of
the struggle of Julian to regain from the Alamanni
the cities on the Lower Rhine which the latter had
occupied, as in the time of Probus, within the Roman
province of Lower Germany. After the decisive
battle of Strasburg, Julian crossed the Rhine at
Mayence and laid waste the country between the
Maine and the Rhine, ' plundering the wealthy farms
' of their crops and cattle, and burning to the ground
' all the houses, *which latter in that district were built*
' *in the Roman fashion.*'[2] He then restored the
fortress of Trajan which protected this part of the
' Limes.' The next year, the Salian Franks having
taken possession of Toxandria, on the Scheldt, Julian
pounced down upon them and recovered possession,
and then set himself ' to restore the fortifications of
' the cities of the Lower Rhine, and to *establish afresh*
' *the granaries which had been burned, in which to stow*

---

[1] ' Quo [Constantio] mortuo,
cunctis qui aderunt adnitentibus,
sed præcipue Eroco Alamannorum
rege, auxilii gratia Constantium
comitato, imperium capit.' *Mon.*

Brit. Excerpta. Ex Sexti Aurelii Victoris *Epitome* (p. lxxii.).

[2] Ammianus Marcellinus, bk.
xvii. c. i. 7.

'*the corn usually imported from Britain.*'[1] This was the occasion on which, according to Zosimus, 800 vessels, more than mere boats, were employed in going backwards and forwards bringing over the British corn, thus proving both the extent of British agriculture and the close connexion between Britain and the province of Lower Germany.

The aggressions of the Alamanni, however, continued, and again we find Ammianus Marcellinus describing how, at the close of a campaign, Valentinian, in A.D. 371, deported into Britain the Bucenobantes, a tribe of the Alamanni from the east banks of the Rhine, immediately north of Mayence. He made them elect Fraomarius as their chief, and then, giving him the rank of a tribune, sent him with his tribe of Alamannic soldiers to settle in Britain, as probably Crocus or Erocus had been sent before him.[2]

This policy of planting colonies of German colonists—even whole clans under their petty chiefs—in the Belgic provinces and Britain, with the double object of keeping up the supply of corn for the empire and soldiers for the legions, was therefore steadily adhered to for several generations. And a further proof of the extent to which the system was carried turns up later in the numerous cohorts of Læti mentioned by Ammianus,[3] and in the '*Notitia*,'[4] as having been drawn from these colonies

---

[1] Am. Marc. bk. xviii. c. ii. s. 3.

[2] *Id.* xxix. c. iv. 7.

[3] *Id.* bk. xx. c. viii. 13.

[4] Among the '*Præfecti Lætorum et Gentilium*' there is mention of the Præfectus Lætorum Teuto- nicianorum, Batavorum, Francorum, Lingonensium, Nerviorum, and Lagensium. *Notitia Occ.* cxl. Böcking, p. 120. See also the valuable annotation '*De Lætis.*' Böcking, 1044 *et seq.*

and placed as garrisons all over Gaul and Germany, but especially on the banks of the Rhine.

It has been necessary to dwell upon this subject because it is needful for the present purpose that it should be fully understood that throughout the German provinces of *Rhœtia*, the *Agri Decumates*, *Upper and Lower Germany*, in *Belgic Gaul*, and in *Britain*, there were large numbers of German semi-servile settlers upon the *Ager Publicus* interspersed among the free coloni and veterans; and that most of the settlers, whether free coloni, veterans, or læti, were engaged in agriculture. Some of them, no doubt, especially since the encouragement said to have been given by Probus to vine culture, may have occupied vineyards in Southern Gaul, or in the valleys of the Rhine and its tributaries.

Lastly, it must also be remembered that there may have been intermixed among the privileged veterans and the overburdened ' læti,' on the public lands, dwindling remains of original Gallic inhabitants, and other free coloni or tenants, not privileged like the veterans, but subject to the various public burdens. Some of these were scarcely to be distinguished, perhaps, in point of law and right from the owners of villas. They may have been holders of slaves, and have had possibly sometimes even free coloni of their own, though varying very much in the size of their holdings, and falling far below the owners of latifundia in social importance. Be this as it may, we shall presently find the free class of landholders, whoever they might be, sinking steadily into a semi-servile condition under the oppression of the Imperial fiscal officers and the burden of the taxation and services

imposed upon them—the *tributum* and *sordida munera*
—the oppressive exaction of which during the later
empire was forcing them gradually to surrender their
freedom, and to seek the shelter of a semi-servile position under the *patrocinium*, sometimes of the fiscal
officer himself, sometimes of the lord of a neighbouring ' villa.'

VI. THE ' TRIBUTUM ' OF THE LATER EMPIRE.

Passing now to the system of taxation and forced
services during the later empire, it will be found to
be of peculiar importance, not only because of its
connexion with the growing manorial tendencies, but
also because the taxation resembled so closely the
system of ' *hidation* ' prevalent afterwards in Saxon
England, and some of the forced services actually
survived in the manorial system.

The system of taxation was modified by the Emperor Diocletian at the very time when the policy of
forced colonisation described in the last chapter was
being carried out.

It was known as the taxation ' *jugatione vel capi-*
tatione '—the tribute or stipendium of so much for
every *jugum* or *caput*.

> The *jugatio* or assess-ment by the *jugum* or *caput*.

' Jugum ' and ' caput ' were names for a hypo-
thetically equal, if not always the same, unit of
taxation.[1]

The ' jugum ' was probably originally taken from
the area which could be cultivated by the single or
double yoke of oxen allotted to the settler, and may

---

[1] *Cod. Theod.* vii. 6, 3. *Per viginti juga seu capita conferant vestem. . .* | *Id.* xi. 16, 6. *Pro capitibus seu jugis suis. . .*

have been a single or double one accordingly. But a person holding a fraction of a *jugum* or *caput* was said to hold only a '*portio*,'[1] and paid, in consequence, a proportion only of the burdens assessed upon the whole jugum.

Now, if the taxation had continued at actually so much per yoke of oxen, the system would have been simple enough; and it would be easy to understand how, whilst the *jugum* represented the unit of taxation for land, the *caput* might be the unit corresponding in value with the jugum, but applying to other kinds of property, such as slaves and cattle, and including the capitation tax levied in respect of wives and children. And this, probably, may be the meaning of the double nomenclature—*jugum vel caput*. At any rate, we know from the Theodosian Code, that the members of a veteran's family were constituent parts of his ' caput.'[2]

The subject is obscure, but the reform of Diocletian seems to have aimed at an equalisation of the taxation according to the value of property.

The *jugum* became a unit of taxation,

This seems to have involved an assessment of various kinds of land in hypothetical *juga*, of the same value (said to be fixed at 2,000 solidi); and this involved a variation in the acreage of the hypothetical *jugum*, according to the richness or otherwise of the land, just as according to Flaccus was the case also as regards the actual centuriæ and allotments.

In one instance in which the figures have been

---

[1] *Cod. Theol.* xi. 17, 4. 'Universi pro portione suæ possessionis jugatio- | nis que ad hæc munia coarctentur.'
[2] *Cod. Theod.* lib. vii. tit. xx. 4.

preserved, viz. for Syria, under the Eastern Empire, the assessment was as follows under the system of Diocletian : [1]—

Of vine-land .	.	5	jugera, or	10	plethra or half-acres.
Arable, first class .	20	,,	40	,,	,,
Arable, second class	40	,,	80	,,	,,
Arable, third class .	60	,,	120	,,	,,

In the east, therefore, sixty jugera, or 120 Greek plethra or half-acres, of ordinary arable land, were assessed as a *jugum.*

This instance makes it clear that while originally the actual allotment to a single or double yoke of oxen may have been taken as the basis of taxation, the ' jugum ' had already become a hypothetical *unit of assessment*, just as, by a similar process, was the case with the English hide. Property had come to be assessed at so many *juga* under the *jugation*, without any attempt to make the assessment accord with the actual number of yokes employed.

The assessment was revised every fifteen years at what was called the *Indiction.*[2]

We have seen that the nominal acreage of the typical holding assigned to the single yoke of two oxen under Roman law on the Continent resembled very closely that of the Saxon yard-land, which also had two oxen allotted with it.[3]

---

[1] See *Syrisch-Römisches Rechts- buch aus dem Fünften Jahrhundert* (Bruns und Sachau), Leipzig, 1880, p. 37; and Marquardt's *Staatsver- waltung*, ii. 220. See also Hy- ginus, *De Limitibus Constituendis*, Lachmann, &c., p. 205, where there is mention of ' *arvum primum, se- cundum,*' &c., in *Pannonia.*

[2] Marquardt, ii. 237.

[3] Not that the Roman jugerum was equal in area to the Saxon acre. It was much smaller, and of quite a different shape, at least in Italy.

We have also seen that the twenty-five or thirty jugera of the single yoke were probably fixed as an eighth of the Roman *centuria*, as the yard-land was the eighth of a double hide.

Analogy of the *jugum* and *centuria* to the yard-land and hide.

The common acreage of the centuria was, as we have seen, 200 or 240 jugera. The latter number may be the simple result of the use of the long hundred of 120 ; or it may have resulted, as suggested above, from the necessity of making the centuria of the free citizen's typical estate divisible into four double holdings of 60 acres, or eight single holdings of 30 acres each.

Be this as it may, the centuria, or typical estate of a free citizen in a regularly constructed Roman colony, seems to have stood to the single or double holding of the common and often semi-servile settler in the same arithmetical relation as the Saxon larger hide of 240 acres did to the yard-land.[1]

We have, then, two kinds of holdings :—

1. The one or more *centuriæ* embraced in the

The acreage of the jugum no doubt varied very much, as did also the acreage of the yard-land.

[1] It is even possible and probable that the Gallic coinage in Roman times, mentioned in the *Pauca de Mensuris* (Lachmann and Rudorff, p. 373), 'Juxta Gallos vigesima pars unciæ denarius est . . . duodecies unciæ libram xx. solidos continentem efficiunt, sed veteres *solidum* qui nunc *aureus* dicitur nuncupabant,'—the division of the pound of silver into 12 ounces, and these into 20 pennyweights— with which we found the Welsh *tunc pound* to be connected, may also have had something to do with the contents of the centuria and jugum. At all events, the division of the pound into 240 pence was very conveniently arranged for the division of a tax imposed upon holdings of 240 acres, or 120 acres, or 60 acres, or 30 acres, or the 10 acres in each field. In other words, the coinage and the land divisions were remarkably *parallel* in their arrangement, as we found was also the case with the *scutage* of the Hundred Rolls, and the *scatt penny* of the villani in the Boldon Book.

latifundia or villas of the large landowners, which, however, when tilled by their coloni, and not by slaves, might well be subdivided into holdings of sixty or thirty acres each.

2. The double and single holdings of the smaller settlers on the 'ager publicus' of fifty or sixty and twenty-five or thirty acres each.

And we may conclude that the system of taxation called the '*jugatio*' was founded upon these facts, though in order to equalise its burden the assessment of an estate or a territory in juga became, under Diocletian, a hypothetical assessment, corresponding no longer with the *actual* number of yokes, just as the Saxon hide *ad geldam*, at the date of the Domesday Survey, no longer corresponded with the actual carucate *ad arandum*.

Another resemblance between the Roman jugation and the Saxon hidage was to be found in the method adopted when it became needful to reduce the taxation of a district.

Thus, the land of the Ædui had been ravaged and depopulated. It had paid the tributum on 32,000 juga; 7,000 juga were released from taxation. In future it was assessed at 25,000 juga only; and so relief was granted.[1]

Further, as the English manorial lord paid the hidage for the whole manor, so the lord of the villa, under Roman law, paid the tributum not only for his own demesne land, but also for the land of his coloni and tenants. Just as the servile tenants of a Saxon thane were called his '*gafol gelders*,' so the semi-

The tributum paid by the lord, who claimed tribute from his tenants, or 'tributarii.'

---

[1] Eumenius, *Pan. Constantini*, Marquardt, S. V., ii. 222.

servile tenants of a Roman lord were called his *tributarii.* In both cases they paid their tribute to their lord, whilst the lord paid the imperial tributum for himself and for them.[1]

Coloni and *tributarii* in Britain.

In a decree of the year 319, issued by Constantine to the 'Vicar of Britain,' words are used which prove that there were *coloni* and *tributarii*[2] on British estates.[3]

Putting all these things together, the analogy between the Roman 'jugation' and the later English hidage can hardly be regarded as accidental.

But to return, at present, to the tribute and the service due from each *jugum* or *caput.*

The Roman 'tributum' and the Saxon 'gafol.'

The tribute was generally paid part in money and part in produce, and was, in fact, a tax. It was a separate thing from the *tithe* of produce, rendered as rent to the State on the tithe-lands of the *Agri decumates* and of Sicily, though all these various annual payments in produce may have been confused together under the term *annonæ.* The *tribute* proper survived probably, as we shall see, in the later manorial '*gafol.*' The *tithe*, or other proportion taken as rent—for the proportion was not always a tenth[4] —more nearly resembled the manorial '*gafol-yrth.*

---

[1] *Cod. Theod.* lib. xi. tit.i. 14.

[2] See also **Ammianus**, xxvii. 8, 7. **Coote**, 131.

[3] *Cod. Theod.* lib. xi. tit. vii. 2. Idem A ad *Pacatianum Vicarium Britanniarum.* Unusquisque decurio pro ea portione conveniatur, in qua vel ipse vel colonus vel tributarius ejus convenitur et colligit ; neque omnino pro alio decurione

vel territorio conveniatur. Id enim prohibitum esse manifestum est et observandum deinceps, quo[d] juxta hanc nostram provisionem nullus pro alio patiatur injuriam. Dat. xii. Kal. Dec. Constantino A. et Licinio C. Coss. (319).

[4] **Hyginus.** Lachmann, &c., i. 205.

But we are not quite ready yet to trace the actual connexion between these Roman and later manorial payments.

VII. THE 'SORDIDA MUNERA' OF THE LATER EMPIRE.

In addition to the payments in kind or rents in produce, called *annonæ*, there were other personal services demanded from settlers in the provinces. They were called '*sordida munera*,' and strangely resembled the base services of later manorial tenants.

There is a special title of the 'Codex Theodosianus' on the 'base services' exacted under Roman law ;[1] so that there is evidence of the very best kind as to what they were.

By an edict of A.D. 328 there was laid upon the *rectores* of provinces the duty of fixing the burden of the services according to three grades of holdings —those of the greater, the middle, and the lowest class—as well as the obligation of seeing that the services were not exacted at unreasonable times, as during the collection of crops. Further, the rectores were also ordered to record with their own hand 'what is the service and how to be performed for 'every "*caput*" [or jugum], whether so many *angariæ* 'or so many *operæ*, and in what way they are to be 'rendered for each of the three grades of holdings.'[2]

---

[1] *Cod. Theod.* lib. xi. tit. xvi, *De Extraordinariis sive Sordidis Muneribus.* See also Godefroy's notes.

[2] Lib. xi. t. xvi. 4. 'Ea forma servata, ut primo a potioribus, dein- de a mediocribus atque infimis, quæ sunt danda, præstentur.' 'Manu autem sua rectores scribere debe- bunt, quid opus sit, et in qua ne- cessitate, per singula capita, vel quantæ angariæ vel quantæ operæ,

———   Certain privileged classes were specially exempted
from these ' base services,' and it happens that edicts
expressly mentioning Rhætia specify from what services they shall be exempt, and so reveal in detail
what the services were.

The province of Rhætia lay to the south of the
Roman *Limes*, and east of the ' Agri decumates ' of
Tacitus, whilst also extending into the Alpine valleys
of the present Graubunden.   The chief city in
North Rhætia, of which we speak (Vindelicia), was
Augusta Vindelicorum (Augsburg), and Tacitus describes the German tribes of the Hermunduri, north
of the *Limes*, as engaged in friendly commerce with
the Romans, and as having perfectly free access not
only to the city, but also to the Roman villas
around it.[1]

What they
were in
Rhætia.   We have seen that in this district south of the
Danube, and in the *Agri decumates* between the
Danube and the Rhine, there were large numbers of
German as well as Roman settlers, occupying land
probably as free ' coloni ' and ' læti,' paying tribute
to the State, in addition to the usual tenth of the
produce and personal services, according to their
grades of holding.   Edicts of A.D. 382 and 390 [2]
represent the tenants and settlers in this Roman province as liable with others to render, in addition to
the tithe of the produce in corn, &c. (*annonæ*), *inter
alia*, the following ' base services ' (*sordida munera*),
viz. :—

---

vel quæ aut in quanto modo præ-
bendæ sint, ut recognovisse se scri-
bant ; exactionis, prædicto ordine
inter ditiores, mediocres, ·atque in-

fimos observando.'
    [1] *Germania*, xli.
    [2] *Cod. Theod.* xi. 16, and 18.

(1) The '*cura pollinis conficiendi, excoctio panis,* and *obsequium pistrini,*' *i.e.* the preparation of flour, making of bread, and service at the bakehouse.

The supply of so many loaves of bread is a very common item of the later manorial services everywhere.

(2) The *præbitio paraveredorum et parangariarum.* These also were services found surviving, in fact and in name, amongst the later manorial services. The *angariæ*[1] and the *veredi*[2] were carrying services, with waggons and oxen or with packhorses, on the main public Roman roads. The *parangariæ* and *paraveredi* were *extra* carrying services *off* the main road. There is a special title of the Codex Theodosianus ' *De Cursu Publico, Angariis et Parangariis,*'[3] in which, by various edicts, abuses are checked and the services restrained within reasonable limits, both as to the weight to be carried and the number of oxen or horses required.

Carrying services also are familiar in manorial records under the name of '*averagium.*' In the Hundred Rolls and the Cartularies, and in the Domesday Survey, they occur again and again ; and in the Anglo-Saxon version of the ' *Rectitudines,*' in describing the services of the ' geneat ' or ' villanus,' the Latin words ' equitare vel *averiare* et summagium

---

[1] From *angarius* = ἄγγαρος, a messenger or courier. The word is probably of Persian origin.

' Nothing mortal travels so fast as these Persian messengers. The entire plan is a Persian invention. . . The Persians give the riding post the name of " *angarum.*" '—*Hero-*

dotus, bk. viii. 98.

See also the *Cyropædia,* bk. viii. c. 17, where the origin of the post-horse system is ascribed to Cyrus.

[2] From the Latin *veredus,* a post-horse.

[3] *Cod. Theod.* lib. viii. t. v.

ducere,' are rendered ' ꝛiꝺan ꞇ aueꝛian ꞇ laꝺe læꝺan.'
Also, in the record of the services of the Tidenham
' geneats ' the words run, ' *ridan, and averian, and lāde*
' *lædan, drāfe drīfan,*' &c.[1] At the same time, on the
Continent the word ' *angariæ* ' became so general a
manorial phrase as to be almost equivalent to ' villein
services ' of all kinds.[2]

The carrying and post-horse services, more strictly
included in the manorial *angariæ* and *averagium,*
extended over Britain, Gaul, and the German provinces.

(3) The ' *obsequia operarum et artificum diver-
sorum* '—the doing all sorts of services and labour
when required—like the Saxon ' boon-work,' which
formed so constant a feature of manorial services
in addition to the gafol and regular week-work. How
could the words be better translated than in the
Anglo-Saxon of the Tidenham record—' and sela ōdra

---

[1] The ' *veredus* ' or post-horse,
from which the *paraveredus* or
extra post-horse, sometimes *parhippus* (all these words occur in the
Codex Justin. xii. 1. [li.], 2 and 4,
De Cursu Publico), may have been
equivalent to the later ' averius ' or
' affrus ' by which the *averagium*
was performed. Cf. ' *Parhippus*
vel Avertarius ' (*Cod. Theod.*
VIII. v. xxii.) and see Id. xlvii.,
' *avertarius* = a horse carrying
' averta ' or saddlebags. Hence,
perhaps, the base Latin *avera,
averiæ, averii, affri,* beasts of
burden, oxen, or farm horses, and
the verb ' *averiare* ' (Saxon of
10th century ' *averian*'), and lastly
the noun ' averagium ' for the
service. See also the Gallic *Ep-o-*
rediæ (men of the horse-course)
mentioned by Pliny iii. 21 (Dr.
Guest's *Origines Celticæ,* i. 381),
and compare this word with *paraveredi.* In modern Welsh ' Rhed '
= a running, a course.

[2] Compare the careful paragraphs on these words in M.
Guerard's Introduction to the *Polyptique de l'Abbé Irminon,* pp. 793
et seq. The sense of the word as
implying a compulsory service is
shown in the Vulgate of Matt. v. 4 :
' Et quicunque te *angariaverit* mille
passus : vade cum illo et alia duo.'

The same word is used in Matt.
xxvii. 32, and Mark xv., where
Simon is *compelled* to bear the
cross.

þinga dón,' '*and shall do other things,*' qualified by the previous words, ' swá him man byt,' ' *as he is bid* ' ? [1]

(4) The ' *obsequium coquendæ calcis* '—lime-burning. This was one of the specially mentioned services of the servi of the Church in Frankish times, under the Bavarian laws, in this very district of Rhætia, as we shall see by-and-by.

(5) The *præbitio materiæ, lignorum, et tabulorum; cura publicarum vel sacrarum ædium construendarum atque reparandarum; cura hospitalium domorum et viarum et pontium* '—the supply of material, wood, and boarding for building, repairing, or constructing public and sacred buildings, and the keeping up of inns, roads, and bridges. Here we have two out of the ' three needs ' marking in England the higher service of the Saxon thane.

Building,
&c., and
support of
inns, roads,
and
bridges.

Such were the chief ' *sordida munera* ' of the settlers in Rhætia and other Roman provinces. But servile as they were, and like as they were to the later manorial services, we must not therefore conclude that the settlers from whom they were due— whether German or Roman, in Romano-German provinces—were under Roman law necessarily *serfs.* They were, as we have said, ' free coloni ' or ' læti,' and below them were the ' servi.' The three grades in which they were classed, ' *ditiores, mediocres, atque infimi,*' marked gradations of wealth,—probably according to the number of yokes of oxen held, or the size of their holdings—not necessarily degrees of freedom.[2]

---

[1] *Supra,* p. 154.

[2] There were probably *servi* on the ' ager publicus ' as there were on the Frankish public lands, called ' *servi fisci.*' See *Decretio Chlotharii regis,* A.D. 511, 558. *Mon, Germ. Hist. Legum Sectio,* ii. p. 6,

VIII. THE TENDENCY TOWARDS A MANORIAL MANAGE-
MENT OF THE 'AGER PUBLICUS,' OR IMPERIAL DOMAIN.

Having now examined into the character of the
holdings, tribute, and 'sordida munera' of the
tenants on what may be called the great provincial
manor of the Roman emperor, it may perhaps be possible to trace some steps in the process by which these
tenants became in some districts practically serfs on
the royal villas or manors of the Teutonic conquerors
of the provinces.

The beginning of the process can be traced apparently at work during the later empire.

The Im-
perial mili-
tary and
fiscal
officers.

The German and Gallic provinces had for long
been considered as in an especial sense *Imperial* provinces, and their 'ager publicus' and tithe-lands had
become regarded to a great extent as the personal
domain of the emperors. They were under the
personal control of his imperial *procuratores*, or
agents.[1]

In fact there had grown up strictly imperial
classes of military and fiscal officers with local jurisdiction over larger or smaller areas. There were the
'duces,' or 'magistri militum,' and 'comites,' and
'vicarii,'[2] whilst in the lowest rank of 'procuratores,'
possibly controlling smaller fiscal districts or sub-

---

[1] Compare Dr. J. N. Madvig's
*Die Verfassung und Verwaltung
des Römischen Staates* (Leipzig,
1882), ii. p. 408.

[2] Madvig, ii. p. 573 ; and *Cod.
Just.* xii. 8–14, and *Cod. Theod.*
xii. i. 38. See also the *Notitia
Dignitatum,* passim.

districts, were the ' *ducenarii*,' and ' *centenarii*.'[1] They seem to have combined military, and judicial, and fiscal duties with functions belonging to a local police.

Whatever at first the exact position and authority of these military and fiscal officers of the Emperor may have been, there is evidence that they easily assumed a kind of manorial lordship over the portion of the public domains under their charge in two distinct ways.

In the first place, the ' villa ' in which a military or fiscal officer lived was the fiscal centre of his district. He was the ' villicus ' by whom the ' annonæ,' tribute, and ' sordida munera ' were exacted. In some instances the services seem to have been rendered in the form of work on his ' villa,' or on the villas of ' conductores,' by whom the special products of some districts were sometimes farmed.[2] And there are passages in the Codes which complain of the tendency in these Imperial officers of higher and lower rank to oppress those under their jurisdiction, even sometimes using their services on their own estates, and thus arrogating to themselves almost the position of manorial lords, whilst reducing their fiscal dependants to the position of semi-servile tenants.[3]

Were apt to assume a sort of lordship in their district.

---

[1] With regard to the *procuratores, ducenarii,* and *centenarii* see Madvig, ii. p. 411. See also *Cod. Just.,* xii. 20 (De agentibus in rebus), where a certain ' magister officiorum ' is forbidden to have under him more than 48 *ducenarii* and 200 *centenarii.* Also *Cod. Just.,* xii. 23 (24). Mr. Coote (*Romans in England,* p. 317 et seq.), identifies the ' centenarii '

with the ' stationarii,' or police of the later provincial rule. Compare this with the distinctly police duties of the ' centenarii ' of the ' *Decretio Clotharii*' (A.D. 511–558), *Mon. Germ. Hist.*—Capitularia, p. 7.

[2] Madvig, ii. 432, and the authorities there quoted.

[3] *Cod. Theod.,* xi. tit. 11. i. ' Si quis eorum qui provinciarum Rectoribus exequuntur, quique in

CHAP.
VIII.

Take per-
sons and
villages
under their
*patro-
cinium.*

In the second place, the practice also was complained of by which the fiscal officers, using their influence unduly, induced tenants on the public lands
of their district, and sometimes even *whole villages*, to
place themselves under their '*patrocinium*,' thereby
practically converting themselves into semi-servile
tenants of a mesne lord who stood between them and
the emperor.[1]

The question would be well worth a more careful
consideration than can be given here how far these
tendencies towards the gradual establishment under

diversis agunt officiis principatus,
et qui sub quocumque prætextu
muneris publici possunt esse terri-
biles, rusticano cuipiam necessitatem obsequii, *quasi mancipio sui
juris*, imponat, aut servum ejus aut
bovem in usus proprios necessitatis-
que converterit... ultimo subjugatur
exitio.' Quoting the above Lehuërou observes :—'Les ducs, les
comtes, les recteurs des provinces,
institués pour résister aux puis-
sants et aux forts, n'usèrent plus
de l'autorité de leur charge que pour
se rendre redoutables aux petits
et aux faibles, et se firent un hon-
teux revenue de la terreur qu'ils
répandaient autour d'eux. Ils en-
levaient sans scrupule, tantôt le
bœuf, tantôt l'esclave du pauvre, et
quelquefois le malheureux lui-même
avec sa femme et ses enfants, pour
les employer tous ensemble à la
culture de leurs *villæ*' (p. 140). See
also *Cod. Theod.* viii. t. v. 7 and
15.

[1] *Cod. Theod.*, xi. tit. 24, *De Pa-
trociniis vicorum.* 'Quicumque ex
tuo officio, vel ex quocumque hominum ordine, *vicos* in suum detecti

fuerint patrocinium suscepisse, con-
stitutas luent pœnas. . . . Quos-
cumque autem vicos aut defensionis
potentia, aut multitudine sua fretos,
publicis muneribus constiterit ob-
viari, ultioni quam ratio ipsa dicta-
bit, conveniet subjugari.'

'Censemus ut qui rusticis patrocinia præbere temptaverit, cujuslibet ille fuerit dignitatis, sive
MAGISTRI UTRIUSQUE MILITIÆ, sive
COMITIS, sive ex *pro-consulibus*, vel
vicariis, vel *augustalibus*, vel *tri-
bunis* (*C. J.* xii. 17, 2), sive ex
ordine *curiali*, vel *cujuslibet alterius
dignitatis*, quadraginta librarum
auri se sciat dispendium pro singu-
lorum fundorum præbito patroci-
nio subiturum, nisi ab hac postea
temeritate discesserit. Omnes ergo
sciant, non modo eos memorata
multa ferendos, qui clientelam sus-
ceperint rusticorum, sed eos quoque
qui fraudandorum tributorum causa
ad patrocinia solita fraude confuge-
rint, duplum definitæ multæ dispendium subituros.' (Dat. vi. Id. Mart.
Constantinop., Theodoro v. c. Coss.
399). See also *Lehuërou*, p. 136
139, and *Cod. Just.*, xi. 54.

the later empire of a manorial relation between the
' coloni ' and ' læti ' on the crown lands, and the fiscal
officer of the district in which they lived, were the
beginnings of a process which ended in the division of
the crown lands practically into ' villæ,' or districts
appendant to the villa of the fiscal officer, which in
their turn may have been the prototypes of the villas
or manors on the ' terra regis ' of Frankish and Saxon
kings.[1]

As we have said, the use of the word ' villa '
in the Salic laws and early capitularies, for the
smallest general territorial unit as well as for the
' villa ' of a private lord, would thus perhaps be most
easily accounted for.   And possibly the continuity
which such a result would indicate between Roman
and Frankish institutions might, after all, be confirmed
by the seeming continuity, in name at least, between
the fiscal officers of the later empire and those of the
Salic and Ripuarian, and other early barbarian codes.
The appearance of the *dux* and the *comes* and the
centenarius in these codes, and in the early capitularies,
as the military, fiscal and judicial officers of the Frankish kings, is at least suggestive of continuity in fiscal
and judicial arrangements, though of course it does
not follow that many German elements may not have
been directly imported into institutions which, even
under the later Roman rule in the Romano-German
provinces, already indirectly and to some extent were

Frankish
' Terra
Regis'
divided
into *Villæ*,
or *Manors*.

---

[1] Madvig, ii. 432. ' Wie lange
die Ackersleute auf den Kaiser-
lichen Grundstücken (*Coloni Cæsaris
Dig.* vi. 6, s. 11, i. 19, 3) eine
grössere persönliche Freiheit be-
wahrten, und seit welcher Zeit das
spätere Kolonatsverhältniss galt,
lässt sich nicht bestimmen, da der
Uebergang schrittweise vor sich
ging.'

no doubt the compound product of both Roman and German ingredients.[1]

The settlement of these difficult points perhaps belongs to constitutional rather than to economic history.

The pro-
cess of
commen-
dation
commenced
under
Roman
rule.
Having noticed the evident tendencies of the fiscal district of the later empire to approach the manorial type, and to become a crown villa or manor with dependent holdings upon it, we must pass on to a further important effect of the oppression of the imperial officers. We have noticed the edicts intended to prevent the tenants on the imperial domain from putting themselves under their direct 'patrocinium.' These edicts did not prevent the over-burdened and oppressed tenant from putting himself under the 'patrocinium' of the lord of a neighbouring villa, thereby becoming his semi-servile tenant, in order to escape from the cruel exactions of the tax-gatherer.

This process was called 'commendation,' and it was carried out on a remarkable scale. It consisted in the surrender by the smaller tenants on the public lands of themselves and their property to some richer landowner; so parting with their inheritance and their freedom whilst receiving back a mere occu-pation of their holding by way of usufruct only as a '*præcarium*,' or for life, as a servile tenement, paying

---

[1] In the *Ripuarian Laws*, tit. li. (53) 'Grafio' = '*comes*' = '*judex fiscalis*,' and the *mallus* was sometimes held 'ante centenarium vel comi-tem, seu ante Ducem Patricium vel Regem,' tit. l. (52). So in the *Salic Laws*, tit. lxxv. 'debet *judex*, hoc est, *comes aut grafio*,' &c., but this occurs in one of the additions to the '*Lex Antiqua.*' Compare the 'cen-tenarius' in his relation to his superior, the 'comes,' and in his position of 'judex' in the mallus with the 'centenarius' under *Cod. Just.*, vii. 20, 4.

to their lord the fixed census or 'gafol' of the servile tenant.

By this process they rapidly swelled the number of servile tenants on villas of the manorial type, and hastened the growing prevalence of the manorial system.[1]

This process of commendation was nothing new. It was an old tribal practice at work long before Roman times in Gaul, and destined not only to outlast the Roman rule, but also to receive a fresh impulse afterwards from the German invasions. And as its progress can be traced step by step from Roman times, through the period of conquest into the times of settled Frankish rule, and its history is closely mixed up with the history of the growth of the Roman villa into the mediæval manor, and with the change of the '*sordida munera*' from public burdens into manorial services, it presents useful stepping-stones over a gulf not otherwise to be easily crossed with security.

Cæsar describes how in Gaul, even before the Roman conquest, the free tribesmen, overburdened by the exactions of chieftains and the tributes imposed upon them (probably by way of 'gwestva' or food-rents), surrendered their freedom, and became little more than 'servi' of the chiefs. And so far had this practice proceeded that he describes the people of Gaul as practically divided into two classes—the chiefs, whom he likened to the Roman 'equites;'

---

[1] M. Lehuërou observes, 'Il y a déjà des *seigneurs*, cachés encore sous l'ancienne et familière dénomination de *patrons*. Cela est si vrai que, non seulement la chose, mais le mot se trouve dans Libanius:— Περὶ τῶν προστασιῶν εἰσι κῶμαι μεγάλαι, πολλῶν ἑκάστη δεσποτῶν.

and the common people, who were in a position little removed from slavery.[1]

Further, there is the evidence of Tacitus himself that oppressive Roman exactions were forcing free tribesmen, even in *Frisia*, to surrender their lands and their children into a condition of servitude.[2]

Again, Gregory of Tours[3] describes how, in a year of famine, the poor surrendered their freedom—*subdebant se servitio*—to escape starvation.

---

[1] *De Bello Gallico*, vi. c. xiii.-xv. 'In omni Galliâ eorum hominum qui aliquo sunt numero atque honore genera sunt duo. Nam plebes pœne servorum habetur loco, quæ per se nihil audet et nulli adhibetur consilio. Plerique, quum aut ære alieno aut magnitudine tributorum aut injuriâ potentiorum premuntur, sese in servitutem dicant nobilibus. In hos eadem omnia sunt jura quæ dominis in servos. . . . Alterum genus est *Equitum*. Hi, quum est usus, atque aliquod bellum incidit (quod ante Cæsaris adventum fere quotannis accidere solebat, uti aut ipsi injurias inferrent aut illatas propulsarent), omnes in bello versantur : atque eorum ut quisque est genere copiisque amplissimus, ita plurimos circum se ambactos clientesque habet. Hanc unam gratiam potentiamque noverunt.'

[2] Tacitus, *Annals*, iv. 72. 'In the course of the year the Frisians, a people dwelling beyond the Rhine, broke out into open acts of hostility. The cause of the insurrection was not the restless spirit of a nation impatient of the yoke ; they were driven to despair by Roman avarice. A moderate tribute, such as suited the poverty of the people, consisting of raw hides for the use of the legions, had been formerly imposed by Drusus. To specify the exact size and quality of the hide was an idea that never entered into the head of any man till Olennius, the first centurion of a legion, being appointed governor over the Frisians, collected a quantity of the hides of forest bulls, and made them the standard both of weight and dimensions. To any other nation this would have been a grievous burden, but was altogether impracticable in Germany, where the cattle running wild in large tracts of forest are of prodigious size, while the breed for domestic uses is remarkably small. The Frisians groaned under this oppressive demand. They gave up first their cattle, next their lands ; and finally were obliged to see their wives and children carried into slavery by way of commutation. Discontent arose, and they rebelled,' &c.

[3] *Hist.*, f. 369.

Lastly, in the fifth century (A.D. 450–90) Salvian [1] describes at great length the process by which Roman freemen were in the practice of surrendering their possessions to great men and becoming tributary to them, in order to escape the exactions of the officers who collected the ' tributum.' He narrates how the rich Romans threw upon the poor the weight of the public tribute, and made extra exactions of their own ; how multitudes in consequence deserted their property and became *bagaudæ*—rebels and out-laws ;—how, in districts conquered by the Franks and Goths, there was no such oppression ; how Romans living in these districts had their rights respected ; how people even fled for safety and freedom from the districts still under Roman rule into these Teutonic districts ; and he expresses his wonder why more did not do this.

Many (he says) would fly from the Roman districts if they could carry their properties and houses and families with them. As they cannot do this (he goes on to say), they surrender themselves to the care and protection of great men, becoming their *dediticii* or semi-servile tenants. And the rich (he complains) receive them under their ' patrocinium ' or overlord-ship, not from motives of charity, but for gain : for they require them to surrender almost all their substance, *temporary possession only being allowed to the parent making the surrender during his life,*[2] while the heirs lose their inheritance. And this (he adds) is not all.

---

[1] Salvian, *De Gubernatione Dei,* ib. v. s. vi.–viii.

[2] ' Hoc enim pacto aliquid paren- tibus temporarie attribuitur, ut in futuro totum filiis auferatur '— Salvian, s. viii.

The poor wretches who have surrendered their property are compelled nevertheless to pay tribute for it to these lords, as if it were still their own. Better is the lot of those who, deserting their property altogether, hire farms under great men, and so become the free *coloni* of the rich. For these others not only lose their property and their status, and everything that they can call their own; they lose also themselves and their liberty.[1]

This evidence of Salvian proves that the surrender by freemen of themselves and their property to an overlord was rapidly going on in Roman provinces during the fifth century, and this as the result of Roman misrule, not of German conquest.

IX. THE SUCCESSION TO SEMI-SERVILE HOLDINGS; AND METHODS OF CULTIVATION.

From the evidence of Salvian we can pass at once, crossing the gulf of Teutonic conquest, to that of the Alamannic and Bavarian laws and the monastic cartularies, in which we shall find the process described by Salvian still going on under German rule, and thereby holding after holding, which had once been free, falling under the manorial lordship of the monasteries.

---

[1] The above is only an abridged summary of the lengthy declamation of Salvian. See Gregory of Tours, ' *De Miraculis S. Martini,*' iv. xi. (1122), where a surrender is mentioned. ' Tradidit ei omnem possessionem suam, dicens: " Sint hæc omnia penes S^{ti.} Martini ditionem quæ habere videor, et hoc tantum exinde utar, ut de his dum vixero alar." '

But before we do so it may be worth while to inquire further into the position, under Roman rule, of the class of semi-servile tenants into which a free possessor of land descended when he made the surrender of his holding. We may ask, What was the rule of succession to semi-servile holdings? and what were the customary methods of cultivation followed by semi-servile tenants, whether upon the villa of a lord or upon the imperial domains?

Salvian distinctly states, as we have seen, that upon the death of the person making the surrender to a lord, the right of inheritance was lost to his children. The holding became, on the surrender, a 'præcarium'—a tenancy at the will of the lord by way of usufruct only. This being so, any actual succession to the holding must naturally have been, not by inheritance, but, in theory at all events, by regrant from the lord to the successor—generally a single successor—for, under the circumstances, the rule of single succession would be likely to be adopted as most convenient to the landlord.

The tenants produced by commendation were, however, hardly a class by themselves. They most likely sank into the ordinary condition of the large class of 'coloni,' &c., on the great provincial estates. And there is a passage in the 'Institutes of Justinian' which incidentally seems to imply that the ordinary 'colonus' of the later empire was very nearly in the position of the 'usufructuarius,' and held a holding which, in legal theory at least, ended with his life.[1]

---

[1] Lib. ii. Tit. i. 36. 'Is ad quem ususfructus fundi pertinet, non aliter fructuum dominus efficitur, quam si ipse eos perceperit; et ideo, licet maturis fructibus nondum tamen perceptis decesserit, ad here-

And if this was the generally received theory of the status of semi-servile tenants on the great estates, the probability is that the practice of single succession by regrant may have followed as a matter of convenience and as an all but universal usage.

Further, if we may suppose this to have been the case on the private estates of provincial landowners, the question remains whether the semi-servile classes of tenants on the imperial domains may not have been subject to the same customary rules.

Tenants on public lands in theory 'usufructuarii.'

Now it must be remembered that the legal theory as regards that part of the provincial land which was not centuriated and allotted to the soldiers of the conquering Roman army as a 'colonia,' but left in the possession of the old barbarian inhabitants, was that the latter were merely usufructuary tenants, paying tribute for the use of the land which belonged now to the conquerors.[1] And although *quasi*-rights of inheritance, founded perhaps more upon barbarian usage than direct Roman law, probably grew up generally in the more settled districts of Gaul and the two Germanies, yet there may well have been grades of tenants, some with rights of inheritance and some without them. It may well be questioned whether, in the case of the 'læti' and other semi-servile tenants, hereditary rights were generally recognised. If we take into account the tendency we have noticed in the management of the provincial domains towards manorial methods and usages, it seems at least probable that the semi-servile classes of tenants under

---

dem ejus non pertinent, sed domino proprietatis adquiruntur. *Eadem* | *fere et de colono* dicuntur.'
[1] Rudorff, ii. 317.

the imperial military and fiscal officers were placed much in the same position as the coloni on private villas ; that, in fact, their tenure was only a usufruct for life or at will—a tenure to which, by custom, the single succession would be a natural incident.

Passing now specially to the tenants on the ' Agri Decumates ' and other tithe lands north of the Alps, and asking what were their rules of succession and methods of husbandry, perhaps sufficient stress has not always been laid upon the elasticity with which Roman provincial management adopted local customs and adapted itself to the local circumstances of a widely extended empire. We know little of the methods and rules adopted in the management of the ' tithe lands,' but if the foregoing considerations be sound, it may be that but little change was needful to convert their tenants into serfs on a manorial estate. They may have had but little to gain or to lose, or even to alter in their habits, in exchanging the rule of the imperial fiscal officers for the lordship of the later manorial lord.

It is much to be hoped that more light may ere long be thrown upon this obscure subject by students of provincial law and the barbarian codes. In the meantime it may be possible, perhaps—so slowly do things change in the East—that an actual modern example taken from thence of the customary mode of managing public tithe lands at the present moment in what was once a Roman province might be a better guide to a correct conception of what went on 1,500 years ago on the ' Agri Decumates ' than we could easily get in any other way.

The Roman province of Syria is peculiarly in-

CHAP.
VIII.

The Syrian
code of
fifth
century.

teresting, because the Roman code[1] applying to it
in the fifth century happens to remain, and to afford
interesting evidence of adaptation to local customs in
a district unique in the advantage that its usages, little
altered by the lapse of time, can be studied as well
in the parables of the New Testament as on its
actual fields to-day.

The
'Pflicht-
theil' in
Syria and
in Bavaria
of Roman
origin.

Sir Henry S. Maine[2] has recently referred to the
parable of the 'Prodigal Son' as illustrating the
custom still followed in Turkey of sons taking their
portions during the parent's lifetime, leaving one
home-staying son to become the single successor to
the remainder, including the family homestead and
land.

The Syrian code,[3] following Roman Law,[4] insisted
upon three-twelfths of a man's property going to his
children equally, and left him at liberty to dispose of
the remaining nine-twelfths among them at his pleasure. But an *emancipated* son had no claim to a
share in the *three*-twelfths.[5] These local or Roman
usages have an interesting connexion with the permission which, as we shall see in the next section, was
given by the Bavarian code of the seventh century,
to free possessors of land ' *after they had made division
with their sons*' to surrender their ' *own portion*,' by
way of commendation, to the Church.[6]

---

[1] *Syrisch-Römisches Rechtsbuch.*
Aus dem fünften Jahrhundert.
Leipzig, 1880.

[2] *Early Law and Customs,* p. 260.

[3] S. 1, s. 9, and s. 27.

[4] *Inst. Just.* ii. xviii. 53, and
compare Sandars' note on this passage.

[5] *Syrian Code,* s. 3.

[6] See also *Lex Burgundiorum,*
i. 2, ' Si cum filiis deviserit et por-
tionem suam tulerit, . . .' and id.
xxiv. 5 and li. 1 and 2. Also
' Urkunden' of St. Gall, No. 360.
' Quicquid contra filios meos in por-
tionem et in meam swascaram

It is remarkable that, to the present day, in those districts of Bavaria where the Code Napoléon has not superseded ancient custom and law, the ' Pflicht-theil ' of not less than one-half or one-third, as fixed by the later Roman law, still remains inalienable from the heirs, whilst a custom for the father to hand over the whole or a part of the family holding to a son during his lifetime also occurs.[1]

These coincidences between customs of Syria and Bavaria—both once Roman provinces—refer to land of inheritance. But there were also in Syria as elsewhere in the fifth century, between the freeholders and the slaves, a class of semi-servile tenants—*adscriptitii*—who were, in a sense, the property of a lord.[2] And besides these, again, from the time of the New Testament[3] to the present, there have been tenants paying a tithe or other portion of the produce in return for a usufruct only of public or private lands.

There is no direct reference to public tithe lands in the Syrian code, but the following description of present customs as regards such lands may be valuable in the absence of earlier evidence. It describes the tenants of the Crown tithe lands in Palestine as having only a usufruct, expiring at their death, and as conducting their husbandry upon an open-field system, which being so widely spread is no doubt very ancient, and likely enough to resemble

---

accepi.' See also Sir H. Maine's *Ancient Law*, pp. 198, 224, 228.

[1] *Reports on Tenure of Land,* 1869-70, p. 226. Just. Nov. 18.

[2] See *Syrian Code*, s. 50.

[3] See the parable of ' The unjust steward,' and *supra*, p. 145.

more or less closely local methods followed on the
' Agri Decumates ' under Roman rule.[1]

Land sys-
tem in
Palestine.

Land tenure in Palestine is of three kinds :—

I. *Ard miri*,[2] or taxed Crown land.

In this class are included nearly all the large and fruitful plains like
those of Jaffa, Ramleh, and Esdraelon. These lands are leased by the
Government to various individuals, or *sometimes to a whole village.* The
lessee pays a *tenth* of the produce of the soil for his right of cultivation.
Miri land, therefore, cannot be sold by the lessee, nor has he the power to
transfer it ; he merely possesses the right of cultivation for a given time,
and this only holds good during the lifetime of the lessee. In the event of
his death, the contract he has made becomes null and void, even though
its term be not expired.

II. *Ard wakûf*, or glebe-land. . . .

III. *Ard mulk*, or freehold, is chiefly composed of small pieces of
ground in the neighbourhood of the villages, such as fig and olive planta-
tions, gardens, and vineyards. . . .

Tithe
lands let to
villages,
and
worked
under the
open-field
system.

It has been already mentioned that by far the greater part of the
cultivated land is not private, but Government property, either *miri* or
wakûf, and that the cultivator is merely the holder. Each district has
certain tracts of such lands, and after the rains they are let to the different
inhabitants in separate plots. The division is decided by lottery. Herr
Schick has given an account of the manner in which this lottery takes
place. All those who are desirous of land assemble in the *sâha* (an open
place generally in front of the inns). The Imam, or *khatîb*, who is writer,
accountant, and general archivist to the whole village, presides over this
meeting. The would-be cultivators notify how many ploughs they can
muster. If a man has only a half-share in one, he joins another man with
a like share. Then the whole number is divided into classes. Supposing
the total number of ploughs to be forty, these would be divided into four
classes of ten, and each class would choose a Sheikh to represent them.
The land of course varies in quality, and this division into classes makes
the distribution simpler. Say there are four classes, the land is divided
into four equal portions, so that each class may have good as well as bad.
When the Sheikhs have agreed that the division is fair, the lots are drawn.
Each of the Sheikhs puts some little thing into the *khatîb's* bag. Then the
khatîb calls out the name of one of the divisions, and some passing child is

---

[1] *Journal of the Palestine Ex-
ploration Society,* January 1883.
' Life, Habits, and Customs of the
Fellahin of Palestine,' by the Rev.
F. A. Klein. From the *Zeitschrift*
of the German Palestine Explora-
tion Society.

[2] Shortened form of *ard emiri*—
land of the Emir.

made to draw out one of the things from the bag, and to whichever Sheikh it belongs, to this class belongs the division named by the *khatib*. This decided, the Sheikhs have to determine the individual distribution of the land. In the case of ten ploughs to a class, *they do not each receive a tenth piece of the whole, but, in order to make it as fair as possible, the land is divided into strips, so that each portion consists of a collection of strips in different parts of the village lands.* The boundaries are marked by *furrows* or stones, and to move a neighbour's landmark is still accounted an ' accursed deed,' as in the days of ancient Israel (Deut. xix. 4). . . .

The measure by which the Fellahin divide their land is the feddân. It is decided by the amount which a man with a yoke of oxen can plough per day, and is therefore a most uncertain measure.

This description of the mode in which public Was it so on the Roman tithe lands? land in Palestine is often let to individual tenants or to whole villages at a rent of a tenth of the produce, and further, the picture it gives of the cultivation of the land let to a village by those villagers who supply oxen for the ploughing on an open-field system so like that of Western Europe, at least may suggest the possibility of a somewhat similar system having been adopted in the management of the tithe lands of the ' Agri Decumates.'

The allusion to the division of the fields into strips, and to the unit of land measurement being the day's work of a pair of oxen, and, we may add, the use of the same unit of measurement throughout the Turkish Empire,[1] may at least prepare us to find

---

[1] The standard measure of land throughout the Turkish Empire is called a *deunum*, and is the area which one pair of oxen can plough in a single day ; it is equal to a quarter of an acre, or a square of forty *arshuns* (nearly 100 feet). There seems to be but one allusion to this fact in the Scriptures ; it is found in 1 Sam. xiv. 14, where the exploit of Jonathan and his armour-bearer is described : twenty of the enemy are stated to have fallen within a space of ' *a half-acre of land* ' of ' *a yoke of oxen,*' an expression better rendered ' within the space of half a *deunum* of land.' This measure is referred to in

indications of a somewhat similar system of cultivation on the tithe lands on the Danube and the Rhine
when we come to examine their conditions under the
early Alamannic and Bavarian laws.

And, lastly, this Eastern illustration of the modern
management of ' tithe lands ' may help us to give due
weight to the suggestion of Sir H. S. Maine [1] that
not only on the ' ager publicus,' but even on the
Roman provincial villa itself, in the organisation of
the mostly barbarian and servile tenants, and of
the husbandry, many features may well have been
borrowed from ordinary and wide-spread customs of
barbarian communities, thus partially explaining
what must again and again strike us in this investigation, viz., the ease with which Roman and barbarian elements combined during the later Roman
rule of the provinces and afterwards in producing a
complex and joint result—the typical manorial estate.

X. THE TRANSITION FROM THE ROMAN TO THE LATER MANORIAL SYSTEM.

Laws of
the
Alamanni,
A.D. 622.
The Alamannic conquest of the province of *Germania Prima*, including what is now Elsass and the
western part of the ' Agri Decumates,' may be described as almost a passive one. The population had
long been partly German, and Roman provincial usages
can hardly have been altogether supplanted in the fifth
century. It was not till the Alamanni were themselves

---

ancient profane writers, so that no
change has occurred in this respect.
Van Lenner's *Bible Customs in*

Bible Lands, i. 75.
  [1] *Early Law and Custom,* p.
332.

conquered by the Franks (who had in the meantime become nominally Christian) that their laws were codified. When this took place in the year 622 it was with special reference to the interests of the Church that the laws were framed, just as in the case of the first codification of Anglo-Saxon laws on King Ethelbert becoming a Christian.

The very first provision of the Alamannic laws was a direct permission to any freeman, without hindrance from ' Dux ' or ' Comes,' to surrender his property and himself to the Church by charter executed before six or seven witnesses ; and it provided further that if he should surrender his land, to receive the usufruct of it back again during life as a benefice charged with a certain tribute or census, his heir should not dispute the surrender.[1]

In the Bavarian laws of slightly later date there is a similar permission to any freeman, *from his own share, after he has made division with his sons*, to surrender to the Church *villas, lands, slaves*, or other property, to be received back as a *beneficium* in the same way,[2] and neither ' rex,' ' dux,' nor ' any other person ' is to prevent it.

---

[1] *Lex Alamannorum* Chlotharii.] 'Ut si quis liber res suas vel semetipsum ad ecclesiam tradere voluerit, nullus habeat licentiam contradicere ei, non dux, non comes, nec ulla persona, sed spontanea voluntate liceat christiano homine Deo servire et de proprias res suas semetipsum redemere. . . .

2. Si quis liber, qui res suas ad ecclesiam dederit et per cartam firmitatem fecerit, sicut superius dictum est, et post hæc ad pastorem ecclesiæ ad beneficium susceperit ad victualem necessitatem conquirendam diebus vitæ suæ : et quod spondit persolvat ad ecclesiam censum de illa terra, et hoc per epistulam firmitatis fiat, ut post ejus discessum nullus de heredibus non contradicat.'— Pertz, *Legum*, t. iii. pp. 45-6.

[2] *Lex Baiuwariorum.* Textus Legis primus.

1. 'Ut si quis liber persona

Who are the people thus permitted to surrender their possessions to the Church? Clearly they are the free possessores or tenants on the public lands, now become ' *terra regis*,' under the fiscal officers who are still called *duces* and *comites*.

Here, then, is still going on, but in the interest of the Church, precisely the process described by Salvian, and with precisely the same results.

Further, these results can be traced with remarkable exactness; for in the charters of *St. Gall* and *Lorsch* and *Wizenburg* there are numerous instances of surrenders made under this law.

In the ' Urkundenbuch' of the Abbey of St. Gall, under date A.D. 754,[1] there is a charter by which a possessor of land in certain ' villas ' in the neighbourhood of St. Gall hands over to the monastery all that he possesses therein, with the cattle, slaves, houses, fields, woods, waters, &c., thereon, together with two servi and all their belongings; and (it proceeds) ' for these things I am willing to render service every ' year as follows :—viz. xxx. seglas of beer (cervesa), ' xl. loaves and a sound spring pig (frischenga), and 'xxx. mannas, and to plough 2 jugera[2] (jochos) per

---

voluerit et dederit res suas ad ecclesiam pro redemptione animæ suæ, licentiam habeat de portione sua, postquam cum filiis suis partivit. Nullus eum prohibeat, non rex, non dux, nec ulla persona habeat potestatem prohibendi ei. Et quicquid donaverit, villas, terras, mancipia, vel aliqua pecunia, omnia quæcumque donaverit pro redemptione animæ suæ, hoc per epistolam confirmet propria manu sua ipse. . . .

' Et post hæc nullam habeat potestatem nec ipse nec posteri ejus, nisi defensor ecclesiæ ipsius *beneficium* præstare voluerit ei.'—Pertz, *Legum*, t. iii. pp. 269–70.

[1] *Urkundenbuch der Abtei St. Gallen*, i. p. 22.

[2] Compare with the Kentish ' yokes' and ' ioclets.' The yoke here is, however, evidently the *juger*, not the *jugum*.

' annum, and to gather and carry the produce to
' the yard, also to do post service (*angaria*) when
' required.'

Here we have not only the public *tributum* con-
verted into a manorial census or ' gafol,' but also the
sordida munera transformed into manorial services.

In another charter, A.D. 759, is a surrender of all a
man's possessions in the place called *Heidolviswilare*,
to the Abbey, ' in this wise that I may receive it back
' from you *per precariam*, and yearly I will pay
' thence *census*, *i.e.* xxx. siclas of beer, xl. loaves,
' a sound spring frisginga, 3 day-works (operæ) of
' one man in the course of the year; and my son
' Hacco, if he survive me, shall do so during his life.'[1]

In another, A.D. 761,[2] the monks of St. Gall re-
grant a ' *villa* ' called ' *Zozinvilare* ' to the original
maker of the surrender at the following *census*, viz.
xxx. siclas of beer and xl. loaves, a friscinga, and
two hens, with this addition—' *In quisqua sicione*[3]
' thou shalt plough *saigata una* (one selion ?) and
' reap this and carry it into [the yard], and in one
' day (jurno)[4] thou shalt cut it, and in another gather
' it and carry it, as aforesaid.'

In the surrender of a holding ' in villa qui dicitur
' *Wicohaim*,[5] the census is . . . siclas of beer, xx.
' maldra of bread and a frisginga, and work at the
' stated time at harvest and at hay-time, two days in
' reaping the harvest and cutting the hay, and in
' early spring one " *jurnalis* " at ploughing, and in
' the month of June to break up [brachan] another,

---

[1] *Urkundenbuch*, pp. 27-8.
[2] *Id.* p. 33.
[3] See also *id.* pp. 76 and 90.

[4] Hence ' *jurnal* ' for *acre*.
[5] *Id.* p. 41.

' and in autumn to plough and sow it—this is the
' census for that villa.'

These grants were clearly surrenders by freemen
like those described by Salvian, which carried with
them whatever coloni or servi there were upon the land.

Thus, under date 771,[1] a priest gives to the
monks all his property *in villa Ailingas* and another
place, except two servi and five yokes of land ; and
in another place he gives ' *servum unum cum hoba*
' *sua et filiis suis et cum uxore sua.*' The *hoba* was
clearly the ' hub ' or yard-land of the serf, and it,
he and his wife and children were all granted over
by their lord to the abbey.

In the same year 771 [2] a man named *Chunibertus*
and his wife surrendered an estate called *Chunibertes-
wilari*, and it is described as including just what a
Roman villa would include, *i.e.* the *villa* itself (*casa*),
surrounded by its court (*curte circumclausa*), together
with buildings, slaves, arable land, meadows, fields,
&c., &c. And yet in this case also he retains possession ' *sub usu fructuario* ' during his life, paying the
same kind of census as in the other cases—xx. siclas
of beer, a maldra of bread, and a *frisking*.

Likeness
of the
census and
services to
the Saxon
' gafol '
and 'gafol-
yrth.' Now, it will at once be seen how like is the census
described in these charters to the Saxon gafol of the
' Rectitudines,' and of the manors of Tidenham or
Hysseburne. There is distinctly the *gafol*, and in
many cases the *gafolyrth* also, but no mention of the
week-work. Add this, and there would be an almost
exact likeness to Saxon serfdom.

But it will be remembered that even under the

---

[1] *Urkundenbuch,* p. 59.   [2] *Id.* p. 60.

laws of Ine the *week-work* was not added to the *gafol* unless the lord provided not only the yard-land, but also the homestead. These surrenders were surrenders by freemen of their own land and homesteads. It was hardly likely that the more servile week-work should be added to their census. How it would fare with their children when they sought to succeed their parents in the now servile holding is quite another thing.

There is, indeed, apparently an instance, under date 787,[1] of the settlement of a new serf—the grant of a fresh holding in villenage from the Abbot of St. Gall to the new tenant. The holding, if we may use the Saxon terms, is ' set ' both ' to *gafol* and to *week-work* ;' for the tenant binds himself (1) to pay to the abbey as *census* (*i.e.* as *gafol*) yearly vii. maldra of grain and a sound spring frisking, to be delivered at the granary of the monastery ; and (2) to plough *every week* (*i.e.* as week-work)[2] at their nearest manor (*curtem*) a '*jurnal* '(or acre strip) in every *zelga* [3] (*i.e.* in each of the three fields) ; and also six days in a year when work out of doors is needed, whether in harvest or hay-mowing, to send two ' *mancipii* ' for the work: also, when work is wanted in building or repairing bridges, to send one man with food to the work, who is to stop at it as long as required. And to these payments and services the new tenant bound ' himself, his heirs, and all their descendants lawfully ' begotten.'

New serf created and 'week-work' added.

---

[1] *Urkundenbuch*, p. 106.

[2] ' Et ad proximam curtem vestram in unaquaque zelga ebdomedarii jurnalem arare debeamus " (p. 107).

[3] Waitz speaks of the three great fields under the ' *Dreifelderwirthschaft* ' as ' Zelgen.'—*Verfassung der Deutschen Völker*, i. 120. And see *infra*, chap. x. s. iii.

This surely is a distinct case of the settlement of a new serf upon the land, rendering in Saxon phrase both *gafol* and *week-work*; and the serfdom created is as nearly as possible identical with that of an English manor of the same date.

But to return to the surrenders. It is clear from the instances quoted that some of these owners who surrendered their holdings were holders of whole *villas or heims*, some of them of *portions of villas or heims*. And yet they placed themselves by the surrender, as Salvian described it, in a servile position, *lower*, as he says, *than that of the coloni of the rich*, for they merely retained the usufruct during their life. The inheritance was lost. And they still had a tribute to pay to their lord, though free from tribute to the public purse. The Frankish kings now stood in the place of the Roman Emperor. The old Roman *tributum* apparently remained, but was payable to the Frankish king. When under the Alamannic laws these surrenders were made to the Church, the tribute also was transferred from the king to the Church.

We have seen that when such a surrender had been made under Roman rule to a rich Roman landowner, the latter became responsible to the public exchequer for the tributum, but he exacted tribute in his turn from his tenant, who thus, as Salvian said, though parting with his inheritance, still paid tribute to his lord. But this tribute can hardly have been the full *tributum* at which the holding was assessed to the *jugatio*. It seems to have been rather a fixed and typical *gafol* or census, marking a servile condition. For in the Alamannic laws there are clauses making the following remarkable provisions :—

Leges Alamannorum Hlotharii [1] (A.D. 622).

XXII.

(1) Servi enim ecclesiæ tributa sua legitime reddant, quindecim siclas de cervisa, porco valente [al. porcum valentem] tremisse uno, pane [al. panem] modia dua, pullos quinque, ova viginti.

(2) Ancillæ autem opera inposita sine neglecto faciant.

(3) Servi dimidiam partem sibi et dimidiam [al. dimidium] in dominico arativum reddant. Et si super hæc est, sicut servi ecclesiastici ita faciant, tres dies sibi et tres in dominico.

XXIII.

De liberis autem ecclesiasticis, quod [al. quos] colonos vocant, omnes sicut coloni regis ita reddant ad ecclesiam.

XXII.

(1) Let servi of the Church pay their tribute rightly, viz., 15 siclæ of beer, with a sound spring pig, of bread two modia, five fowls, twenty eggs.

(2) Let female servi do services required without neglect.

(3) Let servi do ploughing, half for themselves and half in the demesne. And if there be other services, let them do as the servi of the Church—three days for themselves and three days in the demesne.

XXIII.

Concerning the freemen of the Church who are called 'coloni,' let all pay to the Church just as the coloni of the king.

Tribute, services, and three days' 'week-work' under the Alamannic law.

These clauses seem to establish clearly three facts :—

(1) That the slavery of the slaves or *servi* on the ecclesiastical estates had already, in A.D. 622, become modified and restricted as a matter of general ecclesiastical custom to a *three days' week-work.*

(2) That the proper tribute (or *gafol*) of persons becoming servi of the Church by surrender under this edict was to be as stated ; the resemblance of the details of this tribute with those mentioned in the St. Gall surrenders showing the servile nature of the status into which those making the surrender placed themselves thereby.

(3) Freemen of the Church called ' *coloni*' were

to pay to the Church as the *coloni* on the *terra regis* did to the king.

In other words, a *whole villa* or *manor*, with the village community of ' free coloni ' and the ' servi ' upon it, might be handed over *as a whole* to the Church : in which case the free coloni were to remain free and pay tribute to the Church as they would have done to the king if they had been ' coloni ' on the *terra regis*.

After thus becoming ' free coloni ' of the Church they might, if they chose, by a second act surrender their freedom and become *servi* of the Church, just as ' free coloni ' on royal villas or on the *terra regis* might do under this edict.

This evidence relates, it will be remembered, to the district on the left bank of the Rhine, which so abounded with ' *heims* ' and ' *villas*,' as well as to that portion of the ' Agri Decumates ' which was included in the province of Germania Prima.

There is still clearer evidence for the district to the east of the ' Agri Decumates,' comprehended in the Roman province of Rhætia.

Rhætia, it will be remembered, was the province, in edicts relating to which the ' *sordida munera* ' were most clearly defined. We have seen traces of some of these ' base services,' especially the *boon-work* and the ' *angariæ*,' in the St. Gall charters. Still clearer traces of them are found in the services described in the early ' Bavarian laws ' of the seventh century. These laws, as has been seen, expressly allowed ' surrenders ' by freemen of their property to the Church, and the services of the *servi* and *coloni* of the Church are described with remarkable clearness.

The section is headed—

Lex Baiuwariorum, textus legis primus.[1]

13.

De colonis vel servis ecclesiæ, qualiter serviant vel quale [al. qualia] tributa reddant.

Hoc est agrario secundum estimationem iudicis; provideat hoc iudex secundum quod habet donet : de 30 modiis 3 modios donet, et pascuario dissolvat secundum usum provinciæ.[2] Andecenas legitimas, hoc est pertica [al. perticam] 10 pedes habentem, 4 perticas in transverso, 40 in longo arare, seminare, claudere, colligere, trahere et recondere. A tremisse unusquisque *accola*[3] ad duo modia sationis excolligere, seminare, colligere et recondere debeat ; et vineas plantare, fodere, propaginare, præcidere, vindemiare. Reddant fasce [al. fascem] de lino [al. ligno] ; de apibus 10 vasa [al. decimum vas] ; pullos 4, ova 15 reddant. *Parafretos* [al. palafredos] donent, aut ipsi vadant, ubi eis iniunctum fuerit. *Angarias* cum carra faciant usque 50 lewas [al. leugas] ; amplius non minentur.

Ad casas dominicas stabilire [al. stabiliendas], fenile, granica vel tunino recuperanda, pedituras rationabiles accipiant, et quando necesse fuerit, omnino componant.

13.

Concerning the coloni or servi of the Church, what services and tributes they are to render.

This is the tribute *for arable*, according to the estimation of the judge. The judge must look to it that according to what a man has he must give ; for 30 modia he must give 3 modia. And for *pasturage* he must pay according to the custom of the province. Legal andecenæ (the perches being of 10 feet), 4 perches in breadth and 40 in length, [he is] to plough, to sow, to fence, to gather, to carry, and to store. For spring crops every cultivator to prepare for two modia of seed, and sow, gather, and store it. And to plant vines, tend, graft, and prune them, and gather the grapes. Let them render a bundle of flax, of honey the tenth vessel, 4 fowls, and 15 eggs. Let them give post-horses, or go themselves wherever they are told. Let them do carrying service with waggons as far as 50 leugæ. They cannot be compelled to go farther.

In keeping up the buildings in the demesne, in repairing the hayloft, the granary, or the 'tun,' let them take reasonable portions, and when needful let them compound to-

---

[1] Pertz, *Legum*, t. iii. pp. 278–280.

[2] Compare *Chlotharii II. Præceptio* (584–628) s. 11. 'Agraria, pascuaria vel decimas porcorum ecclesiæ pro fidei nostræ devotione concedimus, ita ut actor aut decimator in rebus ecclesiæ nullus accedat.'—*Mon. Germ. Hist. Capitularia,* I. i. p. 19.

[3] This word '*accola*' is often used in charters for '*free coloni.*'

Calce furno [al. calcefurno], ubi prope fuerit, ligna aut petra [al. petras] 50 homines faciant, ubi longe fuerat [al. fuerit], 100 homines debeant expetiri, et ad civitatem vel ad villam, ubi necesse fuerit, ipsa calce trahantur [al. ipsam calcem trahant].

gether. To the limekiln when near let 50 men, and when it is far let 100 men be found to supply wood or [lime-]stone, and where needful let the lime itself be carried to city or villa.

These are the services of the *coloni* or *accolæ* of the Church. Next as to the *servi* :—

Servi autem ecclesiæ secundum possessionem suam reddant tributa. Opera vero 3 dies in ebdomada in dominico operent [al. operentur], 3 vero sibi faciant. Si vero dominus eius [al. eorum] dederit eis boves aut alias res quod habet [al. quas habent], tantum serviant, quantum eis per possibilitatem impositum fuerit; tamen iniuste neminem obpremas [al. opprimas].

Let the servi of the Church pay tribute according to their holdings. Let them work 3 days a week in the demesne, and 3 days for themselves. But if their lord give them oxen or other things they have, let them do as much service as can be put upon them, yet thou shalt oppress no one unjustly.

Gafol-yrth
or plough-
ing of
andecenæ
or acre
strips,
probably
for the
tenths on
the ' tithe-
lands.'

In the face of this evidence it seems impossible to ignore either the continuity of the tribute and services under Roman and German rule on the one hand, or their identity with the *gafol*, the *gafol-yrth*, and the *week-work* of the English manor on the other hand. There is first the tenth of the chief produce due as of old from these occupants of the ' Agri Decumates ' of Tacitus, closely connected with the tribute of ploughing—the Saxon *gafol-yrth* noticed above in the St. Gall charters. This is to be rendered in *lawful andecenæ*, and this measure of the plough-work is reckoned by the Roman rod of ten feet, and takes the precise form, four rods by forty, which belongs to the English acre of four roods ; [1] and this is the

---

[1] In the Glosses this andecena is called a ' *sharwork*.'

strip to be sown, gathered, and stored, just as in the case of the Saxon '*gafol-yrth.*'

The tending of vines is peculiar to the country. The tenth bundle of flax, the tenth vessel of honey, and the fowls and eggs are also familiar items of the *census* or *gafol*, both in the charters of St. Gall and in the services of Saxon manors.

Then there are the pack-horse services (*parafreti*) and the carrying services ('*angariæ cum carra*'), the keeping up of buildings, supply of the limekiln, and the carriage of lime to the villa—all which once public services ('*sordida munera*'), due to the Roman Emperor on whose tithe lands the coloni were settled, were now the manorial services of 'coloni' of the Church. They were called in the Codex Theodosianus '*obsequia*,' and are almost identical with the Saxon '*precariæ*' or boon-works. ◆ 'Sordida munera.'

Lastly, it has been observed that the coloni or *accolæ* did not give '*week-work.*' This was, as has been seen, the distinctive mark of serfdom here in Rhætia, as for centuries afterwards throughout the manors of mediæval Europe.

In other words, in the seventh century there are two classes of tenants on ecclesiastical manors—(1) the *coloni* or *accolæ*, to use the Saxon terms of King Ine's laws, *set to gafol*; and (2) the *servi, set to gafol and to week-work.*

Throw the two classes together, or let the remaining Roman coloni sink, as the result of conquest or otherwise, down into the condition up to which the slaves have risen in becoming serfs, and the serfdom of the mediæval manorial estate is the natural result. At the same time an explanation is given of the persistently double character of the later services, which apparently was a survival of their double origin in the union of the public tribute and *sordida munera* of the Roman *colonus* with the servile work of the Roman slave.

On the estates of the Church in the early years of the seventh century the humanising power of Christian feeling had silently raised the status of the slave. It had dignified labour, and given to him a property in his labour, securing to him not only one day in seven for rest to his weary and heavy-laden limbs, but also *three days in the week* wherein his labour was *his own*. From slavery he had risen into serfdom. And this serfdom of the *quondam* slave had become, in the eyes of the still more weary and heavy-laden free labourers on their own land, so light a burden compared with their own—such was the lawless oppression of the age—that they went to the Church and took upon them willingly the yoke of her serfdom, in order that they might find rest under her temporal as well as spiritual protection.

Such an impulse did this rush for safety into serfdom on ecclesiastical or monastic estates receive from the unsettlement and lawlessness of the period of the Teutonic invasions, that by the time of Charles the Great a large proportion of the land in these once Roman provinces had become included in the manorial estates of the monasteries.

Scores of
free-
tenants on
a single
manor
make sur-
renders
to the
Abbey of
Lorsch.

In the thickly peopled Romano-German lands on both sides of the Rhine, including the present Elsass on the one side, and the district between the Rhine and the Maine (the present Baden and Wirtemberg) on the other, so strong was the current in this direction, that we find in the *Traditiones* of the monasteries of ' *Lorsch* ' and ' *Wizenburg* ' scores of surrenders taking place sometimes in a single village. And these cases are of peculiar interest because *G. L. von Maurer* relies almost solely upon them as the earliest examples available in support of his theory of the original German *mark* and *free village community.* His *only* early instances are taken from the Lorsch Cartulary.[1] He cites 107 surrenders to the Abbey of Lorsch in ' *Hantscuhesheim* ' alone,[2] and concludes that there must have been at least as many free holders resident there in earlier times. In *Loeheim* there were eight surrenders; in other heims thirty-five, five, twenty-three, ten, forty, five, and so on. These must, he concludes, have formed part of originally free village communities on the German mark system.[3]

Now these surrenders to the abbey go back to the reign of Pepin ; and the question is, What were these freemen who made these surrenders? Were they indeed members of *German free village communities?*

In the first place, they lived in a district which for many centuries had been a Roman province. The manners of the people had long been Romanised. Even across the Maine for generations the homesteads had been built in Roman fashion.[4] And it is significant that the fragments surrendered in this district, which since the time of Probus had become devoted to the vine culture, were mostly little *vineyards* ; e.g. ' *rem* ' *meam, hoc est vineam, i. in Hantscuhesheim,* '[5] and so

---

[1] *Geschichte der Dorfverfassung in Deutschland,* i. pp. 6 *et seq.*

[2] *Traditiones in Pago Rhinensi. Codex Lauresham.* pp. 357 *et seq.*

[3] *Dorfverfassung,* pp. 15 *et seq.*

[4] Ammianus Marcellinus, bk. xvii. c. i., A.D. 357.

[5] *Codex Lauresham.* pp. 326, 362, 369, 375 and *passim.*

on. These vineyards were often composed of so many
'*scamelli*,' or little *scamni*—ridges or strips marked out
by the Roman *Agrimensores*. All this is thoroughly
Roman. What looks at first sight so much like a
German free village community, was once a little
Roman ' vicus ' full of people, with their vineyards on
the hills around it. They look like German settlers
or ' free coloni' on the public domains, who had become appendant to the villa of the fiscal officer of the
district, which had in fact by this time become to all
intents and purposes a manor.

A little further examination will confirm this view.

The *villas*
were
manors.

Turning to the record of the earliest donation to
the abbey, in A.D. 763,[1] we find a description of a
whole villa or *heim*—'*Hoc est, villam nostram quæ*
' *dicitur Hagenheim, cum omni integritate sua, terris*
' *domibus ædificiis campis pratis vineis silvis aquis*
' *aquarumve decursibus farinariis litis libertis conlibertis*
' *mancipiis mobilibus et immobilibus, &c.*'

Here there clearly is a villa or manor, and the
tenants of this manor are *liti, liberti, coliberti*,[2] and
mancipii or slaves. There are charters of other
estates which are just as clearly manors with servile
tenements and slaves upon them.

In the similar records of surrenders to the Abbey
of St. Gall, as we have seen, there are also donations
of little free properties in ' *heims* ' and ' *villares*,' but
by far the greater number of the earliest donations
are distinctly of whole manors or parts of manors,
with *coloni* and *mancipii* upon them.

---

[1] *Codex Lauresham.* p. 3.

[2] It is curious to notice that
' coliberti ' appear also in the *western*
counties of England in the Domesday Survey.

The heims of this Romano-German district were therefore distinctly manors. They were also ' *marks.*'

In 773 Charles the Great gave to the Abbey of Lauresham the ' villa' called ' Hephenheim,' ' *in pago* ' *Rinense, cum omni merito et soliditate sua cum terris* ' *domibus ædificiis accolis mancipiis vineis sylvis* ' *campis pratis, &c.*'—that is, the *whole manor*—' *cum* ' *omnibus terminis et marchis suis.*' And then follow the *marchæ sive terminus silvæ,* which pertained to the same villa of Hephenheim, ' as it had always ' been held *sub ducibus et regibus ex tempore antiquo.*' It was then a ' villa ' or manor belonging to the Royal domain, and it was then held as a benefice by a ' comes,' whose predecessor had also held it, and his father before him, of the king.[1]

This is clearly a grant of a whole manor with the tenants and slaves upon it, and a manor of long standing ; and the word *mark* is simply the base Latin word for boundary, like the Saxon word ' gemæra.' Further, the boundaries are given exactly as in the Saxon charters, in the form described in the writings of the Roman *Agrimensores.*

In 774,[2] Charles the Great made a similar grant to the abbey in almost identical terms of the ' villa ' called ' *Obbenheim,*' in the district of Worms, ' *cum omni merito* ' *et soliditate sua, &c., accolis, mancipiis, &c.*,' just as before. This was another whole royal manor granted with its tenants and slaves to the abbey. Yet in 788[3] the holder of a vineyard ('*j petiam de vinea*') in this same Obbenheim surrenders it to the abbey. In 782[4]

---

[1] *Codex Lauresham.* i. pp. 15–16.

[2] *Id.* i. pp. 18 and 19.

[3] *Id.* i. p. 297.

[4] *Id.* i. p. 303.

there is another grant. In 793[1] there is a similar grant of five vineyards, and another[2] of three vineyards ; and scores of other donations of vineyards occur in the reigns of Charles and of his predecessor Pepin.[3]

It is obvious, then, that these surrenders or donations, which were exactly like those of *Hantscuhesheim*, were made by ' free coloni' of the manor, who in the time of Pepin, while the lordship remained in the king, as well as afterwards when the manor had been transferred to the abbey, surrendered their holdings to the abbey, thus converting them either into tenancies on the demesne land, or into servile holdings under the lordship of the abbey. They were not members of a German free village com-

munity, for they were tenants of a manor when they made their surrenders. Nor were they slaves (*mancipii*). The only other class mentioned in the charter was that of the *accolæ*, the word used for ' free coloni' in the Bavarian laws. These *accolæ*, it seems, then, were ' coloni' or free tenants upon a royal manor, part of the old *ager publicus*, now ' *terra regis.*' And as such under the Frankish law it seems that they had power to transfer themselves from the lordship of the king to that of the Church. The Alamannic laws were enacted or at least confirmed after the Frankish conquest, and probably were in force over this particular district at the date of these surrenders. These laws, as we have seen, expressly forbade the *comes* under whom they lived

---

[1] *Codex Lauresham.* i. p. 347.   [2] *Id.* i. pp. 349–350.
[3] *Id.* ii. pp. 232 *et seq.*

to prevent free tenants from making such surrenders
for the good of their souls.

Indeed, among the St. Gall charters there is one
exactly in point.

It is dated A.D. 766,[1] and by it the sons of a person who had surrendered his land to the Abbey under these laws by this charter renewed the arrangement, ' in this wise, that so as we used to do service to ' the king and the comes, so we shall do service ' for that land to the monastery, receiving it as a ' benefice of the same monks *per cartulam precariam.*'

This view of the case may be still further confirmed. In the Lorsch records are contained in some cases descriptions of the services of the two kinds of tenants on the manors surrendered to the Abbey. There are free tenants and servile tenants, and it is a strong confirmation of the continuity of the services from Roman to mediæval times to find some of them so closely identical with the ' *sordida munera* ' of the Theodosian Code and the services described in the Bavarian laws.

To take an example : In *Nersten* the services of
each *mansus ingenualis* may be thus classified : [2]—

(1) *As census,* 5 modii of barley, 1 pound of flax, at Easter 4*d.*, 1 fowl, 10 eggs, 2 loads of wood.

(2) *As work,* 4 weeks a year whenever required.

(3) *As 'gafolyrth,'* to plough 1 acre in each of the [three] fields (*sationes*), and to gather and store it.

(4) *As 'precariæ,'* or *sordida munera*—

> 3 days' work at reaping.
> 2 days' work at mowing.

---

[1] *Urkundenbuch* of St. Gall, i. p. 50.

[2] *Codex Laureshamensis,* iii. 212. See also the services at *Winenheim* (iii. 205), a manor near Heppenheim.

2 days' work at binding and 2 loads of carrying.
The tenant gives a *parafredum.*
Attends in the host.
Carts 5 loads of lime to the kiln.
Carts 5 loads of wood.
Goes messages ' infra regnum' whenever required.

Each *mansus servilis* rendered, on the other hand—

(1) *As census,* 1 uncia, 1 fowl, 10 eggs, a frisking worth 4*d.*
(2) *As boon work,* 'facit moaticum et bracem et picturas in sepe et in
    grania.' In addition the tenant:—
    Ploughs 4 days, and all demesne land.
    Feeds for the winter 5 pigs and 1 cow.
(3) *As week-work,* 3 days a week whenever required.
    For women's work, 1 uncia, 1 load of wood, 1 of grass, 10 eggs.

In total there were eighty-seven ' *mansi et sortes.*'

Their
Roman
connexion. It is evident that these *mansi* and *sortes* were not
allodial lots in the common mark of a free village
community, but the holdings of two grades of *semi-
servile* and *servile* tenants *on a manor*; and it is evident
that some of the services were survivals of the *sordida
munera* exacted under Roman law. Surely the continuity in the mode of surrender and in the services
and tribute on these South German manors, traced
from the Theodosian Code to the Alamannic and Bavarian laws, and found again in the surrenders (identical
with those described by Salvian) made under those
laws, and also in the later surveys of the monastic
estates, excludes the probability of their having been
original settlements of German free village communities on the German mark system, such as G. L. von
Maurer assumes that they were.

These curious and numerous instances on which
this writer relied as evidence of the mark-system,
and as remains of a once free German village community, turn out in fact to be further instances of

the progress under Frankish rule, within a once Roman province, of the practice described by Salvian—a practice which continued from century to century, helping on the threefold tendency (1) in the villa to become more and more manorial, *i.e.* more and more an estate of a lord with a village community in serf-dom upon it; (2) for all land to fall under some manorial lordship or other, whether royal, eccle-siastical, monastic or private, and so to become part of a manorial estate; (3) for the originally distinct classes of ' free coloni' on the one hand, and *slaves* or *servi* on the other hand, to become merged in the one common class of mediæval serfs.

We have yet, however, to examine the German side of this continental economic history as carefully as we have examined the Roman side of it, before we shall be in a position to use continental analogies as the key to the solution of the English economic problem.

It may be that direct and important German ele-ments also entered as factors in the manorial system, both during the period of Roman rule in the German provinces, and also after their final conquest by the German tribes.

CHAPTER IX.

THE GERMAN SIDE OF THE CONTINENTAL EVIDENCE.

I. THE GERMAN TRIBAL SYSTEM, AND ITS TENDENCY TOWARDS THE MANORIAL SYSTEM.

THE description given of the Germans by Cæsar is evidently that of a people in the same tribal stage of economic development as the one with which Irish and Welsh evidence has made us familiar.

'Their whole life is occupied in hunting and warlike enterprise. . . . They do not apply much to agriculture, and their food mostly consists of milk, cheese, and flesh. Nor has anyone a fixed quantity of land or defined individual property, but the magistrates and chiefs assign to tribes and families who herd together, annually, and for one year's occupation, as much land and in such place as they t ink fit, compelling them the next year to move somewhere else.'[1]

He also alludes to the frailty of their houses,[2] another mark of the tribal system in Wales, which

---

[1] *De Bello Gallico*, lib. vi. c. 21 and 22. 'Neque quisquam agri modum certum aut fines habet proprios, sed magistratus ac principes in annos singulos gentibus cognationibusque hominum, qui una coierunt, quantum eis et quo loco visum est agri attribuunt, atque anno post alio transire cogunt.'

[2] *Id.* lib. vi. c. 22.

indeed was a necessary result of the yearly migration
to fresh fields and pastures.

Now what were the tribes of Germans with whom
Cæsar came most in contact?

His chief campaigns against the Germans were (1)
against the *Suevi*, who were crossing the Rhine north of
the confluence with the Moselle, and (2) against Ariovistus in the territory of the *Sequani* at the southern
bend of the Rhine eastward. And it is remarkable
that the *Suevi* were prominent again among the tribes
enlisted in the army of Ariovistus.[1] So that it is
easy to see how the Suevi, coming into close contact
with Cæsar at both ends, came to be considered by
him as the most important of the German peoples.

He describes the *Suevi* separately, and in terms
which show over again that they were still in the early
tribal stage [2] in which an annual shifting of holdings
was practised. Indeed, their semi-nomadic habits
could not be shown better than by the inadvertently
mentioned facts that the Suevi who were crossing the
Rhine to the north brought their families with them;
and that the Suevi and other tribes forming the army
of Ariovistus to the south had not had settled homes
for fourteen years,[3] but brought their families about
with them in waggons wherever they went, the
waggons and women of each tribe being placed
behind the warriors when they were drawn up by
tribes in battle array.[4]

This statement of Cæsar that the Germans of his

---

[1] *De Bello Gallico*, lib. i. c. 51.
[2] *Id.* lib. iv. c. 1. 'Sed privati
ac separati agri apud eos nihil est,
neque longius anno remanere uno in

loco incolendi causa licet.'
[3] *Id.* lib. i. c. 36.
[4] *Id.* lib. i. c. 51.

Chap. IX.
time were still in the early tribal stage of economic
development in which there was an annual shifting
of the households from place to place needs no cor-
roboration or explaining away after what has already
been seen going on under the Welsh and Irish tribal
systems. The ease with which tribal redistributions
were made under the peculiar method of clustering
homesteads which prevailed in Wales and Ireland,
makes the statement of Cæsar perfectly probable.

But how was it 150 years later, when Tacitus
wrote his celebrated description of the Germans of
his time?

The 'Germania' of Tacitus.
The 'Germania' was obviously written from a
distinctly Roman point of view.
The eye of the writer was struck with those points
chiefly in which German and Roman manners differed.
The Romans of the well-to-do classes lived in cities.
City life was their usual life, and those of them who
had villas in the country, whilst sometimes having
residences for themselves upon them, as we have seen,
cultivated them most often by means of slave-labour
under a *villicus*, but sometimes by *coloni*.

The scattered settlements of the free tribesmen.
What struck Tacitus in the economy of the
Germans (and by Germans he obviously meant the
free tribesmen, not their slaves) was that they did
not live in cities like the Romans. ' They dwell' (he
says) ' apart and scattered, as spring, or plain, or
' grove attracted their fancy.'[1] Of whom is he speaking? Obviously of free tribesmen or tribal households, *not of villagers or village communities*, for he

---

[1] 'Colunt discreti ac diversi, ut fons, ut campus, ut nemus placuit.'—
Germania, xvi.

immediately afterwards, in the very next sentence, speaks of the Germans as avoiding even in their villages (*vici*) what seemed to him to be obviously the best mode of building, viz. in streets with continuous roofs. ' Their villages ' (he says) ' they ' build not in our manner with connected and at-' tached buildings. There is an open space round ' every one's house.' And this he attributes not to their fancy for one situation or another, as in the first case, but ' either to fear of fire or ignorance of ' how to build.' [1]

It is obvious, therefore, that the Germans who chose to live scattered about the country sides, as spring, plain or grove attracted them, were not the villagers who had spaces round their houses. We are left to conclude that the first class were the chiefs and free tribesmen, who, now having become settled for a time, were, in a very loose sense, the *landowners*, while the latter, the villagers, must chiefly have been their servile dependants. And this inference is confirmed when Tacitus comes to the second point and tells us that the *servi* of the Germans differed greatly from those of the Romans. There were some slaves bought and sold in the market, and free men sometimes sank into slavery as the result of war or gambling ventures; but in a general way (he says) their slaves were not included in the tribesmen's households or employed in household service, but each family of slaves had a separate home-

---

[1] ' Vicos locant non in nostrum morem, connexis et cohærentibus ædificiis: suam quisque domum spatio circumdat, sive adversus casus ignis remedium, sive inscitia ædificandi.'—*Germania,* xvi.

Chap. IX. stead.[1] They had also separate crops and cattle;
for ' the lord (*dominus*) requires from the slave a
' certain quantity of corn, cattle, or material for
' clothing, as in the case of *coloni*. To this modi-
' fied extent (Tacitus says) the German *servus* is
' a slave. The wife and children of the free tribes-
' man do the household work of his house, not slaves
' as in the Roman households.'

Clearly, then, the *vicus*—the *village*—on the land
of the tribesman who was their lord, was inhabited
by these *servi*, who, like Roman *coloni*, had their
own homesteads and cattle and crops, and rendered
to their lord part of their produce by way of tribute
or food-rent.

The lords—the tribesmen—themselves (as Tacitus
elsewhere remarks) preferred fighting and hunting to
agriculture, and left the management of the latter to
the women and weaker members of the family.[2]

A later
tribal
stage than
Cæsar
described.

Now, if we could be sure that the tribal homestead was a permanent possession, and that the village
of serfs around it had a single tribesman for its lord,
the settlement would practically be to all intents and
purposes a *heim* or *manor* with a village in serfdom
upon it. It was evidently in a real sense the tribesman's separate possession, for, after speaking of blood
relationships which bind the German tribesman's
family and home most strongly together, Tacitus
adds, ' Everyone's children are his heirs and successors

---

[1] 'Ceteris servis non in nostrum morem descriptis per familiam
ministeriis utuntur. Suam quisque
sedem, suos penates regit. Fru-
menti modum dominus aut pecoris
aut vestis ut colono injungit, et
servus hactenus paret : cetera
domus officia uxor ac liberi ex-
sequuntur.'—*Germania*, xxv.

[2] *Id.* xiv. and xv.

' without his making a will; and if there be no
' children, the grades of succession are brothers,
' paternal uncles, maternal uncles.' [1]

But then this was also the case in Wales and
Ireland. There was division among male heirs of the
family land. And yet this family land was not a
freehold permanent estate so long as a periodical
redistribution of the tribe land might shift it over to
someone else.

The embryo manor of the German tribesman,
with its village of serfs upon it, might therefore, if
the same practice prevailed, differ in three ways from
the later manor. It might become the possession of
a tribal household instead of a single lord ; and also
it possibly might, on a sudden redistribution of the
tribal land, fall into the possession of another tribesman or tribal household, though perhaps this is not
very likely often to have happened. Finally, it might
become subdivided when the time came for the unity
of the tribal household to be broken up as it was in
Wales after the final redivision among second cousins.

It must be remembered that land in the tribal
stages of economic progress was the least stable and
the least regarded of possessions. A tribesman's
property consisted of his cattle and his serfs. These
were his permanent family wealth, and he was rich
or poor as he had more or less of them. So long as
the tribe land was plentiful, he as the head of a tribal
household took his proper share according to tribal
rank ; and so long as periodical redistributions took
place, even when the tribal household finally was

---

[1] *Germania,* xx.

broken up, room would be found for the new tribal households on the tribal land. But when at last the limits of the land became too narrow for the tribe, a portion of the tribesmen would swarm off to seek new homes in a new country. Frequent migrations were, therefore, at once the proofs of pressure of population and the safety-valve of the system.

Fresh settle-ments.

The emigrating tribesmen in their new home would form themselves into a new sept or tribe, take possession of fresh tracts of unoccupied land, and perhaps, if land were plentiful, wander about for a time from place to place as pasture for their cattle might tempt them. Then at last they would settle : each tribesman would select his site by plain, wood or stream, as it pleased him. He would erect his stake and wattle tribal house, and daub it over with clay [1] to keep out the weather. He would put up his rough outbuildings and fence in his corn and cattle yard. Round this tribal homestead the still rougher homesteads of his serfs, each with its yard around it, would soon form a straggling village, and the likeness to the embryo manor would once more appear.

The celebrated passage of Tacitus describing German agricul-ture.

Indeed, when we turn to the famous passage in which the German settlements and their internal economy are described, the words used by Tacitus seem in themselves to indicate that he had in his eye precisely this process which the example of the Welsh and Irish tribal systems has helped to make intelli-gible to us. Tracts of country (*agri*), he says, are ' *taken possession of* ' (*occupantur*) by a body of tribes-men (*ab universis*) who are apparently seeking new

---

[1] *Germania*, xvi.

homes ; and then the *agri* are presently divided among Chap. IX. them.

This passage, so often and so variously construed and interpreted, is as follows :—

> ' Agri pro numero cultorum ab universis vicis [or *in* or *per vices*] [1] occupantur, quos mox inter se secundum dignationem partiuntur : facilitatem partiendi camporum spatia præstant.
>
> ' Arva per annos mutant, et superest ager : nec enim cum ubertate et amplitudine soli labore contendunt, ut pomaria conserant et prata separent et hortos rigent : sola terræ seges imperatur.' [2]

It is unfortunate that the first few lines of this passage are made ambiguous by an error in the texts. If the true reading be, as many modern German critics now hold, ' *ab universis vicis* '—by all the *vici* together, or by the whole community in *vici*—there still must remain the doubt whether the word *vicus* should not be considered rather as the equivalent of the Welsh *trev* than of the modern *village*. The Welsh ' trev ' was, as we have seen, a subordinate cluster of scattered households. Tacitus himself probably uses the word in this sense in the passage where he describes the choice of the chiefs, or head men (*principes*) ' qui jura per pagos *vicos*que reddunt.' [3] The *vicus* is here evidently a smaller tribal subdivision of the *pagus*, just as the Welsh *trev* was of the ' *cymwd*,' and not necessarily a village in the modern sense. [4]

---

[1] The Bamberg Codex has ' *ab universis vicis*,' and this is followed by Waitz (*Verfassungsgeschichte*, Kiel, 1880, i. 145). The Leyden Codex has ' in vicem.' Others ' per vices,' which earlier critics considered to be an error for ' per vicos.' See Wietersheim's *Ge-*

schichte der *Völkerwanderung*, with Dahn's notes, i. p. 43. Leipzig, 1880.

[2] *Germania*, xxvi.

[3] *Id.* xii.

[4] The Welsh ' trev ' and German ' dorf' probably are from the same root.

Chap. IX.

Fresh *agri* taken possession of and divided under tribal rules.

If, on the other hand, the true reading be '*ab universis in,* or *per, vices* or *invicem,* the meaning probably is that fresh tracts of land (*agri*) are one after another taken possession of by the tribal community when it moves to a new district or requires more room as its numbers increase.

The new *agri,* the passage goes on to say, are soon divided among the tribesmen or the *trevs,* '*secundum dignationem,*' according to the tribal rules, the great extent of the open country and absence of limits making the division easy, just as it was in the instance of Abraham and Lot.

In any case it is impossible to suppose that Tacitus meant by the words *in vices* or *invicem,* if he used them, that there was any *annual* shifting of the tribe from one locality to another, for it is obvious that the very next words absolutely exclude the possibility of an annual movement such as that described by Cæsar. '*Arva per annos mutant et superest ager.*' They change their *arva* or ploughed land yearly, *i.e.,* they plough up fresh portions of the *ager* or grass land every year, and there is always plenty left over which has never been ploughed.[1] Nothing could describe more clearly what is mentioned in the Welsh triads as '*co-aration of the waste.*' The tribesmen have their scattered homesteads surrounded by the lesser homesteads of their 'servi.' And the latter join in the co-tillage of such part of the grass land as year by year is chosen for the corn crops, while the cattle wander over the rest.

---

[1] ' "*Ager*" dictus qui a divisoribus agrorum relictus est ad pascendum communiter vicinis.' Isodorus, *De Agris.* Lachmann and Rudorff, i. p. 369.

This seems to have been the simple form of the open field husbandry of the Germans of Tacitus.

And this is sufficient for the present purpose ; for whichever way this passage be read, it does not modify the force of the previous passages, which show how manorial were the lines upon which the German tribal system was moving even in this early and still tribal stage of its economic development, owing chiefly to the possession of serfs by the tribesmen. It gives us further a clear landmark as regards the use by the Germans of the open-field system of ploughing. Tacitus describes a husbandry in the stage of ' co-ara-tion of the waste.' It has not yet developed into a fixed *three-course* rotation of crops, pursued over and over again permanently on the same arable area, as in ' the three-field system ' afterwards so prevalent in Germany and England.

These are important points to have gained, but the most important one is that, notwithstanding the strong resemblances between the Welsh and German tribal arrangements, there was this distinct difference between them. The two tribal systems were not working themselves out, so to speak, on the same lines. The Welsh system, in its economic develop-ment, was not directly approaching the manorial arrangement except perhaps on the mensal land of the chiefs. The Welsh tribesmen had as a rule no servile tenants under them. The *taeogs* were mostly the *taeogs* of the chiefs, not of the tribesmen. Thus, as we have seen, when the conquest of Wales was completed, the tribesmen of the till then unconquered districts became freeholders under the Prince of Wales, and with no *mesne* lord over them. The taeogs be-

The ten-dency of the Ger-man tribal system un-like the Welsh to-wards the manor.

came taeogs of the Prince of Wales and not of local landowners. So that the manor did not arise. But even in the time of Tacitus the German tribesmen seem to have already become practically manorial lords over their own *servi*, who were already so nearly in the position of serfs on their estates that Tacitus described them as ' *like coloni.*'

The German and Roman elements easily combined to make the manor.

The manor—in embryo—was, in fact, already in course of development. The German economic system was, to say the very least, working itself out on lines so nearly parallel to those of the Roman manorial system that we cannot wonder at the silent ease with which before and after the conquest of Roman provinces, German chieftains became lords of villas and manors. The two systems, Roman and German, may well have easily combined in producing the later manorial system which grew up in the Roman provinces of Gaul and the two Germanies.

II. THE TRIBAL HOUSEHOLDS OF GERMAN SETTLERS.

Now, if we were to rely upon this evidence of Tacitus alone, the conclusion would be inevitable that the German and Roman land-systems were so nearly alike in their tendencies that they naturally and simply joined in producing the manorial system of later times. And there can be little doubt that, speaking broadly, this would be a substantially correct statement of the case.

Were there other kinds of settlements not so manorial?

But before we can fairly and finally accept it as such, it is necessary to consider another branch of evidence which has sometimes been understood to point to a kind of settlement *not manorial.*

The evidence alluded to is that of *local names* ending in the remarkable suffix *ing* or *ingas*. It is needful to examine this evidence, notwithstanding its difficult and doubtful nature. It raises a question upon which the last word has by no means yet been spoken, and out of which interesting and important results may eventually spring. The impossibility of arriving, in the present state of the evidence, at a positive conclusion, is no reason why its apparent bearing should not be stated, provided that sugges- tion and hypothesis be not confounded with verified fact. At all events, the inquiry pursued in this essay would be open to the charge of being one-sided if it were not alluded to.

The reader of recent literature bearing upon the history of the English conquest of Britain will have been struck by the confidence and skill with which, in the absence of historical, or even, in some cases, traditional evidence, the story of the invasion and occupation of England has been sometimes created out of little more than the combination of physical geography with local names, on the hypothesis that local names ending in '*ing*,' or its plural form '*ingas*,' represent the original *clan settlements* of the German conquerors. Writers who rely upon G. L. Von Maurer's theory of the German *mark-system* have also naturally called attention to local names with this suffix as evidence of settlements on the basis of the *free village community* as opposed to those of a manorial type.

Local names with this suffix, it is hardly needful to say, are found on the Continent as well as in England.

CHAP. IX.

How, it may well be asked, does the evidence they afford of *clan settlements* or *free village communities* comport with the thoroughly manorial character of the German settlements on the lines described by Tacitus?

What Germans did Tacitus describe?

Now, in order to answer this question, it must first be considered how far the description of Tacitus covers the whole field—whether it refers to the Germans as a whole, or whether only to those tribes who had come within Roman influences, and so had sooner, perhaps, than the rest, relinquished their earlier tribal habits to follow manorial lines.

So far as his description is geographical it is very methodical.

Those within the *limes.*

(1) There are the Germans *within* the Roman *limes.*[1] These included the tribes who, following up the conquests of Ariovistus, had settled on the left bank of the Rhine in what was then called the province of Upper Germany, including the present Elsass and the country round the confluence of the Rhine with the Maine and Moselle. These tribes were the Tribocci, Nemetes and Vangiones.[2] Further, there were the tribes or emigrants, many of them German, gradually settling within the limits of the ' Agri Decumates.' Lastly, there were the *Batavi* and other tribes settled in the province of Lower Germany at the mouths of the Rhine, shading off into Belgic Gaul.

Northern tribes outside it.

(2) There were the Northern tribes *outside* the Roman province,[3] some of them tributary to the

---

[1] *Germania*, xxviii. and xxix.
[2] These tribes are mentioned by Cæsar as forming part of the army
of Ariovistus. *De Bello Gallico*, lib. i. c. 51.
[3] *Germania*, xxx.-xxxvii.

Romans and some of them hostile, the *Frisii*, the *Chatti* (or Hessians), and other tribes, reaching from the German Ocean to the mountains, and occupying the country embracing the upper valleys of the Weser and the Elbe, some of which tribes afterwards joined the Franks and Saxons.

(3) There were the *Suevic* tribes[1] so familiar to Cæsar, and amongst whom were the *Angli* and *Varini*, the *Marcomanni* and *Hermunduri*, always hovering over the *limes* of the provinces from the Rhine and Maine to the Danube : some of them hostile and some of them friendly ; some of whom afterwards mingled with the Franks and Saxons, but most of whom were absorbed in the Alamannic and the Bavarian tribes who finally, following the course of the previous emigration, passed over the *limes* and settled within the 'Agri Decumates' in Rhætia, and in the Roman province of Upper Germany.

(4) Behind all these tribes with whom the Romans came in contact were others vaguely described as lying far away to the north and east.

The habits of *which* of these widely different classes of German tribes did Tacitus describe?

Probably it would not be safe to go further than to say that the Germans whose manners he was most *likely* to describe were those chiefly *Suevic* tribes hovering round the *limes* of the provinces, especially of the 'Agri Decumates,' with whom the Romans had most to do. It is at least possible that he left out of his picture, on the one hand, those distant northern or eastern tribes who may still have retained their early nomadic habits, and on the other hand those

---

[1] *Germania*, xxxviii.–xlv.

Germans who had silently and peaceably settled within the *limes* of the Roman provinces, and so had become half Roman.[1]

But to what class are we to refer the settlements represented by the local names with the supposed patronymic suffix?

The previous study of the Welsh and Irish tribal system ought to help us to judge what they were.

In the first place we have clearly learned that in tracing the connexion of the tribal system with local names, the fixing of a particular personal name to a locality implies *settlement*. It implies not only a departure from the old nomadic habits on the part of the whole tribe, but also the absence within the territory of the tribe of those redistributions of the tribesmen among the homesteads—the shifting of families from one homestead to another—which prevailed apparently in Wales and certainly in Ireland to so late a date.

Following the parallel experience of the Irish and Welsh tribal system we may certainly conclude that in the early semi-nomadic and shifting tribal stage described by Cæsar the names of places, like those of the Irish townlands, would follow local peculiarities of wood or stream or plain, and that not until there was a permanent settlement of particular families in fixed abodes could personal names attach themselves to places, or suffixes be used which in themselves involve the idea of a fixed abode.

Then with regard to the nature of the tribal settlements which these local names with a patronymic

---

[1] He regarded the 'Agri Decumates' as 'hardly in Germany.'

suffix may represent, surely the actual evidence of
the Welsh laws and the 'Record of Carnarvon,' as to
what a *tribal household* was, must be far more likely
to guide us to the truth than any theoretical view of
the 'village community' under the German mark-
system, or even actual examples of village communities
existing under complex and totally different circumstances at the present time, valuable as such examples
may be as evidence of how the descendants of tribesmen comport themselves after perhaps centuries of
settlement on the same ground.

Now we have seen that the tribal household in
Wales was the joint holding of the heirs of a common
ancestor from the *great-grandfather* downwards, with
redistributions within it to make equality, first between
brothers, then between cousins, and finally between
second cousins; the youngest son always retaining
the original homestead in these divisions. The *Weles,*
Gwelys, and *Gavells* of the 'Record of Carnarvon' were
late examples of such holdings. They were named
after the common ancestor and occupied by his heirs.
Such holdings, so soon as there was fixed settlement
in the homesteads, were obviously in the economic
stage in which, according to German usage, the name
of the original holders with the patronymic suffix
might well become permanently attached to them.[1]

We may then, following the Welsh example, fairly
expect the distinctive marks of the tribal household to
be joint holding for two or three *generations*, and then
the *ultimate division of the holding among male heirs,*
the *youngest retaining the original ancestral homestead.*

---

[1] This result did not follow in Wales, because in Welsh local names
suffixes are not usual.

We know how persistently the division among male heirs was adhered to in Wales and in Ireland under the custom of Gavelkind,[1] though of the peculiar right of the youngest son to the original homestead we have no clear trace in Ireland. Possibly St. Patrick was strong enough to reverse in this instance a strong tribal custom. But in Wales the succession of the youngest was, as we have seen, so deeply ingrained in the habits of the people that it was observed even among the *taeogs.* The elder sons received *tyddyns* of their own in the *taeog trev* in their father's lifetime, whilst the youngest son remained in his father's tyddyn, and on his death succeeded to it.

The persistence in division among heirs and the right of the youngest were very likely therefore to linger as survivals of the tribal household.

Survival of this equal division and *the right of the youngest.*

Now it is well known that in the south-east of England, and especially in Kent, the custom of Gavelkind has continued to the present day, retaining the division among male heirs and historical traces of the right of the youngest son to the original homestead. In other districts of England and in many parts of Europe and Asia the division among heirs has passed away, but the right of the youngest—*Jüngsten-Recht* —has survived.

Mr. Elton, in his ' *Origins of English History*,' has carefully described the geographical distribution in Western Europe of the practice, not so much of *division among heirs*, as of the *right of the youngest* to

---

[1] *Gavelkind* may be derived from *gabel*, a fork or branch, and the word is used in Ireland as well as in Kent. Irish *gabal, gabal-cined* (Gavelkind). *Manners, &c. of the Ancient Irish.* O'Curry, iii. p. 581.

inherit the *original homestead*, the latter having survived in many districts where the other has not.

In England he finds the right of the youngest
most prevalent in the south-east counties—in Kent,
Sussex, and Surrey, in a ring of manors round London,
and to a less extent in Essex and the East Anglian
kingdom,—*i.e.* as Mr. Elton describes it, in a district
about co-extensive with what in Roman times was
known as the *Saxon shore.* A few examples occur in
Hampshire, and there is a wide district where the
right of the youngest survives in Somersetshire, which
formed for so long a part of what the Saxons called
' *Wealcyn.*' [1]

Further, as the custom is found to apply to copyhold or semi-servile holdings, it would not be an impossible conjecture that previously existing original
tribal households were, at some period, upon conquest, reduced into serfs, the division of the holdings
among heirs being at the same time stopped, so as to
keep the holdings in equal ' yokes,' or ' yard-lands,'
thus leaving the right of the youngest as the only
point of the pre-existing tribal custom permitted to
survive.

A similar process, perhaps in connexion with the
Frankish conquest of parts of Germany, possibly
had been gone through in many continental districts.
Mr. Elton traces the right of the youngest in the
north-east corner of France and in Brabant, in Fries-
land, in Westphalia, in Silesia, in Wirtemberg, in the
Odenwald and district north of Lake Constance, in
Suabia, in Elsass, in the Grisons. It is found also in

---

[1] *Origins of English History,* pp. 188–9.

the island of Borneholm, though it seems to be absent in Denmark and on the Scandinavian mainland.[1]

Attention has been called to this curious survival of the right of the youngest because it forms a possible link between the Welsh, English, and continental systems of settlements in tribal households.

We now pass to the more direct consideration of the local names with the supposed patronymic suffix.

Wide extension and meaning of the patronymic suffix 'ing,' &c.
These peculiar local names are scattered over a wide area; the suffix varying from the English *ing* with its plural ' *ingas*,' the German *ing* or *ung* with its plural *ingas, ingen, ungen, ungun*, and the French ' *ign* ' or *igny*, to the Swiss[2] equivalent *ikon*, the Bohemian *ici*,[3] and the wider Slavonic *itz* or *witz*.

It seems to be clear that the termination *ing*, in its older plural form *ingas*, in Anglo-Saxon, not by any means always,[4] but still in a large number of cases, had a *patronymic* significance.

We have the evidence of the Anglo-Saxon Chronicle itself that if *Baldo* were the name of the parent, his children or heirs would in Anglo-Saxon be called *Baldings*[5] (Baldingas).

There is also evidence that the oldest historical form of settlement in Bohemian and Slavic districts

---

[1] *Origins of English History,* pp. 197–98.

[2] Arnold's *Ansiedelungen*, p. 89.

[3] Palacky's *Geschichte von Böhmen*, Buch ii. c. 6, p. 169.

[4] ' Ing' also meant a low meadow by a river bank, as ' *Clifton Ings*,' near York, &c. Also it was sometimes used like ' ers,' as ' *Ochringen*,' dwellers on the river ' Ohra.'

In Denmark the individual strip in a meadow was an ' ing,' and so the whole meadow would be ' *the ings*.'

[5] See Anglo-Saxon Chronicle *sub anno* 522. ' Cordic was Elesing, Elesa was Esling, Esla was Gewising,' and so on. See also Bede's statement that the Kentish kings were called *Oiscings*, after their ancestor *Oisc*. Bede, bk. ii. c. 5.

was in the tribal or joint household—the undivided family sometimes for many generations herding together in the same homestead (*dědiny*).[1]

And the number of local names ending in *ici*, or *owici*, changing in later times into *itz* and *witz*, taken together with the late prevalence of the undivided household in these semi-Slavonic regions, so far as it goes, confirms the connexion of the patronymic termination with the holding of the co-heirs of an original holder.[2]

The geographical distribution of local names with the patronymic termination is shown on the same map as that on which were marked the position of the 'hams' and 'heims.'

First, as regards England, the map will show that In Eng-land. in the distribution of places mentioned in the Domesday survey ending in *ing*, the largest proportion occurs east of a line drawn from the Wash to the Isle of Wight : just as in the case of the 'hams,' only that in Sussex the greatest number of 'ings' occurs instead of in Essex.

It is worthy of notice that names ending in *ingham* or *ington* are not confined so closely to this district, but are spread much more evenly all over England.[3] Further, it will be observed that the counties where the names ending in *ing* occur without a suffix are remarkably coincident with those where Mr. Elton has found survivals of the *right of the youngest, i.e.* the old 'Saxon shore.'

---

[1] Palacky, pp. 168–9. Compare the word with the Welsh *tyddyn*, and the Irish *tate* or *tath*.

[2] See Meitzen's *Ausbreitung der*

Deutschen, p. 17. Jena, 1879.

[3] See Taylor's *Words and Places*, p. 131.

Next, as to the opposite coast of *Picardy*, the *ings* and *hems* are alike, for very nearly all the *hems* in the Survey of the Abbey of St. Bertin of A.D. 850 are preceded by *ing*, *i.e.* they are *inghems*. The proportion was found to be sixty per cent.[1]   In this north-east corner of France the right of the youngest, as we have seen, also survives.

In the Moselle valley and round Troyes and Langres.   There are also many patronymic names of places in the Moselle valley and in Champagne around Troyes and Langres.[2]

In Frisia.   Next, as to *Frisia*, eight per cent. of the names mentioned in the Fulda records end in '*inga*,' two and a half per cent. in *ingaheim*, and three per cent in *ing* with some other suffix, making thirteen and a half per cent. in all.   In Friesland also there are survivals of the *right of the youngest*.

In Germany most densely in the old Roman provinces of the 'Agri Decumates.'   Over North Germany, outside the Roman *limes*, the proportion is much less, shading off in the Fulda records from six to three, two, and one per cent.

But the greatest proportion occurs within the Roman *limes* in the valleys of the Neckar and the Upper Danube, where (according to the Fulda records) it rises to from twenty to twenty-four per cent.,[3] shading off to ten per cent. towards the Maine, and in the present Elsass, and to nine per cent. southwards in the neighbourhood of St. Gall.[4]

---

[1] It is curious to observe that, taking all the names in the Cartulary (including many of *later date*), only 2 per cent. end in *ing* or *inga*, 6 per cent. in *inghem* or *ingahem*: making 8 per cent. in all.

[2] Taylor's *Words and Places*, pp. 496 *et seq.*

[3] Out of 119 places named in the charters of the Abbey of *Frisinga* earlier in date than A.D. 800, 24 per cent. ended in *inge*, and only 1 per cent. in *heim*.—Meichelbeck, *passim*.

[4] In the St. Gall charters, out of 1,920 names, 9 per cent. end in

This chief home of the 'ings' was the western part of the district of the 'Agri Decumates' of Tacitus and the northern province of Rhætia, gradually occupied by the Alamannic and Bavarian tribes in the later centuries of Roman rule.

Whether they entered these districts under cover of the Roman peace, or as conquerors to disturb it, the founders of the 'ings' evidently came from German mountains and forests beyond the *limes*.

North of the Danube names with this suffix extend chiefly through the region of the old Hermunduri into the district of Grapfeld and Thuringia, where they were in the Fulda records six per cent. *North of the* limes *chiefly in Grapfeld and Thuringia.*

This remarkable geographical distribution in Germany suggests important inferences.

(1) The attachment of the personal patronymic to the name of a particular locality implies in Germany no less than in Ireland and Wales a permanent settlement in that locality, and so far an abandonment of nomadic habits and even of the frequent redistributions and shifting of residences within the tribal territory. *They suggest settlements*

(2) The occurrence of these patronymic local names most thickly *within the Roman limes* and near to it, points to the fact that the Roman rule was the outside influence which compelled the abandonment of the semi-nomadic and the adoption of the settled form of life. *within Roman provinces,*

(3) The addition in some cases—most often in Flanders and in England, which were both Roman *possibly manorial,*

---

inga, 3½ per cent. in *inchova*. The most common other terminations are either *wilare* or *wanga*; only 2 per cent. end in *heim*.

CHAP. IX. provinces—of the suffix *ham* to the patronymic local name, although most probably a *later* addition, and possibly the result of conquest, at least reminds us of the possibility already noticed that even a *villa* or *ham* or manor, with a servile population upon it, might be the possession of a tribal household, who thus might be the lords of a manorial estate.

Offshoots from Suevic tribes who became Alamanni.

(4) Considering the geographical distribution of the patronymic termination, beginning in Thuringia and Grapfeld, but becoming most numerous in Rhætia and the 'Agri Decumates,' it is almost impossible to avoid the inference that it is in most cases connected with settlements in these Roman districts of offshoots from the old Suevic tribe of the Hermunduri—viz. *Thuringi*, *Juthungi*, and others who, settling in these districts during Roman rule, became afterwards lost in the later and greater group of the *Alamanni*.

Forced settlement of Alamanni in Belgic Gaul,

This inference might possibly be confirmed by the fact that the isolated clusters of names ending in 'ing' on the west of the Rhine, correspond in many instances with the districts into which we happen to know that forced colonies of families of these and other German tribes had been located after the termination of the Alamannic wars of Probus, Maximian, and Constantius Clorus. These colonies of *læti* were planted, as we have seen, in the valley of the Moselle, and the names of places ending in 'ing' are numerous there to this day. They were planted in the district of the Tricassi round Troyes and Langres, and here again there are numerous patronymic names. They were planted in the district of the Nervii round Amiens close to the cluster of names ending in 'ingahem,' so many of which in the ninth century are

found to belong to the Abbey of St. Bertin. Lastly—
and this is a point of special interest for the present
inquiry—we know that similar deportations of tribesmen of the Alamannic group were repeatedly made
into Britain, and thus the question arises whether
the places ending in 'ing' in England may not also
mark the sites of peaceable or forced settlements of
Germans under Roman rule.

They lie, as we have seen, chiefly within the
district of the Saxon shore, *i.e.* east of a line between the Wash and the Isle of Wight, just as was
the case also with the survivals of the *right of the
youngest.*

If evidence had happened to have come to hand
of a similar deportation of Alamannic Germans into
Frisia instead of Frisians into Gaul, the coincidence
would be still more complete.

The suggestion is very precarious. Still, it might
be asked, where should clusters of tribal households
of Germans resembling the Welsh *Weles* and *Gavells*
be more likely to perpetuate their character and
resist for a time manorial tendencies than in these
cases of peaceable or forced emigration into Roman
provinces? Who would be more likely to do so than
troublesome septs (like that of the Cumberland
'*Grames*' in the days of James I.) deported bodily to
a strange country, and settled, probably not on private
estates, but on previously depopulated public land,
without slaves, and without the possibility of acquiring
them by making raids upon other tribes?

Now, according to Professor Wilhelm Arnold, the
German writer who has recently given the closest
attention to these local names, the patronymic suffix

' ingen ' is one of the distinctive marks of settlements of Alamannic and Bavarian tribes, and denotes that the districts wherein it is found have at some time or another been conquered or occupied by them. The *heims*, on the other hand, in this writer's view, are in the same way indicative of Frankish settlements.[1]

The view of so accurate and laborious a student must be regarded as of great authority. But the foregoing inquiry has led in both cases to a somewhat different suggestion as to their meaning. The suffix *heim* is Anglo-Saxon as well as Frankish, and translating itself into villa and manor seems to represent a settlement or estate most often of the manorial type. So that it seems likely, that whatever German tribes at whatever time came over into the Roman province and usurped the lordship of existing villas, or adopted the Roman villa as the type of their settlements, would probably have called them either *weilers* or *heims* according to whether they used the Roman or the German word for the same thing.

And in the same way it also seems likely, that *whatever tribes*, at *whatever time*, by their own choice or by forced colonisation, settled in *house communities of tribesmen with or without a servile population under them*, would be passing through the stage in which they might naturally call their settlements or home-

---

[1] Arnold's *Ansiedelungen und Wanderungen deutscher Stämme.* Marburg, 1881. See pp. 155 *et seq.* He considers that the Alamanni were a group of German peoples who had settled in the Rhine valley and the *Agri Decumates*, including among them the *Juthungi*, who had crossed over from the north of the *limes* late in the third century.

CHAP. IX.

steads after their own names, using the patronymic suffix *ing*.

It is undoubtedly difficult to obtain any clear indication of the *time* [1] when these settlements may have been made. Nor, perhaps, need they be referred generally to the same period, were it not for the remarkable fact that the *personal names* prefixed to the suffix in England, Flanders, the Moselle valley, round Troyes and Langres, in the old *Agri Decumates* (now Wirtemburg), and in the old Rhætia (now Bavaria), and even those in Frisia, were to a very large extent *identical*.

This identity is so striking, that if the names were, as some have supposed, necessarily *clan-names*, it might be impossible to deny that the English and continental districts were peopled actually by branches of the same *clans*. But it must be admitted that, as the names to

The names are not *clan* names, but personal names.

---

[1] In the *Erklärung der Peutinger Tafel*, by E. Paulus, Stuttgart, 1866, there is a careful attempt to identify the stations on the Roman roads from *Brigantia* to *Vindonissa*, and from *Vindonissa* to *Regino*. The stations on the latter, which passed through the district abounding in 'ings,' are thus identified; the distances between them, except in one case (where there is a difference of 2 leugen), answering to those marked in the *Table* (see p. 35):—

Vindonissa (Windisch), *Tenedone* (Heidenschlöschen), *Juliomago* (Hüfingen), *Brigobanne* (Rottweil), *Aris flavis* (Unter-Iflingen), *Samulocennis* (Rottenberg), *Grinario* (Sindelfingen), *Clarenna* (Cannstatt), *Ad lunam* (Pfahlbronn),

Aquileia (Aalen) [up to which point there is a remarkable change of names throughout, but from which point the similarity of names becomes striking], *Opie* (Bopfingen), *Septemiaci* (Maihingen), *Losodica* (Oettingen), *Medianis* (Markhof), *Iciniaco* (Itzing), *Biricianis* (Burkmarshofen), *Vetonianis* (Nassenfels), *Germanico* (Kösching), *Celeuso* (Ettling), *Abusena* (Abensberg), *Regino* (Regensburg). But these names in *ing* and *ingen*, and Latin *iaci*, do not seem to be patronymic. So also in the case of the Roman ' *Vicus Aurelii* ' on the *Ohra* river, now 'Oehringen.' Is it not possible that many other supposed patronymics may simply mean such and such or So-and-so's ' ings ' or meadows?

which the peculiar suffix was added were *personal* names and not family or clan names—*John* and *Thomas*, and not *Smith* and *Jones*—it would not be safe to press the inference from the similarity too far. *Baldo* was the name of a person. There may have been persons of that name in every tribe in Germany. The Baldo of one tribe need not be closely related to the Baldo of another tribe, any more than *John Smith* need be related to *John Jones.* The households of each Baldo would be called *Baldings*, or in the old form *Baldingas*; but obviously the Baldings of England need have no clan-relationship whatever to the Baldings of Upper Germany.[1] Nevertheless, the striking similarity of mere personal names goes for something, and it is impossible to pass it by unnoticed. The extent of it may be shown by a few examples.

But the identity of the names throughout is very remarkable.

In the following list are placed *all* the local names mentioned in the Domesday Survey of *Sussex*, beginning with the first two letters of the alphabet in which the peculiar suffix occurs, whether as final or not,[2] and opposite to them similar personal or local

---

[1] The occasional instances in which the patronymic termination is added to the name of a tree or an animal, has led to the hasty conclusion that the Saxons were '*totemists*,' and believed themselves descended from trees and animals; *e.g.* that the *Buckings* of *Bucks* thought themselves descendants of the beech tree. The fact that *personal names* were taken from trees and animals—that one person called himself '*the Beech*,' another '*the*

Wolf'—quite disposes of this argument, for their households would call themselves '*Beechings*' and '*Wolfings*' in quite a natural course, without any dream of descent from the tree or the animal whose name their father or great-grandfather had borne.

[2] The resemblance is equally apparent whether the comparison be made between names without further suffix or whether those with it are included. See the long list

names taken from the early records of *Wirtemberg*,
i.e. the district of the Rhine, Maine, and Neckar, formerly part of the 'Agri Decumates.'

Sussex.	*Wirtemberg.*
Achingeworde	Acco, Echo, Eccho, Achelm
Aldingeborne	Aldingas
Babintone	Babinberch, Babenhausen,
	Bebingon
Basingeham	Besigheim
Bechingetone	Bechingen
Beddingesjham	Bedzingeswilaeri
Belingeham	Bellingon, Böllingerhof
Berchinges	Bercheim
Bevringetone	
Bollintun	Bollo, Bollinga
Botingelle	Böttinger
Brislinga	Brisgau

As regards the supposed patronymic names in
the district between Calais and St. Omer, Mr. Taylor
states that 80 per cent. are found also in England.[1]

We may take as a further example the resemblance
between names of places occurring in Sprüner's maps
of '*Deutschlands Gaue*' in the Moselle valley and those
of places and persons mentioned in early Wirtemberg
charters.

Moselle Valley.	*Wirtemberg.*
Beringa	Beringerus
Eslingis	Esslingen
Frisingen	Frieso, Frisingen
Gundredingen	Gundrud
Heminingsthal	Hemminbah
Holdingen	Holda
Hasmaringa	Hasmaresheim
Lukesinga	Lucas, Lucilunburch

of patronymic names in England, 496–513.
Germany, and France in Taylor's   [1] Taylor's *Words and Places,* pp.
Words and Places, App. B, pp.   131–4, and App. B, p. 491.

Moselle Valley.	*Wirtemberg.*
Munderchinga	Mundricheshuntun, Munderkingen
Ottringas	Oteric, Otrik
Putilinga	Pettili, Pertilo
Uffeninga	Ufeninga
Uttingon	Uto, Uttinuuilare

In Champagne.

The following coincidences [1] occur in the modern Champagne, which embraces another district into which forced emigrants were deported.

Champagne.	*England.*	*Wirtemberg.*
Autigny	Edington	Eutingen
Effincourt	Effingham	Oeffingen
Euffigneux	Uffington	Offingen
Alincourt	Allington	—
Arrigne	Arrington	Erringhausen
Orbigny	Orpington	Erpfingen
Attigny	Attington	Atting
Etigny	Ettinghall	Oettinger
Bocquegney	Buckingham	Böchingen
Bettigny	Beddington	Böttingen

And so on in about forty cases.

A comparison of the fifteen similar names in *Frisia* occurring in the Fulda records, with other similar names of places or persons in *England* and *Wirtemberg*, gives an equally clear result.

In Frisia.

Frisia.[2]	*Wirtemberg.*[3]	*England.*
Auinge	Au, Auenhofen	{ Avington (Berks and Hants)
Baltratingen	Baldhart, Baldingen	Beltings (Kent)
Belinge	Bellingon	{ Bellingdon ⎫ Several { Bellings ⎭ counties
Bottinge	Böttingen	{ Boddington (Gloucester, Northampton)

---

[1] See the lists given in Taylor's *Words and Places*, Appendix B, pp. 496 *et seq.* Taylor says that there are 1,100 of the patronymic names in France, of which 250 are similar to those in England. See pp. 144 *et seq.*

[2] Taken from *Traditiones Fuldensis*, Dronke, pp. 240–243. The above list includes all the names in Frisia with a patronymic and no other suffix.

[3] Taken from the *Wirtembergische Urkundenbuch.*

Frisia.	*Wirtemberg.*	*England.*	Chap. IX.
Creslinge	{ Creglingen, Chrez- zingen }	{ Cressing (Essex) Cressingham (Norfolk)	
Gandingen	——	——	
Gutinge	——	{ Guyting (Gloucester) Getingas (Surrey)	
Hustinga	——		
Huchingen	{ Huchiheim Huc = Hugo }	Hucking (Kent)	
Husdingun	——	——	
Rochinge	Roingus, Rohinc	Rockingham (Notts)	
Suettenge	Suittes, Suitger		
Wacheringe	Uuachar	Wakering (Essex)	
Wasginge	Uuassingun	Washington (Sussex)	
Weingi	Wehingen	——	

The inferences to be drawn from the similarity.

It is impossible to follow out in greater detail these remarkable resemblances between the personal names which appear with a patronymic suffix in the local names in England and Frisia, and certain well-defined districts west of the Rhine, and the local and personal names mentioned in the Wirtemberg charters. The foregoing instances must not be regarded as more than examples. And for the reasons already given it would also be unwise to build too much upon this evident similarity in the personal names, but still it should be remembered that the facts to be accounted for are—(1) The concentration of these places with names having a supposed patronymic termination in certain defined districts mostly within the old Roman provinces. (2) The practical identity throughout all these districts of so many of the personal names to which this suffix is attached.

The first fact points to these settlements in tribal households having taken place by peaceable or forcible emigration during Roman rule, or very soon after, at all events *at about the same period.* The second fact points to the practical homogeneity of the German tribes, whose emigrants founded the settlements which in England, Flanders, around Troyes and Langres, on the Moselle, in Wirtemberg, in Bavaria, and also in Frisia, bear the common suffix to their names.

The facts already mentioned of the survival *to a great extent in the same districts*, strikingly so in England, of the *right of the youngest*, and in Kent of the original form of the local custom of Gavelkind, point in the same direction.

Taking all these things together, we may at least regard the economic problem involved in them as one deserving closer attention than has yet been given to it.

The settlements in tribal households may have been manors.

In conclusion, turning back to the direct relation of these facts to the process of transition of the German tribal system into the later manorial system, it must be remembered that the holdings of tribal households might quite possibly be, from the first, embryo manors with serfs upon them. They might be settlements precisely like those described by Tacitus, the lordship of which had become the joint inheritance of the heirs of the founder. As a matter of fact, the actual settlements in question had at all events become manors before the dates of the earliest documents. We have seen, *e.g.*, that the villas belonging to the monks of St. Bertin, with their almost invariable suffix ' ingahem,' were manors from the time of the first records in the seventh century, and they may never have been anything else. We have seen that in the year 645 the founder of the abbey gave to the monks his villa called *Sitdiu*, and its twelve dependent villas (*Tatinga villa*, afterwards *Tatingahem*, among them) [1] with the slaves and coloni upon them. They seem to

---

[1] *Chartularium Sithiense*, p. 18.

have been, in fact, so many manorial farms just like
those which, as we learned from Gregory of Tours,
Chrodinus in the previous century founded and handed
over to the Church.

We have not found, therefore, in this inquiry into
the character of the settlements with local names
ending in the supposed patronymic suffix, doubtful as
its result has proved, anything which conflicts with the
general conclusion to which we were brought by the
manorial character of the Roman villa and the manorial tendency of the German tribal system as described
by Tacitus, viz. that as a general rule the German
settlements made upon the conquest of what had once
been Roman provinces were of a strictly manorial
type. If the settlements with names ending in *ing*
were settlements of *læti* or of other emigrants during
Roman rule, taking at first the form of tribal households, they at least became manors like the rest during
or very soon after the German conquests. If, on
the other hand, they were later settlements of the conquerors of the Roman provinces, or of emigrants following in the wake of the conquests, they none the less
on that account soon became just as manorial as those
Roman villas which by a change of lordship and
translation of words may have become German *heims*
or Anglo Saxon *hams*.

It is certainly possible that during a short period,
especially if they held no serfs or slaves, tribal
households may have expanded into free village
communities. But to infer from the existence of
patronymic local names that German emigration at
all generally took the form of free village communities
would surely not be consistent with the evidence.

CHAPTER X.

*THE CONNEXION BETWEEN THE OPEN-FIELD SYSTEM
AND SERFDOM OF ENGLAND AND OF THE ROMAN
PROVINCES OF GERMANY AND GAUL.*

I. THE OPEN-FIELD SYSTEM IN ENGLAND AND IN GERMANY COMPARED.

Chap. X. WE now return to the English manorial and open-field system, in order, taking it up where we left it, to trace its connexion with the similar Continental system, and to inquire in what districts the closest resemblances to it are to be found—whether in the un-Romanised north or in the southern districts so long included within the *limes* of the Roman provinces.

Under the manorial system, the open-field system the shell of serfdom. The earliest documentary evidence available on English ground left us in full possession of the Saxon manor with its village community of serfs upon it, inhabiting as its shell the open-field system in its most organised form, *i.e.* with its (generally) three fields, its furlongs, its acre or half-acre strips, its headlands, its yard-lands or bundles of normally thirty acres, scattered all over the fields, the yard-land representing the year's ploughing of a pair of oxen in the team of

eight, and the acre strip the measure of a day's plough-
work of the team.

This was the system described in the ' *Rectitudines* '
of the tenth century, and the allusions to the ' gebur,'
the ' yard-land,' the ' setene,' the ' gafol,' and the
' week-work ' in the laws of Ine carried back the evidence presumably to the seventh century.

But it must not be forgotten that side by side
with this manorial open-field system we found an
earlier and simpler form of open-field husbandry
carried on by the free tribesmen and taeogs of Wales.
This simpler system described in the Welsh laws
and the ' triads ' seemed to be in its main features
practically identical with that described also in the
Germania of Tacitus. It was an annual ploughing
up of fresh grass-land, leaving it to go back again
into grass after the year's ploughing. It was, in fact,
the agriculture of a pastoral people, with a large
range of pasture land for their cattle, a small portion
of which annually selected for tillage sufficed for their
corn crops. This is clearly the meaning of Tacitus,
' *Arva per annos mutant et superest ager.*' It is clearly
the meaning of the Welsh ' triads,' according to which
the tribesman's right extended to his 'tyddyn,' with
its corn and cattle yard, and to *co-aration of the
waste*.

Nor can there be much mystery in the relation
of these two forms of open-field husbandry to each
other. In both, the arable land is divided in the
ploughing into furlongs and strips. There is co-operation of ploughing in both, the contribution of oxen
to the common team of eight in both, the allotment
of the strips to the owners of the oxen in rotation,

CHAP. X.

Three-field system produced by a three-course rotation of crops. producing the same scattering of the strips in both. The methods are the same. The difference lies in the application of the methods to two different stages of economic growth. The simple form is adapted to the early nomadic stage of tribal life, and survives even after partial settlement, so long as grassland is sufficiently abundant to allow of fresh ground being broken by the plough each year. The more complex and organised form implies fixed settlement on the same territory, the necessity for a settled agriculture within a definite limit, and the consequent ploughing of the same land over and over again for generations. The *three-field* system seems to be simply the adaptation of the early open-field husbandry to a permanent three-course rotation of crops.

But there is a further distinguishing feature of the English three-field system which implies the introduction of yet another factor in the complex result, viz. the *yard-land*. And this indivisible bundle of strips, to which there was always a single succession, was evidently the holding not of a free tribesman whose heirs would inherit and divide the inheritance, but of a serf, to whom an outfit of oxen had been allotted. In fact, the complex and more organised system would naturally grow out of the simpler form under the two conditions of *settlement* and *serfdom*.

Now, turning from England to the Continent, we have in the same way various forms of the open-field system to deal with, and in comparing them with the English system their geographical distribution becomes very important.

Happily, very close attention has recently been given to this subject by German students, and we are

able to rely with confidence on the facts collected by
Dr. Landau,[1] by Dr. Hanssen,[2] and lastly by Dr. August
Meitzen in his *Ausbreitung der Deutschen in Deutsch-*
land,[3] and in his still more recent and interesting
review of the collected works of Dr. Hanssen.[4]

Whilst we learn from these writers that much
remains to be done before the last word can be said
upon so intricate a subject, some general points seem
at least to be clearly made out.

In the first place there are some German systems
of husbandry which may well be weeded out at once
from the rest as not analogous to the Anglo-Saxon
three-field system in England.

There is the old '*Feldgraswirthschaft,*' analogous
perhaps to the Welsh co-ploughing of the waste and
the shifting '*Arva*' of the Germans of Tacitus, which
still lingers in the mountain districts of Germany and
Switzerland, where corn is a secondary crop to grass.[5]

There are the '*Einzelhöfe*' of Westphalia and other
districts, *i.e.* single farms, each consisting mainly of
land all in one block, like a modern English farm,
but as different as possible from the old English open-
field system, with its yard-lands and scattered strips.[6]

Further, there is a peculiar form of the open-field
system, chiefly found in forest and marsh districts, in
which each holding consists generally of *one single*

---

[1] '*Die Territorien in Bezug auf
ihre Bildung und ihre Entwicklung,*'
Hamburg and Gotha, 1854.

[2] Dr. Hanssen's various papers
on the subject are collected in
his *Agrarhistorische Abhandlungen,*
Leipzig, 1880.

[3] Jena, 1879.

[4] '*Georg Hanssen,* als *Agrar-
Historiker.*' Von August Meitzen,
1881. Tübingen.

[5] See Hanssen's chapter, '*Die
Feldgraswirthschaft deutscher Ge-
birgsgegenden,*' in his *Agrarhist.
Abhandl.,* pp. 132 *et seq.*

[6] Landau, pp. 16-20.

long strip of land, reaching from the homestead right across the village territory to its boundary.[1] This system, so different from the prevalent Anglo-Saxon system, is supposed to represent comparatively modern colonisation and reclamation of forest and marsh land ; and though possibly bearing some analogy to the English *fen* system, is not that for which we are seeking.

Passing all these by, we come to a peculiar method of husbandry which covers a large tract of country, and which is adopted under both the single farm system and also the open-field system with scattered ownership, but which nevertheless is opposed to the three-field system. It is especially important for our purpose because of its geographical position.

All over the sand and bog district of the north of Germany, crops, mostly of rye and buckwheat, have for centuries been grown *year after year on the same land,* kept productive by marling and peat manure, on what Hanssen describes as the 'one-field system.'[2] This system is found in Westphalia, East Friesland, Oldenburg, North Hanover, Holland, Belgium, Denmark, Brunswick, Saxony, and East Prussia. Over parts of the district under this one-field system the single-farm system prevails, in others the fields are divided into 'Gewanne' and strips, and there is scattered ownership.

Now, possibly this one-field system, with its marling and peat manure, may have been the system described by Pliny as prevalent in Belgic Britain and Gaul before the Roman conquest,

---

[1] See the interesting examples given in Meitzen's *Ausbreitung,* with maps.

[2] See Hanssen's chapter on the 'Einfeldwirthschaft,' *Agrarhist. Abhandl.* pp. 190 *et seq.*

but certainly it is not the system prevalent in England under Saxon rule. And yet this district where the one-field system is prevalent in Germany is precisely the district from which, according to the common theory, the Anglo-Saxon invaders of Britain came. It is precisely the district of Germany where the three-field system is conspicuously absent. So that although Nasse and Waitz somewhat hastily suggested that the Saxons had introduced the three-field system into England, Hanssen, assuming that the invaders of England came from the north, confidently denies that this was possible. 'The Anglo-'Saxons and the Frisians and Low Germans and ' Jutes who came with them to England cannot [he ' writes] have brought the three-field system with ' them into England, because they did not themselves ' use it at home in North-west Germany and Jutland.' He adds that even in later times the three-field system has never been able to obtain a firm footing in these coast districts.[1]

There remains the question, where on the Continent was prevalent that two- or three-field system analogous to the one most generally prevalent on the manors of England ?

The result of the careful inquiries of Hanssen, Landau, and Meitzen seems to be, broadly speaking, this, viz., that setting aside the complication which arises in those districts where there has been a Slavic occupation of German ground and a German re-occupation of Slavic ground,[2] the ancient three-field system, with its *huben* of scattered strips, was most

---

[1] Hanssen, p. 496.

[2] As to this part of the question, see especially Meitzen's *Ausbreitung.*

generally prevalent south of the Lippe and the Teutoberger Wald, *i.e.* in those districts once occupied by the Suevic tribes located round the Roman *limes*, and still more in those districts within the Roman *limes* which were once Roman provinces— the ' Agri Decumates,' Rhætia, and Germania Prima— the present Baden, Wirtemberg, Swabia, and Bavaria, on the German side of the Rhine, and Elsass and the Moselle valley on its Gallic side.[1]

These once Roman or partly Romanised districts were undoubtedly its chief home. Sporadically and later, it existed further north but not generally.

This general geographical conclusion is very important. But before we can fairly assume either a Roman or South German origin, the similarity of the English and South German systems must be examined in their details and earliest historical traces. Further, the examination must not be confined to the shell. It must be extended also to the serfdom which in Germany as in England, so to speak, lived within it.

In previous chapters some of the resemblances between the English and German systems have incidentally been noticed, but the reader will pardon some repetition for the sake of clearness in the statement of this important comparison.

---

[1] Landau, ' *Die Territorien,*' pp. 32 *et seq.*

II. THE BOUNDARIES, OR ' MARCHÆ.'

First as to the whole territory or ager occupied by the village community or township. This, by the presentment of the homage of the Hitchin Manor, was described in the record by its *boundaries*—from such a place to such a place, and so on till the starting-point was reached again.

In the '*gemœra*' of the Saxon charters the same form was used.

In the '*marchœ*' of the manors surrendered to the abbey of Lorsch in the seventh and eighth centuries, the same form was used in the Rhine valley.

It is, in fact, as we have seen, a form in use before the Christian era, and described by the Roman ' Agrimensores' as often adopted in recording the '*limites*' of irregular territories, to which their rectangular centuriation did not extend.

Now, when we consider this method, it implies permanent settlements close to one another, where even the marshes or forests lying between them have been permanently divided by a fixed line, or it implies that a necessity has arisen to mark off the occupied territory from the *ager publicus*. It may have been derived from the rough and ready methods of marking divisions of tribe-land during the early and unsettled stages of tribal life. But the German settlements described by Tacitus seem to have been without defined boundaries. ' Agri' were taken possession of according to the number of the settlers, *pro numero cultorum*. Not till some outside influence compelled final *settlement* would the necessity for well-marked boundaries of territories arise. And **we** have seen that the evidence of local names strongly points to the Roman rule as this settling influence.

In the Lorsch charters the districts included within the 'marchæ' are often, as we have seen, called 'marks.'

III. THE THREE FIELDS, OR 'ZELGEN.'

The three fields.

Next as to the division of the arable land into fields—generally *three* fields [1]—representing the annual rotation of crops.

The homage of the Hitchin Manor presented that the common fields within the township had immemoriably been and ought to be kept and cultivated in three successive *seasons* of—

 (1) Tilth-grain,
 (2) Etch-grain, and
 (3) Fallow.

The three fields are elsewhere commonly known as the—

 (1) Winter corn,
 (2) Spring corn, and
 (3) Fallow.

Universally, the fallow ends at the autumn sowing of the wheat crop of the next season, which is hence called 'winter corn.'

The word *etch*, or *eddish*, or *edish*, occurs in Tusser, and means the stubble of the previous crop

---

[1] Sometimes in Germany, as in England, there were *two* or more. | See Hanssen's chapters on the '*Zwei-, Vier- und Fünffelderwirthschaft.*'

of whatever kind. Thus, in the 'Directions for
February,' he says,—

> ' Eat *etch*, ere ye plow,
> With hog, sheep, and cow.'[1]

This is evidently to prepare the stubble of the last
year's corn crop for the spring sown bean or other
crop ; for under the same month he says,—

> Go plow in the stubble, for now is the season
> For sowing of vetches, of beans, and of peason.[2]

In the directions for the October sowing are the
following lines :—

> Seed first go fetch
> For *edish*, or *etch*.
> White wheat if ye please,
> Sow now upon pease.[3]

And again,—

> When wheat upon *eddish* ye mind to bestow
> Let that be the first of the wheat ye do sow.
> .   .   .   .
> White wheat upon pease-*etch* doth grow as he would,
> But fallow is best if we did as we should.
> .   .   .   .
> When peason ye had and a fallow thereon,
> Sow wheat ye may well without dung thereupon.[4]

' Etch-grain ' is therefore the crop, generally
oats or beans, sown in spring after ploughing the
stubble of the wheat crop, which itself was best
sown if possible upon the fallow, and so was called
the ' tilth-grain.'

The oats or beans grown on the wheat stubble
were sometimes called '*Breach*-corn,' and *Breach*-
land was land prepared for a second crop.[5]

---

[1] Tusser, 'February Abstract.'
[2] *Id.* ' February Husbandry.'
[3] *Id.* 'October Abstract.'
[4] *Id.* ' October Husbandry.'
[5] Halliwell, *sub voce.*

Where shall we find these words and things on the Continent?

Looking to the Latin words used for the three fields, it is obvious that these were sometimes regarded as three separate ploughings—*araturæ*, or *culturæ*,—or as so many sowings—*sationes*,[1]—just as in the north of England they are called 'falls,' or 'fallows,' which have to be ploughed.

In North Germany, where they occur, they are generally simply called '*felder*;'[2] in France around Paris they were called in the ninth century '*sationes*;'[3] but in South Germany and Switzerland the usual word for each field is *Zelg*, which Dr. Landau connects with the Anglo-Saxon '*tilgende*' (tilling), and the later English '*tilth*,' one of the Hitchin words. And he says that *Zelg* strictly means only the ploughed field[4] (*aratura*), though used for all the three. The three fields were thus spoken of as three *tilths*. The word '*Zelg*' we have already found in the St. Gall charters in the eighth century, and Dr. Landau points out other instances of the same date of its use in the districts of Swabia, the middle Rhine, and later in the Inn Valley.

On the other hand, in Westphalia, in Baden, and especially in Upper Swabia and Upper Bavaria, as far as the river Isar, and also in Switzerland, the word *Esch* is the one in use,[5] the word being used in

---

[1] '*Campis Sationalibus*' Charter, A.D. 704. B. M. Ancient Charter, Cotton MS. Augustus, ii. 82. '*Tuican hom*' (Twickenham, in Middlesex).

[2] Landau, 53.

[3] Guerard's *Polyp. d'Irminon.* '*Arat inter tres sationes pertica tres*,'

pp. 134, &c.; and see Glossary, p. 456.

[4] Landau, p. 54.

[5] Landau, p. 54. 'Die alte Form dieses Wortes ist *ezzisc, ezzisca, ezzisch* (gothisch *atisk*), und wird in den Glossen durch *segetes* erklärt.'

Westphalia, also for the whole arable area.[1] *Esch* CHAP. X also was in use at the date of the earliest form of the Bavarian laws (in the seventh century). The hedge put up in defence of the sown field is there called an '*ezzisczun.*'[2] Still earlier, in the fourth century, further East the open fields seem to have been called '*attisk*;' for Ulphilas, in his translation of Mark ii. 23, speaks of the disciples walking over the '*attisk*'—*i.e.* over the '*etch*,' or '*eddish*'—instead of as in the Anglo-Saxon translation over the '*œcera.*' Here, therefore, we have another of the Hitchin words.

In Hesse, according to Dr. Landau, the three 'Brach-fields are spoken of as— frichte.'

(1) In der *Lentzen.*
(2) In der *Brache.*
(3) In der *Rure.*

On the Main, in the fifteenth century, they were spoken of as—

(1) *Lenz* frichte.
(2) *Brach* frichte.
(3) *Rur* frichte.

In Elsass, in the fourteenth century, and on the Danube—

(1) Brochager (Brach field)
(2) Rurager (Fallow field)

were used, and Dr. Landau says that *Esch* is sometimes put in contrast with '*Brach.*'[3] Whatever may be

---

[1] Hanssen's chapter, '*Zur Geschichte der Feldsysteme in Deutschland*,' in his *Agrarhistorische Abhandlungen*, p. 194.

[2] 'Si illum sepem eruperit vel dissipaverit quem *Ezzisczun* vocant,' &c. *Textus Legis Primus*, x. 16.

Pertz, p. 309. In *id.* x. 21 the words '*Semitæ convicinales*' are used of open fields. In the *Burgundian Laws* 'Additamentum Primum*,' tit. 1, 'Agri communes.'

[3] Landau, pp. 54–5.

CHAP. X.

These words point to connexion with South Germany.

the exact meaning of the word *Brach*—whether referring to the breaking of the rotation or the breaking of the stubble—there can be no doubt of the identity of the word with the English *Breach* and *Breach-corn*.

It appears, therefore, that in South Germany, and especially in the districts once Roman province, the three fields representing the rotation of crops for many centuries have been known by names closely resembling those used in England.

IV. THE DIVISION OF THE FIELDS INTO FURLONGS AND ACRES.

Passing next to the divisions of the open fields, we take first the Furlongs or Shots (the Latin *Quarentenæ*).

'Shot.'

The word 'Shot' probably is simply the Anglo-Saxon '*sceot*,' or *division*; but it is curious to find in a document of 1318 mention of 'unam peciam, quod vulgariter dicitur *Schoet*' at *Passau*, near the junction of the Inn with the Danube.[1]

Gewann.'

The usual word in Middle and South Germany' is '*Gewende*,' in Lower Germany '*Wande*' or '*Wanne*,' or '*Gewann*'—words which no less than the Furlong[2] refer to the length of the furrow and the turning of the plough at the end of it.

Headland.

The *headland*, on which the plough was turned,

---

[1] *Passau* received its name from a Roman legion of *Batavi* having been stationed there.—*Mon. Boica*, xxx. p. 83. Landau, p. 49.

[2] In East Friesland, under the one-field system, the word '*flaggen*' is used for 'furlongs.' Hanssen, p. 198.

is also found in the German three-field system as in
England.

In a Frankish document quoted by Dr. Landau, it
is called the ' *Voracker*,' elsewhere it is known as the
' *Anwänder* ' (*versura*), or ' *Vorwart*.' [1]

In the English system the furlongs were divided
into strips or acres by turf balks left in the ploughing, and, as we have seen, on hill-sides, the strips
became terraces, and the balks steep banks called
' linces.' It will be remembered that these were
produced by the practice of always turning the sod
downhill in the ploughing. There are many *linces*
as far north as in the district of the 'Teutoberger
Wald,'[2] and they occur in great numbers as far south
as the Inn Valley, all the way up to St. Mauritz and
Pontresina. Although in many places the terraces
in the Engadine are now grass-land, it is well known
to the peasantry that they were made by ancient
ploughing.

The German word for the turf slope of these
terraces is ' *Rain*,' and, like the word balk, it means
a strip of unploughed turf.[3] It is sometimes used for
the terrace itself. Precisely the same word is used
for the similar terraces in the Dales of Yorkshire,
which are still called by the Dalesmen ' *reeans* ' or
' *reins*.'[4] Terraces of the same kind are found in

---

[1] Landau, p. 32.

[2] There are great numbers to be
seen from the railway from Ems as
far as Nordhausen on the route to
Berlin.

[3] Thus *Rainbalken* is the turf
balk left unploughed as a boundary.

[4] Halliwell. ' *Rain*,' a ridge
(north). See also *Studies*, by

Joseph Lucas, F.G.S., c. viii.,
where there is an interesting description of the ' Reins ' in Nidder-
dale. These terraces occur in
the neighbouring dales of Billsdale,
Bransdale, and Furndale ; and also
in Wharfdale and the valley of the
Ribble, &c.

Scotland; and when Pennant in 1772 asked what they were called, he was told that they were ' *baulks.*' [1]

Both words suggest a wider than merely German origin. ' Balk ' is as thoroughly a Welsh word [2] as it is English and German. ' Rain ' can hardly be other than the Welsh ' *Rhan* ' (a division), or ' *Rhyn* '

The Celtic *Rhan.*

and ' *grwn* ' (a ridge), with which the name of the open-field system in Ireland and Scotland—' *run-rig* ' —is no doubt connected. The English word *lince* or *linch*, with the Anglo-Saxon ' hlinc ' and ' hlince,' is perhaps allied to the Anglo-Saxon ' Hlynian,' or ' Hlinian,' to lean, making its participle ' *hlynigende* ;' and this, and the old High German ' *hlinen*,' are surely connected with the Latin and Italian ' *inclinare* ' and the French ' *enclin.*' As we have seen, the Roman ' Agrimensores ' called these slopes or terraces ' *supercilia.*'

Next let us ask, whence came the English *acre strip* itself ?

The acre strip a day's work.

It represented, as we have seen, a day's work at ploughing. Hence the German *Morgen* and *Tagwerk*, in the Alps *Tagwan* and *Tagwen* ; and hence also, as early as the eighth century, the Latin ' *jurnalis* ' and

---

[1] Pennant's *Tour in Scotland,* p. 281. ' Observed on the right several very regular terraces cut on the face of a hill. They are most exactly formed, a little raised in the middle like a firm walk, and about 20 feet broad, and of very considerable length. In some places were three, in others five flights, placed one above the other, terminating exactly in a line at each end, and most precisely finished. I am told that such tiers of terraces are not uncommon in these parts, where they are called baulks.'

[2] See Pugh's *Welsh Dictionary* : *Balc,* a break in furrow land. *Balcia,* a breaking of furrows. *Balcio,* to break furrows. *Balciog,* having irregular furrows. *Balciwr,* a breaker of furrows. And see *supra,* p. 4.

' *diurnalis.*'[1]   In early Roman times Varro describes
the *jugerum* [or *jugum*]—the Roman acre—as ' *quod*
' *juncti boves uno die exarare possint.*'[2]

The division of arable open fields into day-works
was therefore ancient. It was also widely spread, and
by no means confined to the three-field system. It was
common to the co-aration of both free tribesmen and
' taeogs ' in Wales ; and the Fellahin of Palestine to
this moment divide their open fields into day-works
for the purpose of easy division among them, according to their ploughs or shares in a plough.[3]

In the Irish open-field system, as we have seen,
the land was very early divided into equal ' ridges,'
for in the passage quoted, referring to the pressure of
population in the seventh century, the complaint was,
not that the people received *smaller* ridges than in
former times, but *fewer of them.*   These ridges, however, may or may not have been ' day-works.'

But perhaps, outside of the three-field system, a
still more widely spread practice was that of dividing
the furlongs or larger divisions into *as many strips as
there were sharers,* without reference to the size of the
strips.   This practice seems to be the one adopted in
many parts of Germany, in Russia, and in the East, and
it is in common use in the western districts of Scotland
to this day whenever a piece of land is held by a
number of crofters as joint holders.[4]

---

[1] So in the St. Gall charters,
quoted above. Thus also Dronke,
Traditiones et Antiq. Fuldenses, p.
107, ' xx. diurnales hoc est quod
tot diebus arari poterit.'—Landau,
45.

[2] Varro, *De Re Rustica,* i. 10 ;
and see *Plin. Hist. Nat.* 18, 3. 15.

[3] See *supra,* chapter viii.

[4] I have found it in use on the
coast opposite the Isle of Skye.
Several crofters will take a tract of
land, divide it first into larger
divisions, or ' parks,' and then divide
the parks into lots, of which each
takes one.

It is doubtful whether the division into acre strips representing day-works, and divided from their neighbours by 'raine' or balks, was one of the features of the original German system of ploughing. It is chiefly, if not entirely, in the districts within or near to the Roman 'limes,' or colonised after the conquest of the Roman provinces, that it appears to have been prevalent.[1]

With regard to the word 'acre,' it is probably of very ancient origin.

The German 'acker' has the wider sense of ploughed land in general, but sometimes in East Friesland,[2] and also in South Germany and German Switzerland it has still the restricted meaning of the acre strip laid out for ploughing.[3]

We now pass to the form of the acre strip or day's work in ploughing.

Roman jugerum.
The Roman *actus* or furrow length was 120 feet, or twelve 10-feet rods. The *actus quadratus* was 120 feet square. The jugerum was composed of two of these *actus quadrati*. It was therefore in length still an actus or furrow of 120 feet, and it was twice as broad as it was long; whilst the length of the English acre is ten times its breadth.

Thus the English acre varied much in its shape

---

[1] I am indebted for this information to Professor Meitzen, who informs me that he doubts whether it was a feature of the old purely German open fields. In undisturbed old German districts the 'Gewanne' and strips are of irregular and arbitrary size, and are not separated by permanent turf 'raine' or balks.

[2] Hanssen, p. 198.

[3] In the Engadine, in reply to the question what the flat strips between the linches were called, the driver answered, '*acker.*' When it was pointed out that they were *grass*, the reply was, 'Ah! but a hundred years ago they were ploughed.'

from the Roman jugerum. Its exact measurements
are found in the *mappa*, or measure of the day-work of
the tenants of the abbot of St. Remy at Rheims, which
is described in the Polyptique of the ninth century
as forty perches in length and four in width.[1] It
occurs again in the ' *napatica* ' of the Polyptique of
the abbey of St. Maur, near Nantes, which was of
precisely the same dimensions.[2] And we have seen
that the ' andecena,' or measure of the day's work of
ploughing for the coloni and servi of the Church, was
described by the Bavarian laws in the seventh century as of precisely the same form as the English
acre, forty rods in length and four rods in width, only
that the rods were Roman rods of 10 feet.

We have to go, therefore, to Bavaria in the seventh
century for the earliest instance of the form of the
English acre.   And in this earliest instance it had a
distinctly *servile* connexion, as it had also in the
French cases quoted.   In all it fixed the day's task-
work of semi-servile tenants.

Further, the Bavarian ' andecena,' if the spelling
of the word may be trusted, may have another curious
and interesting connexion with the Saxon acre, to
which attention must be once more turned.

We have seen that the tithes were to be paid in
Saxon times in the produce of ' every tenth acre as it

---

[1] M. Guérard's Introduction to
the *Polyptique d'Irminon*, p. 641.

[2] *Id.* p. 641 ; and Appendix,
i. p. 285. The Irish acre is of the
same form as the English—4 rods
by 40—but the rod is 22 feet. See
the *Cartulaire de Redon* in Brittany,
No. cccxxvi. (p. 277), where a church

is given to the abbey ' cum sedecim
porcionibus terræ quæ lingua eorum
"acres" nominantur' (A.D. 1061–
1075). In Normandy, in the twelfth
and thirteenth centuries, there were
acres of four roods, ' vergées.' *Id.*
p. cccxi. Compare also the form of
the Welsh erw.

CHAP. X.

The form in which the 'agrarium' or tithe-rent was taken.

is traversed by the plough.'   The Roman land-tribute in Rhætia and the 'Agri Decumates' also consisted of tithes.   If these latter tithes were paid as the Saxon ecclesiastical tithes were, by every tenth strip being set aside for them in the ploughing, the words of the Bavarian law have an important significance.   The *judex* or *villicus* is required by the laws to see that the *colonus* or *servus* shall render by way of *agrarium* or land tribute according to what he has, from every thirty modii three modii (*i.e.* the tenth)—'lawful ' *andecenæ* (*andecenas legitimas*), that is (the rod having ' ten feet) four rods in width and forty in length, to ' plough, to sow, to hedge, to gather, to lead, and to ' store.'[1]

Now why is the peculiar phraseology used 'from ' 30 modii 3 modii'?   Surely either because three modii, according to the 'Agrimensores,' went to the juger, or because the actual acre of the locality was sown with three modii of seed,[2] so that in either case it was a way of saying 'from every ten acres one acre.' Further, the form and measure of the acre is described, and it is called the '*lawful andecena*.' The word itself in its peculiar etymology possibly contains a reference to the *one strip set apart in ten for the tithe*.   Be this as it may, here again, in another point connected with the 'acre,' we find the nearest and earliest analogies in South Germany within the old Roman province.

---

[1] Pertz, 278. *Lex Baiuwariorum textus legis primus*, 13.

[2] The Agrimensores reckoned 3 modii of land to the jugerum. *Gromatici Veteres*, i. p. 359 (13). In general 5 modii of wheat seed was sown on the jugerum, but the '*lawful andecena*,' being only about three-fifths of a jugerum, would require only 3 modii of wheat seed to sow it.

Lastly, we have still to explain the reason of the difference between the form of the Roman 'actus' and 'jugerum' and that of the early Bavarian and English acre.

The Egyptian arura was 100 cubits square.[1]

The Greek πλέθρον was 10 rods or 100 feet square.[2]

The Roman actus was 12 rods or 120 feet square.

The Roman 'jugerum' was made up of two 'actus' placed side by side, and was the area to be ploughed in a day.

In all these cases the yoke of two oxen is assumed, and the length of the acre, or 'day-work,' is the length of the furrow which *two* oxen could properly plough at a stretch.[3]

The reason of the increased length of the Bavarian and the English acre was, no doubt, connected with the fact of the larger team.[4]

If the Bavarian team was of eight oxen, like that of the English and Welsh and Scotch common plough, it would seem perfectly natural that with four times the strength of team the furrow might also be assumed to be four times the usual length. In this way the Greek and Roman furrow of 10 or 12 rods may naturally have been extended north of the Alps into the 'furlong' of forty rods.

Form of the acre or day's-work connected with the number of oxen in the team.

---

[1] Herod. ii. 168.

[2] According to Suidas it was equal to four ἄρουραι, and Homer mentions τετράγυον as a usual field representing a day's work. (Od. xviii. 374.) Hence τετράγυον = 'as much as a man can plough in a day.'

[3] 'Sulcum autem ducere longiorem quam pedum centumviginti contrarium pecori est.'—Col. ii.

11, 27.

[4] The Rev. W. Denton, in his *Servia and the Servians,* p. 135, mentions Servian ploughs with six, ten, or twelve oxen in the team. See also mention of similar teams of oxen or buffaloes in Turkey— *Reports on Tenures of Land,* 1869–70, p. 306.

Now, there is a remarkable proof that long furrows, and therefore probably large teams, were used in Bavaria, then within the Roman province of Rhætia, as early as the second century. The remains of the Bavarian 'Hochäcker' are described as running uninterruptedly for sometimes a kilomètre and more, *i.e.* five times the length of the English furlong. And a Roman road with milestones, dating as early as A.D. 201, in one place runs across these long furrows in a way which seems to prove that they were older than the road.[1]

The Bavarian 'Hochäcker' and their long furrows.

Professor Meitzen argues from this fact that these 'Hochäcker' with long furrows are pre-German in these districts, and in the absence of evidence of their Celtic origin he inclines to attribute them to the husbandry of officials or contractors on the imperial waste lands, who had at their command hundreds of slaves and heavy plough teams.

This may be the solution of the puzzling question of the origin of the Bavarian 'Hochäcker,' but the presence of the team of eight oxen in Wales and Scotland as well as in England, and the mention of teams of six and eight oxen in the Vedas[2] as used by Aryan husbandmen in the East, centuries earlier, makes it possible, if not probable, that the Romans, in this instance as in so many others, adopted and adapted to their purpose a practice which they found already at work, connected perhaps with a heavier soil and a clumsier plough than they were used to south of the Alps.[3]

---

[1] '*Der älteste Anbau der Deutschen.*' Von A. Meitzen, Jena, 1881.

[2] Zimmer's *Altindisches Leben*, p. 237.

[3] There are two other points which bear upon the Roman connexion with the *acre*.

(1) If the length of the furrow

V. THE HOLDINGS—THE YARD-LAND OR HUB.

We now pass from the strips to the holdings.
The typical English holding of a serf in the open
fields was the yard-land of normally thirty acres (ten

was to be increased, it would be natural to jump from one well-known
measure to another. The *stadium*,
or length of the foot race, was one-
eighth of a mile, and was composed of ten of the Greek ἄμμα.
The 'furlong' is also the one-eighth
of a mile, and contains ten chains.
But the stadium contained 625
Roman feet or 600 Greek feet—
about 607 English statute feet.
How does this comport with its
containing 40 rods? The fact is,
the rod varied in different provinces,
and the Romans adopted probably
the rod of the country in measuring
the acre. ' Perticas autem juxta
loca vel crassitudinem terrarum,
prout provincialibus placuit videmus
esse dispositas, quasdam decimpedas,
quibusdam duos additos pedes, aliquas vero xv. vel x. et vii. pedum
diffinitas.'— *Pauca de Mensuris,
Grom. Vet.*, Lachmann, &c., p. 371.
Forty rods of 10 cubits, or 15 feet
each, would equal the 600 feet of
the Greek stadium. In fact, the
English statute furlong is based
upon a rod of 16½ feet. There is
also the further fact that the later
Agrimensores expressly mention a
'stadialis ager of 625 feet' (Lachmann, Isodorus, p. 368; *De Mensuris excerpta*, p. 372). So that it
seems to be clear that the stadium,
like the furlong, was used not only

in measuring distances, but also in
the division of fields.

(2) We have seen that the acre
strips in England were often called
'balks,' because of the ridge of unbroken turf by which they were
divided the one from the other. We
have further seen that the word
'balk' in Welsh and in English
was applied to the pieces of turf left
unploughed between the furrows
by careless ploughing. There is a
Vedic word which has the same
meaning.

The Latin word 'scamnum' had
precisely this meaning, and also it
was applied by the Agrimensores
to a piece of land broader than its
length. The 'scamnum' of the
Roman 'castrum' was the strip
600 feet long and 50 to 80 feet
broad—nearly the shape of the
English and Bavarian 'acre'—set
apart for the 'legati' and 'tribunes.'
The fields in a conquered district,
instead of being allotted in squares
by 'centuriation,' were divided into
'scamna' and 'striga;' and the fields
thus divided into pieces broader
than their length were called 'agri
scamnati,' while those divided into
pieces longer than their breadth
were called 'agri strigati.' Length
was throughout reckoned from
north to south; breadth from east
to west. Frontinus states that the

scattered acres in each of the three fields), to which
an outfit of two oxen was assigned as '*setene*' or
'*stuht*,' and which descended from one generation to
another as a complete indivisible whole.

The hub or yard-land.

The German word for the yard-land is *hof* or *hub*;
in its oldest form *huoba, huba, hova*.[1] And Aventinus,
writing early in the sixteenth century of the holdings
in Bavaria in the thirteenth century, distinguishes the
hof as the holding belonging to a *quadriga*, or yoke
of four oxen, taxed at sixty 'asses,' from the *hub* or
holding of the *biga* or yoke of two oxen, and taxed

'arva publica' in the provinces were cultivated 'more antiquo' on this method of the 'ager per strigas et per scamna divisus et assignatus,' whilst the fields of the 'coloniæ' of Roman citizens or soldiers planted in the conquered districts were 'centuriated.' See Frontinus, lib. i. p. 2, and fig. 3 in the plates, and also fig. 199; and see Rudorff's observations, ii. 290–298. The whole matter is, however, very obscure, and it is difficult to identify the 'ager scamnatus' with the Romano-German open fields. Frontinus was probably not specially acquainted with the latter.

[1] The meaning of 'hub' is perhaps simply 'a holding,' from 'haben.'

The term 'yard-land,' or 'gyrdlandes,' seems to be simply the holding measured out by the 'gyrd,' or rod; just as gyrd also means a 'rood.' Compare the 'vergée' of Normandy.

The Roman 'pertica' was the typical rod or pole used by the Agrimensores, and on account of its use in assigning lands to the members of a colony, it is sometimes represented on medals by the side of the augurial plough. By transference, the whole area of land measured out and assigned to a colony was known to the Agrimensores as its 'pertica' (Lachmann, Frontinus, pp. 20 and 26; Hyginus, p. 117; Siculus Flaccus, p. 159; Isodorus, p. 369).

The Latin 'virga,' used in later times instead of '*pertica*' for the measuring rod, followed the same law of transference with still closer likeness to the Saxon 'gyrd.' Both 'virga' and 'gyrd'=a rod and a measure. Both 'virga terræ' and 'gyrd landes'=(1) the rood, and (2) the normal holding—the virgate or yard-land. The word 'virgate, or 'virgada,' was used in Brittany as well as in England. In the *Cartulaire·de Redon* it is, however, evidently the equivalent of the Welsh 'Randir.' See the twelve references to the word 'virgada in the index of the *Cartulary*.

at thirty ' asses.'[1] If the tax in this case were one
' *as* ' per acre, then the *hof* contained sixty acres, and
the *hub* thirty acres. So that, as in the yard-land,
ten acres in each field would go under the three-field
system to the pair of oxen.

The *hub* of thirty *morgen* seems to have been the
typical holding of the serf over a very wide area,
according to the earliest records. Whilst as a rule
absent from North Germany, Dr. Landau traces it in
Lower Saxony, in Engern, in Thuringia, in Grapfeld,
in Hesse, on the Middle Rhine and the Moselle, in
the old Niederlahngau, Rheingau, Wormsgau, Lob-
dengau and Spiergau, in Elsass, in Swabia, and in
Bavaria.[2]

The double *huf* of sixty *morgen* also occurs on
the Weser and the Rhine in Lower Saxony and in
Bavaria.[3] The word ' huf' first occurs in a document
of A.D. 474.[4]

The passage in the Bavarian laws of the seventh
century, already referred to, declaring the tithe to
be ' three modii from every thirty ' modii—or one
' lawful andecena' from each ten that, in the typical
case taken, ' a man has '—would seem to suggest that
ten *andecenæ* or acre strips in each field (or thirty in
all) was a typical holding, whilst the use of the
Roman rod of ten feet points to a Roman influence.

Further, the fact of the prevalence of the double
and single *huf* or *hub* of sixty and thirty acres over
so large an area once Roman province, irresistibly
suggests a connexion with the double and single yoke

---

[1] Du Cange, under ' Huba.'
[2] Landau, p. 36. [3] *Id.* 37–8.
[4] In the will of Perpetuus.
Meitzen, *Ausbreitung,* &c., p. 14.

Chap. X.

The double 'hub' of sixty morgen. The outfit of oxen.
of oxen given as outfit to the Roman veteran, with such an allowance of seed as to make it probable, as we have seen, that the double yoke received normally fifty or sixty jugera, and the single yoke twenty-five or thirty jugera.

It is worth remembering, further, that in the Bavarian law before quoted, limiting the week-work of the *servi* on the ecclesiastical estates to three days a week, an exception is made allowing unlimited week-work to be demanded from *servi* who had been supplied with their outfit of oxen *de novo* by their lord. So that there is a chain of evidence as to the system of supplying the holders of ' yard-lands,' ' huben,' and ' yokes,' with an outfit of oxen, of which the Kelso ' *stuht*,' the Saxon ' *setene*,' the outfit of the *servus* under this Bavarian law, and that of the Roman veteran, are links.[1]

It is hardly needful to repeat that it does not follow from this that the system of allotting about thirty acres (varying in size with the locality) to the pair of oxen was a Roman invention. The clear fact is that it was a system followed in Roman provinces under the later empire, as well as in Germany and England afterwards ; and, as the holding of thirty acres was found to be the allotment to each ' tate ' or household under the Irish tribal system, it may possibly have had an earlier origin and a wider prevalence than the period or extent of Roman rule.

The scattering of the strips composing a *yard-land*, or *hub*, over the open fields should also be once more mentioned in comparing the two. It was not

---

[1] The practice was long continued in what was called the ' steel bow tenancy ' of later times.

confined to the ' yard-land ' or ' hub.' It arose, as we have seen, in Wales, from the practice of joint ploughing, and was the result of the method of dividing the joint produce, probably elsewhere also, under the tribal system. It is the method of securing a fair division of common land in Scotland and Ireland and Palestine to this day, no less than under the English and German three-field system. And the remarkable passage from Siculus Flaccus has been quoted, which so clearly describes a similar scattered ownership, resulting probably from joint agriculture carried on by ' *vicini*,' as often to be met with in his time on Roman ground. This passage proves that the Roman holding (like the Saxon *yard-land* and the German *hub*) might be composed of a bundle of scattered pieces ; but this scattering was too widely spread from India to Ireland for it to be, in any sense, distinctively Roman. It perhaps resulted, as we have seen, from the heaviness of the soil or the clumsiness of the plough, and the necessity of co-operation between free or semi-servile tenants, in order to produce a plough team of the requisite strength according to the custom of the country ; and this necessity probably arose most often in the provinces north of the Alps.

Another point distinctive of the ' yard-land ' and the ' hub ' was the absence of division among heirs, the single succession, the indivisibility of the bundle of scattered strips in the holding. And this finds its nearest likeness perhaps, as we have seen, in the probably single succession of the semi-servile holder, or mere ' usufructuarius ' under Roman law, and especially under the semi-military rule of the border provinces.

The single succession to the ' hub ' and ' yardland.'

CHAP. X.

The Saxon
'Gebur'
and the
High Ger-
man
'Gipur.'

Lastly, before leaving the comparison between the *yard-land* and *hub* it may be asked why the serf who held it in England was called a *Gebur.*

The word *villanus* of the Domesday Survey is associated with other words, such as *villicus, villata, villenage,* all connected with serfdom, and all traceable through Romance dialects to the Roman ' *villa.*'

But the Anglo-Saxon word was ' *Gebur.*' It was the *Geburs* who were holders of yard-lands.

We trace this word *Gebur* in High German dialects. We find it in use in the High German translation of the laws of the Alamanni, called the ' *Speculi Suevici,*' where free men are divided into three classes :—

(1) The ' *semperfrien* ' = lords with vassals under them.

(2) The ' *mittlerfrien* ' = the men or vassals of the lords.

(3) The ' *geburen* ' = *liberi incolœ,* or ' fri-lant-sæzzen ' [*i.e.* not slaves].[1]

The word ' gebur ' or ' gipur ' occurs also in the High German of Otfried's ' Paraphrase of the Gospels,'[2] of the ninth century, and in the Alamannic dialect of Notger's Psalms for *vicinus.*[3]

Here, again, the South German connexion seems to be the nearest to the Anglo-Saxon.

---

[1] *Juris Prov. Alemann.* c. 2. Schilteri editio.
[2] Otfried, v. 4, 80; ii. 14, 215.
[3] Notger, Psalm xliii. 14; lxxviii. 4; lxix. 7.

VI. THE HIDE, THE HOF, AND THE CENTURIA.

From the yard-land, or *hub*, the holding of a serf, we may pass to the typical holding of the full free landholder, connected in England with the full team of eight oxen.

The Saxon *hide*, or the *familia* of Bede, was Latinised in Saxon charters into '*casatum.*' We have found in the St. Gall charters the word '*casa*' used for the homestead. The present Romanish word for house is '*casa*,' and for the verb 'to dwell,' '*casar.*' And there is the Italian word '*casata*,' still meaning a family. Thus the connexion between the '*familia*' of Bede and the '*casatum*' of the charters is natural Bede wrote more classical Latin than the ecclesiastical scribes in the charters. The hide was the holding of a family.[1] Hence it was sometimes, like the yard-land or holding of a servile family, called a '*hiwisc*,' which was Anglo-Saxon, and also High German for family.[2] But the Saxon hide, also, was translated into *ploughland* or *carucate*, corresponding with the full team of eight oxen.

Generally in Kent, and sometimes in Sussex, Berks, and Essex, we found in addition to or instead of the hide or carucate, or '*terra unius aratri*,' *solins*, *sullungs*, or *swullungs*—the land pertaining to a '*suhl*,' the Anglo-Saxon word for plough. This word is

---

[1] Compare *Cod. Theod.* IX. tit. xlii. 7 : 'Quot mancipia in prædiis occupatis . . . quot sint *casarii vel coloni*,' &c.

[2] See *Ancient Laws of England*, Thorpe, p. 79, under *wer-gilds*, s.

vii., where 'hiwisc' = 'hide.' See also '*hiwiski*,' '*hiwischi*,' for *familia*,' in '*St. Paules Glossen*,' sixth or seventh century. Braune's *Althochdeutsches Lesebuch*, p. 4.

surely of Roman rather than of German origin. The Piedmontese '*sloira*,' and the Lombardic '*sciloira*,' and the Old French ' *silleoire*,' are surely allied to the Romanish '*suilg*,' and the Latin ' *sulcus*.'

The 'gioc,' or 'jugum.' Again, in Kent the quarter of a ' sulung ' (answering to the yard-land or virgate of other parts) is called in the early charters a ' gioc,' ' ioclet,' or ' iochlet,' [1] *i.e.* a yoke or small-yoke of land. We have seen in the St. Gall charters, also, mention of ' juchs ' or ' jochs,' which, however, were apparently jugera. This word *gioc* is surely allied to the Italian ' *giogo*,' and the Latin *jugum*.

The 'hide' and 'centuria' the typical free holding. Here, then, we have the *hide* the typical holding of a *free* family, as the *centuria* was under Roman law. A free Saxon thane might hold many hides, and so might and did the lord of a Roman villa hold more than one ' centuria ' within its bounds. Still Columella took as his type of a Roman farm the ' centuria ' of 200 acres,[2] and calculated how much seed, how many oxen, how many *opera*, or day-works of slaves, or ' coloni ' were required to till it. The hide, double or single, was also a land measure, and contained eight or four yard-lands, and so also was the ' centuria ' a land measure divisible into eight normal holdings allotted with single yokes. Both also became, as we have seen, units of assessment. But in England the hide was the unit. Under the Roman system of taxation the *jugum* was the unit.

---

[1] *B. M. Ancient Charters*, ii. Cotton MS. Aug. ii. 42, A.D. 837. The Welsh *short yoke* was that of two oxen, *i.e.* a fourth part of the full plough team.

[2] Columella, ii. 12. The calculation in this passage, how many *opera* or day-works a farm requires shows striking resemblance to the later manorial system.

This variation, however, confirms the connexion.
The Roman *jugum*, or yoke of two oxen, made a
complete plough. Nothing less than the hide was
the complete holding in England, because a team
of eight oxen was required for English ploughing.
The yard-land was only a fractional holding, incom-
plete for purposes of ploughing without co-operation.
Hence it would seem that the complete *plough* was
really the unit in both cases.

How closely the English hidation followed the The Saxon
lines of the Roman '*jugatio*' has already been seen. 'hidation'
When to the many resemblances of the hide to the Roman
'centuria,' and of the 'jugum' to the virgate, re- jugatio.'
garded as units of assessment, are now added the
other connecting links found in this chapter, in things,
in figures, and in words, between the Saxon open-
field system, and that of the districts of Upper
Germany, so long under Roman rule, the English
hidation may well be suspected to go back to
Roman times, and to be possibly a survival of the
Roman *jugation*. When Henry of Huntingdon, in
describing the Domesday Survey, instead of saying
that inquiry was made how many hides and how
many virgates there were, uses the words ' quot
jugata et quot virgata terræ,'[1] he at any rate used
the exact words which describe what in the Codex
Theodosianus is spoken of as taxation 'per *juga-
tionem.*'[2]

Not, as already said, that the Romans introduced into Britain the division of land according to
plough teams, and the number of oxen contributed

---

[1] Du Cange, ' Jugatum.' | [2] See Marquardt, ii. 225 *n.*

to the plough team. It would grow, as we have seen, naturally out of tribal arrangements whenever the tribes settled and became agricultural, instead of wandering about with their herds of cattle. It was found in Wales and Ireland and Scotland, in Bohemia, apparently in Slavonic districts also and further east.[1] It is much more likely that the Romans, according to their usual custom, adopted a barbarian usage and seized upon an existing and obvious unit as the basis of provincial taxation.

The Frisian tribute of hides was perhaps an example of this. The Frisians were a pastoral people, and a hide for every so many oxen was as ready a mode of assessing the tribute as counting the plough teams would be in an agricultural district. The word ' hide,' which still baffles all attempts to explain its origin, may possibly have had reference to a similar tribute.

Roman *tributum* in Frisia paid in hides.

Even in England it does not follow that it was in its origin connected with the plough team. Its real equivalent was the *familia*, or *casatum*—the land of a family—and in pastoral districts of England and Wales the Roman tribute may possibly have been, if not a hide from each plough team, a hide from every family holding cattle ; just as in A.D. 1175 Henry II. bound his Irish vassal, Roderic O'Connor, to pay annually ' *de singulis animalibus decimum corium placabile mercatoribus*'—perhaps a tenth of the hides he himself received as tribute from his own tribesmen.[2] The supposition of such an origin of the connexion of the word ' hide ' with the ' land of a family '

---

[1] Meitzen, *Ausbreitung*, pp. 21 and 33.

[2] *Fœd.* vol. i. p. 31. Robertson's *Historical Essays*, p. 133.

or of a plough team is mere conjecture; but the *fact* of the connexion is clear. All these three things, the *hide*, the *hiwisce*, and the *sullung*, and their sub-division the *yard-land*, were the units of British ' hidation,' just as the *centuria* and the *jugum* were the units of the Roman ' jugatio.'

VII. THE GAFOL AND GAFOL-YRTH.

Passing now to the serfdom and the services under which the ' yard-lands ' and the ' huben ' were held, it may at least be said that their practical identity suggests a common origin.

We learned from the *Rectitudines* and from the *Laws of Ine*, to make a distinction between the two component parts of the obligations of the ' gebur ' in respect of his yard-land.

There was (1) the *gafol*, and (2) the *week-work*.

The *gafol* was found to be a semi-servile incident to the yard-land. The week-work was the most servile one.

A man otherwise free and possessing a homestead already, could, under the laws of Ine, hire a yard-land of demesne land and pay *gafol* for it, without in-curring liability to *week-work*. But if the lord found for him both the yard-land and the homestead, then he was a complete ' gebur ' or ' villanus,' and must do *week-work* also.

Taking the *gafol* first, and descending to details, it was found to be complex—*i.e.* it included *gafol* and *gafol-yrth*.

The *gafol* of the ' gebur,' as stated in the *Rectitudines*, was this :—

> For *gafol proper* :—
> 10*d.* at Michaelmas.
> 23 sesters of beer }
> 2 fowls   } At Martinmas.
> 1 lamb at Easter, or 2*d.*
> For *gafolyrthe* :—the ploughing of 3 acres, and sowing of
> it from the ' gebur's ' own barn.

Comparing the *gafol* proper with the *census* of the St. Gall charters, and the *tribute* of the ' servi ' of the Church under the Alamannic laws of A.D. 622, the resemblance was found to be remarkably close.

The tribute of the ' servi ' of the Church was thus stated in the latter :—

> 15 siclæ of beer.
> A sound spring pig.
> 2 modia of bread.
> 5 fowls.
> 20 eggs.

As regards this tribute *in kind* the likeness is obvious, and it further so closely resembles the food-rent of the Welsh free tribesmen as to suggest that it may have been a survival of ancient tribal dues—a suggestion which the word ' gafol ' itself confirms. It seems to be connected with the *Abgabe*, or food gifts of the German tribesmen.[1]

Possible connexio with Roman *tributum.*

We saw that the word *gafol* was the equivalent of *tributum* in the Saxon translation of the Gospels. ' Does your master pay tribute ? ' *' Gylt he gafol?'*

Further, the French evidence seems to show

---

[1] Diez, p. 150. ' *Gabella*,' Portuguese, Spanish, and Provençal = tax. French *gabelle* = salt-tax. Italian ' *gabellan*,' to tax, from v. b. *gifan*, Goth. *giban*.

that the later manorial payments in kind and services
upon Frankish manors were, to some extent, a survival of the old Roman exactions in Gaul.[1] And
the tribute of the Alamannic and Bavarian laws, and
of the St. Gall and other charters, was found to be
equally clearly a survival of the Roman *tributum*
in the German province of Rhætia and the 'Agri
Decumates.'

But in addition to the 'gafol' in kind, there was The Saxon
'gafol-
yrth' and
the Roman
'agra-
rium' or
tithe-rent.
the *gafol-yrth*; and of this also we found in the St.
Gall charters numerous examples. In the many cases
where the owner of homesteads and land surrendered
them to the Abbey, and henceforth paid tribute to
the Abbey, there was not only the tribute in kind,
but also the *ploughing of so many acres*, sometimes
of one, sometimes of two, and sometimes of one in
each *zelga* or field—to be ploughed, and reaped, and
carried by the tenant. The combination of the dues
in *kind* and in *ploughing*, with sometimes other
services, made up the *tributum in servitium*—*i.e.* the
gafol of the *tributarius*, or '*gafol-gelder*,' which he
paid under the Alamannic laws to his lord, the latter
thenceforth paying the public *tributum* for the
land to the State.

Perhaps we may go one step further.

From the remarkable resemblance of the English Not always
a tenth.
gafol-yrth and its South German equivalent the inference was drawn that this peculiar *rent taken in
the form of the ploughing of a definite number of
acres*, was probably a survival of the Roman tenths,

---

[1] See Guérard's *Polyptique d'Irminon,* i. chap. viii. Also Lehuérou's
Institut. Meroving. liv. ii. c. 1; and

M. Vuitry's *Etudes sur le Régime
Financier de la France,* Premiere
Etude.

or other proportion of produce claimed as rent from settlers on the *ager publicus* of the ' Agri Decumates,' and of Rhætia. Indications were found that the *agrarium*, or tenth of the arable produce, may have been taken *in actual acres* like the Saxon tithes—*i.e.* in the produce of so many ' *andecenæ*,' the ploughing, sowing, reaping, and garnering of which were done by the tenant.

But under Roman usage the proportion taken was not always a *tenth*. The State rent was nominally a tithe. But it was in fact so extortionately gathered as sometimes in Sicily to *treble* the tithe.[1] Hyginus also says that the ' vectigal,' or tax, was taken in some provinces in a certain part of the crop, in some a fifth, in others a seventh.[2] In Italy the dues from the *Agri Medietates* perhaps surviving in the later *metayer* system, amounted sometimes to *one-half*. At any rate, the proportion varied.

Now the Saxon ' gafol-yrth ' of the yard-land of thirty acres seems, according to the ' Rectitudines,' as we have seen, to have been the produce of three acres in the wheat-field, ploughed by the 'gebur' and sown with seed from his own barn. For it will be remembered that the first season after the yard-land was given there was to be no gafol, and in the gebur's outfit only seven out of the ten acres in the wheat-field

---

[1] So Cicero asserted against Verres. The seed, he argued, was fairly to be taken at about a *medimnus* to each jugerum. Eight medimni of corn per acre would be a good crop ; ten would be the outside that under all possible favour of the gods the jugerum could yield. Therefore the tithe ought not to exceed at the highest estimate one medimnus per jugerum. But the tax-gather had taken *three* medimni per jugerum, and so by extortion had *trebled the tithes.*—*In Verrem*, act. ii. lib. iii. c. 47, 48, 49.

[2] *Hygini de Limitibus Constituendis*, p. 204.

were to be handed over to him already sown, leaving
three unsown, *i.e.* probably *the three* which otherwise he must have sown for the *gafol-yrth* due to
his lord. As ten acres of the yard-land were probably always in fallow, three acres of wheat was a
heavier *gafol-yrth* than a fairly gathered tithe would
have been.

It would therefore seem probable that as the
'gafol' in kind may be traced back to the Roman
tributum, itself perhaps a survival of the tribal food-
rents of the conquered provinces, so the ' gafol-yrth '
may be traced back to the Roman *decumæ*, or other
proportion of the crop due by way of land-tax or
rent to the State. And this survival of the complex
tribute or gafol, made up of its two separate elements,
from Roman to Saxon times, becomes all the more
striking when it is considered also that it was due
from a normal holding with an outfit of a pair of
oxen, both in the case of the Saxon *yard-land* and of
the Roman veteran's allotment.

VIII. THE BOON-WORK AND WEEK-WORK OF THE SERF.

Proceeding still further, besides the *gafol* and
gafol-yrth, and yet distinct from the *week-work*, was
the liability of the serfs on the Saxon manor to certain *boon-work* or services *ad preces*; sometimes in
ploughing or reaping a certain number of acres of the
lord's demesne land in return for grass land or other
advantages, or without any special equivalent;
sometimes in going errands or carrying goods to
market or otherwise, generally known as *averagium*.
' He shall land-gafol pay, and shall *ridan* and *averian*

The Saxon
' boon-
work ' and
the Roman
' sordida
munera.'

' and *lade lædan*' for his lord.   So this boon-work in addition to ' gafol' is described in the ' Rectitudines.'

The various kinds of manorial 'averagium' were, as we have seen, often called in mediæval Latin *angariæ*, a going on errands or postal service ; *paraveredi*, or packhorse services ; and *carroperæ*, or waggon services.

We have seen how these services resembled the *angariæ* and the *parangariæ* and *paraveredi*, which were included among the ' *sordida munera*' or ' *obsequiæ*' of the Theodosian Code in force in Rhætia in the fourth century, found still surviving, though transformed into manorial services, in the same districts in the seventh century and afterwards, under the Bavarian laws and in the monastic charters. The carrying services and other boon-work on Saxon manors closely resembled those of the Frankish charters and the Bavarian laws, and probably therefore shared their Roman origin.

The week-work of the serf.

There remains to complete the serfdom its most servile incident, the *week-work*—that survival of the originally unrestricted claim of the lord of the Roman villa to his slave's labour which, limited, as we have seen, according to the evidence of the Alamannic laws, under the influence of Christian humanity by the monks or clergy, in respect of the servi on their estates, to three days a week, became the mediæval *triduanum servitium*.   The words of the Alamannic law are worth re-quoting.

' *Servi dimidiam partem sibi et dimidiam in dominico arativum reddant.   Et si super hæc est*, SICUT SERVI ECCLESIASTICI *ita faciunt, tres dies sibi et tres in dominico*.'

Let *servi* do plough service, half for themselves and half in demesne. And if there be any further [service] let them work *as the servi of the Church*, three days for themselves, and three in demesne.

This remarkable passage in the Alamannic code of A.D. 622 seems to be the earliest version extant of the Magna Charta of the agricultural servus, who thus early upon ecclesiastical estates was transformed from a slave into a serf.

IX. THE CREATION OF SERFS AND THE GROWTH OF SERFDOM.

There is yet another point in which the corre- Serfdom spondence between British and Continental usages is recruited from above worth remarking. and from below.

The community in serfdom on a lord's estate was both by Saxon and Continental usage recruited from above and from below.

Free men from above, by voluntary arrangement Free-men with a lord, could and did descend into serfdom. serfs. The Saxon free tenant could, by free contract, arrange to take a yard-land, and if he were already provided with a homestead and oxen, he became a 'gafol-gelder,' or *tributarius* of his lord, without incurring the liability to the more servile ' week-work,' just as was the case when, under the Alamannic laws, free men made surrender of their holdings to the Abbey of St. Gall. In both cases, as we saw, week-work was added if the lord found the homestead and the outfit.

On the other hand, whenever a lord provided his Slaves be-slave with an outfit of oxen, and gave him a part in come serfs. the ploughing, he rose out of slavery into serfdom. To speak more correctly, he rose into that middle class of tenants who, by whatever name they were known at first, afterwards became confounded together in the ranks of mediæval serfdom.

Grades in serfdom during the period of transition.

There were, in fact, grades in the community in serfdom not only like those of the Saxon geburs and cottiers, but also corresponding to the historical origin of the serfs. Thus, as we have seen in the 'Polyptique d'Irminon' and in many other cartularies and surveys of monastic estates, there are *coloni* and

'Tributarii,' 'coloni,' and 'liti.'

liti among the serfs, names bearing witness to the historical origin of the serfs, though the difference between them had all but vanished.

Slaves made into these.

There is a passage in the Ripuarian laws, 'If any one shall make his slave into a "tributarius," or a "litus," &c.'[1] The 'lidus' of the 'Lex Salica' was under a lordship, and classed with 'servi,' and by a legal process he could be set free.[2] We have noticed the passage in the Theodosian Code which speaks of 'coloni' and 'tributarii' on British estates, and also the mention by Ammianus Marcellinus of 'tributarii' in Britain. We have noticed also the three grades of

The læts of the laws of Ethelbert.

'læts,' the only class of tenants mentioned in the laws of Ethelbert.

Now, whatever doubt there might be as to what were the 'læts' on Kentish 'hams' and 'tuns' in the sixth century, if they stood alone as isolated phenomena; taken together with the 'tributarii' and 'coloni' and 'liti' on Continental manors, there can be hardly any doubt that they belonged to the same middle

---

[1] Tit. lxii.

[2] *Lex Salica*, tit. xxxviii. 'De homicidiis *servorum* et ancillarum. v. Si quis homo ingenuus *lidum alienum* expoliaverit,' &c. See also tit. xvi. See also tit. xxvi. 'De libertis extra consilium Domini sui dimissis' (xxxv. 'De libertis dimissis ingenuis '). 'Si quis *alienum lætum* ante rege per dinarium *ingenuum demiserit*,' &c.

class of semi-servile tenants to which allusion has
been made. Their presence on the manorial 'hams'
and 'tuns' of England revealed in the earliest historical record after the Saxon Conquest, taken in
connexion with the many other points brought
together in this chapter, makes the inference very
strong indeed that they, like the 'coloni,' 'tributarii,'
and 'liti' on Continental manors, were a survival from
that period of transition from Roman to German rule,
during which the names of the various classes of
semi-servile tenants, afterwards merged in the common
status of mediæval serfdom, still preserved traces of
their origin.

X. THE CONFUSION IN THE STATUS OF THE TENANTS ON ENGLISH AND GERMAN MANORS.

In one sense both in England and Germany the
holders of the 'yard-lands' and 'huben,' though serfs,
were *free*. As regards their lords they were serfs.
As regards the slaves they were free. In this respect
they resembled very closely the Roman 'coloni' on a
private villa.

On the Frankish manors there were two classes of
these semi-servile tenants—'mansi ingenuiles,' who
were free from the 'week-work;' and 'mansi serviles,'
from whom 'week-work' was due. Probably owing
to the nature of the Saxon conquest the first of these
classes seems to have practically become absorbed in
the other. The laws of Ine, indeed, mention the gafol-
gelder who, providing his own homestead, did not
become liable to 'week-work' like the 'gebur.' But

in the statements of the services on the manors of
Hisseburne and Tidenham no such class appears.
In the 'Rectitudines' there is no class mentioned between the *thane*, who is lord of the manor, and the
'geneats'—*i.e.* the 'gebur' and the 'cotsetl.' In the
Domesday Survey there are no tenants above the
villani, as a general rule, except in the Danish districts, where the 'Sochmanni' and the 'liberi homines' appear.

Comparing the status of English and German
holders of 'yard-lands' and 'huben,' the resemblances
are remarkable, and they confirm the suggestion
of a common origin. Both are 'adscripti glebæ.' In
both cases there is the absence of division among
heirs. In both the succession is single, and in theory
at the will of the lord. In both there are the gafol
and customary services.

In both cases there is the distinction in grade of
serfdom between the man who freely becomes the
holder of a yard-land or hub by his own surrender, or
by voluntary submission to the semi-servile tenure,
and the man who is a *nativus* or born serf.

In both cases there is a regular contribution towards military service or the equipment of a soldier,
and apparently no bar in status from actual service,
though doubtless in a semi menial position.

The con-
fusion per-
haps
partly a
survival
from
Roman
provincial
conditions.

In all these points we have noticed strong analogies
between the semi-free and semi-servile conditions of
the various classes of tenants on Roman villas, and on
the Roman public lands, which we have spoken of as
the great provincial manor of the Roman Empire.
And the natural inference seems to be, that even the
curious confusion of the free and servile status may

be, in part, a survival of the like confusion in the
Roman provinces. It naturally grew up under the
semi-military rule of the German provinces, and possibly in Britain also; whilst the Saxon conquest of
the latter, no doubt, as we have said, tended to reduce
the confusion into something like simplicity by fusing
together classes of semi-servile tenants of various
historical origins, in the one common class of the later
' geneats ' or ' villani,' in whose status the old confusion, however, survived.

XI. RESULT OF THE COMPARISON.

To sum up the result of the comparison made in
this chapter between the English and the Continental
open-field system and serfdom. The English and
South-German systems at the time of the earliest
records in the seventh century were to all intents
and purposes apparently identical.

Strong evi-
dence of
connexion
between
Britain and
the South
German
provinces
during
Roman
rule, in the
serfdom
and in the
open-field
system
which was
its shell.

The mediæval serf, judging from the evidence of
his gafol and services, seems to have been the compound product of survivals from three separate
ancient conditions, gradually, during Roman provincial rule and under the influence of barbarian
conquest, confused and blended into one, viz. those of
the *slave* on the Roman villa, of the *colonus* or other
semi-servile and mostly barbarian tenants on the
Roman villa or public lands, and of the *slave* of the
German tribesman, who to the eyes of Tacitus was
so very much like a Roman *colonus.*

That peculiar form of the open-field system,
which was the shell of serfdom both in England and
on the Continent, also connects itself in Germany

distinctly with the Romano-German provinces, whilst at the same time conspicuously absent from the less Romanised districts of Northern Germany.

It seems therefore inconceivable that the three-field system and the serfdom of early Anglo-Saxon records can have been an altogether new importation from North Germany, where it did not exist, into Britain, where it probably had long existed under Roman rule.

The Saxon invaders from North Germany hardly brought the three-field system into England. We have already quoted the strong conclusion of Hanssen that the Anglo-Saxon invaders and their Frisian Low-Saxon and Jutish companions could not introduce into England a system to which they were not accustomed at home. It must be admitted that the conspicuous absence of the three-field system from the North of Germany does not, however, absolutely dispose of the possibility that the system was imported into England from those districts of Middle Germany reaching from Westphalia to Thuringia, where the system undoubtedly existed. It is at least possible that the invaders of England may have proceeded from thence rather than as commonly supposed, from the regions on the northern coast. But if it be possible that a system of agriculture implying long-continued settlement, and containing within it numerous survivals of Roman elements, could be imported by pirates and the emigrants following in their wake, the possibility itself implies that the immigrants had themselves previously submitted to long-continued Roman influences.

On the whole we may adopt as a more likely theory the further suggestion of Hanssen, that if the three-field system was imported at all into England,

the most likely time for its importation was that same
period of Roman occupation during which he considers that it came into use in the Roman provinces
of Germany.[1]

Nor is there anything inconsistent with this
suggestion in the irregular lines of the English open
fields and their divisions, so different from those
produced by the rectangular centuriation of Roman
'Agrimensores.' We must not forget that the open
field system in its simpler forms was almost certainly
pre-Roman in Britain as elsewhere ; so that what the
Romans added to transform it into the manorial
three-field system probably was rather the three-course
rotation of crops, the strengthening of the manorial
element on British estates, and the methods of
taxation by 'jugation,' than any radical alteration
in the land-divisions or in the system of co-operative
ploughing.[2]

---

[1] 'Soll die Dreifelderwirthschaft nach England importirt sein, so bliebe wohl nur übrig an die Periode der römischen Okkupation zu denken, wie ich eine ahnliche Vermuthung, die sich freilich auch nicht weiter begründen lasst, fur Deutschland ausgesprochen habe (p. 153). Einfacher ist es den selbstständigen Ursprung der Dreifelderwirthschaft in ganz verschiedenenen Ländern als einen auf einer gewissen wirthschaftlichen Kulturstufe wie von selber eintretenden Fortschritt sich zu denken' (*Agrarhist. Abhand.* p. 497).

[2] Mr. Coote has adduced apparently clear evidence of centuriation in many parts of England ; but we have already seen that only the land actually assigned to the soldiers of a *colonia* was centuriated. There would seem to be no reason to suppose that they disturbed the generally existing open fields still cultivated by the conquered population.

CHAPTER XI.

RESULT OF THE EVIDENCE.

I. THE METHOD OF THE ENGLISH SETTLEMENTS.

IT may perhaps now be possible to sum up the evidence, without pretending to more certainty in the conclusion than the condition of the question warrants.

The tribal system in Wales and Germany.

At the two extreme limits of our subject we have found, on one side, the tribal system of Wales and Ireland, and, on the other side, the German tribal system.

In the earliest stage of these systems they were seemingly alike, both in the nomadic habits of the tribes, and the shifting about of the households in a tribe from one homestead to another. Sir John Davis describes this shifting as going on in Ireland in his day, and Cæsar describes it as going on in Germany 1,700 years earlier.

Co-aration of the waste on the early open-field system.

In both cases, such agriculture as was a necessity even to pastoral tribes was carried on under the open-field system in its simplest form—the ploughing up of new ground each season, which then went back into grass. The Welsh triads speak of it as a *co-aration* of portions of *the waste*. Tacitus describes it in the words, ' Arva per annos mutant, et superest ager.' In neither case, therefore, is there *the three-field system*, which implies fixed arable fields ploughed again and again in rotation.

The three field system evidently implies the surrender of the tribal shifting and the submission to fixed settlement. Further, as wherever we can examine the three-field system we find the mass of the holdings to have been fixed bundles, called *yard-lands* or *huben*—bundles retaining the same contents from generation to generation—it seems to follow either that the tribal division of holdings among heirs, which was the mark of free holdings, had ceased, *or* that the three-field system was from the first the shell of a community in serfdom.

The three-field system implies fixed settlements and rotation of crops, which came probably with Roman rule. The yard-land or hub implies servile tenants.

The geographical distribution of the three-field system—mainly within the old Roman provinces and in the Suevic districts along their borders—makes it almost certain that, in Germany, *Roman rule* was the influence which enforced the settlement, and introduced, with other improvements in agriculture, such as the vine culture, a fixed rotation of crops.

In Wales the necessity for settlement did *not* generally produce the three-field system *with holdings in yard-lands*,[1] because, as the Welsh tribesmen, though they may have had household slaves, as a rule held no taeogs or prædial slaves, it produced no serfdom. But under the German tribal system, even in the time of Tacitus, the tribesmen in the semi-

---

[1] There are undoubtedly manors and yard-lands in some districts, but of later and English introduction.

Romanised districts, at all events, already had prædial slaves.

The Roman villa another factor and grew into the manor. The manorial system, however, was not simply a development from the tribal system of the Germans; it had evidently a complex origin. A Roman element also seems to have entered into its composition.

The Roman *villa*, to begin with, a slave-worked estate, during the later empire, whether from German influence or not, became still more like a manor by the addition of *coloni* and other mostly barbarian semi-servile tenants to the slaves.

There may have been once free village communities on the 'ager publicus,' but, as we have seen, the management of the public lands under the fiscal officers of the Emperor also tended during the later Empire to become more and more manorial in its character, so much so that the word 'villa' could apparently sometimes be applied to the fiscal district.

Roman and German elements combined. Whichever of the two factors—Roman or German—contributed most to the mediæval manor, the manorial estate became the predominant form of land ownership in what had once been Roman provinces. And the German successors of Roman lords of villas became in their turn manorial lords of manors; whilst the 'coloni,' 'liti,' and 'tributarii' upon them, wherever they remained upon the same ground, apparently became, with scarcely a visible change, a community of serfs.

Both 'ager publicus' and 'terra regis' manorial. On the other hand, the fact that the *terra regis* also was divided under Saxon and Frankish kings into *manors* probably was the natural result of the growing manorial management of the public lands under the fiscal officers of the Emperor during the later Empire, quickened or completed after the barbarian conquests. The fiscal districts seem to have become in fact royal manors, and the free 'coloni,' 'liti,' and 'servi' upon them appear as manorial tenants of different grades in the earliest grants to the monasteries.

The fact that as early as the time of Tacitus, the German chieftains and tribesmen were in their own country lords of serfs, in itself explains the ease with which they assumed the position of lords of manors on the conquest of the provinces.

The result of conquest seems thus to have been chiefly a change of lordship, both as regards the private villas and the public lands. The conquered districts seem to have become in a wholesale way practically *terra regis*. There is no evidence that the modes of agriculture on the one hand or the modes of management on the other hand were materially changed. The conquering king would probably at once put followers of his own into the place of the Roman fiscal officers. These would become *quasi-*lords of the royal manors on the *terra regis*. Then by degrees would naturally arise the process whereby under lavish royal grants manors were handed one after another into the private ownership of churches and monasteries and favourites of the king, thus honey-combing the *terra regis* with private manors.

This seems to have been what happened in the Frankish provinces, and in the Alamannic and Bavarian districts, where the process can be most clearly traced. And the result seems to have been the almost universal prevalence of the manorial system in these districts. Even the towns came to be regarded as in the demesne of the king. And gradually manorial lordship extended itself over the free tenants as well as over the various semi-servile classes who were afterwards confused together in the general class of serfs.

The community of serfs was fed from above and from below. Free 'coloni,' by their own voluntary surrender, and free tribesmen, perhaps upon conquest or gradually by the force of long usage, sank into serfs. Slaves, on the other hand, by their lord's favour, or to meet the needs of agriculture, were supplied with an outfit of oxen and rose out of slavery into serfdom.

But what was this serfdom? It was not simply the old prædial slavery of the Germans of Tacitus. Nor was it merely a continuance of the slavery on the Roman villa.

Slavery mitigated by Christian humanity.

For finally, in the period of transition from Roman to German lordship, a new moral force entered as a fresh factor in the economic evolution. The silent humanising influence of Christianity seems to have been the power which mitigated the rigour of slavery, and raised the slave on the estates of the Church into the middle status of serfdom, by insisting upon the limitation of his labour to the three days' week-work of the mediæval serf.

Thus, from the point of view alike of the German and the Roman 'servi,' mediæval serfdom, except to the freemen who by their own surrender or by conquest were degraded into it, was a distinct step upward in the economic progress of the masses of the people towards freedom.

Applying these results especially to England, we

have once more to remember that there was settled
agriculture in Belgic Britain before the Roman
invasion : that the fact vouched for by Pliny, that *marl*
and *manure* were ploughed into the fields, is proof
that the simplest form of the open-field system—the
Welsh co-aration of the waste, and the German
shifting every year of the ' *arva* '—had already given
place to a more settled and organised system, in
which the same land remained under tillage year
after year. Pliny's description of the marling of the
land, however, points rather to the *one-field system* of
Northern Germany than to the three-field system, as
that under which the corn was grown which Cæsar
found ripening on British fields when he first landed
on the southern coast.[1]

In the meantime Roman improvements in agriculture may well have included the introduction into
the province of Britain of the three-course rotation
of crops. The open fields round the villa of the
Roman lord, cultivated by his slaves, ' coloni,' ' tributarii,' and ' liti,' may have been first arranged on the
three-field system ; and, once established, that system
would spread and become general during those centuries of Roman occupation in which so much corn
was produced and exported from the island.

The Roman *annonæ*—founded, perhaps, on the
earlier tribal food-rents—were, in Britain, as we know
from the ' Agricola ' of Tacitus, taken mostly in corn ;

---

[1] The ' *one-field system* ' of *per-manent arable* must not be confused with the improvement of the early Welsh and Irish ' co-aration of the waste,' by which the land was cropped perhaps two or three or four years before it was *left to go back into grass*. This resembles the German *Feldgraswirthschaft* and not the German one-field system.

and the *tributum* was probably assessed during the later empire on that system of *jugation* which was found to be so like to the *hidation* which prevailed after the Saxon conquest.

Conquest the rule. The invaders become lords of *hams* or manors.

Putting aside as exceptional the probably peaceful but at best obscure settlements in tribal households, and regarding conquest as the rule, the economic evidence seems to supply no solid reason for supposing that the German conquerors acted in Britain in a way widely different from that which they followed on the conquest of Continental Roman provinces. The conquered territory here as elsewhere probably became at first *terra regis* of the English, Saxon, or Jutish kings. And though there may have been more cases in England than elsewhere of extermination of the old inhabitants, the evidence of the English open-field system seems to show that, taking England as a whole, the continuity between the Roman and English system of land management was not really broken. The Roman provincial *villa* still seems to have remained the typical form of estate ; and the management of the public lands, now *terra regis*, seems to have preserved its manorial character. For whenever estates are granted to the Church or monasteries, or to thanes of the king, they seem to be handed over as already existing manors, with their own customs and services fixed by immemorial usage.

It is most probable that whenever German conquerors descended upon an already peopled country where agriculture was carried on as it was in Britain, their comparatively small numbers and still further their own dislike to agricultural pursuits and liking for lordship, and familiarity with servile tenants in the old country, would induce them to place the conquered people in the position of serfs, as the Germans of Tacitus seem to have done, making them do the agriculture by customary methods. If in any special cases the numbers in the invading hosts were larger than usual, they would probably include the semi-servile dependants of the chieftains and tribesmen. These, placed on the land allotted to their lords, would be serfs in England as they had been at home.

At this point, as we have seen, the internal evidence of the open-field system, at the earliest date at which it arises, comes to our aid, showing that as a general rule it was the shell, not of household communities of tribesmen doing their own ploughing like the Welsh tribesmen by co-aration, but of serfs doing the ploughing under an over-lordship.

Here the English evidence points in precisely the same direction as the Continental. For, as so often repeated, the prevalence, as far back as the earliest records, of yard-lands and *huben*, handed down so generally, and evidently by long immemorial custom, as *indivisible bundles* from one generation to another, implies the *absence* of *division among heirs*, and is accordingly a mark of the servile nature of the holding.

Further, whenever a place was called, as so many places were, by the name of a single person, it seems obvious that at the moment when its name was acquired it was under a *land ownership*, which, as regards the dependent population upon it, was a *lordship*. We have seen that in the laws of King Ethelbert the ' *hams* ' and ' *tuns* ' of England are spoken of as in a single ownership, whilst the men tion of the three grades of ' læts ' shows that there were semi-servile tenants upon them. And in the vast number of instances in which local names consist of a personal name with a suffix, the evidence of the local name itself is strong for the manorial The earlier character of the estate. When that suffix is *tun*, or 'hams' and 'tuns' *ham*, or *villa*, with the personal name prefixed, the manors. evidence is doubly strong. Even when connected with an impersonal prefix, these suffixes in themselves distinctly point, as we have seen, to the manorial character of the estate, with at least direct, if not absolutely conclusive, force.

Whatever doubt remains is not as to the generally manorial character of the *hams* and *tuns* of the earliest Saxon records, or as to the serfdom of their tenants; as to this, it is submitted that the evidence is clear and conclusive. Whatever doubt remains is as to which of two possible courses leading to this result was taken by the Saxon conquerors of Britain.

As regards the methods of their conquest, there happens to exist no satisfactory contemporary evidence. They may either have conquered and adopted the Roman villas, whether in private or imperial hands, with the slaves and ' coloni ' or ' tributarii ' upon them, calling them ' hams,' or they may have destroyed the Roman villas and their tenants, and have established in their place fresh ' hams' of their own, which in mediæval Latin records, whether in private or royal possession, were also afterwards called ' villas.' In some districts they may have followed the one course, in other districts the other course. Either of the two might as well as the other have produced manors and manorial serfdom.

But when the internal evidence of the Anglo-Saxon
land system is examined, even this doubt as to which
of the two methods was generally followed is in part
removed. For it may at least be said with truth
that the hundred years of historical darkness during
which there is a simple absence of direct testimony,
is at least bridged over by such planks of *indirect*
economic evidence as the apparent connexion between
the Roman 'jugation' and the Saxon 'hidage,' the
resemblance between the Roman and Saxon allotment of a certain number of acres along with single
or double yokes of oxen to the holdings, the prevalence of the rule of single succession, the apparent
continuance of the Roman *tributum* and *annonæ*, and
even some of the *sordida munera* in the Saxon *gafol,*
gafol-yrth, averagium, and other manorial services ;
and, lastly, the fact that in Gaul and Upper Germany
the actual continuity between the Roman *villa* and
the German *heim* can be more or less clearly traced.

The force of this economic evidence, it is submitted, is at least enough to prove either that there
was a sufficient amount of continuity between the
Roman villa and the Saxon manor to preserve the
general type, or that the German invaders who destroyed and re-introduced the manorial type of estate
came from a district in which there had been such
continuity, and where they themselves had lived long
enough to permit the peculiar manorial instincts of
the Romano-German province to become a kind of
second nature to them.

It is as impossible to conceive that this complex
manorial land system, which we have found to bristle
with historical survivals of usages of the Romano-

German province, should have been suddenly introduced into England by *un-Romanised* Northern
piratical tribes of Germans, as it is to conceive of the
sudden creation of a fossil.

The most reasonable hypothesis, in the absence of
direct evidence, appears therefore to be that the
manorial system grew up in Britain as it grew up in
Gaul and Germany, as the compound product of
barbarian and Roman institutions mixing together
during the periods first of Roman provincial rule, and
secondly of German conquest.

This hypothesis seems at least most fully to
account for the facts.   Perhaps, it is not too much to
say that whilst the large tracts of England remaining
folk-land or *terra regis*, in spite of the lavish grants to
monasteries complained of by Bede, are in themselves
suggestive of the comparatively limited extent of
allodial allotments among the conquering tribesmen,
the existence and multiplication upon the *terra regis*,
not of free village communities, but of royal manors
of the same type as that of the Frankish villas, with
a serfdom upon them also of the same type, and connected with the same three-field system of husbandry
in both cases, almost amounts to a positive verifica-
tion when the historical survivals clinging to the
system in both cases are taken into account.

The large extent of folk-land evidence against extensive allodial allotments.

Even on the supposition that the Saxons really
exterminated the old population and destroyed every
vestige of the Roman system, it has already become
obvious that it would not at all follow that they
generally introduced free village communities ; for in
that case the evidence would go far to show that
they most likely brought slaves with them and settled

The in-
vaders
either
adopted
the natives
as serfs or
brought
serfs with
them.

them in servile village communities round their own
dwellings, as Tacitus saw the Germans of his time
doing in Germany. But, again, it must be remembered that however naturally this might produce the
manor and serfdom, still the survivals of minute provincial usages hanging about the Saxon land system
would remain unaccounted for, unless the invaders of
the fifth century had already been thoroughly Romanised before their conquest of Britain.

We cannot, indeed, pretend to have discovered *English*
in the economic evidence a firm bridge for all pur- *history*
poses across the historic gulf of the fifth century, *with free*
and to have settled the difficult questions who were *ties but*
the German invaders of England, whence they came, *dom.*
and what was the exact form of their settlements
in one district or another. But the facts we have
examined seem to have settled the practical economic question with which we started, viz. whether
the *hams* and *tuns* of England, with their open
fields and yard-lands, in the earliest historical times
were inhabited and tilled in the main by free village communities, or by communities in villenage.
However many exceptional instances there may have
been of settlements in tribal households, or even free
village communities, it seems to be almost certain
that these 'hams' and 'tuns' were, generally speaking, and for the most part from the first, practically
manors with communities in *serfdom* upon them.

It has become at least clear, speaking broadly, that *The yard-*
the equal 'yard-lands' of the 'geburs' were not the *the allodial*
'alods' or free lots of 'alodial' freeholders in a com- *of a free*
mon 'mark,' but the tenements of serfs paying 'gafol' *tribesman.*
and doing 'week-work' for their lords. And this is

English history begins not with free communities but with serfdom.

The yard-land not the allodial allotment of a free tribesman.

equally true whether the manors on which they lived were bocland of Saxon thanes, or folk-land under the 'villicus' of a Saxon king.

II. LOCAL EVIDENCE OF CONTINUITY BETWEEN ROMAN AND ENGLISH VILLAGES.

There yet remains one test to which the hypothesis of continuity between the British, Roman, and English village community and open-field system may be put.

Doubts as to the extermination of the British population by the English invaders. It has sometimes been inferred, perhaps too readily, that the English invaders of Roman Britain nearly exterminated the old inhabitants, destroying the towns and villages, and making fresh settlements of their own, upon freshly chosen sites. If this were so, it would, of course, involve the destruction of the open fields round the old villages, and the formation of fresh open fields round the new ones.

The passage in Ammianus Marcellinus has sometimes been quoted, in which he describes the Alamanni, who had taken possession of Strasburg, Spires, Worms, Mayence, &c., as encamped outside these cities, shunning their inside 'as though they had been graves surrounded by nets.'[1] But this was in time of war, and no proof of what they might do when in peaceable possession of the country.

Mr. Freeman also has drawn a graphic picture of Anderida, with the two Saxon villages of Pevensey and West Ham outside of its old Roman walls, and no dwellings within them. But it would so obviously be

---

[1] Amm. Marc. xvi. c. ii.

much easier to build new houses outside the gates of a ruined city, or, perhaps, we should say rather fortified camp, than to clear away the rubbish and build upon the old site, that such an instance is far from conclusive. Nor does the fact that in so many cases the streets of once Roman cities deviate from the old Roman lines prove that the new builders avoided the ancient sites. It proves only that, instead of removing the heaps of rubbish, they chose the open spaces behind them as more convenient for their new buildings, in the process of erecting which the heaps of rubbish were doubtless gradually removed.

But, in truth, cases of fortified cities are not to the point. What we want to find out is whether, in the *rural* districts, the British villages, with their open fields around them, were generally adopted by the Romans, and whether, having survived the Roman occupation, the Saxons adopted them in their turn.

Is there evidence of continuity in the rural villages?

It may be worth while to recur to the district from which was taken the typical example of the open fields, testing the point by such local evidence as may there be found.

e.g. in the Hitchin district.

Among the ancient boundaries of the township of Hitchin, or rather of that part which included the now enclosed hamlet of Walsworth, was mentioned the Icknild way—that old British road which, passing from Wiltshire to Norfolk, here traverses the edge of the Chiltern hills. It sometimes winds lazily about uphill and down, following the line of the chalk downs. In many places it is merely a broad turf drift way. Here and there a long straight stretch of a mile or two suggests a Roman improvement upon

The Icknild way and other ancient roads.

its perhaps once more devious course. Here and there, too, are fragments of similar broad turf lanes leading nowhere, having lost the continuity which no doubt they once possessed. Sometimes crossing it, sometimes branching off from it, sometimes running parallel to it, are also frequently found similar winding broad turf drift ways, or straight roads of apparently British or Roman origin. It crosses Akeman Street at Tring, Watling Street at Dunstable, and Irmine Street at Royston. Neither Dunstable nor Royston, however, are examples of continuity, being comparatively modern towns, neither of them mentioned in the Domesday Survey. Hitchin lies about half-way between the cross-roads.

The district under its Belgic kings.

The district included in the annexed map, of which Hitchin is the centre, was a part of Belgic Britain. According to Cæsar this had been under the rule of the same king as Belgic Gaul, and upon the evidence of coins and certain passages in Roman writers, it is pretty well understood to have been, soon after the invasion of Cæsar, under the rule of Tasciovanus,[1] whose capital was Verulamium, and after him of his son Cunobeline, whose capital was Camulodunum. The sons of the latter (one of them Caractacus) were prevented from succeeding him by the advance of the Roman arms.[2] The intimate relations of the two capitals at Verulam and at Colchester explain the existence of the roads between them.

The dykes which cross the Icknild way at in-

---

[1] Evans' *Ancient British Coins*, p. 220 *et seq.*
[2] *Ibid.* p. 284 *et seq.*

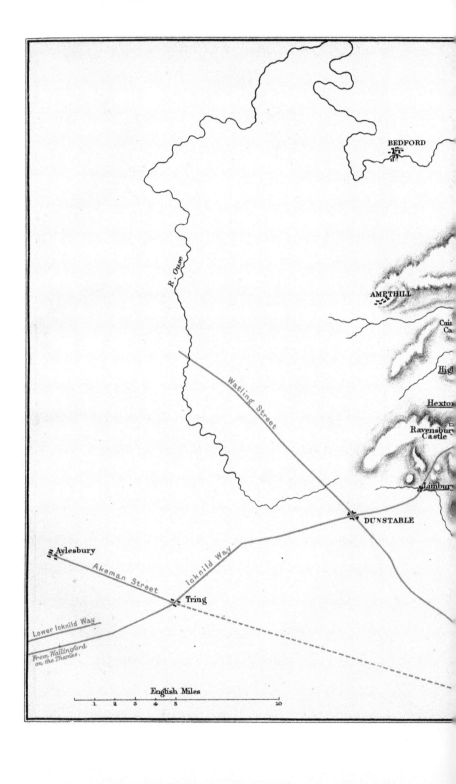

BEDFORD

R. Ouse

AMPTHILL

Cai
Ca

Hig

Watling Street

Hexto

Ravensbur
Castle

Limbur

DUNSTABLE

Aylesbury

Akeman Street

Icknild Way

Tring

Lower Icknild Way

From Wallingford
on the Thames.

English Miles

1   2   3   4   5   10

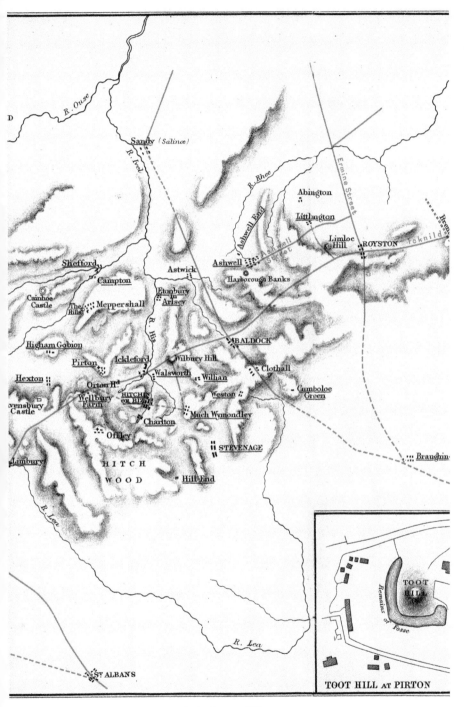

R. Ouse

Sandy (*Salinæ*)

R. Ivel

R. Rhee

Abington

Littlington

Ashwell End

Limloe Hill

ROYSTON

Ashwell

Shefford

Astwick

Harborough Banks

Ashwell Street

Ermine Street

Icknild

Campton

Cainhoe Castle

The Hills

Meppershall

Etonbury or Arlsey

R. Hiz

Higham Gobion

BALDOCK

Pirton

Ickleford

Wilbury Hill

Clothall

Hexton

Walsworth

Willian

Cumboloe Green

Orton H?

Weston

Wellbury Farm

HITCHIN or BIZ

ravensbury Castle

Charlton

Much Wymondley

Braughin

Limbury

Offley

STEVENAGE

HITCH WOOD

Hill End

R. Lea

R. Lea

ST ALBANS

TOOT HILL

Remains of Fosse

TOOT HILL AT PIRTON

London, Longmans & C?

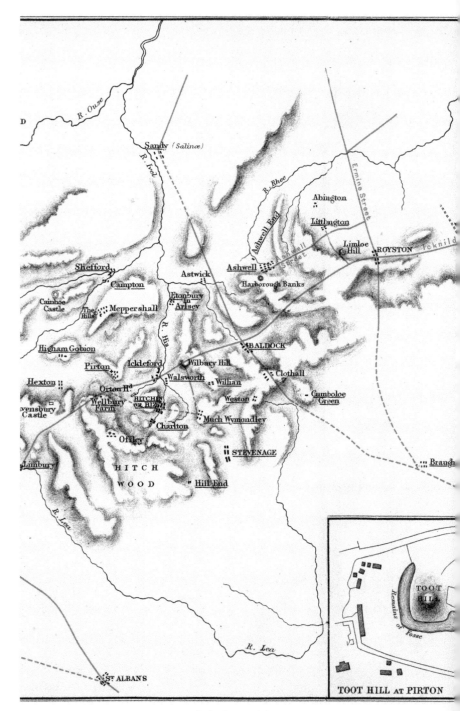

TOOT HILL AT PIRTON

London: Longmans & C°

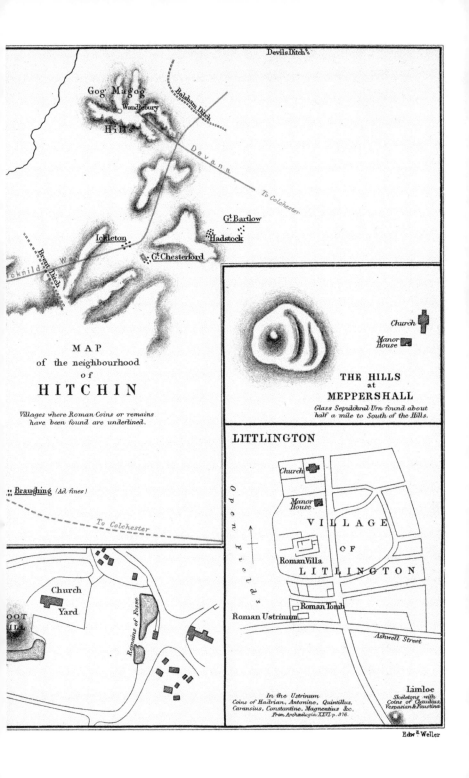

Devils Ditch

Gog Magog
Wandlebury
Hills

Balsham Ditch

Devana

To Colchester

Gt. Bartlow
Hadstock

Ickleton
Gt. Chesterford

Brent Ditch
Icknild W.

MAP
of the neighbourhood
of
HITCHIN

Villages where Roman Coins or remains
have been found are underlined.

Braughing (Ad fines)

To Colchester

Church
Yard

OOT
ILL

Remains of Fosse

THE HILLS
at
MEPPERSHALL

Glass Sepulchral Urn found about
half a mile to South of the Hills.

Church

Manor
House

LITTLINGTON

Church

Manor
House

Roman Villa

VILLAGE
OF
LITLINGTON

Open Fields

Roman Tomb
Roman Ustrinum

Ashwell Street

Limloe
Skeletons with
Coins of Claudius,
Vespasian & Faustina

In the Ustrinum
Coins of Hadrian, Antonine, Quintillus,
Carausius, Constantine, Magnentius &c.
From Archæologia XXVI. p. 376.

Edwd. Weller

tervals, East of Royston—the Brent dyke, the Balsham dyke (parallel to the *Via Devana*), and the
Devil's dyke, near Newmarket—seem to indicate that
here was the border land between this district and
that of the Iceni (Norfolk and Suffolk).

Sandy (the Roman *Salinæ*), at the north of the
district in the map, is known, from the evidence of
coins of Cunobeline, to have been an important British
centre. A gold coin of Tasciovanus, and other
British coins, have been picked up on the Icknild
way, between Hitchin and Dunstable. A gold coin
of Cunobeline, and many fragments of Roman pottery,
have been found about half a mile to the east of
Abington, a village a little to the north of the Icknild
way, near Royston.[1] Coins of Cunobeline have also
been found at Great Chesterford. A copper coin of
Cunobeline was picked up in a garden in Walsworth,
a hamlet of Hitchin, and British urns of a rude type
have been recently found on the top of Benslow Hill,
the high ground on the east of the town.

The map will show in how many directions the
district is cut up by Roman roads, which, as they
evidently connect the various parts of the domain
of the before-mentioned British kings, were probably,
with the Icknild way itself, British tracks before they
were adopted by the Romans.

Almost every commanding bluff of the chalk
downs retains traces of its having been used as a hill
fort, probably in pre-Roman times, as well as later,
while the numerous tumuli all along the route of the
Icknild way testify, probably, to the numerous battles
fought in its neighbourhood.

---

[1] I am indebted to the Rev. W. G. F. Pigott for this information.

Chap. XI.

Its Roman
conquest
under
Claudius
and Aulus
Plautius,
about
A.D. 43. Probably this district fell under direct Roman rule after the campaigns of Aulus Plautius and Claudius, about A.D. 43.[1] The direction of the advance was probably across the Thames at Wallingford, and along the Icknild way, from which the descent upon Verulam could well be made from Tring or Dunstable down what were afterwards called Akeman Street and Watling Street. Under the tumulus near Litlington, called Limloe, or Limbury Hill, skeletons were found, and coins of the reign of Claudius, and of later date. It is possible that the battle was fought here in a later reign which brought the further parts of the district under Roman rule.

The date of the Saxon conquest of this district may be as definitely determined. It preceded the conquest of Bath, Cirencester, and Gloucester by a very few years. It may be pretty clearly placed at about A.D. 571, when, according to the Saxon Chronicle, 'Cuthwulf fought with the Brit-weals at Bedcan-ford (Bedford), and took four towns. He took Lygean-birg (Lenborough) and Aegeles-birg (Aylesbury), and Bænesingtun (Bensington) and Egonesham (Eynsham).' This was the time when Bedfordshire, Buckinghamshire, and Oxfordshire fell into the hands of the West Saxons.

The old boundary of the ecclesiastical division of the country before the time of the Norman conquest included this district, with Bedford, in the diocese of Dorchester. The boundary probably followed the lines of the old West Saxon kingdom, and shut it off

---

[1] See the paper on 'The Campaign of Aulus Plautius,' in Dr. Guest's *Origines Celticæ*, vol. ii.

from Essex and the rest of Hertfordshire, which were
included in the diocese of London.

The district, therefore, seems to have remained nearly 400 years under Roman rule, and under the British post-Roman rule another 100 years, till within twenty-five or thirty years of the arrival of St. Augustine in England, and the date of the laws of King Ethelbert, and within little more than 100 years of the date of the laws of King Ine, which laws presumably applied to this district as a part of the West Saxon kingdom.

The question is whether the position of the Roman remains which have been discovered in this neighbourhood points to a continuity in the sites of the present villages between British, Roman, and Saxon times. This question may certainly, in many instances, and, perhaps, generally, be answered distinctly in the affirmative. Do the Roman remains suggest continuity?

Take first the town of Hitchin itself. Its name in the Domesday Survey was ' Hiz,' and there can be little doubt that it is a Celtic word, meaning 'streams.'[1] The position of the township accords with this name. The river ' Hiz ' rises out of the chalk at Wellhead, almost immediately turns a mill, and, flowing through the town, joins the Ivel a few miles lower down in its course, and so flows ultimately into the Ouse. The Orton[2] rises at the west extremity of the township, in The town of Hitchin, or 'Hiz,' *i.e.* 'of the streams.'

---

[1] Compare supra, p. 161: the change of ' Hisse-burn ' or ' Icenan-burn ' into ' Itchin River,' and of ' æt Icceburn ' into 'Ticceburn,' and 'Titchbourne.' May not Icknild Way, or 'Icenan-hild-wæg,' mean highway ' by the streams,' and Ricknild Way mean highway ' by the ridge'? See map, *supra*, ch. v., s. v. They are sometimes parallel as an upper and lower road.

[2] Formerly 'Alton.' See Survey of the Manor of Hitchin. 1650. Public Record Office.

a few hundred yards turns West Mill, and forms the
boundary of the parish till it meets the Hiz at Ickleford, where the two are forded by the Icknild way.
The Purwell, rising from the south east, forms the
boundary between the parishes of Hitchin and Much
Wymondley, and then, after turning Pearl Mill, and
dividing Hitchin from Walsworth Hamlet, also joins
the Hiz before it reaches Ickleford. Thus two of
these three pure chalk streams embrace the township, and one passes through it giving its Celtic name
Hiz to the town.[1]

Its Celtic
name.

It is not likely that either the Romans or the
Saxon invaders gave it this Celtic name.

British and
Roman re-
mains.

As already mentioned, on the top of the hill, to
the east of the town, British sepulchral urns have
been recently found.

A Roman cemetery, with a large number of
sepulchral urns, dishes, and bottles, and coins of
Severus, Carausius, Constantine, and Alectus, was
turned up a few years ago on the top of the hill on
the opposite side of the town, in a part of the open
fields called 'The Fox-holes'[2]—a plot of useless
ground being often used for burials by the Romans.

Another Roman cemetery, with very similar
pottery and coins, has been found on Bury Mead,
near the line where the arable part ceases and the

---

[1] In Hampshire the old Celtic
or Belgic names of rivers in many
cases gave their names to places
upon them. The '*Itchin*' to Itchin
Stoke, Itchin Abbas, Itchbourne,
&c. The '*Meona*' (*Cod. Dip.*
clviii.) to Meon Stoke, East and
West Meon, &c. The '*Candefer*'
(*Cod. Dip.* mcccix.) to three 'Can-
dovers.' So also the *Tarrant* gives
its names to several places.

[2] Now part of the garden of
Mr. W. T. Lucas, in whose possession many of them now remain.
Three skeletons, one of them of
great size, were found near the urns.

Lammas meadow lands begin. Bury field itself (*i.e.* the arable) has been deeply drained, but yielded no coins or urns.

Occasional coins and urns have been found in the town itself.

This, so far as it goes, is good evidence that Hitchin was a British and a Roman before it was a Saxon town.

In the sub-hamlet of Charlton, near Wellhead, the source of the Hiz, small coins of the lower Empire have been found. As already mentioned, a coin of Cunobeline was found in the village of Walsworth. In even the hamlets, therefore, there is some evidence of continuity. At Ickleford, where the Icknild way crosses the Hiz, Roman coins have been found.

The next parish to the east, divided from Hitchin by the Purwell stream, is Much Wymondley.

The evidence of continuity, as regards this parish, is remarkably clear. The accompanying map [1] supplies an interesting example of open fields, with their strips and balks and scattered ownership still remaining in 1803. These open arable fields were originally divided off from the village by a stretch of Lammas land.

Between this Lammas land and the church in the village lie the remains of the little Roman holding, of which an enlarged plan is given. It consists now of several fields, forming a rough square, with its sides to the four points of the compass, and contains, filling in the corners of the square, about 25 Roman

---

[1] For permission to reproduce this map I am indebted to the present lord of the manor, C. W. Wilshere, Esq., of the Fryth, Welwyn.

CHAP. XI. jugera—or the eighth of a centuria of 200 jugera— the extent of land often allotted, as we have seen, to a retired veteran with a single pair of oxen. The proof that it was a Roman holding is as follows :— In the corner next to the church are two square fields still distinctly surrounded by a moat, nearly parallel to which, on the east side, was found a line of black earth full of broken Roman pottery and tiles. Near the church, at the south-west corner of the property, is a double tumulus, which, being close to the church field, may have been an ancient ' toot hill,' or a terminal mound. In the extreme opposite corner of the holding was found a Roman cemetery, contain- ing the urns, dishes, and bottles of a score or two of burials. Drawings of those of the vessels not broken in the digging, engraved from a photograph, are appended to the map, by the kind permission of the owner.[1] Over the hedge, at this corner, begins the Lammas land.[2]

How many other holdings were included in the Roman village we do not know, but that the village was in the same position in relation to the open fields that it was in 1803 is obvious.

Ashwell. Ashwell also evidently stands on its old site round the head of a remarkably strong chalk spring, the clear stream from which flows through the village as the river *Rhee*, a branch of the *Cam*. Early Roman coins and sepulchral urns have been found in the hamlet called ' Ashwell End,' and a Roman road, called ' Ashwell Street,' passes by the town parallel

---

[1] Mr. William Ransom, of Fair- field, near Hitchin.

[2] As regards Roman cemeteries, as placed in the extreme corner of a holding, *see* Lachmann, pp. 271-2; *De Sepulchris Dolabell.* p. 303.

WILLIAN

LETCHWORTH

HITCHIN

HITCHIN

IPPOLLITTS

N.B. The property of the Lord of the Manor
is coloured Red.

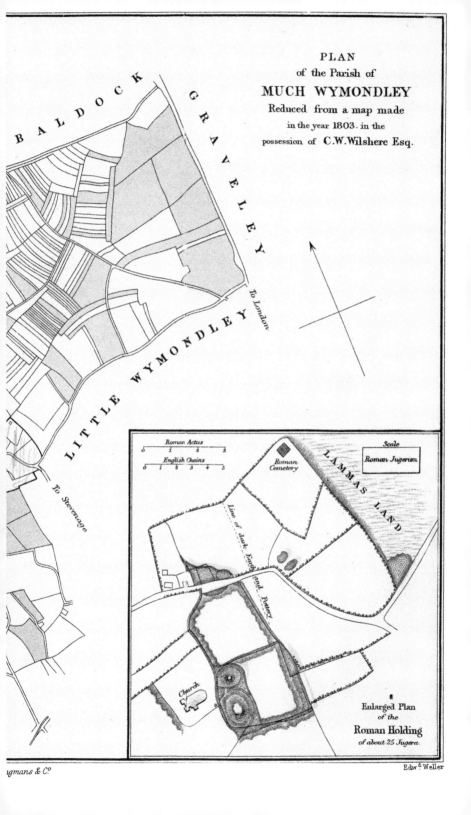

PLAN
of the Parish of
MUCH WYMONDLEY
Reduced from a map made
in the year 1803. in the
possession of C.W.Wilshere Esq.

BALDOCK

GRAVELEY

LITTLE WYMONDLEY

To London

To Stevenage

Roman Actus

English Chains

Scale
Roman Jugerum

Roman Cemetery

LAMMAS LAND

Line of dark Earth and Pottery

Church

Enlarged Plan
of the
Roman Holding
of about 25 Jugera.

Longmans & C⁰

Edwᵈ Weller

to the Icknild way. Near to the town is a camp, with a clearly defined vallum, called Harborough Banks, where coins of the later Empire have been found. A map of the parish, made before the enclosure, and preserved in the place, shows that it presented a remarkably good example of the open-field system.

An instance of continuity as remarkable as that of Much Wymondley occurs at Litlington,[1] the next village to Ashwell, on the Ashwell Street. The church and manor house in this case lie near together on the west side of the village, and in the adjoining field and gardens the walls and pavements of a Roman villa were found many years ago. At a little distance from it, nearer to the Ashwell Street, a Roman *ustrinum* and cemetery were found, surrounded by four walls, and yielding coins of Hadrian, Antoninus Pius, Quintillus, Carausius, Constantine the Great, Magnentius, &c. A map of this village is appended.

When the Roman villa was discovered, the open fields around the village were still unenclosed, and the position of Ashwell Street was pushed farther from the village at the time of the enclosure.

The tumulus called 'Limloe,' or 'Limbury Hill,' lies at the side of the road leading from the Icknild way across the Ashwell Street to the village, and immediately under it skeletons with coins of Claudius, Vespasian, and Faustina were found, as already mentioned.

A few miles further east than Royston are two villages, Ickleton on the Icknild way, and Great

---

[1] *Archæologia,* vol. xxvi. p. 376

F F

Chesterford a little to the south of it.   That both these places are on Roman sites the foundations and coins which have been found attest.[1]   There are remains of a camp at Chesterford, and coins of Cunobeline as well as numerous Roman coins have been dug up there.[2]

Hadstock.
At Hadstock, a village near, in a field called ' Sunken Church Field,' Roman foundations and coins have been found.[3]

Other instances of continuity in the sites of villages.
Proceeding further east the list of similar cases might be greatly increased.   But keeping within the small district, in the following other cases the finding of Roman coins in the villages seems to be fair proof of continuity in their sites, viz.:—Sandy, Campton, Baldock, Willian, Cumberlow Green, Weston, Stevenage, Hexton, and Higham Gobion.

Ancient mounds and earth works.
Two remarkable instances of ancient mounds or fortifications close to churches occur at Meppershall and Pirton, of both of which plans are given.   The Pirton mound is called in the village the ' toot hill.' These mounds in the neighbourhood of churches may be much older than the Saxon conquest.   Open air courts were by no means confined to one race.[4]   Roman remains have been found in the neighbourhood of both these places, but how near to the actual village sites I am unable to say.[5]

Leaving out these two and many more doubtful cases, and without pretending to be exhaustive, there have been mentioned nearly a score in which Roman

[1] *Journal of British Archæological Association*, iv. 356, and v. 54.
[2] *Archæologia*, xxxii. p. 350.
[3] *Id.*, p. 352.
[4] *See* Mr. Gomme's interesting work on *Primitive Folkmotes*, c. ii.
[5] A remarkably fine *glass* funeral urn was found about half a mile below the Meppershall Hills in 1882 by the tenant of the neighbouring farm.

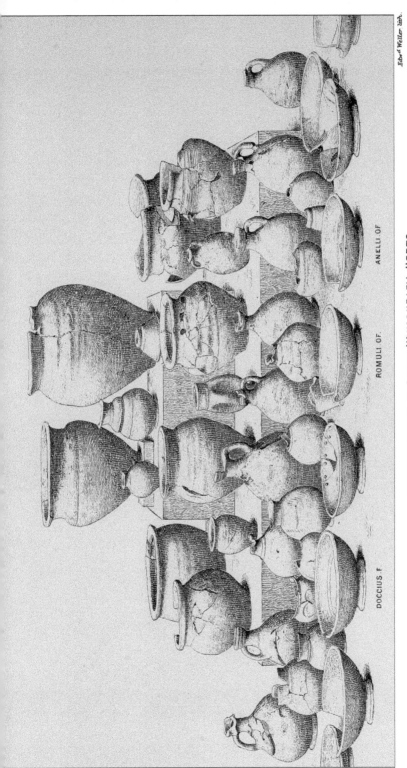

ROMAN POTTERY FOUND AT GREAT WYMONDLEY, HERTS.

MARCH 1882.

In the possession of William Ransom, Esq.

London, Longmans & Cº

DOCCIUS.F

ROMULI.OF

ANELLI.OF

Edwd Weller lith.

remains or coins have already been found on the
present sites of villages in this small district.

So far the local evidence supports the view that
the West Saxons, who probably conquered it about
A.D. 570, succeeded to a long-settled agriculture ; and
further it seems likely that, assuming the lordship
vacated by the owners of the villas, and adopting the
village sites, they continued the cultivation of the open
fields around them by means of the old rural population on that same three-field system, which had probably been matured and improved during Roman
rule, and by which the population of the district had
been supported during the three generations between
the departure of the Roman governors and the West
Saxon conquest.

But it may perhaps be urged that these districts,
conquered so late as A.D. 570, may have been exceptionally treated. If this were so, it must be borne in
mind that the whole of central England—i.e. the counties described in the second volume of the Hundred
Rolls as to which the evidence for the existence of the
open-field system was so strong—was included in the
exception. Indeed, if the line of the Icknild way be
extended along Akeman Street to Cirencester, Bath,
and Gloucester, the line of the Saxon conquests which
were later than A.D. 560 would be pretty clearly
marked. The laws of Ine, pointing backwards as
they do from their actual date, reach back within
two or three generations of the date of the Saxon
conquest of this part of his kingdom.

It would be impossible here to pursue the question in detail in other parts of England. Perhaps it
will be sufficient to call attention to the many cases

Chap. XI.

The
Hitchin
district
hardly
excep-
tional.
mentioned in Mr. C. Roach Smith's valuable ' Collectanea,'[1] in which Roman remains have been found in
close proximity to the churches of modern villages,
and to his remark that a long list of such instances
might easily be made.[2]

The number of such cases which occur in Kent is
very remarkable, and Kent was certainly not a late
conquest.

I will only add a passing allusion to the remarkable case at Woodchester, in Gloucestershire, where
the church, present mansion, and Roman villa are
close together,[3] and mention that in two of the hamlets on the manor of Tidenham—Stroat and Sedbury
(or Cingestun)—Roman remains bear testimony to a
Roman occupation before the West Saxon conquest.[4]

The fact seems to be that the archæological evidence, gradually accumulating as time goes on, points
more and more clearly to the fact that our modern
villages are very often on their old Roman and sometimes probably pre-Roman sites—that however much
the English invaders avoided the walled towns of
Roman Britain, they certainly had no such antipathy
to the occupation of its villas and rural villages.

---

[1] Vol. i. pp. 17, 66, 190; vol.
iii. p. 33; vol. iv. p. 155; vol. v.
p. 187; vol. vi. p. 222.

[2] *Collectanea,* v. p. 187. The
recently discovered Roman villa
on the property of Earl Cowper,
at Wingham, near Canterbury,
is a striking instance. See Mr.
Dowker's pamphlet thereon. See
also *Archæologia,* xxix. p. 217, &c.,
where Mr. C. Roach Smith mentions several other instances.

[3] *Account of the Roman An-
tiquities at Woodchester,* by S.
Lysons. Lond.: MDCCXCVII.

[4] See Mr. Ormerod's *Archæological Memoirs.*

III. CONCLUSION.

The economic result of the inquiry pursued in this essay may now be summed up in few words. Economic result.

Its object was not to inquire into the origin of village and tribal communities as the possible beginning of all things, but simply to put English Economic History on true lines at its historical beginning, viz. : the English Conquest.

Throughout the whole period from pre-Roman to modern times we have found in Britain two parallel systems of rural economy side by side, but keeping separate and working themselves out on quite different lines, in spite of Roman, English, and Norman invasions—that of the *village* community in the eastern, that of the *tribal* community in the western districts of the island. Two rural systems throughout—the village community in the east, and the tribal community in the west.

Both systems as far back as the evidence extends were marked by the two notes of community and equality, and each was connected with a form of the open or common field system of husbandry peculiar to itself. These two different forms of the common field system also kept themselves distinct throughout, and are still distinct in their modern remains or survivals. Community and equality in both. Each had its own open-field system.

Neither the village nor the tribal community seems to have been introduced into Britain during a historical period reaching back for 2,000 years at least. Both pre-Roman.

On the one hand, the village community of the eastern districts of Britain was connected with a settled agriculture which, apparently dating earlier The English village community in serfdom, and its

CHAP. XI.

three-field
system.

than the Roman invasion and improved during the Roman occupation, was carried on, at length, under that three-field form of the open-field system which became the shell of the English village community. The equality in its yard-lands and the single succession which preserved this equality we have found to be apparently marks not of an original freedom, not of an original allodial allotment on the German 'mark system,' but of a settled serfdom under a lordship —a semi-servile tenancy implying a mere usufruct, theoretically only for life, or at will, and carrying with it no inherent rights of inheritance. But this serfdom, as we have seen reason to believe, was, to the masses of the people, not a degradation, but a step upward out of a once more general slavery. Certainly during the 1,200 years over which the direct English evidence extends the tendency has been towards more and more of freedom. In other words, as time went on during these 1,200 years, the serfdom of the old order of things has been gradually breaking up under those influences, whatever they may have been, which have produced the new order of things.

A step out
of slavery
towards
the free-
dom of the
new order
of things.

The tribal
community
and its
'run-rig'
system

On the other hand, the tribal community of the western districts of Great Britain and of Ireland, though parallel in time with the village community of the eastern districts, was connected with an earlier stage of economic development, in which the rural economy was pastoral rather than agricultural. This tribal community was bound together, perhaps, in a unique degree, by the strong ties of blood relationship between free tribesmen. The equality which followed the possession of the tribal blood involved an equal division among the sons of tribesmen, and was main-

tained in spite of the inequality of families by frequent
redistributions of the tribal lands, and shiftings of the
tribesmen from one homestead to another according
to tribal rules. We have traced the curious method
of clustering the homesteads in arithmetical groups
mentioned in the ancient Welsh laws, and still practised in Ireland in the seventeenth century, and we
have found many survivals of it in the present names
and divisions of Irish townlands. We have found
the simple form of open-field husbandry used under
the tribal system, and suited to its precarious and
shifting agriculture, still surviving in the 'rundale' opposed to
the new
or 'run-rig' system, by which, to this day, is effected order of
things.
in Ireland and western Scotland that infinite subdivision of holdings which marks the tenacious ad-
herence to tribal instincts on the part of a people still
fighting an unequal battle against the new order of
things.

The new order has, no doubt, arisen in one sense The new
order op-
out of both branches of the old, but neither the posed to
community
manorial village community of the eastern district, and
nor the tribal community of the west, can be said to equality.
be its parent. Its fundamental principle seems to be
opposed to the community and equality of the old order
in both its forms. The freedom of the individual and
growth of individual enterprise and property which
mark the new order imply a rebellion against the
bonds of the communism and forced equality, alike
of the manorial and of the tribal system. It has
triumphed by breaking up both the communism of
serfdom and the communism of the free tribe.

Nor, it would seem, can the new order be regarded Belongs to
a wider
with any greater truth as a development from the range of

Chap. XI.

development.

germs of any German tribal or ' mark ' system imported in the keels of the English invaders. It would seem to belong to an altogether wider range of economic development than that of one or two races. Its complex roots went deeply back into that older world into which the Teutonic invaders introduced new elements and new life, no doubt, but, it would seem, without destroying the continuity of the main stream of its economic development, or even of the outward forms of its rural economy.

This, from an economic point of view, is the important conclusion to which the facts examined in this essay seem to point. These facts will be examined afresh by other and abler students, and the last word will not soon have been said upon some of them. They are drawn from so wide a field, and from lines reaching back so far, that their interest and bearing upon the matter in hand will not soon be exhausted or settled. But if the conclusion here suggested should in the main be confirmed, what English Economic History loses in simplicity it will gain in breadth. It will cease to be provincial. It will become more closely identified with the general economic evolution of the human race in the past. And this in its turn will give a wider interest to the vast responsibilities of the English-speaking nations in connexion with the progress of the new order of things and the solution of the great economic problems of the future.

The communism of the old order a thing of the past,

What are the forces which have produced, and are producing, the evolution of the new order, and to what ultimate goal the ' weary Titan ' is bearing the ' too full orb of her fate,' are questions of the highest rank of economic and political importance, but questions upon which not much direct light has been thrown, perhaps, in this essay. Still the knowledge what the community and equality of the English village and of the Keltic tribe really were under the old order may at least dispel any lingering wish or hope that they may ever return. Communistic systems such as these we have examined, which have lasted for 2,000 years, and for the last 1,000 years at least have been gradually wearing themselves out, are hardly likely—either of them—to be the economic goal of the future.

The reader of this essay may perhaps contemplate the few remaining balks and linces of our English *like the open-field* common fields, and the surviving examples of the *system.* ' run-rig' system in Ireland and Scotland, with greater interest than before, but it will be as historical survivals, not of types likely to be reproduced in the future, but of economic stages for ever past.

APPENDIX.

'AT the Court [Leet and] of the View of Frank pledge   1819.
' of our Sovereign Lord the King with the General Court   Oct. 21.
' Baron of William Wilshere, Esquire, Lord Firmar of the
' said manor of his Majesty, holden in and for the manor
' aforesaid, on Thursday, the twenty-first day of October,
' One thousand eight hundred and nineteen, Before Joseph
' Eade, Gentleman, Steward of the said manor, and by ad-
' journment on Monday, the first day of November next
' following, before the said Joseph Eade, the Steward afore-
' said.

   ' The jurors for our Lord the King and the Homage of
' this Court having diligently enquired into the boundaries,
' extent, rights, jurisdictions, and customs of the said manor,
' and the rights, powers, and duties of the lord and tenants
' thereof, and having also enquired what lands in the town-
' ship of Hitchin and in the hamlet of Walsworth respectively
' within this manor are subject to common of pasture for the
' commonable cattle of the occupiers of messuages, cottages,
' and land within the said township and hamlet respectively,
' and for what descriptions and number of cattle, and at what
' times of the year and in what manner such rights of com-
' mon are by the custom of this manor to be exercised, and
' what payments are by such custom due in respect thereof,
' they do upon their oaths find and present as follows :—

   'That the manor comprises the township of Hitchin and
' the hamlet of Walsworth, in the parish of Hitchin, the

' lesser manors of the Rectory of Hitchin, of Moremead,
' otherwise Charlton, and of the Priory of the Biggin, being
' comprehended within the boundaries of the said manor of
' Hitchin, which also extends into the hamlets of Langley
' and Preston in the said parish of Hitchin, and into the
' parishes of Ickleford, Ippollitts, Kimpton, Kingswalden,
' and Offley.

Bounda-
ries.

'That the following are the boundaries of the township
' of Hitchin with the hamlet of Walsworth (that is to say),
' beginning at Orton Head, proceeding from thence to Bur-
' ford Ray, and from thence to a water mill called Hide Mill,
' and from thence to Wilberry Hills; from thence to a place
' called Bossendell, from thence to a water mill called Pur-
' well Mill, and from thence to a brook or river called Ippol-
' litts' Brook, and from thence to Maydencroft Lane, and
' from thence to a place called Wellhead, and from thence to
' a place called Stubborn Bush, and from thence to a place
' called Offley Cross, and from thence to Five Borough
' Hills, and from thence back to Orton Head, where the
' boundaries commenced. And that all the land in the
' parish of Hitchin lying on the north side of the river which
' runneth from Purwell Mill to Hide Mill is within the ham-
' let of Walsworth, and that the following lands on the south
' side of the same river are also within the same hamlet of
' Walsworth (vizt.), Walsworth Common, containing about
' fourteen acres; the land of Sir Francis Sykes called the
' Leys, on the south side of Walsworth Common, containing
' about four acres; the land of William Lucas and Joseph
' Lucas, called the Hills, containing about two acres; and
' nine acres or thereabouts, part of the land of Sir Francis
' Sykes, called the Shadwells, the residue of the land called
' the Shadwells on the north side of the river.

Jurisdic-
tion.

' That the lord of the manor of Hitchin hath Court Leet
' View of Frank pledge and Court Baron, and that the juris-
' diction of the Court Leet and View of Frank pledge ex-
' tendeth over the whole of the township of Hitchin and the
' hamlet of Walsworth. That a Court Leet and Court of the
' View of Frank pledge and Great Court Baron are accus-
' tomed to be holden for the said manor within one month

' after the Feast of Saint Michael the Archangel in every
' year, and may also be holden within one month after the
' Feast of Easter. And that general or special Courts Baron
' and customary Courts are holden at the pleasure of the lord
' or of his steward.

' That in the Court Leet yearly holden after the Feast of
' St. Michael the Archangel the jurors for our Lord the King
' are accustomed to elect and present to the lord two con-
' stables and six headboroughs (vizt.), two headboroughs for
' Bancroft Ward, two for Bridge Ward, and two for Tilehouse
' Street Ward (each such constable and headborough having
' right and being bound to execute the office through the
' whole leet), and likewise two ale conners, two leather
' searchers and sealers, and a bellman who is also the watch-
' man and cryer of the town. And they present that Ban-
' croft Ward contains Bancroft Street, including the Swan
' Inn, Silver Street, Portmill Lane, and the churchyard,
' church and vicarage house, and the alley leading out of
' Bancroft now called Quaker's Alley. That Bridge Ward
' contains the east and north sides of the market place, and
' part of the south side thereof to the house of John Whitney,
' formerly called the Maidenhead Inn, Mary's Street, other-
' wise Angel Street, now called Sun Street, Bull Street, now
' called Bridge Street, to the river ; Bull Corner, Back
' Street, otherwise Dead Street, from the south to the north
' extremities thereof; Biggin Lane with the Biggin and
' Hollow Lane. And that Tilehouse Street Ward contains
' Tilehouse Street, Bucklersbury to the Swan Inn, and the
' west side and the remainder of the south side of the market
' place.

PRESENTMENTS OF THE HOMAGE.

' And the Homage of this Court do also further present
' that freeholders holding of the said manor do pay to the
' lord by way of relief upon the death of the preceding tenant   Reliefs.
' one year's quitrent, but that nothing is due to the lord
' upon the alienation of freehold.

' That the fines upon admissions of copyholders, whether   Fines on
' by descent or purchase, are, and beyond the memory of   admissions.

' man have been, certain (to wit), half a year's quitrent ; and
' that where any number of tenants are admitted jointly in
' one copy, no greater fine than one half year's quitrent is
' due for the admission of all the joint tenants.

Power of
leasing.

' The Homage also present that by the custom of the
' manor the customary tenants may without licence let their
' copyholds for three years and no longer, but that they may
' by licence of the lord let the same for any term not ex-
' ceeding twenty-one years; and that the lord is upon every
' such licence entitled to a fine of one year's quitrent of the
' premises to be demised.

Forfeiture.

' The Homage present that the freehold tenants of the
' said manor forfeit their estates to the lord thereof for
' treason and for murders and other felonies ; and that the
' copyholders forfeit their estates for the like crimes, and for
' committing or suffering their copyholds to be wasted, for
' wilfully refusing to perform their services, and for leasing
' their copyholds for more than three years without licence.

' The Homage also present that by the custom of this
' manor copyholds are granted by copy or court roll for the
' term of forty years, and that a tenant outliving the
' said term is entitled to be re-admitted for the like term
' upon payment of the customary fine of half a year's quit-
' rent.

Heriots.

' The Homage present that there are no heriots due or
' payable to the lord of this manor for any of the tenements
' holden thereof.

Woods and
trees.

' The Homage also present that all woods, underwoods,
' and trees growing upon the copyhold lands holden of the
' said manor were by King James the First, by his Letters
' Patent, under the Great Seal of England, bearing date the
' fourteenth day of March, in the 6th year of his reign (in
' consideration of two hundred and sixty-six pounds sixteen
' shillings paid to his Majesty's use), granted to Thomas
' Goddesden and Thomas Chapman, two copyholders of the
' said manor, and their heirs and assigns, in trust to the use
' of themselves and the rest of the copyholders of the said
' manor; and that the copyhold tenants of the said manor
' are by virtue of such grant entitled to cut all timber and

' other trees growing on their copyholds, and to dispose
' thereof at their will.

' The Homage also present that no toll has ever been
' paid or ought to be paid for any kind of corn or grain sold
' in the market of Hitchin.

Grain sold
in the
m⸱rket
toll free.

' They also present that from the time whereof the
' memory of man is not to the contrary, the lord of this
' manor has been used to find and provide a common pound
' and stocks for the use of the tenants of this manor.

Common
pound
and stocks.

' And the Homage do further present that by the custom
' of this manor the lord may, with the consent of the Homage,
' grant by copy of court roll any part of the waste thereof, to
' be holden in fee according to the custom of the manor, at
' a reasonable rent and by the customary services, or may
' with such consent grant or demise the same for any lesser
' estate or interest.

COMMONS WITHIN THE TOWNSHIP OF HITCHIN.

' And the Homage of this Court do further present that
' the commonable land within the manor and township of
' Hitchin consists of—

' Divers parcels of ground called the Green Commons,
' the soil whereof remains in the lord of the said manor (that
' is to say):

1st. Green
Commons
in the
township
of Hitchin.

' Butts Close, containing eight acres or thereabouts;
' Orton Mead, containing forty acres or thereabouts, exclu-
' sively of the Haydons, and extending from the Old Road
' from Hitchin to Pirton by Orton Head Spring west unto
' the way which passes through Orton Mill Yard east; and
' that the Haydons on the east of the last mentioned way,
' containing four acres or thereabouts, are parts of the same
' common, and include a parcel of ground containing one
' rood and thirteen perches or thereabouts adjoining the
' river, which have been fenced from the rest of the common
' by Samuel Allen; and the ground called the Plats lying
' between Bury Mead and Cock Mead, containing two acres
' or thereabouts, including the slip of ground between the
' river and the way leading to the mill of the said John

'Ransom, lately called Burnt Mill, and now called Grove
'Mill, which hath been fenced off and planted by John
'Ransom.

2nd.
Lammas
Meadows.

' And of the lands of divers persons called the Lammas
'Meadows in Cock Mead, which contain eighteen acres or
'thereabouts, and in Bury Mead, which contains forty-five
'acres or thereabouts, including a parcel of land of the Rev.
'Woollaston Pym, clerk, called Old Hale.

3rd. Com-
mon
fields.

' And of the open and unenclosed land within the several
'common fields, called Purwell Field, Welshman's Croft, Bur-
'ford Field, Spital Field, Moremead Field, and Bury Field.

Right of
common.

' That the occupier of every ancient messuage or cottage
'within the township of Hitchin hath a right of common for
'such cattle and at such times as are hereinafter specified
'upon the Green Commons and the Lammas Meadows, but
'no person hath any right of common within this township
'as appurtenant to or in respect of any messuage or cottage
'built since the expiration of the 13th year of the reign of
'Queen Elizabeth, unless the same shall have been erected
'on the site of an ancient messuage then standing.

' That any person having right of common in respect of
'the messuage or cottage in his actual occupation may turn
'on the Green Commons and the Lammas Meadows two
'cows and one bullock, or cow calf under the age of two
'years.

Common
bull.

' That the rectors impropriate of the rectory of the parish
'of Hitchin or their lessees of the said rectory are bound to
'find a bull for the cows of the said township, and to go with
'the herd thereof, and that no other bull or bull calf may be
'turned on the commons.

' That Butts Close is the sole cow common from the 6th
'day of April, being Old Lady-day inclusive to the 12th day
'of May also inclusive, and after that time is used for col-
'lecting in the morning the herd going out to the other
'commons.

' That Orton Mead, including the Haydons, is an open
'common upon and from the thirteenth day of May, called
'Old May-day, till the fourteenth day of February, called
'Old Candlemas Day.

' That the Plats are an open common upon and from
' Whitsunday till the 6th day of April.

' That Cock Mead and Bury Mead became commonable
' on the thirteenth day of August, called Old Lammas Day,
' and continue open till the 6th day of April.

' That the common fields called Bury Field and Welsh-
' man's Croft are commonable for cows only from the time
' when the corn is cut and carried therefrom until the twelfth
' day of November, called All Saints', and that the close of
' Thomas Wilshire, gentleman, called Bury Field Close, is part
' of the common field called Bury Field, and the closes of
' John Crouch Priest, called Ickleford Closes, are part of
' Welshman's Croft, and are respectively commonable at the
' same times with the other parts of such respective common
' fields.

' That every occupier of an ancient messuage or cottage
' hath right of common upon the Green Commons, except
' Butts Close, for one gelding from and after the thirteenth
' day of August until the fourteenth day of February.

' That no person entitled to common for his cattle may
' turn or suffer the same to remain on any of the commons
' between the hours of six in the evening and six in the
' morning.

' That it is the duty of the Homage at every Great Court
' Baron holden next after the Feast of St. Michael to appoint
' a herdsman for this township, and that every commoner
' turning his cows upon the commons is bound to pay a
' reasonable sum, to be from time to time assessed by the
' Homage, for the expenses of scouring the ditches, repairing
' the fences and hedges, and doing other necessary works for
' the preservation of the commons and for the wages of the
' herdsman. And the Homage of this Court assess and present
' such payments at one shilling for every head of cattle
' turned on the commons, payable by each commoner on the
' first day in every year on which he shall turn his cattle
' upon the commons, to be paid to the foreman of the Homage
' of the preceding Court Baron, and applied in and towards
' such expenses. And that the further sum of threepence be
' paid on Monday weekly for every head of cattle which any

' commoner shall turn or keep on the commons for the wages
' of the herdsman.

' That the cattle to be depastured on the commons ought
' to be delivered or sent by the owners to Butts Close between
' the hours of six and eight of the morning from the sixth
' day of April to the eleventh day of October, both inclusive ;
' and after the eleventh of October between the hours of
' seven and nine of the morning. And that it is the duty of
' the herdsman to attend there during such hours, and to
' receive into his care the cattle brought to him, and to
' conduct them to the proper commons, and to attend and
' watch them there during the day, and to return them to
' the respective owners at six o'clock in the evening or as
' near thereto as may be; but no cow which is not brought
' to the herdsman within the hours before appointed for
' collecting the herd is considered as part of the herd or to
' be under the herdsman's care ; and that no horned cattle
' ought to be received into the herd without sufficient knobs
' on their horns.

SHEEP COMMONS.

The com-
mon fields.

' That every occupier of unenclosed land in any of the
' common fields of the said township hath common of pasture
' for his sheep levant and couchant thereon over the residue
' of the unenclosed land in the same common field, in every
' year from the time when the corn is cut and carried until
' the same be again sown with corn, and during the whole of
' the fallow season, save that no sheep may be depastured on
' the land in Bury Field and Welshman's Croft between the
' harvest and the twelfth day of November, the herbage
' thereof from the harvest to the twelfth day of November
' being reserved for the cows.

The three
seasons.

' That the common fields within the township of Hitchin
' have immemorially been and ought to be kept and culti-
' vated in three successive seasons of tilthgrain, etchgrain,
' and fallow.

' That the last fallow season of Purwell Field and Welsh-
' man's Croft was from the harvest of 1816 until the wheat
' sowing in the autumn of 1817 ; and that the fallow season

' of those fields commenced again at the close of the last
' harvest. That the last fallow season of Burford Field and
' Spital Field was from the harvest of the year 1817 until the
' wheat sowing in the autumn of the year 1818. And the
' last fallow season of Moremead Field and Bury Field was
' from the harvest of 1818 until the wheat sowing of 1819.

' That no person hath any right of common for sheep on
' any of the Green Commons or Lammas ground within this
' township except on Old Hale and on the closes of John
' Crouch Priest, called Ickleford Closes, which are common-
' able for sheep at the same time with the field called Welsh-
' man's Croft.

' The Homage find and present that every owner and
' every occupier of land in any of the common fields of this
' township may at his will and pleasure enclose and fence
' any of his land lying in the common fields of this township
' (other than and except land in Bury Field and Welshman's
' Croft), and may, so long as the same shall remain so enclosed
' and fenced, hold such land, whether the same belong to one
' or to more than one proprietor, exempt from any right or
' power of any other owner or occupier of land in the said
' township to common or depasture his sheep on the land so
' enclosed and fenced (no right of common on other land
' being claimed in respect of the land so enclosed and fenced).

Right of enclosure giving up right of common.

' The Homage also find and present that the commonable
' lands in the hamlet of Walsworth within this manor con-
' sist of—

' A parcel of meadow ground called Walsworth Common,
' containing fourteen acres or thereabouts, the soil whereof
' remains in the lord of the manor.

Walsworth Common.

' And of certain parcels of meadow called Lammas
' Meadow (that is to say), the Leys, part of the estate of Sir
' Francis Sykes adjoining to Walsworth Common, and con-
' taining four acres or thereabouts; Ickleford Mead, contain-
' ing two acres or thereabouts; Ralph's Pightle, adjoining
' to Highover Moor, containing one acre or thereabouts,
' Woolgroves, containing three acres or thereabouts, lying
' near to the mill of John Ransom, heretofore called Burnt
' Mill, and now called Grove Mill.

‘ A close called the Hills, containing two acres or
‘ thereabouts, on the west side of the road from Hitchin to
‘ Baldock, and a parcel of land called the Shadwells on the
‘ east side of the same road, and divided by the river, con-
‘ taining twelve acres or thereabouts.

‘ And they find and present that four several parcels of
‘ land hereinafter described have been by John Ransom en-
‘ closed and fenced out from the said Lammas ground called
‘ Woolgroves, and are now by him held in severalty.

‘ And that the same are and always have been parts of
‘ the commonable land of the said hamlet (to wit): A piece
‘ of land containing twenty-one perches or thereabouts on
‘ the south-west side of the present course of the river, and
‘ between the same and the old course ; a piece of land
‘ containing twelve perches or thereabouts, now by the altera-
‘ tion of the course of the river surrounded by water ; a piece
‘ of land on the north-east side of Woolgroves, containing
‘ one rood and twenty-two perches or thereabouts ; and a
‘ piece of land at the south-east corner of Woolgroves, con-
‘ taining one rood or thereabouts.

‘ And the Homage find and present that the occupier of
‘ every ancient messuage or cottage within the hamlet of .
‘ Walsworth hath a right to turn and depasture on the com-
‘ monable land thereof, in respect of and as appurtenant to
‘ his messuage or cottage, two cows and a bullock or yearling
‘ cow calf upon and from the thirteenth day of May, called
‘ Old May-day, until the sixth day of April, called Old Lady-
‘ day, and one horse upon and from the said thirteenth day
‘ of May until the thirteenth day of August, called Old
‘ Lammas-day, and hath a right to turn the like number of
‘ cattle upon the Lammas ground in Walsworth upon and
‘ from Old Lammas-day until Old Lady-day. That no person
‘ hath a right to common or turn any sheep upon the said
‘ common called Walsworth Commons, and that no sheep
‘ may be turned on the Lammas ground of Walsworth be-
‘ tween Old Lammas-day and the last day of November.

‘ The Homage also present that it is the duty of the
‘ Homage of this Court at every Great Court Baron yearly
‘ holden next after the Feast of St. Michael, upon the appli-

' cation and request of any of the persons entitled to common
' the cattle upon the commons within the hamlet of Wals-
' worth, to appoint a herdsman for the said hamlet, and to
' fix and assess a reasonable sum to be paid to him for his
' wages, and also a reasonable sum to be paid by the com-
' moners for draining and fencing the commons.

 ' This Court was then adjourned to Monday, the first day
' of November next.

' Signed   THOS. JEEVES (Foreman).

SAMUEL SMITH.

JOHN MARSHALL.

WILLM. DUNNAGE.

WM. BLOOM.

ROBT. NEWTON.

WILLM. HALL.

WM. MARTIN.

THOS. WALLER.

GEO. BEAVER.

W. SWORDER.

JOHN MOORE.'

INDEX AND GLOSSARY.

EBEDIW, Welsh death payment or heriot, 195

Edward the Confessor, his dying vision of the open fields round Westminster, 100

Einzelhöfe, German single farms in Westphalia, 371

Enclosure Acts, 4,000 between 1760–1844, 13

English settlements, methods of, 412–423

Ergastulum, prison for slaves on Roman villa, 264

Erw, Welsh acre, the actual strips in open fields described in Welsh Laws, 119

Etch, crop sown on stubble, 377

Ethelbert, Laws of, *hams* and *tuns* in private ownership and mention of læts, 173-174

FABER, or village blacksmith, holds his virgate free of services, 70

Fleta (temp. Ed. I.), description of manor in, 45

Forera (Saxon foryrthe), or headland, 20, 108

Frankpledge, View of, 10

Franks, their inroads, 283; deported into Belgic Gaul, 284

Frisians, 285. Tribute in hides, 306, *n.*

Furlong (shot, or quarentena), division of open fields 'a furrow long,' divided into strips or acres, 4; in Saxon open fields, 108; German, Gewann, 380

GAFOL (from German *Gaben, Abgaben*, food gifts under German tribal system), tribute, 144, 145; in money and in kind, of villani, on English manors, 78; of *gebur*, on Saxon manors, 132, 140-142, 155, 162. Marked a semi-servile condition, 146, 326

Gafol-land, 137. *See* Geneat-land

Gafol-gelder, payer of gafol or tribute, 145

Gafol-yrthe, the ploughing of generally three acre strips and sowing by the gebur, from his own barn, and reaping and carrying of crop to lord's

barn by way of rent; in 'Rectitudines,' 132-140; on Hysseburne Manor of King Alfred, 162; in South Germany in seventh century, 326 *et seq.* Possibly survival of the *agrarium* or tenth of produce on Roman provincial tithe lands, 399–403

Gavael, the tribal homestead and holding in N. Wales, 200–202

Gavelkind, Irish *gabal-cined*, distinguished by equal division among heirs, 220, 352

Gebur, villanus proper, or owner of a yard-land normally of thirty acres with outfit of two oxen and seed, in 'Rectitudines,' 131-133. His services described, 131-133, and 137-143; his gafol and week-work in respect of yard-land, 142; his outfit or 'setene,' 133, 143; in laws of Ine, 147. Services and gafol on Tidenham Manor of King Edwy, 154. In High German 'Gebur and Gipur' = vicinus, 394, and compare 278

Gedal-land, land divided into strips (Laws of Ine), 110. *See* Doles

Geneat, a wide term covering all tenants in villenage, 129, 137, 154. Servile condition of, liable to have life taken by lord, 146

Geneat-land, land in villenage as opposed to 'thane's inland,' or land in demesne, 116. Sometimes called 'gesettes-land' and 'gafol-land,' 128, 150; 'gyrds of gafol-land,' 150

Gesettes-land, land set or let out to husbandmen, 128. *See* 'Geneat-land'

Gored Acres, strips in open fields pointed at one end, 6, 20; in Saxon open fields, 108

Gwely, the Welsh family couch (lectus), also a name for a family holding, 195; in Record of Carnarvon, 194

Gwentian Code, of South Wales. *See* 'Wales, Ancient Laws of'

Gwestva, food rent of Welsh tribesmen, and *tunc pound* in lieu of it, 195; early evidence of, in Ine's laws, 209–213

Gyrd (a rod-virga)

Gyrdland. *See* Yardland. *See* 169–172

HAM (hem, heim, haim), in Saxon, like 'tun,' generally = villa or manor, 126, 254. A private estate

and yard-lands, 110–117. Scattering of strips in a holding the result of co-operative ploughing, 117–125. The three-field system would grow out of the simple form of tribal system, by addition of rotation of crops in three courses, settlement, and serfdom, 368–370. *Welsh open-field system*, 181, 213, with division into '*erws*,' or acres, 119. Scattering of strips in a holding arising from co-aration, 121. The system 'co-aration of the waste,' *i.e.* of grass land which went back into grass, 192, 227, 244, 251. Like that of the Germania of Tacitus, 369, 412. No fixed 'yard-lands' or rotation of crops, 251, 413. *Irish and Scotch open-field system* like the Welsh; modern remains of, in *Rundale* or *Run-rig* system, 214–231. *German* open-field systems, 369–411; different kinds of. *Feldgraswirthschaft* resembling that described by Tacitus and Welsh 'co-aration of waste,' 371. One-field system of N. Germany, 372–373. Forest and marsh system, 372. Three-field system in S. Germany, 373. Comparison of, with English, and connexion with Roman province, 375–409. Absent from N. Germany, and so could not have been introduced into England by the Saxon invaders, 373, 409, 411. Rotation of crops, perhaps of Roman introduction, 410, 411. Wide prevalence of forms of open-field system, 249. Description of, in Palestine, 314. Mention of, by Siculus Flaccus, 278. Possibly in use on Roman tithe lands, 315. Remains of the simple tribal form of, in modern rundale or run-rig of Ireland and Scotland, quite distinct from the remains of the three-field form in England, 437–439. Described by Tusser as uneconomical, 17, and by Arthur Young, 16

PARANGARIÆ, extra carrying services, *see* 'angariæ'
Paraveredi, extra post-horses (*see* Roman 'sordida munera'), 297, from *veredus* a post-horse, 298. Manorial *Parafretus*, 325–334
Patrocinium. See 'Commendation'
Pfahl-graben, the Roman *limes* on the side of Germany, 282

Pflicht-theil, survival of late Roman law, obliging a fixed proportion of a man's property to go equally to his sons. In Bavaria, 313. Compare Bavarian laws of the seventh century, 317, and Syrian code of fifth century, 312
Piers the Plowman, his 'faire felde,' an open field divided into half-acre strips and furlongs, by balks, 18–19
Plough-bote, or *Plough-erw*, the strips set apart in the co-ploughing, for the carpenter, or repair of plough, 121. (*See* Carpenter)
Plough team, normal English manorial common plough team of 8 oxen (*see* 'Caruca'). Welsh do., also of 8 oxen, 121–2. Scotch also, 62–66. 6, 10, or 12 oxen in Servia, 387 *n.* In India, 388. Single yoke of 2 oxen in Egypt and Palestine, 314, 387; and in Sicily, 275, and Spain, 276
Polyptique d'Irminon, Abbot of St. Germain des Prés, and M. Guérard's Introduction quoted, 265, 298, 641
Præpositus of a manor elected by tenants, 48. Holds one wista without services at Alciston, 50. Holds his two bovates free (Boldon Book), 70. Word used for Welsh 'maer,' 184
Precaria, a benefice or holding at will of lord or for life only, 319, 333
Precariæ or Boon-works, work at will of lord, 78. On Saxon Manors, 140, 157. In South Germany, 327. Sometimes survivals of the Roman 'sordida munera,' 327, 403
Priest, his place in village community often with his yard-land, 90–111, 115
Probus introduces vine culture on the Rhine, 288. Deports Burgundians and Vandals into Britain, 283. Colonised with Læti Rhine Valley and Belgic Gaul, 283
Punder, keeper of the village pound, 69, 70

QUARENTENA. See Furlong. Length of furrow 40 poles long

RAIN, German for 'balk' as in Yorkshire 'reean' = linch, 381
Randir, from *rhan* = a division, and *tir*, land; a share of land under Welsh

laws, 200. A cluster of three homesteads in South Wales, 204 ; and four
randirs in the *trev*, 204 ; but in
North Wales a subdivision of the
homestead, 200
' *Rectitudines Singularum Personarum* '
(10th century ?), evidence of, 129 *et
seq.* Dr. Leo's work upon, 164
Redon, Cartulaire de, quoted, 385
Rhætia, semi-servile barbarian settlers
in, 288. *Sordida munera* in, 296–
299. Roman custom, in present
Bavaria as to land tenure, 313.
Transition from Roman to Mediæval
manor in, 316–335
Rig, strip in Irish and Scotch open
fields, 3. Hence Run-rig system
Roman jugatio sive capitatio, 289, 295.
See Roman tributum
Roman ' sordida munera,' 295–299.
Some of them survive in manorial
services, 324, 325, 327, 334, 404
Roman tributum of later Empire, 289–
295. Roman *jugatio* and Saxon
hidage compared, *id.*, and 397
Roman Veterani settled on *ager pub-
licus* with single or double yokes of
oxen and seed for about 30 or 60
jugera, 272–276
Roman Villa. See Villa
Run-rig or *Rundale*, the Irish and
Scotch modern open-field system, 3.
Survival of methods of tribal system
now used in subdivision of holdings
among heirs, 226, 230, 438–440

ST. BERTIN, Abbey of Sitdiu at,
Grimbald brought by King Alfred
from thence, 160 ; Chartularium
Sithiensis, and surveys of estates of,
255–6 ; villa or manor of Sitdiu,
272, 366 ; suffix ' inghem ' to names
of manors, 356
St. Gall, records of Abbey, surrenders
to, 316–324
St. Paul's (Domesday of), A.D. 1222,
51
Salian Franks in Toxandria, 286
Scattered Ownership, in open fields, 7.
Characteristic of ' yard-land ' in
Winslow manor rolls, 23. In Saxon
open fields, 111. In Welsh laws, 118.
Resulted from co-ploughing, 121.
Under runrig system, 226–229
Scutage, 1*d.* per acre or 1*l.* per double
hide of 240 a., or 40*s.* per *scutum*, to

which four ordinary hides contributed, 38
Seliones, the acre or half-acre strips into
which the open fields were divided,
separated by turf *balks*, 2, 3, 19,
119
Servi (*slaves*), in Domesday Survey, 89,
93–95. Saxon *Theow*, 164–166, 175.
Welsh *caeth*, 199, 238. On Roman
Villa, 263. Arranged in *decuriæ*,
264. Under Alamannic and Bavarian
laws, 317, 323–326
Services of villani, chiefly of three
kinds: (1) Gafol, (2) precariæ or boon-
work, (3) week-work (refer to these
heads), 41. In Hundred Rolls, 41.
Domesday of St. Paul's, 53. Gloucester and Worcester records, 58. In
Kelso records, 67, Boldon Book,
68. Liber Niger of Peterborough, 73.
Summary of post-Domesday evidence, 78. On Saxon manors, in
' Rectitudines,' 130, 137–147. On
Tidenham manor of King Edwy, 154.
On Hysseburne manor of King Alfred,
162. In Saxon ' weork-ræden,' 158.
Of cottiers (or bordarii) in Hundred
Rolls, 44. Gloucester and Worcester,
58, 69. Of Saxon ' cotsetle,' 130,
141. On German and English manors
compared, 399–405
Setene, outfit of holder of Saxon yard-
land, 133, 139. See Stuht
Shot, 4 (*see* furlong), Saxon ' sceot,' a
division, occurs at Passau, 380
Siculus Flaccus mentions open fields
irregular boundaries, and scattered
ownership, on *agri occupatorii*, 274–
278
Sochmanni, a class of tenants on manors
chiefly in the Danish districts, 34.
Mentioned in Hundred Rolls in Cambridgeshire, 34; in Domesday Survey,
87, 102
Solanda, in Domesday of St. Paul's =
double hide of 240 a., 54
Solin, sullung, of Kent, plough land
from ' Suhl,' a plough, 54; divided
into 'yokes' (=yard-lands), 54; sullung = 4 gyrdlands and to ½ sullung,
outfit of four oxen, A.D. 835, 139. See
also, 395
Stuht, Kelso records, outfit of two
oxen, &c., with husband-land (yard-
land), 61. Compare ' *setene* ' of the
Saxon gebur with yard-land, 133 and
139, and outfit of Roman veteran,

274; and see under Bavarian Laws, 326

Succession to holdings, under the tribal system to all sons of tribesmen equally, 193, 234, 340; to yard-lands and other holdings in serfdom *single* by regrant, 23–24, 133, 176; so probably in the case of semi-servile holdings of *usufructuarii* under Roman law, 308

Supercilia, or linches, mentioned by *Agrimensores,* 277

Syrian Code of fifth century, 291–294

*T*ACITUS, description of German tribal system in the *Germania,* 338–343

Taeogs (or aillts), Welsh tenants without Welsh blood or rights of inheritance, not tribesmen—their 'register land' (tir cyfrif), 191; arranged in separate clusters or trevs with equality within each, 197; their 'register land,' 197; their dues to their lord and other incidents, 198–199

Tate, or Tath, the Irish homestead, analogous to Welsh 'tyddyn,' 214, 231. *See* Tribal system, Irish

Thane, Lord of a ham. Thane's inland = Lord's demesne land, 128. Thane's law or duties in 'Rectitudines,' 129; his services, 134; a soldier and servant of king, 135; his 'fyrd,' 136; *tri-noda necessitas,* 134

Theows, slaves on Saxon estates, 144; their position, 164. Example from 'Ælfric's Dialogue,' 165

Three-Field System. (*See* Open-field system.) Form of the open-field system with three-course rotation of crops

Tidenham, Manor of King Edwy. Description of, and of services of geneats and geburs upon, A.D. 956, 148–159. *Cytweras* and *hæcweras,* for salmon fishing, 152

Tir-bwrdd = terra mensalia, 198

Tir-gwelyawg, family land of Welsh free tribesmen, 191

Tir-cyfrif, register land of taeogs, 101

Tir-kyllydus, Welsh geldable land, 191

Tithes of Church under Saxon laws taken in actual strips or acres 'as they were traversed by the plough,' 114; acres of tithes in Domesday

Survey, 117; Ethelwulf's grant, 114

Tithe lands of Sicily, 275; of modern Palestine, 314. (*See* '*Agri decumates.*')

Trev, cluster of Welsh free tribesmen's homesteads, four in North Wales, 200–202; twelve in South Wales, 204. *Taeog* trevs, 203

Treviri, 284

Tricassi, 284

Tribal System in Wales, 181–213. Welsh districts and traces of, in Domesday Survey, 182, 206–7. Food rents in D.S., 185. Welsh land system described by Giraldus Cambrensis, 186–189. In Ancient Laws of Wales, 189 *et seq.* The free tribesmen of Welsh blood, 190. Homesteads scattered about, but grouped into clusters for payment of food rents, 190. Their family land (tir-gwelyawg), 190–191. Their right to a tyddyn (homestead), five free 'erws' and co-tillage of waste, 192. The tribal household with equality within it among brothers, first cousins, and second cousins, 193. The gwely or family couch, 194. The *gwestva,* or food rent, and tunc pound in lieu of it, 195. Other obligations of tribesmen, 195. The *taeogs or aillts* (see these words) not tribesmen, their tenure and rules of equality, 197. Land divisions under Welsh Codes connected with the *gwestva* and food rents, 199–208. Early evidence of payment of gwestva and of food rents of taeogs, 208–213. Shifting of holdings under tribal system, 205. Cluster of twelve tyddyns in Gwent and sixteen in N. Wales pay *tunc pound,* 202, 203. *In Ireland and Scotland,* 214–231. Clusters of sixteen tates or taths (Welsh tyddyn) 215–217. Sir John Davies's surveys and description of tribal system, Tanistry, and Gavelkind, 215–220. Example of a Sept deported from Cumberland, 219. Ancient division of Bally or townland into *quarters* and *tates,* 221, 224. Quarters and names of tates still traceable on Ordnance Survey. 223–224. Names of tates not personal, owing to tribal distributions and shiftings of tribal households from tate to tate, 224.

LONDON: PRINTED BY
SPOTTISWOODE AND CO., NEW-STREET SQUARE
AND PARLIAMENT STREET

For EU product safety concerns, contact us at Calle de José Abascal, 56–1°,
28003 Madrid, Spain or eugpsr@cambridge.org.

www.ingramcontent.com/pod-product-compliance
Ingram Content Group UK Ltd.
Pitfield, Milton Keynes, MK11 3LW, UK
UKHW042210180425
457623UK00011B/126